BOSTON *Celtics*

ENCYCLOPEDIA

by

Peter C. Bjarkman

Sports Publishing L.L.C.
www.Sportspublishingllc.com

Book Layout and Design: Erin J. Sands
Developmental Editor: Terrence C. Miltner and Mark Zulauf
Dustjacket Design: Julie L. Denzer

ISBN: 1-58261-564-0

Every effort has been made to determine ownership of copyrighted photos. If we failed go give adequate credit, we will be pleased to make corrections in future printings.

Published in the United States

Sports Publishing L.L.C.
www.SportsPublishingLLC.com

TABLE OF Contents

Acknowledgments...iv

Chapter I: Celtic Mystique 1

Chapter II: An Era of Transition 32

Chapter III: Auerbach's Hall of Famers 40

Chapter IV: Sixth Men, Role Players and Memorable Auerbach Steals 66

Chapter V: The Russell Era 97

Chapter VI: The Bird Era.. 119

Chapter VII: A Dozen-Plus Games for the Ages..................... 135

Chapter VIII: The Coaches 155

Chapter IX: A Trio of Legendary Sidecourt Personalities........................... 173

Chapter X: Statistical Appendices.. 185

Annotated Bibliography 242

ACKNOWLEDGMENTS ———————

acknowledgments

My thanks go to Terrence Miltner and Erin Sands at Sports Publishing for their efforts to make this book happen. Terrence provided a critical editor's eye and his assistance in rounding up the photos was invaluable. Erin did a tremendous job in melding my text and the photos into the finished product you hold in your hands.

As for those photos, my thanks go to Harris Lewine at AP/Wide World Photos, Mark Rucker at Transcendental Graphics and Frank P. McGrath, Jr. for their help in digging up all of these photos. I would also like to thank Mike Pearson at Sports Publishing for the opportunity to write this book.

Peter C. Bjarkman

BOSTON *Celtics*

ENCYCLOPEDIA

Larry Bird rides in the parade truck through the streets of Boston during the city's celebration of the team's 16th NBA Championship title.

BOSTON Celtics
Boston Celtics

CHAPTER I

Celtic Mystique:
Concise History of a Half-Century of Celtics Magic

*"Other teams have histories;
Boston alone has a mystique."*
- Bob Ryan

To begin a history of baseball one might start logically with the Cincinnati Reds, the diamond sport's oldest and most storied senior circuit franchise. Or the argument might be easily made to focus first and foremost on the New York Yankees, owners of more pennants and World Series flags than any other ballclub by far. And a case could even be made for American League teams in Detroit and Boston or National League clubs in Chicago or St. Louis—at least when it comes to picking the sport's most storied and legendary franchise. Then again, what baseball club has a more colorful past on both east coast and west than the Ebbets-Rickey-O'Malley Dodgers?

In the sport of basketball no such paradox exists. The story of professional basketball—in the large bulk of its chapters—reduces neatly to the story of the Boston Celtics. Hands down, no contest, no challenge. In the late '50s and throughout the decade of the '60s here was not only the first great dynasty club of the infant professional roundball sport, but unarguably the greatest dynasty in the history of American sports. Eight straight world championships, eleven titles in but thirteen seasons. It was the era of Bob

Cousy, certainly the single ballplayer next to George Mikan who had the greatest individual impact on how the game was subsequently played. And it was also the era of Bill Russell, a mysterious and controversial legend who single-handedly turned basketball into a defensive game.

Throughout the '70s the lustrous tradition continued as Tom Heinsohn succeeded Auerbach and Russell at the reins and the proud Celtics rebounded from a temporary slide to remain a dominant force during pro basketball's true lost decade. Now it was the era of John "Hondo" Havlicek, basketball's greatest "sixth man" soon turned into a franchise player in his own right, and of Dave Cowens, the second great redhead of Boston hardwood legend. And finally in the '80s came the return to glory behind the brilliant play and floor leadership of Larry Bird.

Yet it is for a single epoch that the Boston Celtics are most memorable. For card-carrying basketball fans only one dynasty team comes immediately to mind when complete domination of a league or an era is the topic—the '60s—era Celtics of coach Arnold "Red" Auerbach. Nowhere in all of

Celtics mastermind Red Auerbach counsels his attentive troops—including Bill Russell (#6) and Sam Jones at far right—during the 1965 NBA playoffs.

American sport, in fact, is there to be found another dynasty franchise to compare with those Boston teams formed and masterminded by Auerbach and led into court action over a 13-year stretch by Cousy and Russell.

The collegiate ranks of the roundball sport seems to offer a competitor for the title. Nowhere in the history of college athletics is there anything more remarkable than John Wooden's string of NCAA championships with the UCLA Bruins. But the marks established by Wooden and his UCLA titans fall a fraction short of those posted by Auerbach and the Celtics. Seven NCAA titles in a row and 10 in 12 seasons, versus eight straight NBA crowns and 11 in 13 seasons. (But for an injury to Russell in 1958, the Celtics string would likely have been ten in a row.) It seems a close call, and yet the Wooden teams were not a "dynasty" in the same sense as the Auerbach teams. There were really three different teams at UCLA, constantly shifting personal, and a constantly shifting playing field of opponents in each new two or three year span. The Celtics roster during the Auerbach string remained largely intact; the rival Hawks, Sixers and Lakers squads they battled were almost as stable. And certainly what Auerbach's Boston juggernaut accomplished has never been matched (or even closely approximated) anywhere in professional sports competition.

When the period from 1957 to 1969 is conjured up in the collective memory of hoop fans in every corner of the nation, the first great glory era of the pro game is colored by a bright shade of kelly green. The undying and all-pervasive symbol of the era was the shamrock; its undeniable signature was the parquet floor of the nation's most legendary indoor sporting arena. The collage of images is indeed indelible: "The Cooz" dribbling through traffic and passing behind his back, Russell outplaying Wilt in crucial contest after crucial contest, Sudden Sam Jones "stoppin' and poppin'" and Hondo Havlicek stealing the ball in the single most heart-stopping moment of franchise history. Boston teams did more than dominate the postseason play of this period; Celtics ballclubs of the era were indeed arguably the entire story of professional basketball for almost an entire generation of roundball fans.

BOSTON The Cousy Era

Arnold "Red" Auerbach—a Jewish kid from Brooklyn who maintained a Washington, D. C. address during his entire four decade tenure on the Celtics bench and in the club's front office—would be the eventual author of the world's greatest sports dynasty ever. But Boston's most celebrated redhead certainly did not work his miracle overnight. In fact, the Red Auerbach Era in Boston got off to anything but a blazing start.

And even when it hit full stride the Celtics "mystique" was a phenomenon that never generated the full appreciation it merited until decades after the original triumphs had been etched into the record books. Boston was always foremost a baseball town and a hockey town and the Celtics were rarely front-page news, even when they were writing the most unmatchable sports story in the city's history. Rarely did the hoops club sell out its games during the championship string of the '60s (six or seven thousand was a good crowd; sellouts of 13,909 were a rare event reserved for a few playoff games), despite the fact that the hockey Bruins rarely had a seat available during the same epoch. Bill Russell for all his prowess was far too rebellious and

Bob Cousy was Boston's first superstar and a ballhandling wizard whose moves were copied on every playground in the land.

controversial a figure to generate widespread fan appeal. And although the Red Sox were at a low point of franchise history they remained first in the city's heart. Only Bob Cousy seemed to rise above the Celtics' back-page status. From 1951 through 1963—even in the heyday of Ted Williams—Bob Cousy was the most famous and revered athlete Beantown had ever known. From the beginning of his Holy Cross days in 1946 through his tearful Celtics retirement in 1963, Cooz was the one totally popular and beloved sports hero that Boston could call its own.

Auerbach's NBA coaching career began before Boston, and even before the NBA was called the NBA. It all started for Auerbach in Washington, where the former George Washington University backcourt star first enjoyed a bundle of early successes, both as high school mentor at St. Alban's Prep and Roosevelt High and then in the fledgling professional ranks. The Basketball Association of American had been launched by East Coast hockey club owners just as peacetime followed on the heels of World War II, and in the nation's capital hockey arena owner Mike Uline turned to the 28-year-old Auerbach to take over a first edition of the Washington entry in the new circuit. Auerbach had just returned from his own military stint and had convinced Uline of his worthiness for the post by boasting that he could deliver talented ex-service ballplayers to fill up the club roster. Auerbach delivered well enough and his Washington Caps posted the circuit's best first-year record at 49-11. After two additional winning campaigns in Washington (including a title matchup with the Minneapolis Lakers in his final season) Auerbach was next off for a brief tenure with Ben Kerner's Tri-Cities Blackhawks. It was with the Illinois-and-Iowa-based ballclub that Red suffered through the only losing record of his career (28-29) during a first season of the newly reconstituted National Basketball Association. The Auerbach-Kerner relationship was anything but smooth, however, and Red quit by season's end in a spat over a trade made by Kerner and objected to by Auerbach. Later the flamboyant coach would get his full measure of revenge, both by beating the transplanted St. Louis Hawks on several occasions in the NBA playoffs and also by fleecing Kerner in the infamous Bill Russell deal.

The arrival of a new coach named Auerbach in Boston in 1950 brought promises of immediate improvement for a lackluster team that had failed to better 25 wins in any of its first four seasons under coaches Honey Russell and Doggie Julian. But when Boston Garden owner Walter Brown gambled on the feisty yet successful Auerbach he introduced considerable upheaval into the heretofore staid

No Celtics weapon during the glory-era of the 1960s more intimidated NBA rivals than the sight of the fiery redhead along the sidelines.

young Boston franchise as well.

For one thing, it was clear from the moment of Red's arrival who the basketball boss in Boston would always be. Red's first clash with the locals came over a hot-shot prospect named Bob Cousy who had led Holy Cross to the 1947 NCAA title and was now becoming available in the second-ever NBA draft. There was considerable hometown pressure to draft Cousy but Auerbach had little use for a hotshot dribbler as the type of ballplayer to build a franchise around. There are two accounts of Red's exact words to the press on the occasion of his introduction as Boston's new coach, words uttered when the issue of Boston's draft selection immediately came up. One version has Red snapping: "I'm not interested in drafting someone just because he happens to be a local yokel." The second quotes Auerbach as retorting: "Am I supposed to win ballgames here, or please the local yokels?" But, either way, there is little doubt today about Auerbach's initial assessment of Cousy's limitations. The new Boston coach refused to tab Cousy with Boston's territorial draft selection and the Celtics opted instead for center Charlie Share of Bowling Green (traded to Fort Wayne for the rights to Bill Sharman) and guard Chuck Cooper of Duquesne (the first black player ever drafted by the league).

It was an ironic move, of course, since Red's key to success would be his installing of the controlled fast-breaking game he had learned as a player under Bill Reinhart at George Washington University. And Cousy was the perfect ballhandler to run just such an offense—one dependent on pinpoint passing, controlled dribbling, and rapid movement of the ball to an open man. It was one case were Auerbach was clearly wrong in his assessment of talent, but in this instance the stubborn coach was saved by fate from his own erroneous ways. Cousy was drafted by Auerbach's former employer, Ben Kerner's Tri-Cities Hawks. Almost immediately the Hawks traded Cousy to the Chicago Stags and before the season could even open that struggling club was out of business. Cousy's name was next thrown into a hat along with Chicago stars Max Zaslofsky and Andy Phillip and offered to teams (Boston, Philadelphia and New York) having claims against the insolvent Chicago franchise. The folding of a franchise and the subsequent dispersal draft and coin flip had stuck Auerbach and Boston with Cousy anyway, much to Red's dismay and owner Walter Brown's equal displeasure. Auerbach was already a brilliant basketball mind—keen on judging talent—but on a few occasions he was more lucky than anything else.

But blind luck aside, Auerbach's vault to the top came largely through rare talent. Auerbach had two strong suits above all others. The first was an ability to keep his domineering personality in check and thus allow his extremely talented players free reign to develop and utilize their athletic skills. Boston players of the glory era (1957-1966) universally hated Auerbach's penchant for lighting up a victory cigar on the bench as soon as a ballgame appeared to be well in hand. Cousy later commented often on how this practice fired up opponents and enemy fans alike and saddled the Boston players with added oncourt pressures they didn't need. But on all other counts Auerbach was a true players' coach and his teams adored him for it. With his strongest Boston clubs he kept the offense simple (Boston had six or seven plays and rarely ran them all) and relied instead on great physical conditioning and Cousy's abilities to run the fast-break offense which Auerbach had designed. In crucial situations, especially in late moments of a game, the coach also relied on players to suggest the offensive plays. Auerbach thus soon had five talented coaches on the floor at once. And as Tom Heinsohn put it, if a player suggested the play in the huddle then he had that much more pride at stake in making sure that it worked out on the floor.

Auerbach's other unmatched strength was as master trader and stellar manipulator of the college player draft. Knowing that Russell was exactly what he needed and that Rochester was already sold on Sihugo Green with their own first pick in 1956 lottery, Auerbach engineered a huge deal with Kerner and the Hawks to land his coveted centerpiece ballplayer. And it was only the first of many such history-shaping transactions. Red was never afraid to give up something to get something in return and he gave up plenty in the Russell deal. But he also made the best acquisition in NBA history. Later the redhead would build another dynasty team by having the foresight to draft Larry Bird early (as an unavailable underclassman, taken with the sixth overall pick) and also to acquire Parish and McHale (both via Golden State) just two drafts later. Red got McHale by fleecing Detroit coach (and later TV personality) Dick Vitale out of a number one 1980 selection (for Bob McAdoo), then trading that pick (along with the 1980 number 13 selection obtained from Washington) to the Warriors for Parish and also a Golden State first-round selection (third overall). Golden State used that number one slot to select disappointing Joe Barry Carroll while Auerbach banked the number three selection for future Hall-of-Famer

McHale. And there was yet one more clever Auerbach deal that only the cruel hand of fate expunged from the record. Red arranged a trade (Gerald Henderson for Seattle's first overall 1986 selection) that allowed the acquisition of number one pick Len Bias out of the University of Maryland. Red seemed to have done it again, but this one time pure chance intervened to stop him in a way that the league's other executives never seemingly could.

Even before Auerbach's greatest teams arrived on the scene, the Boston Celtics did have one important date with history. That was the team's somewhat muddled role in the integration of the NBA with the drafting of Duquesne forward Chuck Cooper in 1950. Cooper's pioneering role in basketball's destruction of the color line has often been unfortunately misrepresented by historians who simply haven't done their homework and have thus overanxiously labelled Cooper as basketball's Jackie Robinson. Cooper's role was somewhat less central than Robinson's: the Celtics' first black was indeed also the first player of his race tabbed by the formal NBA drafting procedure; on the other hand, he was not the first black to ink an NBA contract (New York signed Harlem Globetrotter Nate "Sweetwater" Clifton only hours after Boston had drafted but not yet signed Chuck Cooper). More importantly, neither Cooper nor Clifton were the first blacks to set foot on an NBA floor for game action. That honor fell to Earl Lloyd, a West Virginia State 6-6 leaper taken a few slots after Cooper in the same 1950 draft. Due to a quirk in the league schedule, Lloyd's Washington Caps ballclub opened play a night earlier than either Cooper's Celtics or Clifton's Knicks, giving Lloyd a cherished if overlooked slot in the history books.

Thus Boston was not actually the first NBA team to integrate its roster on the playing floor as is so often reported. On the other hand, it is an unfair distortion to suggest that Boston and Auerbach later made efforts to keep Celtics teams lily white in the '70s and '80s. Boston's role in integrating the sport is, in fact, quite the reverse. A schedule-maker's trick might indeed have kept Boston from being technically the first team to field a black athlete in their gameday lineup. But more importantly, Boston was the league's first team (in 1963-64) to put five black men on the floor at the same time (Heinsohn was the only white starter, but he often gave way to Willie Naulls). And then a season later Boston's Celtics fielded the first all-black starting lineup in NBA history. This was the five made up of Russell, Sanders, Naulls, K.C. Jones and Sam Jones. And it was Boston, of course, that could boast the first black coach (the first in any major U.S. pro sport) when Russell assumed the post in 1966. Unlike Boston's baseball Red Sox a few seasons earlier, the Celtics were anything but a racial foot-dragger.

The first building block of a future dynasty club was

put in place almost by accident. That block was Bob Cousy, a player the new coach didn't really want and thus only acquired quite by accident and through more than a small dose of outrageous good fortune. But once Cousy was on the scene his impact on basketball was truly immense, certainly greater than any player of the league's first decade save Mikan. Mikan had actually forced major rule changes and encouraged rule-bending playing tactics. Cousy's revolutionary impact was more subtle but none the less dramatic. And here was also the greatest ballhandler and passer the game has ever known, right down to the present moment. As Heinsohn often points out, Cousy's passing was so superb that only the players receiving his "soft assists" could truly appreciate them. Russell was the missing element to round off the plan for Auerbach's fast-breaking offense. But without Cousy there wouldn't even have been a plan.

With his unmatched wingspan and steelspring legs, Bill Russell turned the arts of shotblocking and defense into basketball's most potent force.

good supporting players on board, like Arnie Risen and Bill Sharman. Risen was an accomplished point-maker who had already helped other teams in Rochester and Indianapolis. The skinny 6-9 center was a fixture, between 1947 and 1957, in the league's top ten rankings in both rebounding and scoring. And Sharman was the best pure outside shooter of the entire decade. Especially on the freethrow line was Sharman truly invincible. The University of Southern California graduate had once hoped to play baseball as a hard-hitting outfielder and had advanced to the top minor leagues, but was eventually stuck behind Jackie Robinson in Brooklyn. (Sharman holds the trivial distinction of having once been thrown out of a major league game for heckling from the bench—while on a late-season call-up with the Dodgers in the early '50s—while actually never having played in a big league contest.) But on the basketball court Sharman's talents were never overshadowed by others. Beginning in 1951 the crack-shooting Texan teamed with Cousy to create a balanced backcourt combo that surpassed Bob Davies and Bobby Wanzer in Rochester as the best outside duo of that early era. While Cousy ran the offense and did the passing, Sharman simply shot the lights out. He regularly lead the club in scoring throughout the first phase of the Celtics dynasty run (1956-1959).

Before Russell reshaped the notions of big-man play, diminutive Bob Cousy had already "written the book" on the wizardry of backcourt style. And while Russell was destined to be marked as a sure-fire all-time great before ever actually setting foot in the league, Cousy was the greatest of unanticipated surprises—especially for the Boston Celtics, who twice passed up the opportunity to have him on their roster (they didn't want him in the college draft and didn't want him in the dispersal draft several months later) and yet were still fortunate enough to end up with Cousy almost in spite of themselves. With Cousy and Russell in tow, the Celtics were almost unbeatable. Not quite, of course, but it certainly appears that way in hindsight. The unit that Auerbach molded by the end of the 1950s developed a unique freelancing fast-break style which altered forever the strategies by which basketball was played. It might even be said that it was the Celtics' fast-break offense (Russell rebounding and outletting to Cousy who found Heinsohn or Ramsey ahead of the pack) more than any other single feature which eventually allowed the professional game to overtake the rival collegiate version of roundball in fan popularity.

With Cousy at the helm, the Boston clubs of the mid-fifties were respectable and competitive. They also had some

With Cousy and Sharman running the show in the season's immediately before Russell's arrival the Boston Celtics were always respectable if not ever overwhelming. For six straight years the team played over .500 and finished either second or third in the Eastern Division each season (1951-1956). But before Russell these guard-heavy Boston teams were also always easy victims of more physical ballclubs like Minneapolis, Rochester or Syracuse, in either round one or round two of the league championship series.

And the pre-Russell Celtics were not entirely without a big man either. For several seasons prior to Bill Russell's fortuitous arrival and the resulting dramatic reversal in Celtic fortunes, there was yet another slightly more modest big man who guided the Boston club into annual league warfare. Some would even date the first emergence of the dynasty-driven Celtics to coincide with the now long-forgotten deal that brought "Easy Ed" Macauley to his new home in Boston Garden. The St. Louis University star played the NBA's first season with the hometown St. Louis Bombers and was acquired by Boston through the dispersal draft which followed the folding of the St. Louis outfit. Macauley was an exceptional shooter for his period, and his offensive battles with Mikan foreshadowed the Russell-Chamberlain duels that lay waiting just down the road.

Yet clearly the greatest contribution of Boston's first exceptional pivot man to the emerging Celtics dynasty would rest ironically in Macauley's departure rather than his arrival on the Boston scene. With Macauley and Risen in the forecourt and Cousy doing the playmaking the Celtics were already an offensive whirlwind team that could score quicker and more continuously than any team in the league. But such offensive proficiency didn't seem to pay large postseason dividends in a league that was still based far more on muscle and intimidation than on finesse. There was a large missing piece in Boston and Auerbach seemed to know precisely what the piece was. "Easy Ed" Macauley would soon serve as the valuable trade bait with which Auerbach could hook the incomparable big man around whom he would construct his greatest Boston championship teams.

Auerbach owned the third pick of the 1956 college draft, and it was no secret that the scheming Boston mentor coveted San Francisco University center Bill Russell as the single component needed to convert his team from also-rans into champions. It was also no secret that penny-pinching Rochester management, owning the league's first pick, would bypass the huge center who would demand an unthinkable salary for his services. St. Louis was willing to deal their number two shot at Russell (since Ben Kerner had apparently not yet learned to distrust his ex-employee), but the price would be steep. Hawks management required Macauley (who earlier starred at St. Louis University) and promising Cliff Hagan as well, but it was a price Auerbach didn't flinch at paying. The result would not only be Celtic invincibility but a new national stature for NBA basketball to boot.

Once the Celtics had Russell they had the key to a dynasty that would soon dwarf achievements posted by the then-reigning Minneapolis Lakers. Only Auerbach seemed to know what he was doing at the time. But the impact of his move would quickly transform the league and the sport forever.

The Russell Era

No team has ever so dominated a professional sport for any period that extended beyond a single decade. Over the course of 13 winters—the span of most lengthy careers for individual players—Boston would breeze by the opposition with an incredible 11 world titles. Eight of these championships would come in unbroken succession. In this same 13-year span the Celtics would average 55 victories per campaign; they would never lose more than seven home contests over this stretch during any single season; and for 12 straight years their winning percentage would remain well above the .600 mark. This was total domination as it has never before or since been experienced in any major league sport in North America.

And if one isn't quite sure where the Celtics stand in regard to the modern-day Bulls or Lakers, or perhaps how they stack up with other sports dynasties like the Yankees of baseball or Dolphins of football or Canadiens of hockey, consider one additional fact that speaks necessary volumes. At the end of the 1980s the NBA was 44 years old and had enshrined 47 players and coaches in the Naismith Basketball Hall of Fame. Exactly 8 of those players (plus the coach)—a full 17 percent—were from one team. Not one franchise, but **one team** which Red Auerbach sent out on the floor during the 1960-61 NBA campaign. Name another ballclub in the entire realm of professional sports where the complete starting lineup was composed of Hall-of-Famers. Or one where three Hall-of-Famers (Frank Ramsey, Sam Jones, and K. C. Jones) were on the roster and didn't even start! Name, in fact, a team in any sport that has drafted three Hall-of-Famers in a single season—Auerbach's rare feat when he pegged Russell, Heinsohn and K. C. Jones in 1956. It was like a Yankees roster with Ruth, Mantle, Gehrig, Ted Williams, Ty Cobb, Willie Mays, Cy Young and Walter Johnson all in the same starting lineup and pitching rotation. On personnel factors alone the early-'60s Celtics were the greatest ballclub ever to share the same locker room of any sporting arena.

And there would be still further domination in the years to come, as Boston would rebound from the early 1970s doldrums to capture two more titles and five divisional crowns in the next decade. But as storied as the Celtics saga had remained for almost four decades since Red Auerbach first appeared on the Boston scene, still nothing can quite match the glories of those first 10 seasons of Auerbach and Russell-led Boston championship teams. Between the beginning of the 1956-57 season and the close of the following decade, one unbeatable Celtics lineup seemed to merge into another (as Heinsohn gave way to Sanders and Havlicek and Cousy-Sharman merged with the Jones Boys). One postseason heroic moment merely set the stage for more dramatic ones to follow. Year after year it was the same coach, the same stars, the same championship venue, and precisely the same result.

Perhaps the only reasonable method of reviewing this period of complete Celtics domination on the hardwood courts of the NBA seems to involve an approach which avoids the chronological continuum in favor of other more distinctive milepost measures of the era. These measures are the images, personalities and magical moments that even today remain indelible—the coaches, superstar performers, largely unheralded role players, legendary rivalries, and titanic postseason clashes which still form the sport's most treasured era.

The coaches of the period who together define "the Celtic Mystique" were only two—Auerbach and his pet project and short-term successor, Bill Russell. The Celtics dynasty saga not only begins with Red Auerbach, but it might very well have ended with Auerbach as well. To his lasting credit, Red's vision included not only the drafting of Russell but also the selection of Russell as his coaching successor (and also the first black man to serve as an NBA mentor) a decade later. It was a bold move that surprised and even shocked almost the entire basketball community. To give Red credit for nothing more than bare expediency, it seems that at the time the resident Celtics genius knew better than anyone that only Bill Russell as coach could adequately handle Bill Russell the player.

Red Auerbach himself would remain the guiding light of the Celtics franchise throughout the seasons and the decades to follow that great glory-span of 1956-66— first as general manager, later as elder statesman and patriarch, always as spiritual father and visible touchstone of the revered Celtic ideal. In future seasons Auerbach would mold and direct other Celtics dynasty teams from his secure front office post. First came the selection of Russell's rookie teammate Tommy Heinsohn for the plum Boston coaching slot at the outset of the 1970s. Heinsohn would reward his boss with two more world titles and five divisional flags during his own eight seasons at the helm. All of Red's coaches right down to the end of the 80s (Russell, Heinsohn, Sanders, Cowens, K. C. Jones) would be his former players, with the single notable exception of Bill Fitch who also earned a world title. Later came the acquisition of frontcourt star Dave Cowens, a brash rookie out of

Even the league's most talented slashing drivers like Dolph Schayes of Syracuse had to contend with Bill Russell's impenetrable roadblocks under the Boston basket.

Transcendental Graphics

Florida State plucked with the fourth overall pick of the 1970 college draft. And then, of course, the surprise 1978 drafting of Larry Bird (only a college junior at the time, who would not play for another full season) to assure a return to Celtic glory throughout the decade of the 1980s. Finally, the shrewd acquisition of Robert Parish (plus draft rights to Kevin McHale) through yet another bold 1980 trade with the San Francisco Warriors.

If fate had not intervened in the mid-1980s, Auerbach's genius might have built still another team the equal of those of the Russell-Cousy or Cowens-Havlicek-Jo Jo White eras. This time around it would be an unbeatable tandem of Bird and prized rookie Lennie Bias from the University of Maryland. Bias seemed to have all the tools for immediate stardom when grabbed by Auerbach in the 1986 draft, and was poised to enter the Celtics' starting lineup with all the flare and fury of Tom Heinsohn in 1956, John Havlicek in 1962, and Cowens in 1970. But Len Bias died suddenly of a drug-induced heart attack only days after the draft-day festivities, thus stunning the entire sports world. On this single tragic occasion Auerbach's ingenious draft manipulations had come up absolutely empty.

Russell, on the other hand, was arguably the greatest player-coach in all of sports history. Certainly no one else who managed bench strategy while also taking a full-time role in the game's playing action ever contributed so heavily in both roles towards winning championship honors—at least not over the stretch of more than a single season. When Auerbach stepped away from the Boston bench he knew for certain that any replacement would have to make peace with his eccentric center, since Russell was undoubtedly the very heart and soul of the Boston team. It was Red's great genius that he saw the immediate solution and turned directly to Russell himself with the task. And in the three years that followed (1966-67 through 1968-69) Russell would surprisingly prove much more like his mentor as a bench strategist than anyone could have ever imagined.

But it was certainly as a player in the previous decade under Auerbach that Bill Russell was absolutely insuperable. Russell's failure to achieve lofty scoring numbers will perhaps always bar him from wide support as the greatest NBA player of all time. Never once in his career did the big man average 20 points per game; rarely did he enjoy a 30-point scoring outburst. The huge supporting cast strung around him for so long not only lifted the offensive burden somewhat from his shoulders but also stole some of the luster from his own often inde-scribable defensive performances. For those who saw him time after time dominate against the very man most frequently nominated for all-time best—Wilt Chamber-lain—there can be no convincing argument that Chamberlain or anyone else was ever any better than Bill Russell. Not if team victory in a team sport is any weighty consideration for canonization. On defense there has never been another basketball player to challenge Russell's total control over the area of floor and sky around the opponent's basket. Celtics players later referred to it as their "Hey, Bill" style of defense—gamble up front and know that if your man got away from you you could always look over your shoulder and shout "Hey, Bill" for a sure defensive stop. Russell would pocket five season MVP awards (1958, 1961-63, 1965) before he was done, a feat matched in league history only by Kareem Abdul-Jabbar and Michael Jordan. Fans of slam dunks and miraculous off-balance shots would likely select Air Jordan or Oscar Roberston or even Magic Johnson to pace their modern-day dream team; fans or coaches wishing to win the single money contest would always opt for Bill Russell to key their prized cham-pionship lineup.

But there were other larger than life Celtics stars of this era, many of whom would have been franchise players for any other ballclub. In Boston, however, these men always lived in the long shadows cast by Russell and Cousy. Tom Heinsohn, for example, was a hard-as-nails force who first defined the NBA prototype of the power forward and who well earned his colorful nicknames of "Tommy Gun" and "Ack-Ack" (the sound of a machine gun). Heinsohn loved to shoot, and across nine brilliant seasons (1955-56 through

Red Auerbach enjoys another moment of jubilation on the Boston bench, this time as the invincible Celtics clinch the 1963 Eastern Division title against Cincinnati.

AP/Wide World Photos

1964-65) he fired up an endless stream of running hook shots and line-drive jumpers that seemed always to find the proper range. While Heinsohn was perpetually shooting, his eventual replacement, John "Hondo" Havlicek, was a man of true perpetual motion. For 16 incredible seasons (1962-63 through 1977-78) Hondo piled 20-point year upon 20-point year as he climbed among the NBA's dozen all-time highest scorers with over 26,000 career points. And no other player ever displayed more raw stamina than Havlicek. None ever left a more colorful collage of memorable career moments either. And none ever discovered more ways to beat you than the man who ceaselessly ran circles around the rest of the league for almost two decades.

Bill Sharman, in turn, teamed with Bob Cousy to form the first truly memorable guard combo in league annals. While Cousy was the passing wizard of the duo, Sharman was the premier shooter of the 1950s, flawless at the foul line (.883 over an 11-year career and three seasons above 90 percent accuracy) and nearly as picture-perfect from the field. So obvious was his offensive prowess to the fans that few understood Sharman's equal reputation among opponents and teammates alike as a matchless defensive backcourt man. And there was another little-known aspect to Sharman's game which elevated him above less talented players of his era. Such was his devotion to scientific conditioning that he was truly decades ahead of his rivals in his approached to preparing himself for the rugged game of professional basketball.

All the important cogs in the Celtics' wheels were not front-line starters, of course. It would be with reliable Frank Ramsey that Red Auerbach would soon build a vital component of his prototype winning team, a component that first became a Celtics trademark and later a true NBA fixture. For Kentucky University's Frank Ramsey was the first and perhaps the foremost of the league's storied "sixth-man" specialists—the super-sub who charges from the bench in early action to shift a game's momentum with talented and spirited play. Ramsey added the dimensions of speed and intelligence to the Celtics attack, then handed the mantle to John Havlicek who took sixth-man performance to an even loftier level during his earliest years in the league. Ramsey's lasting signature was also Havlicek's—an unwavering ability to arrive cold off the bench and immediately hit several long-range shots to break the spirit or momentum of a charging opponent.

Great teams are noted for their uncanny abilities to repeatedly find replacement parts waiting in the wings to sustain a well-tuned winner. By the early 1960s, as Cousy faded and Sharman disappeared completely from the scene, a new pair of backcourt wizards made the dominant perimeter duo of the 1950s almost unnoticed for their absence. Sharman's successor was Sam Jones, a relentless scoring machine out of tiny North Carolina College who patiently played a backup role for half a dozen winters and then burst forth as a prolific scorer of the Bill Russell-coached squads. Here was a player whose trademark was the soft touch with which his shots kissed the glass and the lightening first step with which he left defenders scrambling in his wake. So large was Jones's reputation among peers and opponents that he would be a clear choice in 1971 for the all-time NBA silver anniversary mythic all-star team. And by the mid-1960s one guard named Jones was found teaming with another, as Russell's former San Francisco teammate K. C. Jones was now more than adequately handling Cousy's former playmaking duties.

The rivalry between Russell and Chamberlain was the NBA's biggest drawing card throughout the 1960s.

AP/Wide World Photos

Another memorable element in the history of the first great Boston dynasty era was the great Celtics rivalries with a series of worthy title challengers, each featuring marquee players of their own. At the top of the list was the late-1950s matchup between the Celtics paced by Russell and the high-flying St. Louis Hawks featuring the rare offensive tandem of Bob Pettit and Cliff Hagan (NBA Finals—1957, 1958, 1960, 1961). When the Hawks and Pettit quickly faded from the scene and shed their role as legitimate challengers, there quickly arose other rivals most worthy of titanic confrontations with Auerbach's men. First came the Warriors from Philadelphia and their own young tower of power, Wilt Chamberlain (Eastern Division Finals—1957, 1960, 1962; NBA Finals—1964). When Chamberlain later

took his act back to Philadelphia from his brief West Coast tour in San Francisco (new home of the Warriors after 1962), still another Eastern Division challenge arose in the guise of the newly relocated Syracuse Nationals, who now played wearing the logo of the Philadelphia 76ers (Eastern Divisions Finals—1958, 1959, 1961, 1965, 1966, 1967, 1968). Wilt would challenge Bill Russell and his Boston mates yet a third time under the banner of the Los Angeles Lakers (NBA Finals—1962, 1963, 1965, 1966, 1968, 1969) during the decade's final two seasons.

The centerpiece—quite literally, of course—of the memorable Celts-Warriors, Celts-76ers, and Celts-Lakers rivalries during the tempestuous 1960s was unquestionably the head-to-head clash of the league's two greatest big men. From his abbreviated rookie season of 1956-57 (when he reported two months late due to a stint on the US Olympic team), Bill Russell remained a dominant defensive force the likes of which basketball had never seen before. A late entry into competition during that first season had cost "Big Bill" the league's rookie-of-the-year honors (won by teammate Tom Heinsohn) and a rebounding title (when his total of 943 caroms placed him fourth among league board sweepers, even though his per game average of 19.3 was two per game better than official league leader Maurice Stokes). But Russell had served notice from his earliest moments in the league that his defensive presence was every bit as vital as that offered by Wilt on offense. And it was in the semi-final or title rounds of league postseason play that the Russell-Chamberlain clashes would reach their most dramatic moments during seven of the decade's seasons.

Each head-to-head matchup of Russell and Chamberlain during this decade-long battle for supremacy was indeed a titanic struggle. Between November 1959 and May 1969 the two squared off in league and postseason competition a total of 142 times. The point tally on almost every occasion fell to Wilt, yet the final scoreboard count just as frequently pointed in the favor of Russell and his mates. The measure of Russell's own individual greatness, of course, was that for 10 straight seasons (1957-1966) after his rookie debut his ballclub outlasted all rivals to race into the league's final championship round. Only twice (1964 and 1969) in this stretch, however, did the two behemoths —Mr. Defense and Mr. Offense—lock horns in the season's final title matchup. On four other occasions Russell's Celtics were able to dominate Chamberlain and company (first the Warriors and then the 76ers) during the hard-fought Eastern Division finals, twice in matchups that stretched the full seven required games.

Chamberlain, for his part, raced to seven consecutive scoring crowns after following Russell into the league in 1959, yet not once in this span did his club walk away with a championship banner. Only after the Warriors had abandoned an East Coast home in Philadelphia for a West Coast abode in San Francisco did Wilt finally shake his annual dreaded early departures from the playoffs at the hands of the division-rival Celtics and at long last reach a championship-round confrontation with Russell. But the Celtics were at the zenith of their game in the spring of 1964 and although Wilt averaged 34.7 points throughout 12 playoff games that spring to Russell's 13.1 in 10, Wilt's offensive superiority would matter little. The Warriors simply didn't have the manpower to match up with Boston at the other four positions, and the Celtics breezed to an easy title in five lopsided contests.

Russell enjoyed his finest outing against Chamberlain in the first game of their first-ever NBA Finals confrontation in 1964: for 21 consecutive minutes throughout the second and third periods of that contest Russell held the game's greatest offensive force absolutely scoreless. At one point Russ blocked a Wilt fall-away jumper and when huge Nate Thurmond picked up the loose ball and tried to stuff it back at the hoop Russ blocked that one too.

Rising from the midst of this memorable series of individual and team rivalries was an almost unbroken chain of unforgettable playoff contests, as well as truly memorable single moments of intense court action still vivid more than three decades later for the generation of fans that witnessed them first-hand. This string of remarkable moments must certainly begin with events which transpired on the Saturday afternoon of April 13, 1957—the scene of Boston's first-ever NBA title celebration. What unfolded that afternoon must still be considered perhaps the most exciting and nerve-racking Celtics game ever played.

Boston had just posted their first-ever division title and had also compiled the best record in the entire league for the very first time in the club's 11-year history. St. Louis, behind third-year frontcourt star Bob Pettit, had finished in a three-way tie for the Western Division crown, then cruised by Fort Wayne and Minneapolis in single-game tie-breakers to earn a first-round playoff bye. While Boston was blanking Syracuse in three straight for the Eastern title, St.

Louis was doing the same to the Lakers over in the West. The stage was then set for what appeared to the experts as an effortless Boston flight to the club's first title flag. But the Hawks were not prepared to be easy victims, and an overtime St. Louis victory (125-123) in the title series opener on the Boston home court provided the momentum that Pettit's club needed to extend Boston to a full seven games. Some additional color was added to the already high-spirited series when Auerbach punched his old boss Ben Kerner in the mouth at courtside preceding game three, the spat resulting from Auerbach's complaints that one of the Kiel Auditorium goals had been intentionally set too low.

Then came the game they still debate and dissect on Congress Street and on the steps of Faneuil Hall. No single NBA contest has been more often relived, its climactic moments more often retold, than that Saturday afternoon finale in which the Celtics more than a half-dozen times seemed to take command of the game's ebb and flow, only to have St. Louis roar back on each and every occasion. Pettit sent the contest into overtime with two clutch free throws in the closing seconds. Foul troubles then mounted for St. Louis as Jack McMahon and Cliff Hagan went to the bench, yet Hawks forward Jack Coleman forced a second overtime period with his dramatic jumper moments before the second buzzer sounded. Then it was the hometown Celtics' turn for unprecedented heroics as Jim Loscutoff sank a pair of clutch free throws to give Boston a final 125-123 advantage, a margin of victory which held up only when Pettit's last-second shot bounced harmlessly off the Boston rim.

If Boston's hitherto lowly Celtics were something of a surprise frontrunner in 1957, the league's championship mantle once more shifted quite suddenly to the river city of St. Louis for the following season. Boston again breezed to the Eastern title with a league-best 49 victories. This was the season, as well, when Bill Russell emerged as an undisputed league MVP. The Boston post-man topped the circuit in rebounding with a 22.7 average and directed the Cousy-led fast-break offense with endless pinpoint outlet passes from beneath the defensive goal. Bob Pettit—now also at the very top of his game—was simply too much for the Celtics and MVP Russell during the April championship round, however. Slowed by an ankle injury in game three, Russell was stripped of his mobility and reduced to a token role down the final playoff home stretch. Without Russell to harass him, Pettit was truly unstoppable during the sixth and final game as he poured in a postseason record 50 points and thus single-handedly dethroned the Celtics after but one season as the league's champions.

The final two seasons of the decade witnessed continuation of the dramatic Boston-St. Louis playoff tap dance. During the campaign which opened in October 1958 and folded in April 1959 both clubs raced to double-digit final leads in their respective divisions. Boston established a new league milestone by becoming the first team to amass 50 victories in a single season since Minneapolis and Syracuse had first turned the trick 10 years earlier. Yet if fans anticipated a titanic Pettit-Russell postseason rematch they were to be sorely disappointed. A revived Minneapolis outfit behind phenomenal rookie Elgin Baylor soon shocked the basketball world by torpedoing the Hawks during a six-game series that turned on a Lakers' thrilling game-five overtime victory in St. Louis. Elgin Baylor was no match for the well-balanced Celtics, however, and the Minneapolis Cinderella story ended abruptly in the face of Boston's scoring onslaught led by Sharman, Cousy and Heinsohn. Boston had already thumped Minneapolis 18 straight leading into the 1959 NBA Finals and the string included an embarrassing 173-139 February pasting that had prompted charges of point tampering. Minneapolis avoided such embarrassment this time around by keeping all games close (the point spreads were 3, 20, 3 and 5), but the result was nonetheless a lopsided four-game Boston sweep—the first of NBA Finals history.

Neither Boston nor St. Louis would lighten up even one iota on their respective division rivals during the decade-ending 1959-60 campaign. Bob Cousy would later inform reporters that throughout his entire tenure with the club the Celtics were never even once willing to coast anytime during season's play. They hated to lose two in a row, Cousy observed, and a single regular-season defeat (whether the victor was the rival Hawks or the hapless Cincinnati Royals) would cause them to approach the following contest as though it were playoff sudden-death. And that philosophy was never more evident than in 1960 when Cousy and his mates rattled off a then-record 59 wins to bury division-rival Philadelphia by 10 full games.

The Hawks and Pettit had kept pace, however, with 46 victories of their own and a lengthy 16-game spread over Detroit. And this time out there would be no upset-minded villain to spoil the anticipated Hawks-Celtics final show-down. True to season-long form, Boston set out to control the final series with a 140-122 opening-game romp. St. Louis would not bend easily, however, and held on to force a seventh-game showdown, one which only resulted in a Boston 20-point victory waltz. Russell had 22 points and 35 rebounds in the 122-103 laugher; Ramsey added 24 points and 13 boards; Heinsohn posted 22 points and 8 caroms; Cousy took advantage of an injury to Hawks playmaker Slater Martin to tally 19 points alongside his 14 assists. But the biggest number for Boston was the "two" which stood for repeat. The 1950s would thus end with the

This time the celebration is not another championship banner but instead a new NBA record for single-season victories (60), earned at the close of the 1961-62 season.

first back-to-back champion since the Mikan-led Lakers had accomplished the feat at the outset of the decade. The league's first ten-year span would also bow out with the Boston Celtics holding claim to three titles in four tries, duplicating the very feat with which Minneapolis and Mikan had opened the pioneering league's earliest seasons.

Beginning with the spring of 1959 the Celtics were off and running to their unmatched string of eight consecutive league championships. That unrivalled string began in 1959 with an altogether easy sweep of the fading Minneapolis Lakers who were only one season away from their history-making West Coast odyssey. It was punctuated by the victories over St. Louis in both 1960 and 1961—a suffi-cient measure of revenge for the stunning 1958 title upset in which Bob Pettit had singlehandedly benched the Boston championship machine while Russell sat in limbo with a wounded ankle. The next five seasons saw the "Celtics Express" roll on undaunted past the Lakers who were now residents of Los Angeles on four separate occasions, with only a single title-round appearance of Wilt Chamberlain and the San Francisco Warriors sandwiched in between. As these championship years peeled off the calendar one by one the old Celtics cast of stars departed a single actor at a time. Sharman hung up his black high-top sneakers in 1961 and Cousy took his last dribbles in the NBA Finals of 1963. Ramsey and Loscutoff bowed out at the conclusion of the 1964 championship year; then Heinsohn also decided to retire his battle-weary body a single season later. By the time the second half of the decade opened in the fall of 1965, only Auerbach on the bench and Russell in the pivot remained from the original championship club of Russell's rookie season.

But old heroes were relentlessly being replaced with new ones in Boston, and one year's thrills seemed little more than prelude to another's. In an age before television was a household staple and in a sport with comparatively few memorable single moments, one defensive sleight-of-hand by John Havlicek, for example, rates right up there in our sports annals alongside Red Grange's five-touchdown afternoon against Michigan or Babe Ruth's called shot in the 1932 World Series. The moment in question was ironically set upon the stage of one of the more classic Russell-Chamberlain battles, as Philadelphia and Boston entered the wanning moments of a seventh and deciding game in the 1965 Eastern Division Finals. Chamberlain had poured in six vital points during the game's final two minutes and sliced a once-safe Boston lead to the narrowest of possible margins. There were but five seconds standing between Philadelphia and an end to Boston's six-year championship string. With the scoreboard reading 110-109 in favor of Boston, Russell had attempted an inbounds pass that had uncharacteristically gone astray against a basket support wire. Philadelphia now had the inbounds play and was poised for the clincher; one more Philly basket would mean that the Boston dynasty would at long last—at least temporarily—be at an end. It was at this moment that Havlicek's brilliant career seemed to crystalize into a single reflexive action, as the perpetually moving defender sliced in front of Philly's Chet Walker to steal away an inbounds pass. Hondo's superhuman play had sealed yet another miraculous Boston triumph and thus clinched yet another Finals opportunity to claim still one more Boston championship banner.

Hondo's last-second steal not only fixed the memory of his own career but also cemented a reputation for the man who dramatically called the moment from the radio broadcast booth for New England's legions of diehard fans. Years of replay on highlight films and audio tapes have now immortalized the call of Celtics long-time announcer Johnny Most, whose raspy voice caught the raw emotion and sudden shock of the moment—"Havlicek stole the ball! Havlicek stole the ball!" Only Russ Hodges's equally dramatic call of Giant Bobby Thomson's 1951 playoff homer remains a more famous moment in the history of American sports broadcasting.

Havlicek's heroics would also allow the Celtics' string of uninterrupted titles to remain intact and stretch to an unprecedented seven straight once Boston breezed past Los Angeles in a short and anticlimactic 1965 five-game finale. The inevitable fall of the proud and seemingly invincible Celtics would not come until two seasons later, when an aging Boston team was finally overrun by a fresh 1967 Philadelphia Sixers squad which many still regard as the finest single-season unit of NBA history. The stage was thus set for the most memorable Celtics playoff series of the Auerbach-Russell era, the one marked by the amazing comeback of the 1968 season. The flawless Sixers had buried a fine Boston club in both the regular and postseason action of 1967, and again in the 1968 campaign Philadelphia had cruised to regular-season victory with a comfortable eight-game margin over Boston in the season-long divisional race. And March of 1968 would also mark the first season in a decade that Boston did not enter the playoffs as the league's defending champion.

Serious questions were already being raised about Russell's coaching style and leadership effectiveness after the apparent Boston collapse in postseason play a year earlier. Russell did, in fact, seem a lackluster bench boss when compared to his legendary predecessor. The Boston big man had never been much of a practice player and seemed to possess even less intensity as a practice coach. But Bill Russell had always maintained a "second-season philosophy" concerning the playoffs and once more had his team primed for a postseason rematch against Philly. The Sixers jumped to a 3-1 lead in the division title pairing (which had begun the day after the assassination of Dr. Martin Luther King) and looked as invincible as they had one winter earlier. But when Boston stormed back to force a seventh game the momentum had clearly already reversed and the Sixers were now themselves reeling. Before a screaming final-game crowd in Philadelphia's Spectrum, Russell punctuated his head-to-head mastery over Chamberlain with a second half of play in which Wilt managed to attempt but two harmless shots.

AP/Wide World Photos

A familiar Boston Garden celebration scene has Red Auerbach carried off the floor by his ecstatic players after Boston's clinching victory in game five of the 1961 championship series.

At the final buzzer Boston was on top by four—100 to 96—and Russell had his team back in the Finals once more. As was so often the case during the Russell-Chamberlain era, the final series with Los Angeles proved largely redundant as the Lakers simply couldn't handle either an intense-if-aging Russell or a hot-shooting Havlicek who averaged 25.9 ppg for postseason play. When the dust had cleared, Boston's Celtics now wore their 10th league crown in a span of but 12 short years.

When it comes to sheer drama, the 1969 playoffs which followed twelve months later provided perhaps the most inspired Celtics title series of the entire endless string of postseason derbies. Certainly this final '60s championship fling would remain the most rewarding of all for legions of Boston supporters. The time had finally come when no one in Boston or elsewhere else around the NBA actually expected the Celtics to win any longer—Russell was now 35 (and had secretly decided at mid-year that this would be his swansong), Sam Jones was 36 and had announced upcoming retirement, Bailey Howell was 32 and Satch Sanders 30. At 28, Havlicek was the only starter who had not reached his fourth decade. A fourth-place regular-season finish (48-34) was the lowest for the club in 20 years. But Boston followers had also long since come to realize that Russell-led teams played at a different level when championships were on the line. They knew as did the players themselves that age was no measure of Celtic pride and spirit.

With the postseason fully launched, Boston summoned a last reserve of individual and team strength to glide by Philadelphia in five games and then past the young yet talented New York Knicks in six. What loomed on the horizon, however, was a different matter altogether, a crack Lakers team which still boasted Elgin Baylor and Jerry West in the forecourt and had added Russell's old nemesis, Chamberlain, to anchor the frontcourt line.

But Russell always found a way to thwart the less defensively minded Wilt, and if Bill had not pushed his aging team during December and January he certainly lit a fire under them in April. The key game was the fourth, and the decisive moment came when Sam Jones stole victory with a last-second basket that prevented a 3-1 Los Angeles series lead. Game seven was again a classic in which the old warriors from Boston were once more able to work championship magic against a younger and more talented team, while at the same time faced with a hostile enemy crowd. Chamberlain again proved of questionable character as he retired to the bench with a minor injury in the final quarter and saw no further action down the crucial final moments of the disappearing season. (Russell later criticized Wilt for removing himself from the game and the tension between the two over the incident largely ruined their earlier off-court friendship.) Boston would barely hang on to a

dwindling lead as the clock shrank and an off-balance jumper by reserve Don Nelson in the final seconds was barely enough to preserve the last and easily the most incredible championship of the incomparable Bill Russell era.

The true extent of the Celtic mystique is perhaps best measured by the mythic status which the team of Russell, Cousy, Havlicek and Heinsohn has now acquired for later generations of NBA fans. Since those halcyon days when Red Auerbach first acquired Bill Russell off the campus of San Francisco University and overnight converted the struggling ballclub that Walter Brown had founded a decade earlier into a true titan of the neophyte NBA, the Celtics have remained the most successful and perhaps best-loved franchise in all of professional sports. Auerbach's teams have done far more than capture 16 world championship flags in the 43 seasons he has served as coach, general manager and finally franchise president. Boston's Celtics forever remain the benchmark by which the public conception of true dynasty teams will forever more be measured. Michael Jordan, Kareem Abdul-Jabbar and Magic Johnson aside, no one has ever again seen basketball—the total team game—as it was once played to perfection by the Boston Celtics of the Bill Russell era.

The Finkel-Havlicek Era

The Celtics were not completely dead after the departure of Bill Russell. It did certainly appear that way, of course, in the immediate wake of Russell's inevitable exit. But the collapse was brief enough and in fact lasted only a single season.

Without Russell on the bench, and more importantly without the big man stacking the defensive odds their way on the court, the Boston team fell like a lead weight in '69-'70, crashing all the way to sixth spot in the Eastern Division standings, barely ahead of a perennially poor Detroit Pistons outfit. It was a rough beginning for new head coach Tom Heinsohn whom Auerbach had lured away from a lucrative insurance business back in Worcester, Massachusetts. Heinsohn's inherited lineup of Tom "Satch" Sanders and Don Nelson up front, gentle seven footer "High Henry" Finkel at Russell's center slot, and Havlicek and Larry Siegfried at the guards could muster only 34 victories. Boston fans who had yawned their way through a decade of taken-for-granted glory now turned their wrath largely on Finkel, a moderately talented giant who had the great misfortune (like millions of other folks around the land) of not being Bill Russell. The iron-fingered and lead-footed Finkel averaged only 9.7 ppg but easily led the circuit in hometown booing and was cause for sarcastic jabs

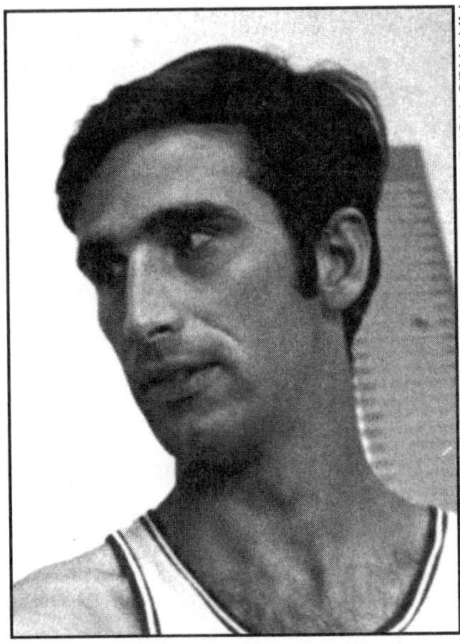

AP/Wide World Photos

Henry Finkel inherited basketball's most impossible task in 1969 as Bill Russell's replacement.

from the Boston press. Of course the name didn't help much either, and it wasn't long before some scribes were callously writing about "The Finkel Era" that had now descended on Boston Garden.

But if Henry Finkel was an all-too-easy scapegoat it was also true that there was now indeed sufficient reason for fan letdown at the Garden. It was Boston's first losing record in 20 years and also the first miss of the playoffs in the same span. And to make matters more embarrassing, the Cincinnati team that finished a slot ahead of the now ramshackle Celtics was coached by Russell's and Heinsohn's old running mate, Bob Cousy.

The road back for Heinsohn and the Celtics was not much delayed in coming, however, and it began almost immediately with the '70-'71 and '71-'72 rebuilding seasons. In only Heinsohn's second campaign at the helm the ballclub improved ten full games, climbed above .500, and finished third in the division. This turn-around had been in large part triggered when Auerbach unloaded Larry Siegfried, Bailey Howell and Emmette Bryant and installed rookie Dave Cowens in the center slot, moved the versatile Havlicek up front with the improving Nelson, and went with a revamped backcourt featuring youngsters Don Chaney and Jo Jo White. Havlicek responded by upping his game a full notch to superstar status. The former stellar role player enjoyed his best offensive season (28.9 ppg, 2338 points, 730 rebounds—all career highs) and was the league's second best scorer behind Alcindor.

By Year Three of the Heinsohn régime it hardly seemed that there had been any downturn at all. The 1972 campaign would next bring the first in a run of five straight regular-season first-place finishes. There was already no question that the apparent lull in Boston had been temporary and that the Celtics were back to their old tricks. Havlicek (27.5 ppg) enjoyed another banner scoring year, this time finishing third behind the renamed Abdul-Jabbar in Milwaukee and a new little-man sensation named Nate "Tiny" Archibald in Cincinnati. The new Boston lineup of Havlicek, Nelson, Cowens, Chaney and White was suddenly as potent as any in the entire league, although the bench of Sanders, Finkel, Steve Kuberski and others was perhaps too thin for any realistic title hopes. Boston did outdistance runner-up New York by eight games in the new Atlantic Division (the league had shifted to a four-division alignment a season earlier) and did survive one round of the playoffs before tumbling in five games to the more experienced Knicks team they had already outdistanced in regular-season combat.

But experience as well as raw talent would soon enough once again be residing up in Beantown. While Auerbach's old rivals, the Lakers, were celebrating their first-ever championship out on the west coast at the end of the '71-'72 season, Boston's proud Celtics were now themselves about to re-emerge with true vengeance. It had been an all-too-short period of rebuilding—at least if you didn't live in or around Boston and rooted for any of the league's 16 other ballclubs.

Renewed Celtic glory was kindled as much as anything by the emerging stardom of undersized pivot-man Dave Cowens, now the league's premier rebounder and shot blocker as well as Boston's unrivalled floor leader. Cowens was a bigger (6-feet-8 1/2 inches) version of Havlicek who could run all day, outhustle as well as out-maneuver any other NBA center, and was a prized left-handed shooter to boot. With such reinforcements the 1973 Boston team

Author's Collection

If Henry Finkel failed to fill Bill Russell's shoes, flamboyant Dave Cowens proved far more successful at the task a season or two later.

soared to a franchise-record 68 victories that still stands as the unsurpassed mark for regular-season winning in Boston. Cowens was the league's MVP and Havlicek had another brilliant season as well. But the biggest plus perhaps was the rebounding of forward Paul Silas, another Auerbach "steal" who had been obtained from Phoenix in compensation for the signing of original Boston draft choice Charlie Scott.

Yet for all their rapid improvement the Celtics still couldn't quite handle the veteran New York Knicks contingent of Bill Bradley, Willis Reed, Dave DeBusschere, Earl Monroe and Walt Frazier in postseason action. Boston again lost a second-round matchup in seven dramatic games. Perhaps the turning point this time, however, came only when Havlicek was felled by a shoulder injury during the see-saw third game of the series.

The first Boston title under Heinsohn, earned during the following 1974 season, didn't come all that easily either. Milwaukee in its penultimate year with Alcindor (now known as Kareem Abdul-Jabbar) and its final year with Oscar Robertson (soon to retire) would muster enough brilliant offensive play to extend Heinsohn's men to a full seven final-round championship games. Boston had again climbed into the postseason by outdistancing New York to win the Atlantic Division. And in the Eastern Finals this time around it was the Knicks who were knocked out by injuries—to Willis Reed and Dave DeBusschere—assuring a quick five-game Boston victory. Thus the title match-up between Boston with Cowens and Havlicek and Milwaukee with Jabbar and Oscar was precisely the one everyone had expected. And it proved a thrilling tug-of-war right down to the final contest.

Boston held a large advantage against Milwaukee from the start: the Bucks had lost one backcourt star when Lucius Allen was cancelled out by a knee injury and were suffering at the other guard slot as well. "The Big O" was now at the end of his string and could not be counted on for much firepower in his fourteenth and final campaign. Victories were traded through the first six contests, with Milwaukee gamely forcing a rubber match by eking out a 102-101 double-overtime win in game six. In the finale Cowens outdueled Jabbar 28-26 and the Celtics cruised 102-87 for NBA title number 12, after only a five-year temporary hiatus.

The Celtics of the seventies had been able to staff their yearly rosters with a whole new contingent of bright superstars. Havlicek was still in high gear for most of the decade and gloried in his new team-leader and superstar roles. But a new hero figure had also arrived with peerless Dave Cowens. Cowens soon proved one of the greatest Celtics warriors of all—the franchise player of the '70s and undoubtedly the best center in club history after the immortal Russell. It was soon clear, in fact, that a new Boston Celtics powerhouse had now been reconstructed by

Auerbach (from his front-office perch) largely around the most mobile and unconventional center in league history. When Cowens arrived as an unheralded rookie off the campus of Florida State University in the fall of 1970 he immediately revolutionized inside play by moving the conventional pivot position a full 20 feet from the basket. This strategy soon proved infallible as Cowens utilized his rugged style of play to transform the Celtics from a dull and lifeless outfit into the fast-breaking thoroughbred of old, a team suddenly capable of seizing two more championships (1974 and 1976) before the decade of the 1970s rolled into its second half.

And there were other heroes as well. Don Nelson was a mainstay early in the decade and perhaps one of Auerbach's greatest bargains. The future highly successful NBA coach was picked up off waivers (at Tom Heinsohn's suggestion) in 1965 and logged 11 seasons as a steady double-figure scorer and deadly jump-shot artist. Nelson's most outstanding individual campaign was perhaps his penultimate year of '74-'75 when he paced the league in field goal percentage at the advanced age of 34 and also proved one of the circuit's most valued sixth-man performers as backup to Havlicek and Silas. High-scoring Charlie Scott (whose 34.6 ppg ABA mark in 1972 was the highest ever for a guard until Michael Jordan came along) enjoyed three fine Boston years at mid-career, joining the Celtics just in time to contribute heavily to the 1976 championship ballclub. Originally drafted by Auerbach in 1970, Scott opted to star in the ABA; but Boston cleverly traded NBA rights to the North Carolina whirlwind to Phoenix for Paul Silas, then re-acquired Scott for Paul Westphal in May of 1975. Paul Silas himself was a main man in the middle part of the decade and teamed with Cowens on the 1976 championship club to provide Boston with two of the league's top four rebounders. And finally there was Jo Jo White, a stellar guard out of the University of Kansas who continued the lineage of Cousy and Sam Jones when he manned the controls of the Celts' fast-breaking offensive throughout the entire decade of the '70s. White was a fine defender, pumped in better than 14,000 career points with his patented in-front-of-the-face jumper, and averaged better than 20 ppg six different times in postseason play. Next to Cowens, Jo Jo White was unquestionably the "glory player" of the Celtics decade between Russell and Bird.

During this period Tom Heinsohn also carved out a new spot for himself in Celtics history. One of the club's most successful players also now became one of its mastermind coaches. In his eight-plus years on the bench Heinsohn compiled the second most victories in club history (427), the fifth highest winning percentage (.619), and the third highest total of postseason victories (47). If Heinsohn stands in the top six among all-time Boston playing greats (alongside Russell, Cousy, Bird, Cowens and

Havlicek), he certainly rates that distinction among the legendary Boston coaches as well.

The peak of the 1970s, however, came with the 1975-76 Boston campaign. Regular-season action would find Heinsohn's men posting only 54 victories, something of a slide after the 60-win campaigns of 1973 and 1975, yet still a good enough mark to stand second best overall (Golden State won 59 in the Pacific Division) and to outpace Atlantic Division runners-up Buffalo and Philadelphia by a comfortable eight games. Boston's backcourt had now taken on a new look as Don Chaney jumped to the ABA and Auerbach adjusted to this loss by trading Paul Westphal to Phoenix for Charlie Scott. The bench (Nelson, Kevin Stacom, Glenn McDonald, Steve Kuberski, Jim Ard) was now dangerously thin but the front line was still solid and balanced as Havlicek, Cowens, Scott and White all averaged between 17 and 19 ppg and Cowens and Silas both cracked the 1000 rebound plateau.

Tom Heinsohn

But if this seemed like just another run-of-the-mill Boston title outfit, there would be nothing at all commonplace about the postseason shootout with Phoenix which soon followed. The Boston-Phoenix Finals would in fact be highlighted by one of the greatest individual games in NBA annals. This would be the pivotal fifth game, staged in Boston Garden on June 4th with fan interest at an all-time high and the two contenders locked up at two games apiece. What transpired was later to be known among hoopologists far and wide as "The Fabulous Fifth"—one of only two triple-overtime NBA Finals slugfests ever witnessed. It was truly an epic battle of determination and endurance laced with plenty of raw luck. Fortunately for the Celtics faithful most of that luck was good for Boston and not quite so good for Phoenix.

It was a game that had something memorable for fans of all tastes—heroic game-saving shots, expected and unexpected last-second heroes, and a near breakdown of law and order to boot. There was also the delightful story line of the rugged, roughhouse, heavily-favored "Goliath" in the form of the Celtics and the slick-shooting and determined

underdog "David" in the guise of the Suns. Boston roared to a big 22-point first quarter lead and then faded slightly, yet managed to hold onto a 16-point half-time spread. The pesky Suns cut the margin to 68-64 late in the third quarter and rallied furiously down the stretch behind ex-Celtic Westphal. A foul shot by Havlicek knotted the contest with only seconds remaining and both teams (Havlicek and Sun's forward Gar Heard) missed final shots to force the first overtime. Curtis Perry then canned four points in the waning seconds to force a second overtime period after Boston again seemed to have a safe lead within the final minute of play. Action reached a frenzied peak in the second extra session as Dick Van Arsdale's only score of the night and another bucket by Perry gave the visitors a 110-109 edge with but five seconds remaining. Havlicek (playing with a broken bone in his foot) upped tensions a notch higher, however, by canning an off-balanced jumper for the apparent dramatic game-winner.

But it was not quite over yet. Referee Richie Powers was able to quell the jubilant Boston victory celebration with the news that two seconds remained on the scoreboard clock. But not before near-riot conditions had enveloped the Garden and police had to storm the playing floor to restore order among unruly fans. With play resumed Suns' coach John MacLeod took advantage of a rules technicality and called a time out which his ballclub no longer had. Jo Jo White's resulting technical foul shot gave Boston a two-point margin, but the ploy also allowed Phoenix a mid-court inbounds pass to Heard which he promptly sank to force the third extra session. Cowens and Silas had now fouled out for Boston and it was time - in finest Celtics tradition—for the unheralded role players to step forward into their unaccustomed heroes' robes. Jim Ard assumed the center slot and hit 3 of 6 baskets and both his foul shots under extreme pressure. And little-used forward-guard Glenn McDonald enjoyed 64 seconds of lasting glory with three key baskets and two clutch free throws of his own. The Suns stormed back one last time

Legendary Celtics Coaches
(Ranked by Total Victories with Boston)

Name	Regular Season	Post-Season	Championships	(Years)
Red Auerbach	795-397 (.667)	90-58 (.608)	9	('57, '59-'65)
Tom Heinsohn	**427-263 (.619)**	**47-33 (.588)**	**2**	**(1974, 1976)**
K. C. Jones	308-102 (.751)	65-37 (.637)	2	(1984, 1986)
Bill Fitch	242-86 (.738)	26-19 (.578)	1	(1981)
Chris Ford	222-188 (.542)	13-16 (.448)	0	
Bill Russell	162-83 (.661)	28-18 (.609)	2	(1968, 1969)

with two final clutch baskets by Westphal, but these were split by the two charity tosses of Jim Ard. Ard's tosses represented the final margin (128-126) in one of basketball's most draining games. Two days later Boston also captured the most anti-climactic finale in NBA championship history, an 87-80 victory in Phoenix. Boston's lucky thirteenth NBA world championship had certainly been one of the hardest earned, and perhaps also the one that turned more on a few lucky bounces than any other.

Just as the Boston club stumbled a the end of the '60s, so would it stumble again at the very end of the '70s (and ironically at the end of the '80s as well). The first decline had coincided with the career swansong of player-coach Bill Russell. The second came when Havlicek and Cowens faded from the scene. John Havlicek would take his final curtain call on the longest and most productive playing career in proud Celtics history during the 1977-78 campaign (which was also ironically Heinsohn's last as a coach). Cowens would perform in Boston Garden for two additional seasons after Havlicek's retirement, then spend one final year in Milwaukee after being traded away for guard Quinn Buckner. A third such collapse would of course come a full decade later, with the demise of Larry Bird.

Two final seasons of the '70s thus witnessed the Celtics once again hit rock bottom with a trip into the league's lower rungs, a place they had not known very often during the first three decades of club history. While Havlicek's and Heinsohn's final campaign saw the team slide no further than third in the Atlantic Division, a ledger 18-games under .500 was the worst Boston finish since the inaugural year of NBA play back in 1950. A year later the team now coached by Tom Sanders (Heinsohn's replacement 35 games into the 1977-78 season) logged three victories less and tumbled all the way into the divisional cellar. It was clearly time for another rebuilding campaign and for Red Auerbach to pull another miracle rabbit (or perhaps this time a Bird) out of his seemingly ceaseless bag of tricks.

The Bird Era

Great teams in any sport seem to find an endless flow of renewed heroes, like the Yankees with Ruth and Gehrig and DiMaggio and Mickey Mantle, each passing the cloak of honor on to the next legend standing in line, an endless inheritance of immortals spread over three and perhaps more decades. For the Celtics the fifties celebrated Cousy, the sixties Russell, and the seventies Havlicek. And on the horizon in the 1980s was perhaps the brightest one-man team of all—number "33" Larry Joe Bird.

When Larry Bird entered the NBA in the fall of 1979, on the heels of one of the worst Boston seasons ever, he was about to rescue far more than a single once-noble franchise. The league itself had fallen on exceedingly slow times. Dr. J had receded from his prime, Jabbar was piling up milestones but was too placid a performer to inspire fan passions, David Thompson had flamed out early on his promise to be Jordan before Jordan, Kevin Porter and John Lucas were the premier backcourt aces but had painfully little of the trappings of legend about them. NBA basketball needed new heroes and it needed a large dose of new drama as well. Bird would be largely responsible (along with an old collegiate rival now operating out west) for providing the quick fix that basketball sorely needed. And it would be a role he would willingly share. For Larry Bird would always be linked in basketball history with his greatest rival— Earvin Magic Johnson of the Los Angeles Lakers.

The salvation of the sagging league would be a glamorous rivalry of two new superstars who could now replay and even upgrade the earlier tussles of Russell and Chamberlain. The scenario would now be quite different, of course, as the nature and style of the professional game had drastically altered. Russell and Chamberlain were the latter-day towering giants who epitomized a stationary game of shot blocking and board sweeping. Magic and Bird were the mobile shooting and playmaking wizards who captured the flare of the true transition game. And, of course, no small part of the rivalry would be due to the magic of television itself. TV provided a proper forum for the fast-paced and colorful entertainment spectacle of one-on-one fullcourt play. And now the NBA finally possessed precisely the action-packed spectacle that was right for the times.

Larry and Magic brought to the NBA stage and screen a heated rivalry already well established for a hungry audience of college hoops fans. They had both starred for two seasons in the midwestern hotbed of collegiate hoops. Bird had led an unheralded small school to sudden national prominence while Johnson had shone as a sophomore and paced Michigan State to a rare Big Ten title. And soon the two were on a collision course which took them to one of the most storied Final Four meetings in NCAA history. That game was a vintage head-to-head battle in which Magic had captured round one in storybook fashion: the Spartans cruised to an NCAA title 75-64, and Magic won the individual duel plus tourney MVP honors while racking up 31 points.

Both had also entered the NBA under most surprising circumstances at the conclusion of stellar (and in Magic's case, abbreviated) college careers. Bird would be claimed by the Celtics on draft day of 1978, a full season before his collegiate career was over (but in the year when his original college class was due to graduate). And Johnson would opt for the NBA as a "hardship case" in the same season when Bird would now debut, even though he still had two years of university eligibility remaining.

Larry Bird and Earvin "Magic" Johnson together revived a sagging NBA at the outset of the 1980s when they moved their spirited rivalry from collegiate courts to professional arenas.

It was the sort of glamor that seemed to be so long missing from the NBA venues. Clearly there was a lack of the kind of recognizable superstars that had filled the Celtics epoch of the 1960s and the "big man" era at the outset of the 1970s. Jabbar was still around, though the rookie luster of Lew Alcindor in Milwaukee had seemed to fade into the methodical veteran efficiency of a West Coast Kareem. George Gervin had now been the league's scoring leader for three seasons but lacked anything approaching pizzazz or personality. Kids could hardly be expected to take to the alleys and schoolyards aping every move of a colorless player like "Iceman" Gervin. Phoenix forward Truck Robinson had recently captured the league rebounding title. Detroit guard Kevin Porter was the current NBA pacesetter in assists. These were hardly household names either. Bird and Magic brought sorely needed charisma back into the vapid league. Larry Bird displayed the freewheeling flash and flair associated with the street game of urban New York playgrounds and not the rural Indiana game of the heartlands that had spawned him. And Magic was the most infectious personality ever to hit big-time professional sports.

Bird's arrival in Boston could not help but remind the veteran NBA watcher of Russell's fateful journey into Boston a quarter-century earlier—unprecedented rookie, revived veteran lineup, sudden title surge. The mastermind was again Auerbach, of course. The renowned redhead had once again manipulated the draft to his advantage to find a franchise player. Magic Johnson would perhaps draw first blood in the new rivalry and win the first team title of the new decade. But Larry Bird would enjoy a bit of magic of his own during a phenomenal rookie season (21.3 ppg, 1745 points, 10.4 rpg, 143 steals, 4.5 apg). And it would be Bird who would salvage some measure of pride in Boston with coveted rookie-of-the-year honors.

The Celtics, for their own part, enjoyed a marvelous resurrection during Bird's rookie campaign. In this year dedicated to revival, it was the Celtics who made the greatest individual turnaround. Embarrassing victory totals of 32 and 29 during two previous campaigns were dramatically supplanted with a league-best 61 in the win column. Veteran guard Nate "Tiny" Archibald in his second Boston season was a catalyst as he bounced back with a surprising shooting display (14.1 ppg) and stellar play as a veteran

floor general. Dave Cowens confounded the experts by proving there was still spark and power left in his rugged inside game. Cedric "Cornbread" Maxwell was a huge offensive force (16.9 ppg) in the frontcourt, this time with plenty of assistance from the rookie phenom Bird. First-year coach Bill Fitch provided glue to hold it all together as he molded his charges into a winning unit around Bird and the squad of aging veterans. Few were surprised by the choice of Bill Fitch as NBA coach of the year. And fewer still could debate Bird's selection as the circuit's stellar rookie.

The message had thus been sent out in 1980 that the Celtics were now back in business. And by the time Bird's sophomore campaign was underway it was clear everywhere in the NBA just how far back the team had actually come. The second season of the Bird-Magic era would see the balance shift from Los Angeles to Boston. The key to the Celtics' immediate future had begun on draft day when Auerbach engineered a blockbuster maneuver similar to the one that had earlier brought Bird himself to Boston. First the Celtics sent veteran Bob McAdoo to Detroit for a top first-round pick. The prime draft slot was then peddled to Golden State (who would use it to acquire Purdue seven-footer Joe Barry Carroll) in exchange for established workhorse big man Robert Parish and another first-round selection who was pencilled in as Minnesota All-American forward Kevin McHale. The front-line pieces were now suddenly in place, ready to be installed around Bird. What had been an excellent team was suddenly a nearly invincible one.

Bird established his future penchant for postseason heroics during the 1981 semi-final rematch with the resurgent Philadelphia Sixers. It was Philadelphia with the ageless Julius Erving that had prevented a Bird-Magic rookie title shootout a season earlier, by thumping Boston in five during the Eastern Conference Finals. Boston would this time scrap back all the way from a seemingly hopeless 3-1 deficit to capture the dramatic series on a last-minute jumper by none other than icewater-veined Larry Joe Bird. After the Philadelphia series laced with Bird's last-second heroics, a championship round with Houston's Rockets was predictably anticlimactic. Bird himself was slowed by a clever and relentless Houston defense anchored by Robert

Cedric "Cornbread" Maxwell plants a kiss on the NBA championship trophy in Houston moments after being named Most Valuable Player in the 1981 NBA title series.

Reid. But Cornbread Maxwell was suddenly white hot at just the right time and Boston found little enough resistance from an enthusiastic but overmatched Houston team, one that had actually finished under .500 during regular-season play. Bird was still testing the league waters when Boston now had a 14th world title banner already hanging from the rafters of the ancient Boston Garden.

The Celtics and Lakers would continue to own the league for much of the remainder of the decade. The Lakers would enjoy four more titles; Boston would claim another two. Three times they would meet head-to-head in the title round. Through it all Bird and Magic would time and again renew their battles for supremacy. In the end Larry Bird would lug away the bulk of the personal honors, at least if one looked at career stats alone. Bird would never win an individual NBA scoring title, yet would consistently rank high up among the best point producers. Magic would dominate in the assists category and show great strength of overall play. And they each walked off with three league MVP trophies.

Bird, of course, was not the whole show in Boston in the eighties. Auerbach had constructed another juggernaut from his front office perch, and despite the presence of a budding superstar, this was again a balanced team shaped in the true Celtics mold. McHale continued the great Boston sixth-man tradition of Ramsey and Havlicek before him. Parish was the quintessential team-oriented center, perhaps the best in the league since Cowens. The backcourt was also more than adequate. Dennis Johnson was a championship caliber competitor who had already proved his winning ways in both Seattle and Phoenix. Jerry Sichting and Danny Ainge provided spark and ballhandling under fire. And Bill Walton and M.L. Carr among others stepped in as the kind of role players that Loscutoff and Gene Conley and Don Nelson had long ago been.

And on the coaching lines Auerbach had again followed the formula that had already served him so well in the past. As with Russell and then Heinsohn, he had again found a bench boss among the stars of his great dynasty team of the

AP/Wide World Photos

Dennis Johnson wrote a new chapter in the saga of stellar Boston backcourt play during the 1980s. DJ here drives for a bucket during the 1984 NBA Finals against the Lakers.

'60s. K.C. Jones was now at the Boston helm and he proved a most adequate leader fashioned precisely in the Auerbach image.

The three seasons of 1984-86 were among the greatest in ballclub history. Three straight winters the team held the best regular-season league won-loss mark. And all three years the win totals (62, 63, 67) equalled or surpassed the best ledger of the '60s Russell era (62-18 in 1965). The true highlight year of the Bird-Magic rivalry, however—at least from the Boston perspective—had to be the campaign of 1983-84. Bird led the club from wire to wire as rookie coach K. C. Jones enjoyed the best record in the league, a ten-game spread over Eastern runner-up Philadelphia, and convincing victories over Washington, New York and Milwaukee in the first three postseason rounds.

The 1984 NBA Finals offered a showcase Bird-Magic faceoff, the first long-anticipated matchup of the two rival stars during an NBA finale. Bird and Magic were now in their fifth season in the league and had yet to re-enact their 1979 NCAA duel in front of the nation's TV cameras. Boston had first stumbled against Philly in 1980, blocking the hoped-for celebrity shootout. The following year the Lakers had stumbled out of the gate in the playoff's opening round, and then in 1982 Boston and Bird had again been shot down by Erving and the Sixers in the Eastern Finals. But when it finally did become a reality in 1984, the long-anticipated Boston and Los Angeles championship matchup was a true TV bonanza.

This was not only a personal title rematch of Bird and Johnson, but also the first championship rematch of Boston and LA since the storied days of Bill Russell a decade and a half earlier. The Lakers won easily in the first and third games but somehow let both the second and fourth contests get away from them in overtime. Boston then edged ahead 121-103 in game five, only to have Los Angeles once more reverse the momentum by an almost identical 119-108 count in game six. The deciding battle would provide the setting for a record television audience, as well as for yet another testing ground on which Boston could demonstrate its four-decade rubber match superiority against all comers. This time it was again Boston, 111-102, as the Celtics once more protected their miraculous string of never having lost the seventh game of a title series. Bird finally enjoyed his revenge over Magic—and a championship ring and playoff MVP trophy to boot. In Boston it now all seemed to have been well worth the lengthy wait.

For the next three straight seasons Bird would lead the ballclub back to the championship round each and every year. First there would be a rematch loss to the Lakers, then another title earned against Houston. And finally another defeat at the hands of Los Angeles. In the end it was a run almost as glorious as the one once made by Cousy, Russell, Heinsohn and company.

The 1985 playoff season provided pro hoop fans with the richest of fare—another Boston and Los Angeles classic grudge match. Both juggernauts had cruised to easy defense of their conference titles in divisional playoffs. The Celtics looked unbeatable yet again as they crushed the Lakers 148-114 in historic Boston Garden in the championship series opener. Dating back to Minneapolis days, Laker teams had now faced Boston's green and white for the NBA title eight times, and after each and every encounter yet another banner flew proudly from the rafters of venerable Boston Garden. It looked in the face of the one-sided opener that there was little reason to expect anything different this ninth time around. But a feisty Los Angeles squad soon fought back to carry a three-games-to-two lead back into Boston for the final two deciding contests. Like so many of the championship showdowns between these two proud teams in the past, this one again would hinge upon key injury as well as an unexpected heroic performance by a wily overlooked veteran.

It was Bird who would go down with injury this time around, as elbow and finger inflammations would hamper Larry's shooting throughout the round-robin week. And it was Jabbar who would suddenly rise to the occasion with an unanticipated 29 points (backed by James Worthy's 28) in the deciding game six. Magic Johnson again played no

AP/Wide World Photos

Boston's most valuable player, Larry Bird, flies high with a rebounding effort during his stellar MVP performance in the 1982 NBA All-Star contest at New Jersey's Meadowlands Arena.

small role, with a triple-double in the title-clinching match—14 points, 14 assists, 10 rebounds. At the final buzzer the score stood at Los Angeles 111, Boston 100, and the years of Laker frustration were finally relegated to history. Incredible as it may seem, Los Angeles had become the first team in 16 tries to cop an NBA title against the Celtics while playing on the Celt's charmed parquet floor in ghost-ridden Boston Garden.

The Celtics would bounce back in '85-'86, but not before a serious scare early in the campaign. A back injury would slow Bird in the early going and although he didn't miss any games the pain reduced his overall effectiveness and seemed to lower his stature from titan to mere league all-star. Chiropractic treatments were enough to correct the problem in mid-season, however, and a rejuvenated Bird now roared to his third straight season's MVP. The club's 67 victories were also the second best total of franchise history.

The toughest postseason challenge for Bird and his mates came in the opening-round matchup with Jordan and the Chicago Bulls. Returning from his own season of knockout injuries (a broken foot which cancelled all but 18 of his games), Air Jordan nearly stole the show with stellar offensive performances of 49 points and then 63 points (an NBA record) during the opening two contests. But Jordan alone was not enough against the veteran Boston club to prevent a three-game Celtics sweep. The Hawks and Bucks also fell easily and the Celts again entered the NBA Finals against the surprising Houston Rockets (upset winners over the Lakers out West) riding the crest of an 11-1 postseason roll. The roll only continued when the outmanned Rockets fell in a series best remembered for a fifth-game free-for-all featuring towering center Ralph Sampson and Boston's pugnacious Jerry Sichting. The 1986 NBA title flight would be Bird's last great moment as a champion and Larry took full advantage. With a 25.9 playoff scoring onslaught Bird added yet another postseason MVP trophy to his personal stash. And the combined regular and postseason victory total of 82 games now owned by Boston was the highest total in all of NBA history.

The see-saw alternation between NBA titles and bridesmaid losses in the NBA Finals soon continued for a fourth straight year. Again it would be a Magic-Bird and Lakers-Celtics confrontation, the third of the decade. But this time the cards were too heavily stacked against the Beantowners from the outset. McHale was playing on a broken foot while Parish was reduced to limited effectiveness by a severely sprained ankle. The Lakers ran away from the Celts in each of the first two games, as might have been expected with Boston's lineup so hobbled. Boston would gamely rebound to take two of three on the home floor. But a dramatic last-second game-winning mini-hook by Magic Johnson in vital game four would prove pivotal. The 1987 Finals provided in the end a last thunderous triumph of sorts for Boston, although perhaps no one would have predicted it at the time. Bird poured in a sparkling 27 points per postseason contest but couldn't match Johnson for last-minute heroics or overall MVP effectiveness. When the crowd roars had finally died away the Bird-Magic playoff sideshow had played its last fitting act with Johnson now holding a lasting 2-1 advantage.

Bird would enjoy one more glorious campaign in 1987-88 and thus appear to be still operating at the very top of his matchless game. Larry would pace the ballclub in

Back pain and other assorted injuries during the late '80s and early '90s would often leave a frustrated Larry Bird pensively watching the games from the sidelines.

scoring for a record ninth straight time, finish third in the league's scoring race, and post a career-high point total. It was enough for Boston to run away with an Atlantic Division title also, the fifth straight (and last under coach K. C. Jones) in a division where no one else broke .500 or stood within 19 games of Bird and company. But in the playoffs the Celts would nonetheless be toppled by Detroit in a six-game Eastern Conference Final. Actually Boston had been lucky to get out of the second round, where only a 20-point fourth quarter rampage by Bird saved a seventh-game showdown with Atlanta. And it all proved to be something of a prophetic final hurrah for both Bird and his Celtic mates. Larry would be struck down by repeated nagging injuries over the course of the next several seasons. Bone spurs in his foot ended Bird's subsequent 1989 campaign after only six games and Boston slipped to third place and a quick first-round playoff exit (0-3 against eventual champion Detroit) when forced to play without their star forward.

Bird was restored to health for 1990 and again paced the ballclub with a standard Bird season (24.3 ppg, 9.5 rpg, 7.5 apg). But now another loss hit hard as last year's rookie star Brian Shaw opted (along with Cleveland's Danny Ferry) to escape the NBA for a more lucrative European contract and professional play in Italy. Kevin McHale took up some slack with an excellent year as a stellar sixth-man performer, and second-year coach Jimmy Rodgers guided his forces to a close second-place finish behind Philadelphia. But age was now becoming a factor as Bird, McHale and Parish all showed considerable wear and tear from their combined 35 winters on the circuit. Again there was a first-round playoff elimination, this time at the hands of New York in five games. Age and physical pain had especially overtaken Bird, a victim of continued bone spur problems, and the '90-'91 season would be his last at anything like full strength. Again Bird paced the team in scoring, and again the Celtics were back atop the Atlantic Division. But a year later Larry Joe Bird was finally done and retirement had seemed to come all too early to one of the game's greatest modern-era superstars.

With Bird gone and McHale and Parish in the twilight of their own careers, it was not surprising that Boston would again take their predictable end-of-the-decade tumble. This time, however, it would be one of the quickest and deepest falls of all, the kind of collapse that was regular fare in other NBA cities but which Boston fans had almost no clue how to handle. First there would be two more seasons near the top of the Atlantic Division under new coach Chris Ford; and Reggie Lewis would inherit at least a fraction of Bird's stardom as the ballclub's new top scorer and "main man" on offense. But Boston no longer had the firepower to make much noise in postseason play. The 1992 season did bring a lengthy visit to the second round of playoff festivities and a disappointing seventh-game drubbing in the Conference semi-finals by Cleveland. But in 1993 Boston was again quickly and rudely dumped, this time by an expansion team from Charlotte in the opening set of postseason games.

The 1993-94 season was one of the worst in Boston history. The element of personal tragedy that seem to latch onto the team in the eighties and nineties now struck yet again with the unexpected death of team captain Reggie Lewis. Lewis had collapsed on the court during the 1993 postseason series with Charlotte and had been diagnosed with possible heart problems. Then during a private shooting workout in August Lewis suffered a fatal heart attack at age 27. The team would dedicate the 1993-94 season to their fallen comrade, but such a gesture did little to revive sagging ballclub fortunes. There would even be a new club record for consecutive home-court defeats. By the end of a dismal campaign Chris Ford's Celtics were buried in fifth place with an embarrassing 32-50 mark, the fewest wins, lowest standing and first postseason absence since a nearly identical season in 1978-79. It was, in fact, the first time Boston had sunk below 3rd (there had actually been only one finish below 2nd) in the Atlantic Division in fifteen years. And to put a definitive end to a glorious era, ancient center Robert Parish was not resigned at the close of season's play. (Parish would quickly ink a hefty contract with Charlotte's Hornets for an 18th and perhaps final campaign.) The only bright spot perhaps was a late summer signing of aging superstar Dominique Wilkins to lead a '94-'95 rebuilding campaign.

It would now once again be a long climb back. Yet however deep the Boston club might now occasionally tumble, any Boston Celtics fan (and no fans of the hoop sport are more numerous or fanatic, or found in more distant corners of the globe) didn't have to search far for consolations. There were all those championship banners on view in Boston Garden each night. There was the venerable Garden itself—basketball's most hallowed shrine and still going strong as the only original NBA arena of the 1950s. And there was the uniform itself and its constant reminder of basketball's noblest tradition. That green and white jersey with the block-lettered "Celtics" on the front

had remained the same since the primitive days of the league nearly a half-century ago; it was a rare mark of stability in a sport of almost constant change. The only problem now was a growing concern that if any more numbers were retired there would hardly be enough numerals left to outfit those expected great Boston teams of the near future.

Best Trade in Franchise History

There is no hesitation here, no room for debate or counterclaim. It was simply the smartest, luckiest, most famous and most lucrative trade in all basketball history. Acquiring the rights to Bill Russell (in the form of a number two draft selection owned by St. Louis) for established scorer "Easy Ed" Macauley and promising newcomer Cliff Hagan may have seemed like something of a gamble for Auerbach and the Celtics at the time. The move would give the rival Hawks a potent front line of Macauley, Pettit and Hagan and make them a championship contender. And not everyone was convinced that a man who specialized in positioning himself for rebounds and in swatting down enemy shots was a true franchise player.

But here was the first sign of Auerbach's budding genius. Choosing first in the draft lottery would be the Rochester Royals, and Auerbach and Boston owner Walter Brown knew that Royals management (they were a small market team living on the edge of financial survival) would avoid getting into a bidding war with the Harlem Globetrotters for Russell's services. It was also obvious to the Celtics braintrust that Russell was precisely the type of ballplayer they needed—Boston had been a high-scoring outfit for several seasons but had gone nowhere in postseason play without a rebounder to put the ball in Cousy's hands and without a solid defense to shut down opponents' onslaughts. Russell seemed like the man for the job. Of course no one—not even Auerbach—could envision quite how great Russell's impact on the league would actually be. It was a deal that truly made Auerbach, that made the Celtics, that even made the NBA. It was a deal that put pro basketball squarely on the map.

Worst Trade in Franchise History

On October 16, 1984, Boston traded competent guard Gerald Henderson to Seattle's SuperSonics for a high draft pick (number two overall), the one used to select Len Bias, star forward from the University of Maryland. Tragedy then struck suddenly as Bias was found dead in his university dormitory room only days after the heralded draft pick, a victim of recreational drug overdose. For once Auerbach had manipulated the draft day scenario in his favor, made his coveted selection, and then uncharacteristically been left with nothing at all. Of course, it was only unforeseen fate that ruined this latest move by Auerbach. Over four decades as a coach and general manager the unflappable redhead was never really out-traded by any mere mortals. He had clearly won on his draft-related gambles with Russell, Bird, Cowens, McHale, Cedric Maxwell, Brian Shaw and others. One disaster was probably inevitable somewhere along the line, even for Auerbach.

Boston Celtics
Historical Oddity

The true nature of the Boston Celtics' famed "mystique" can be measured by one simple and indelible fact alone. The Boston franchise now owns seventeen NBA titles and boasts twenty former players (Kevin McHale was the latest) enshrined in the James Naismith Memorial Basketball Hall of Fame in Springfield. Eighteen former Celtics players (plus one owner and one coach) have also had their uniform numbers officially retired by the franchise. Yet despite all these trappings of glory the Boston Celtics have amazingly never had a single player win an individual NBA scoring title. No team has owned a larger collection of truly great players, yet no team has so elevated dedicated and selfless teamwork over the opportunities for personal stardom. It is the Red Auerbach way, and it has been the most successful formula of American sports history.

Boston Celtics
Half-Century Chronology

What the New York Yankees are to big league baseball and the Notre Dame Fighting Irish are to college football, the Boston Celtics are to professional basketball. The sport's most glorious dynasty run was etched in Celtics' green; a bulk of the league's most memorable stars—Russell, Cousy, Heinsohn, Sam and K.C. Jones, Cowens, McHale and Bird—have played virtually all of their careers in Boston; the most colorful coach ever to trod the sidelines is synonymous with this franchise; and no arena of past or present epochs evokes such nostalgic memories of legends past as does the once venerable Boston Garden. Throughout much of pro basketball's modern-era half-century, a history of the Boston Celtics has reasonably substituted for a history of the National Basketball Association itself. Below are the year-by-year highlights which capsulize both the history of a marquee franchise and the history of the league which houses it.

Jack "Dutch" Garfinkel sports unfamiliar Boston Celtics togs worn by the first franchise team for the 1946-47 BAA season.

1946-47 (BAA)

Celtics' franchise born on June 6, 1946, as part of bold experiment known as the Basketball Association of America (BAA). New venture intended to capitalize on postwar economic boom and exploding popularity of college basketball. Franchises also placed in ten other eastern cities, all connected with National Hockey League and American Hockey League franchises and arenas. Coached by **John "Honey" Russell** and with only single double-figure scorer (**Connie Simmons,** 10.3 ppg.), Boston's entry ties Toronto for worst record (22-38) in Eastern Division. **Al Brightman** first to score 20 points in December 1 loss to Chicago. Half-century later only Boston and New York Knickerbockers among pioneering BAA (NBA) franchises remain in same city and sport same name they started with.

1947-48 (BAA)

Walter Brown's fledgling franchise survives second shaky season with some evidence of on-court improvement if too little progress at box office. Twenty wins earn third spot in East and first brief playoff appearance versus Chicago Stags. Lanky **Ed Sadowski** (previously center for Toronto and Cleveland teams which didn't survive beyond first BAA season) proves first Celtics star attraction as league's third-best scorer (19.4) and second most accurate field goal shooter.

1948-49 (BAA)

BAA takes major step toward solvency by pirating Minneapolis Lakers franchise with star center George Mikan from rival National Basketball League. **Ed Sadowski** departs to Philadelphia Warriors, leaving rookie **George Kaftan** (local favorite from Holy Cross College) as scoring leader (14.5) in part-time playing role (21 games). Team cracks century mark for first time in 102-83 win over St. Louis Bombers (February 25) at Boston Arena. **Alvin (Doggie) Julian** replaces **Honey Russell** on bench and team adds five wins but loses seven more times during expanded schedule.

1949-50

Six NBL teams merged into league, which expands to three divisions and changes name to National Basketball Association (NBA). Second season under **Doggie Julian** brings first unshared basement finish (22-46 in Eastern Division). **Sonny Hertzberg** (10.2) and **Bob Kinney** (11.1) top offense on team with little pizzazz and no frontline gate attractions. First Celtics team of NBA era would nonetheless be last lackluster Boston club for next full quarter-century.

1950-51

NBA shakes down from 17 to 11 teams and Rochester surprises as replacement for Minneapolis Lakers in postseason winner's circle. But biggest news made in Boston, where new coach **Red Auerbach** (signed for $10,000 after coaching Washington and Tri-Cities) produces first club winning record (39-30), and where several personnel moves signal franchise on the rise. **Ed Macauley** selected from St. Louis Bombers in dispersal draft and becomes team's first 20-per-game scorer. More historic if not immediately more consequential transaction is draft day choice of Duquesne's **Chuck Cooper**, NBA's first black picked from college ranks. **Bob Cousy** also comes on board when selected in October lottery after Chicago Stags ballclub folds. Such transactions launch transition to powerhouse ballclub soon able to dominate league for next two decades. First-ever NBA All-Star Game staged at Boston Garden (March 2) and Ed Macauley leads East to 111-94 victory as game's MVP.

1951-52

Bill Sharman joins Celtics after trade with Fort Wayne Pistons (October 14). Sharman and Cousy play together in backcourt for first time (November 4) as Celtics manhandle Indianapolis Olympians 97-65 in Boston Arena. Boston Garden again hosts All-Star Game, won by East 108-91 behind Philadelphia's Paul Arizin (26 points). NBA's barnstorming flavor demonstrated in Boston Garden when Celtics and Fort Wayne tip-off at midnight for "Milkman's Special" game staged after evening's main event of Ice Follies.

1952-53

Parquet floor which **Walter Brown** commissioned in 1946 moved from original home at Boston Arena (Celtics played numerous games there during first several seasons) to Boston Garden in December. **Ed Macauley** records career-best 46 points against Minneapolis (March 6). Celts win first-ever postseason series (2-0 versus Syracuse) as Cousy scores 50 in four-overtime marathon (March 21).

1953-54

Boston Garden brawl between **Bob Cousy** and Philadelphia Warriors center Neil Johnston requires police intervention on arena floor (November 11). Cousy MVP of league All-Star Game at New York with 10 points in overtime period. Ugly Boston-Syracuse overtime match results in 46 fouls against Nats and 35 called on Celtics (March 17). Wild player melee interrupts Celtics-Nats playoff game for half-hour and Syracuse stars Dolph Schayes and Paul Seymour forced from contest by brawl-related injuries (March 27).

1954-55

Twenty-four-second shot clock used for first time (October 30) in Rochester Royals' 98-95 win over Boston. **Bill Sharman** chosen All-Star Game MVP after brilliant fourth-quarter effort in Madison Square Garden. Cousy All-Star Game's high scorer with 20. Boston dips to even .500 ledger for first time under **Red Auerbach** yet wins division semifinal-round playoffs versus New York before falling to Syracuse in late postseason play. Cousy posts NBA's second-best scoring average (21.2, after Neil Johnston) and paces league in assists, while Sharman NBA free-throw leader.

1955-56

Highest scoring team in the league (106.0 ppg.) paced by **Bill Sharman** (19.9, 6th in NBA) and **Bob Cousy** (18.8, 7th in NBA) but Boston also worst team on defense (105.3) due to run-and-gun style. **Ed Macauley** (17.5, 8th in NBA) adds to offensive punch but his lack of rugged board play exposes Boston's defensive liabilities. **Bob Cousy** is league's assists leader for fourth straight year. **Bill Sharman** tops circuit in free-throw accuracy for fourth straight time also.

1956-57 (NBA Champions)

Biggest transaction in NBA history occurs when Auerbach trades **Ed Macauley** and untested **Cliff Hagan** to

St. Louis for draft rights to **Bill Russell** (who signs for reported $19,500). Russell debuts on December 26 (versus St. Louis Hawks on national television) after leading USA Olympic team to gold medal in Australia. Celtics start season with 14 straight victories. All-Star Game returns to Boston and Cousy claims second MVP trophy with brilliant playmaking. Sharman also cans 80-foot shot in same All-Star event. **Red Auerbach** punches Hawks' owner Ben Kerner in mouth prior to game 3 playoff loss (April 6) in St. Louis. Auerbach's forces capture first NBA banner (April 13) in dramatic double-overtime game seven, with rookie-of-the-year **Tom Heinsohn** collecting 23 rebounds and 37 points to offset Bob Pettit's 39-point performance. **Larry Bird** born in French Lick, Indiana (December 7, 1956).

1957-58
Sam Jones drafted (8th overall) from college ranks (North Carolina Central). **Bill Russell** collects team-standard 49 boards versus Philadelphia Warriors (December 16). Russell again grabs postseason club-record 40 rebounds in game against Philadelphia (March 23). Russell's ankle injury in third game of playoff Finals forces him to sidelines for two contests and tips championship battle in favor of St. Louis Hawks. Celtics dethroned in game six (April 12) when Russell hobbled by game-three injury and Bob Pettit proves unstoppable force with record 50 clutch points.

1958-59 (NBA Champions)
Elgin Baylor cans record 64 points as Boston falls 136-115 in Minneapolis (November 8). Celtics post league-record 173 points (February 27) versus Minneapolis as **Bob Cousy** authors 28 assists. Cousy sets team playoff assists record with 19 versus Minneapolis in Boston Garden (April 9). Boston's four-game sweep of Minneapolis in NBA Finals is first in league history.

1959-60 (NBA Champions)
Celtics collect team-record 91 in single half during 151-118 pasting of Cincinnati Royals (November 11). Celts grab team-record 109 rebounds while pounding Detroit 150-106 in Boston Garden (December 24). Record-tying 17-game winning streak ends New Year's Day versus Cincinnati in Detroit. Boston adds third championship trophy of Auerbach Era with easy 122-103 victory over St. Louis in deciding seventh game, with **Bill Russell** collecting 35 rebounds and 22 points.

1960-61 (NBA Champions)
Boston tabs **Tom Sanders** (New York University) in college draft (8th overall). Wilt Chamberlain (facing **Bill Russell**) amazes with league-record 55 rebounds in 132-129 win over Boston at Philadelphia (November 24). Boston's fourth NBA crown product of five-game rout of

St. Louis Hawks, ending with 121-112 win at Boston Garden. Russell logs 30 points and 38 rebounds in championship finale.

1961-62 (NBA Champions)
Wilt Chamberlain averages above 50 ppg. for entire season, Oscar Robertson averages season's triple-double, and in Boston Auerbach and company post record fourth-straight championship. **Tom Heinsohn** collects career-high 45 points in 127-122 win at Syracuse (Christmas Day). Boston tops 60-win mark for first time in club history. Elgin Baylor records 61 points at Boston Garden in game five of tense NBA Finals. Fifth NBA title earned in dramatic fashion with overtime squeaker in deciding final round contest (April 18). Outcome turns on missed last-second shot by Frank Selvy that could have won for Los Angeles in regulation time.

1962-63 (NBA Champions)
Old rivals take on new look as Philadelphia Warriors with Wilt Chamberlain transfer to San Francisco (and out of Eastern Division) and Cincinnati Royals shift to Eastern Division as replacement. **John Havlicek** of Ohio State, Boston's college draft pick (7th). **Bob Cousy** announces in October this will be his final season. Emotional "Bob Cousy Day" celebrated on last regular-season playing date and unforgettable "We luv ya Cous!" rings from Boston Garden rafters (March 17). Celtics garner sixth NBA crown with game-six victory in Los Angeles. Bob Cousy provides heroics in his final Celtics game by dribbling out the final seconds of the championship victory and tossing the ball towards the rafters as the final horn sounds.

1963-64 (NBA Champions)
Syracuse Nationals relocate to become Philadelphia 76ers. Numbers of **Bob Cousy** (14) and **Ed Macauley** (22) retired and raised to rafters in Boston Garden (October 26). **John Havlicek's** career-best 43 points come in Madison Square Garden victory over Baltimore (December 17). Boston Garden hosts NBA All-Star Game for first time in seven winters, with Auerbach at helm and Heinsohn and Russell in starting lineup for victorious East squad. Seventh NBA title comes easily in brief five-game series with Wilt Chamberlain's San Francisco Warriors. **Frank Ramsey** and **Jim Loscutoff** close out hall-of-fame careers.

1964-65 (NBA Champions)
Franchise founder **Walter Brown** dies (September 7) in Cape Cod hospital. Honorary "Number 1" retired for Brown during lavish Boston Garden ceremony (October 17). Season's 62-18 ledger sets new franchise landmark. Most legendary moment of franchise history (April 15) captured by **Johnny Most's** famed radio call: *"Havlicek stole*

John Havlicek's memorable "steal" came late in the 1965 season, but more than a decade later he was still harassing the opposition's offenses, as with this pilfering of a pass during 1978 Boston Garden action vs. Cleveland.

the ball! Havlicek stole the ball!" Memorable moment comes with **John Havlicek's** pilfering of inbounds pass during final seconds of Eastern Division deciding game with Philadelphia. NBA Finals end (April 25) in only five games with Boston whipping Los Angeles Lakers once again for eighth championship crown. **K.C. Jones** announces retirement two days after playoffs end.

1965-66 (NBA Champions)

Team purchased by Ruppert-Knickerbocker Breweries and National Equities (June 24). **Bill Russell** signs first $100,000 contract in league history (August 25). **Don Nelson** signs as a free agent (October 28) after being released by Los Angeles Lakers one week earlier. **Sam Jones'** career-high 51 points can't prevent Pistons' 108-106 win in Detroit (October 29). Auerbach Era ends (April 28) with final championship victory cigar during 95-93 seventh-game win over Los Angeles in Boston Garden. Russell logs typical 32 rebounds and 25 points in Auerbach's final game.

1966-67

Rugged forward **Bailey Howell** obtained from Baltimore Bullets in exchange for journeyman center Mel Counts (September 1). Ceremony retires uniform numbers of **Tom Heinsohn** (15) and **Bill Sharman** (21) at Boston Garden (October 15). Only regular-season triple overtime in Boston Garden history won by Celtics 137-136 over San Francisco (February 10). Celtics fail to win championship for only time during entire decade when divisional series dropped to Philadelphia in five games. Wilt Chamberlain fails to top NBA in scoring for first time in career yet nonetheless anchors championship 76ers team many still call strongest in league history.

1967-68 (NBA Champions)

Defending champion Philadelphia 76ers dethroned by Boston in seventh game of Eastern Division finals at The Spectrum. Celtics thus become first team ever to win final three contests of seven-game postseason series. Tenth NBA championship comes with 124-109 sixth-game victory in Los Angeles (May 2). **Bill Russell** thus captures first title as head coach, and also first Celtics title banner won without Auerbach on the bench.

1968-69 (NBA Champions)

Ballclub sold as part of deal between Ballantine Brewing and Investors Funding Company. Franchise victory 1,000 earned (October 19) with 106-96 win against Bulls in Chicago. **Sam Jones** hits one of most dramatic shots in franchise history (April 29) to deadlock championship series with Lakers after four games. **Bill Russell** and **Sam Jones** bow out as winners together with seventh-game championship win over Los Angeles. Russell played all 48 minutes (21 rebounds, 6 points) of game which earns him and Boston franchise 11th crown in 13 seasons. **Don Nelson's** last-minute desperation heave provides deciding shot of most surprising Celtics championship ever.

1969-70

Era ends when **Bill Russell** announces retirement as player and coach (August 4). **Jo Jo White** becomes Boston property in college draft (7th pick). **Tom Heinsohn** debuts on bench as Auerbach's hand-picked choice to replace Russell, but first losing season since 1950 ends on sour note with 144-106 thrashing by San Francisco in Boston Garden. Also first season in two decades that team not coached by Auerbach or Russell. Playing rights to long-retired **Bob Cousy** traded (November 18) to Cincinnati Royals in exchange for journeyman forward **Bill Dinwiddie**.

1970-71

Future hall-of-famer **Dave Cowens** surprise Boston selection in college draft. Cowens shares rookie-of-the-year honors with Portland's Geoff Petrie in first-ever tie for freshman honors. Milwaukee's Lew Alcindor nets 53 in Boston Garden (January 27) for third highest output ever against Celtics. Team reverses losing record (44-38) in second year under Heinsohn but again fails to reach postseason. NBA celebrates 25th season and now operates for first time with two conferences and four divisions. NBA Silver Anniversary team features Auerbach, Cousy, Russell, Sharman and Sam Jones.

1971-72

Lew Alcindor (now Kareem Abdul-Jabbar) again posts 50-plus (55) versus Boston in Milwaukee (December 10). **Bill Russell's** "Number 6" retired in closed ceremony when Russell refuses to attend "public" pre-game honors (March 12). Boston captures first regular-season division banner in seven years yet still outclassed by New York Knicks in five-game Eastern Conference Finals. **John Havlicek** (27.5 ppg.) leds club in scoring (3rd in NBA) fourth straight season, matching string posted by **Bill Sharman** in mid-fifties.

1972-73

Dave Cowens both All-Star Game MVP and regular-season MVP, but **John Havlicek** again offensive leader (23.8 ppg.) on perhaps most potent Boston team ever. Key pre-season deal (September 19) with Phoenix obtains **Paul Silas** for rights to **Charlie Scott** (still playing in ABA, after being drafted by Boston in 1970). **Don Nelson's** team-record 465-game ironman streak ends early in season (December 16). Regular-season Atlantic Division title results from highest victory total (68-14) in club annals. Havlicek collects team-record 54 points in opening playoff game with Atlanta (April 1). Shoulder injury to Havlicek (April 20) costs Boston dramatic East Conference Finals series with New York Knicks. **Tom Heinsohn** named second NBA coach-of-the-year in franchise history.

1973-74 (NBA Champions)

Era ends with Wilt Chamberlain's retirement and another begins with Boston's return to NBA pinnacle. **John Havlicek** records 20,000th regular-season career point in Boston Garden versus Los Angeles Lakers (January 11). Havlicek finishes half-dozen-year string as club's leading pointmaker. Dramatic postseason game (April 12) won by two **Jo Jo White** free throws with no time left on clock to eliminate pesky Buffalo Braves during Eastern Conference semifinals. Kareem Abdul-Jabbar's spectacular last-second sky-hook in Boston Garden (May 10) ends game six of NBA finals and forces deciding match at Milwaukee. Boston wins 12th title in lopsided game seven (102-87) of highly memorable title series.

1974-75

Celtics post 60 wins for fifth time in club annals but stumble in conference finals with Washington Bullets after losing homecourt advantage in Boston Garden opener. **Dave Cowens** (20.4) replaces **John Havlicek** (19.2) as offensive leader and **Don Nelson** is league pacesetter in field goal accuracy. **Charlie Scott** obtained from Phoenix at season's end (May 23) in exchange for **Paul Westphal**. **Dave Cowens** edged out for league rebounding crown (by Washington's Wes Unseld) as well as MVP honors (by leading scorer Bob McAdoo of Buffalo Braves).

1975-76 (NBA Champions)

Postseason slip of previous campaign is righted on strength of **Dave Cowens'** second-best all-around season (19.0 ppg., 1246 rebounds) and **Charlie Scott's** added offensive power (17.6 ppg.). Greatest NBA Finals game of all-time (June 4) extends through three overtimes before Celtics prevail against Phoenix Suns in game five at Boston Garden. **Charlie Scott** scores 25 as Celtics capture 13th title banner in game six (June 6). At end of 30 league seasons Boston had been beaten only once in 14 NBA Finals appearances.

1976-77

Tom Heinsohn's team falls out of regular-season first place for first time in half-dozen years, trailing Julius Erving-led Philadelphia Sixers in Atlantic Division by six games. **Sidney Wicks** (15.1) purchased from Portland (October 12) and joins **Jo Jo White** (19.6), **Charlie Scott** (18.2), ageless **John Havlicek** (17.7), **Dave Cowens** (16.4), and **Curtis Rowe** (10.1) with double-figure scoring. Rowe obtained (October 20) in three-way trade with Detroit and Denver which also sends **Paul Silas** to Nuggets. Havlicek reaches final career milestone with 25,000 lifetime points (April 6).

1977-78

First losing season since opening of decade brings change on both bench and playing floor. **Tom Heinsohn** first Celtics coach to be released in mid-season (January 3) when replaced by **Tom "Satch" Sanders**. Jo Jo White's team-record ironman stint also ends (January 31) at 488 games. Collapsed roof of Hartford Civic Center causes several March games to be moved back to Boston Garden. Biggest transition comes at season's end (April 9) when **John Havlicek** plays final career game.

1978-79

Pre-season news involves drafting of Indiana State University junior **Larry Bird** (June 9) who still has one collegiate season remaining. Buffalo Braves and Celtics also swap owners during off-season (July 7) and **Red Auerbach** turns down front office position (July 13) with New York Knicks. Pre-season trade with San Diego/Buffalo franchise acquires **Nate Archibald, Marvin Barnes** and **Billy Knight,** and also draft rights later used (in 1981) to obtain **Danny Ainge. John Havlicek's** uniform "17" retired before loss to Cleveland Cavaliers (October 13). **Bill Fitch** named eighth Boston head coach at season's end (May 23), replacing interim mentor **Dave Cowens**.

1979-80

Larry Bird signs first Boston Celtics contract (June 8) and future GM and head coach **M.L. Carr** also signs as free-agent player. Bird debuts as rookie sensation and follows footsteps of Heinsohn and Cowens as team's third NBA top rookie selection. **Chris Ford** nets first-ever NBA three-point field goal in same game (October 12) as **Larry Bird's** inaugural regular-season appearance. Bird and Magic Johnson meet head-to-head for first time as professionals (December 28) in 123-105 Los Angeles Lakers victory.

1980-81 (NBA Champions)

Pre-season trade with Golden State Warriors (June 9) lands future hall-of-famer **Robert Parish** and also results in drafting of **Kevin McHale. Pete Maravich** (September 21) and **Dave Cowens** (September 30, with letter to Boston newspapers) announce retirements on eve of new season. NBA 35th Anniversary Team includes Havlicek, Russell, Cousy and Auerbach. **Larry Bird** held scoreless for only time in career (January 3) by Golden State Warriors. Memorable Eastern Conference Finals conclude with one-point victory over Philadelphia Sixers in Boston's third-straight comeback from second-half double-digit deficit. **Larry Bird** connects one of most famous shots ever (flying followup in which ball is switched from right to left hand) in game one of NBA Finals versus Houston (May 5). Bird with 27 and **Cedric Maxwell** with 19 pace sixth-game victory against Rockets in Houston to clinch championship number 14.

1981-82

Larry Bird earns All-Star Game MVP nod in Meadow-lands Arena. Boston connection of Bird, **Robert Parish** and **Nate Archibald** spark fourth-quarter drive that wins for East All-Stars. Celtics begin club-best 18-game winning streak by crushing Utah 132-90 (February 24). **Jo Jo White's** number (10) retired at Boston Garden before victory over New Jersey Nets (April 9). Regular-season mark of 63 victories is second highest in lengthy franchise annals.

1982-83

Larry Bird nets 50-plus (53 versus Indiana on March 30) for first time in career. Celtics fail to win 60 games for first time in four seasons under **Bill Fitch** and also fall out of first place in division for first time since Fitch's arrival. **Larry Bird** (23.6) paces team in scoring for fourth of record nine-straight times. Season ends on sour note with four straight defeats by Milwaukee in Eastern Conference semifinals. **Howie McHugh**, team's PR man since 1946, passes away (May 7) five days after season's sad ending.

1983-84 (NBA Champions)

Larry Bird picks up first NBA MVP trophy. **K.C. Jones** named new head coach and orchestrates first of his five straight division first-place finishes. **Robert Parish** posts 10,000 career points by crossing milestone in Phoenix (February 26). Long-anticipated championship showdown between Larry Bird and Magic Johnson spices seven-game NBA Finals. **Kevin McHale** captures first-ever NBA Sixth-Man postseason award. Off-season news highlighted by **Jan Volk** replacing **Red Auerbach** as General Manager. NBA changes name of coach-of-the-year trophy to honor Auerbach.

1984-85

Larry Bird (28.7 ppg.) is league MVP for second consecutive season while finishing second to New York's Bernard King in NBA scoring race. Bird also NBA runnerup in three-point field goal accuracy. "Number 2" retired in honor of **Red Auerbach** (January 4) during gala Red Auerbach Weekend in Boston. All-time NBA great Michael Jordan makes Boston Garden debut (January 9). Larry Bird wins consecutive games versus Portland and Detroit with pair of improbable buzzer-beating shots (January 27 and 29). Bird misses rare quadruple-double (30 points, 12 rebounds, 10 assists, 9 steals) by refusing to enter meaningless fourth quarter of rout over Utah (February 18). **Kevin McHale** posts short-lived team record 56 points against Detroit in Boston Garden (March 3) but **Larry Bird** nails 60 versus Atlanta in New Orleans only nine days later. **Scott Wedman** hits 11 straight 3-point goals (March 31) for new NBA record.

1985-86 (NBA Champions)

Larry Bird captures third consecutive MVP trophy, thus matching **Bill Russell** (1962-64) and Wilt Chamberlain (1967-69) in that department. Bird nets 50 for second time in career (March 10) but Dallas Mavericks beat Boston for first time ever. Bird also sets new NBA career mark for 3-point field goals. Michael Jordan enjoys perhaps most spectacular career night with record 63 points during Chicago's playoff loss in Boston Garden (April 20). Sixteenth and final world title to date earned in six games against Houston Rockets with "Twin Towers" stars Akeem (later Hakeem) Olajuwon and Ralph Sampson.

1986-87

Tragedy marks off-season as top lottery pick **Len Bias** of Maryland (2nd overall) dies of drug overdose two days after NBA draft. Franchise regular-season victory 2,000 collected over Detroit Pistons in Boston Garden (March 1). Boston and Seattle combine for NBA-record 97.1% from charity stripe in Celtics' 112-108 victory at Boston Garden (March 20). Defending NBA champs capture fourth division title in row under **K.C. Jones**. Third Bird vs. Magic showdown in NBA Finals falls to Magic (MVP for season and playoffs) in six games. **Reggie Lewis** (Northeastern) plucked from college draft at end of season.

1987-88

"Larry Legend" enjoys best offensive season (29.9) while **Kevin McHale** and **Robert Parish** rank first and second in NBA field goal percentage. Bird-McHale-Parish credentials as best frontline in league history now established beyond doubt. **Danny Ainge** sets NBA record with at least one 3-point goal in each of 23-straight games. Hall-of-famer **Artis Gilmore** begins brief stint with Celtics (January 8). **Kevin McHale** records career point 10,000 versus Chicago Bulls one night before **Robert Parish** also reaches 15,000 milestone in 143-105 rout of Detroit (January 12-13). **Larry Bird** has statue unveiled at Ritz-Carlton Hotel, then wins third Long Distance Shootout at All-Star Weekend later in same week.

1988-89

Robert Parish collects 10,000th regular-season rebound in Sacramento (February 22). Major late-season trade (February 23) ships veterans **Danny Ainge** and **Brad Lohaus** to Sacramento for **Joe Kleine** and **Ed Pinckney**. **Jimmy Rodgers** succeeds **K.C. Jones** on bench and team falls as low as third in division for first time in decade. With Bird lost to injury for all but six early games, **Kevin McHale** supplants "Larry Legend" as team scoring leader for only time in Bird's dozen full seasons.

1989-90

Larry Bird's team-record consecutive free-throw streak of 71 comes to end (February 13) in Houston. **Dee Brown** leaps to All-Star Weekend Slam Dunk title in Miami. Celtics convert all 35 free throws during 139-118 victory over Miami Heat (April 12). Boston sets several playoff scoring records (April 28) with 157-128 pasting of New York Knicks in first-round matchup.

At the outset of the 1990s an often-injured Larry Bird was still a considerable offensive force for Boston, as in this November 1990 Garden action against the Sacramento Kings.

1990-91

Brian Shaw rejoins team after spending season in Italian league. Era ends as Bird and Magic meet for final time (February 15) with Boston winning 98-95 in Los Angeles Forum. **Dave Cowens** and **Nate "Tiny" Archibald** elected to Naismith Memorial Basketball Hall of Fame (February 8). **Chris Ford** comes on board as eleventh Celtics head coach and guides team back to regular-season divisional title.

1991-92

Robert Parish reaches exclusive 20,000-point plateau versus Philadelphia in Boston Garden (January 17). Fractured cheekbone ends **Larry Bird's** string of 219 straight games played and started (March 2). Nine Celtics break double figures in 125-100 smashing of Orlando in Boston Garden (March 4). **Reggie Lewis** (20.8) replaces Larry Bird as team's leading scorer. Second straight divisional title under **Chris Ford** is team's last to date. Bird's final season stalls in seventh game of Eastern Conference semifinals with Cleveland.

1992-93

Broadcasting legend and Celtics radio voice **Johnny Most** passes away (cancer) and immediately honored in somber memorial service (January 6). **Larry Bird** retirement ceremony (February 4) held in Boston Garden and legendary number "33" jersey raised to place of honor in rafters. Bird undergoes career-threatening back surgery at New England Baptist Hospital (March 5). **Kevin McHale** makes last Boston Garden appearance (May 1) during loss to Charlotte. One day later **Reggie Lewis** diagnosed as having cardiac abnormalities. Lewis collapses and dies of heart ailment during off-season (August 27).

1993-94

Kevin McHale's number "32" retired before Boston Garden victory over Phoenix (January 30). Guard **Sherman Douglas** enjoys best night (April 3) in Boston uniform with 27 points and 22 assists as Celtics blast Sixers 135-112. **Robert Parish** plays last game (April 21) at Boston Garden with Celtics in 95-89 loss to his future team, the Charlotte Hornets. **Dee Brown** fifth Celtics player to score 40-plus since 1979 during double-overtime thriller (April 22) versus Bulls in Chicago.

1994-95

Storied Boston Garden rivalry ends as Celtics and Lakers meet for final time (January 20) in legendary building. **Dominique Wilkins** enjoys single late-career season with Boston as team's top scorer (17.8) and also collects final two points in history of storied Boston Garden. **Reggie Lewis'** number (35) retired in Boston Garden ceremony (March 22). New York Knicks provide opposition in last Boston Garden regular-season contest (April 21), with Boston losing 99-92. Boston suffers worst-ever defeat in 124-77 opening playoff loss to Orlando. Garden doors close for final time with 95-92 playoff loss to Orlando Magic (May 5) which also marks end of **Chris Ford's** five-year coaching tenure.

1995-96

Croatian import **Dino Radja** big gun (19.7) on "Jekyll and Hyde" team which posts fifth highest scoring average but second worst defensive totals in entire NBA. **Dana Barros** ranks among league's top free throwers (4th) but no other star performers emerge. **M.L. Carr** begins two-year coaching stint which quickly proves perhaps bleakest epoch in franchise annals.

1996-97

Brief lackluster **M.L. Carr** reign as both head coach and vice-president ends with disastrous 15-67 season—worst in franchise history. Rookie **Antoine Walker** (17.5 ppg.) leads solid offense featuring seven double-figure scorers which is NBA's sixth most productive, but Celtics also allow most points (107.9) in entire league. Season marks start of league's and team's second half-century.

1997-98

Franchise turns new page with signing of **Rick Pitino** as 13th head coach and club president. **Red Auerbach** stripped of any remaining active control of franchise with "promotion" from club president to board vice-chairman. Kentucky All-American **Ron Mercer** picked in draft (sixth overall) as another major step toward rebuilding moribund franchise. **Larry Bird** cuts ties with Boston to become head coach of rival Indiana Pacers in his home state. Rebuilding season kicks off with thrilling 92-85 season-opening win over defending champion Chicago Bulls. Year culminates with 21-win improvement which is second biggest turnaround in team's half-century history.

1998-99

All-American forward **Paul Pierce** (early departure from Kansas) drafted with tenth overall pick. Youthful lineup of Pierce, **Antoine Walker** and **Ron Mercer**, bolstered by veterans **Kenny Anderson** and **Dana Barros**, spurs late-season failed run toward first playoff appearance in four years. Rick Pitino already has his revamped Celtics pointing toward renewed respectability in only second season at helm.

BOSTON Celtics
BOSTON Celtics

CHAPTER II

An Era of Transistion:
Bridging the Gap from Bird to Pitino

Perhaps the darkest hours ever known in Boston Celtics annals were the pair of retirement bows that fell almost a quarter-century apart—on May 5 of 1969 and August 18 of 1992. The first—Bill Russell's unannounced swan song (no one knew at the time that he would not play or coach another season)—was tempered by the sweet championship victory over the heavily favored LA Lakers which punctuated Boston's ruthless domination throughout the 1960s. Russell's farewell game also marked (in hindsight, at least) only a temporary shedding of invincibility from which the franchise still directed by Red Auerbach would quickly enough recover during the coming decade under the leadership of replacement coach Tom Heinsohn. Celtics rooters would not have to wait long after Russell hung up his familiar number "6" before Celtics pride was being restored in full measure under a new imposing center named Dave Cowens and the usual gang of reinforcements headed by John Havlicek and Don Nelson and a remarkable cast of dozens. But the retooling process which was naturally expected to follow Larry Bird's 1992 departure is still being wistfully awaited in Boston almost a decade later.

There is yet another factor which distinguishes the Boston Celtics' smooth transition between the glorious Russell-led '60s-era to the rebuilding Heinsohn-led '70s-era from the more recent downsliding which has separated Bird-McHale-Parish in the '80s from a flock of hopeless also-ran pretenders in the 1990s. Russell's teams had nobly run out their string and, if anything, had hung around at the top far longer than anyone ever expected they would. Yet for all the achievements of the Bird era, Boston's second greatest hero would witness his career end most prematurely and with many still unmet expectations. Boston fans of the early 1990s (and those everywhere else around the NBA) were not quite yet ready to let go of Larry Bird.

And Bird's premature swan song seemed only the latest chapter in a series of inexplicable curses that had somehow turned Celtics charm and endless Boston good fortune into an unexpected and nearly unendurable (for Boston faithful, at any rate) ongoing nightmare. It had started with the tragic death of prize draftee Len Bias. Had Bias joined the Celtics lineup as planned on the heels of the 1986 draft, a new renaissance in basketball fortunes would almost surely have blossomed up in Beantown. Just as Auerbach had once

Top Celtics lottery pick Len Bias out of the University of Maryland poses on draft day in Boston with Coach K.C. Jones. Two days later Bias was dead of a drug overdose.

AP/Wide World Photos

retooled overnight by finding Cowens to replace Russell, and then a decade later had gambled with draft choices and trades that resulted in the windfall represented by Bird, McHale and Parish, now the Celtics' head honcho had found Bias to underpin The Big Three front wall during their final diminishing seasons. Bias might even inherit Bird's mantle—or at least that was the optimistic plan for the brief span of days that surrounded the June 17, 1986, college draft.

Bias carried a resume that included a 6-8 and 220-pound rock-solid frame, an astounding 38-inch vertical leap, an unstoppable inside power game combined with a finesse-filled outside shooting game that provided considerable double-threat offensive skills. He might provide all the answers for Auerbach and head coach K. C. Jones for a decade or more to come. And Bias himself was reportedly most enthusiastic about playing in Boston. He had apparently even pleaded with GM Jan Volk before a Boston-Houston playoff game to draft him on June 17 (when the Celtics had the number two overall pick, which they had cleverly acquired in still another of Auerbach's deft trade maneuvers). When Cleveland pegged North Carolina's Brad Daugherty and Auerbach announced selection of Len Bias it seemed that Red had one more time struck gold for the team proudly glad in green

Len Bias died two days later of cardiac arrest brought on by a cocaine overdose during wild partying in his University of Maryland residence hall. With him died not only a potentially brilliant NBA career but also the best-laid plans of the Boston basketball braintrust. Auerbach's vision was undoubtedly to repeat ancient history by debuting Bias as a "sixth man" as he had first done with Frank Ramsey in the mid-'50s and later repeated with John Havlicek in the mid-'60s. It would have been a perfect ploy to spell Bird and McHale while the rookie phenom logged 25 quality minutes night-in and night-out. It would have been a strategy almost guaranteed to have also extended the careers of the two resident future hall of famers. And eventually Bias would most likely also have followed Havlicek's exact mold and graduated to frontline stardom as a durable starter—perhaps even as the next Larry Bird.

The Bias tragedy had been followed by a string of late-career misfortunes for the two remaining franchise superstars, six-time All-NBA defensive selection McHale and the legendary Larry Bird. Two seasons after the Len Bias tragedy Bird had missed an entire campaign (all but the first six games) after undergoing Achilles tendon surgery on both heels. Bill Walton—another future hall of famer—enjoyed one brilliant season in Boston during the championship drive of 1986 before his own career-long foot problems returned to cancel any further effectiveness in the Boston lineup. McHale, too, suffered a broken foot which cost him the first 18 games of 1987-88 (and hobbled him

for several months after his return). With no relief from a departed Walton, Parish as well was slowed drastically with elbow, leg and ankle ailments that robbed any effectiveness from his late-eighties playoff performances. And while Bird had regained most of his legendary form for the early months of the first season under new coach Chris Ford in 1990-91, by year's end he was once again crippled, this time by his recurring chronic back problems. Bird tragically ended the postseason lying on the floor in front of the Celtics' bench during his moments away from the on-court action. McHale was also shackled in the same playoff series with Detroit (the Eastern Conference semifinals, won easily 4-2 by the Pistons) by a bad ankle sprain he had earlier suffered way back in February.

And things would now get even worse. Next came the tragic saga of Reggie Lewis, who along with Bias was seemingly destined to be a rising franchise star of the new decade, yet who also like Bias would soon become one of the decade's saddest sports tales. Lewis out of Northeastern University had been the top Boston pick at the end of the first round in the 1987 draft, and guard Brian Shaw from California-Santa Barbara also came on board by the same route one year later. While Lewis started somewhat slowly as a rookie (enjoying limited playing time and averaging under five points a game), he was already a near 20-point scorer by his second NBA campaign. Shaw logged a single rookie season of some promise (8.6 ppg. and All-NBA Rookie 2nd Team) before escaping to Europe and a bigger paycheck, but was once more back in the fold a year later (due to a federal court ruling enforcing his Boston contract) and was providing enough flash and speed to cause GM Jan Volk to unload popular Danny Ainge to Sacramento. In the end Shaw would never pan out quite as hoped and his rocky stay in Beantown would last only two-plus seasons before culminating with a mid-year 1992 trade to Miami for Sherman Douglas. But Lewis, in stark contrast with the apparent ingrate Shaw, was loaded with seemingly unlimited potential as both a scorer and playmaker and quick to demonstrate considerable team spirit; he was thus also clearly cut to fit much better into the preferred Auerbach mold designed for successful Boston players. Yet he was also—most unfortunately—marked for eventual tragedy of almost epic proportions.

The first two seasons under new head coach Chris Ford still seemed to hold out promise that the rebuilding of a championship lineup was perhaps only a very short trip around the next corner. There had been enough potential talent on the Boston roster of 1989-90 for bench boss Jimmy Rodgers to suffer the brunt of the blame for a humiliating collapse in the postseason's first round shootout versus New York. Bird seemed to be both healing and retooling for an expected late career run toward further spectacular playoff heroics. Lewis had emerged as a true superstar-in-waiting; Shaw had been forced back into the Boston lineup by the law courts; Ed Pinckney and Joe Kleine had been brought over from Sacramento in the Ainge trade to spell Parish and McHale. But most important was the hiring of Chris Ford himself as replacement for the overmatched Rodgers. The latter had seemingly over-coached and eventually lost both control and respect of his sagging ballclub. Ford—a solid ten-year player in the league and a fan-favorite in his final three seasons with Boston—thoroughly understood organizational philosophy (learned both as a player and as seven-year assistant under both K. C. Jones and Rodgers) and quickly reinstituted a relentless running game that was the hallmark of the longstanding Boston championship style.

In both 1991 and 1992 the revamped Boston teams—with Lewis taking up the slack for Bird and McHale—seemed like anything but ballclubs now on the downside. There were two more seasons at the top of the Atlantic Division ladder and two more trips into the postseason second round. And postseason results—hard-fought conference semifinals series with first a fading Detroit club and then a rebuilding Cleveland team—only seemed to indicate that the Boston ballclub was now only perhaps a player or two away from grander successes. Chicago with the league's new superstar in Michael Jordan was the brand new NBA frontrunner. But Boston had the second-best 1991 overall record in the Eastern Conference. It was perhaps only injuries that did in Boston that year during the postseason run, where they had struggled in a first-round series with Indiana and then failed to maintain momentum against defending champion Detroit after grabbing an early 2-1 series led. Ford's team jumped on top of the Pistons with consecutive home and road victories, but then ran out of steam for three straight games, despite almost coming back from lengthy fourth-quarter deficits each

time. Injuries to both Parish (a pair of badly sprained ankles) and Bird were too much to overcome during an overtime loss that finally ended the series and the season.

Although the 1991 Celtics edition fell short in the championship chase against Detroit they had nonetheless played with plenty of heart and displayed familiar Celtics pride right up to the final whistle. A season later Ford's second outfit would again sit atop the Atlantic Division during regular-season play, but only by virtue of a dead heat in the standings with surprising New York, which had improved a dozen games in its own ledger and climbed from the middle to the top of the pack. Once again the stopping point for Bird and company would be the conference semifinals, this time after seven games with the equally improved Cleveland Cavaliers. Cleveland, behind the hefty scoring of Brad Daugherty and Mark Price, had trailed the defending champion Chicago Bulls in the Central by ten lengths, yet nonethelesss had a record better than Boston's (by six games) and had improved by a whopping 24 games over the previous season. Bird's last NBA game came in Cleveland in the form of a one-sided loss (122-104) that ended a wire-to-wire series which was never quite as close as the full schedule of games might have suggested.

Reggie Lewis had already developed into a first rate star by the time Larry Bird's own career had finally wound down to premature retirement. In 1991 Lewis (18.7 ppg.) had carried much of the scoring load along with Bird (first with 19.4) and McHale (third at 18.4). A year later he was the team's top pointmaker (20.8), a shade ahead of Bird (20.2), as he averaged above 20 for the first time in his five-year career. It was also only the second time in his own thirteen-year stint that "Larry Legend" was not Boston's top offensive machine. And there was also another bright newcomer on board in the person of highflying 6-2 guard Dee Brown, who had been the

Larry Bird and Michael Jordan meet for the final time in Chicago Stadium during March 1992 late-season action.

AP/Wide World Photos

number 19 overall pick in the 1990 college draft. As a rookie Brown (a top ten career scorer at Jacksonville University) was the third highest freshman pointmaker in the league behind New Jersey's Derrick Coleman and Sacramento's Lionel Simmons. But instant notoriety came for Brown in the form of surprise victory in the 1991 All-Star Weekend Gatorade Slam Dunk festivities in Charlotte. And in the postseason of his first year Brown had also stepped up his offensive game (averaging 12.2, compared to his season's 8.7) and thus become an important all-around team contributor.

It was in the 1992-93 season, however, that things started to go completely sour around Boston Garden. Bird had reluctantly left his playing career behind on the eve of the new campaign. The body of the recognized "best all-around forward ever to play the game" had broken down too many times in too many places and was simply no longer able to perform its passing, shooting and rebounding magic. Reggie Lewis nonetheless continued his stellar play with a second 20.8 scoring average and the top team marks (often by wide margins) in points, average, single-game scoring high, minutes played, and free-throw percentage, while also ranking second on the club in blocked shots (after Parish) and steals (behind Dee Brown). But Coach Ford's third edition was never a serious challenger to New York in the Atlantic Division year-long championship chase, finishing a dozen lengths behind the new East Coast powerhouse. And in the spring playoffs there was a resounding and thus embarrassing first-round pasting at the hands of the lowly expansion Charlotte Hornets. More serious still, there was also a frightfully bad omen early in the short postseason series as star Reggie Lewis suddenly collapsed to the floor (on April 29) during Boston's game-one 112-101 road victory. The dazed team leader had toppled over with 6:26 remaining in the first quarter, yet the cause of Lewis's ailment was not at first readily apparent and he recovered quickly enough on the bench to return to action briefly in both the first and third quarters before finally being dispatched more permanently to the locker room.

Boston's most recent hall-of-famer, Kevin McHale, won three NBA championships as part of the greatest front line trio (along with Robert Parish and Bird) in NBA annals.

Most painful of all—at least until the time of Lewis's sudden illness—the campaign was also the last go-around for hall-of-fame-bound Kevin McHale. McHale had logged his 30,000th NBA minute shortly before season's end. After more than a dozen campaigns there wasn't much left in those lanky arms or legs that had so long rained terror on opposing forwards and low-post defenders. McHale's scoring during his 13th season had slipped to a career-low total of only 760 points and his 10.7 scoring average was also only a shade above his rookie-season low-water mark. His rebounds as well were down to his part-time rookie-season level. McHale would battle most heroically in four postseason games but was outmanned by a youthful Charlotte front line featuring Larry Johnson and Alonzo Mourning.

But if McHale's imminent departure was expected, even if dreaded, Reggie Lewis's certainly was not. A much bigger dip in club fortunes now lay just around the next bend. Only a week after the season's disastrous ending, Reggie Lewis (who never returned to action after the opening game of the fateful Charlotte series) was diagnosed (May 2) as having detectable cardiac abnormalities by a team of a dozen specialists at New England Baptist Hospital. The entire franchise was quite naturally set on its heels by the almost incomprehensible news, especially in light of the still-lingering memories of Len Bias's fate only a half-decade earlier. Then on July 27 came one of the most shocking moments in Boston's century-long professional sports annals. While casually shooting baskets in the Brandeis University gymnasium Lewis had suffered a fatal heart attack. Suddenly Reggie Lewis—like Len Bias before him—was unexplicably gone in the prime of his young and promising life. The somber summer thus ended with Lewis's funeral services (August 2) at Northeastern University's Matthews Arena, a touching event which was attended in sweltering heat by 7,000 Bostonians and featured a full round of most painful if eloquent eulogies. It was truly an unmatched low point in Boston Celtics usually proud team history.

The one-season appearance in Celtics colors by high-scoring Dominique Wilkins was hardly enough to revive the fading glories of a team only recently built around Bird, Parish and McHale.

The Boston franchise never completely recovered in the months and then seasons that followed. On the playing floor the team soon collapsed without Lewis and McHale. The final ledger for 1993-94 was eight games below the break-even mark and 16 below the previous season's standard. And the result was also an inevitable rapid freefall in the divisional standings. By year's end the final member of The Big Three was also taking his final bow up in Boston. Robert Parish would leave the team as well after the season's close, although retirement was not yet on the docket for the seemingly ageless warrior who had now logged 18 NBA seasons and was rapidly closing in on most of the league's longevity standards. Parish would soon post another pair of seasons in Charlotte and even eventually pick up still another championship ring with Chicago.

Ford himself would last only one additional season, a year marked by an ever-so-slight rebound in the league standings and also by the strange apparition of future Naismith Hall of Famer Dominique Wilkins now wearing a Boston Celtics uniform. The high-flying and high-scoring Wilkins was in the twilight of his own highly visible career (he had been traded from Atlanta to the LA Clippers a season earlier and then signed on with Boston as a free agent) but still managed to carry the scoring load for a much watered-down Boston lineup that boasted European

import Dino Radja, Dee Brown, Sherman Douglas and Eric Montross rather than the likes of Bird, McHale, Parish and Lewis. Boston climbed back into the playoffs after a single-season absence but didn't last long during a series most noted for the fact that it closed out five decades of glorious Boston Garden history.

For the fourth straight year the Boston season would end with a painful swan song. Bird had bowed out in 1992, McHale and Lewis logged their last game minutes in '93, and '94 in turn had witnessed Robert Parish's departure. Now it was time to also close out the fabled building that had been indisputably the most glorious venue for a full half century of NBA history. There might have been even more nostalgia than there was surrounding the event up in Boston had the Celtics not already slipped quite so far in the general public estimation—both at home and abroad. Thus instead of a glorious final night's celebration the occasion was played out as something of a somber anticlimax, one in which a strangely unfamiliar crew of inept Celtics ended their historic season by falling to Orlando's expansion pretenders in lackluster postseason action.

The grand finale of the grand old building atop Boston's North Station came on the 5th of May in 1995 and was witnessed by the usual packed house that accounted for consecutive sellout number 661 (stretching out the string that had begun with the launching of the Bird Era). It was the fourth and final game of an all-too-brief series with Orlando which was thoroughly dominated by

Boston forward Derek Strong blocks a shot by Orlando star Shaquille O'Neal during the 95-92 loss which ended the 1994-95 season and closed out storied Boston Garden on a decidedly low note.

the young Florida-based expansion franchise. Dominique Wilkins was the night's hero for Boston with 22 points and 18 rebounds and sparked a third-quarter rally which almost gave control of the game to the outmanned home forces. Boston fought to a slim lead in the closing minutes of the final frame, gaining a final 91-90 advantage on a three-pointer by Sherman Douglas with two and a half minutes left on the game clock. But Anfernee Hardaway's dunk ultimately vaulted the surging Magic into final control of the contest which was settled in the end by a pair of Horace Grant free throws. The final tally read 95-92, Orlando, in what was also Boston's last postseason appearance to date. It was anything but a fitting ending in a building where only the rarest playoff series down through the years had ever ended with a disappointing Boston defeat.

The opening of the new FleetCenter promised an exciting new chapter in the ongoing Celtics saga, but the scenario couldn't have played out much worse. The inaugural game itself was an uninspired 101-100 defeat at the hands of the Milwaukee Bucks. Decades of Celtics' pride and tradition overnight seemed to have evaporated with the final closing of doors in venerable Boston Garden. Auerbach himself had now also stepped into the wings by relinquishing the last vestiges of daily ballclub operations. And there was yet another changing of the guard on the coach's end of the bench—the voluntary departure of Chris Ford and the self-appointment by Director of Basketball Operations M. L. Carr as Ford's replacement— that seemingly offered little if any reason to expect a hoped-for miraculous transformation back to past-era glories.

The lineup of ballplayers was now also truly uninspired, especially by Boston NBA standards. Dee Brown (shooting guard) and Sherman Douglas (playmaker) manned the backcourt; Rick Fox (small forward) and Dino Radja (power forward) handled the front court assignments; and Eric Montross was the current experiment in the center slot: none of this crew could by any stretch be considered among the league's better players. The new coach himself was a Bird-era standby who had once been a popular Celtics player but nonetheless brought little experience to the new assignment and also compromised his effectiveness with added front office responsibilities. In brief, from the very start the coaching tenure of M. L. Carr was seemingly destined to be a total disaster both on and off the playing floor.

Croatian import Dino Radja was now the new Boston

Rick Pitino

offensive star, but despite a near 20-point scoring average he was hardly Bird or McHale, or even Lewis or Parish—or for that matter, even the selfish if productive Dominique Wilkins. By Carr's second season on the job the depleted Boston team was not surprisingly suffering its most embarrassing campaign in a full half-century of team history. There was almost no reason for optimism or enthusiasm from any quarter with a ballclub that lost 67 contests (the previous low-water marks were 50 and 53 just before Bird's arrival) and rang down the curtain 46 games behind the division-leading Miami Heat. And it was altogether evident that drastic changes would have to be made if fans were expected to continue packing games in the impressive spanking-new but tradition-poor Fleet Center arena.

A bold departure came next with the hiring of Rick Pitino to replace M. L. Carr on the bench and also take over much of the front office load for the swooning franchise. Changing coaches and/or general managers was about the only adjustment that could be made, since pro basketball offers little opportunity—even in today's era of rampant free-agency—for stockpiling an entire quality team with a single off-season move or two. Auerbach had often worked such miracles in the past with Russell, Cowens and Bird—and also with Bailey Howell, Paul Silas, Bill Walton, Kevin McHale and Robert Parish—but such draft day or waiver wire magic had now seemingly dried up completely in Boston. And, at any rate, there were no one-man saviors anywhere to be found around the league or down in the college ranks during the second half of the talent-thin 1990s. Pitino certainly had a track record for amazing successes in recent collegiate campaigns. He had not only won another national championship for the tradition-rich Kentucky Wildcats but had nearly expunged an irreplacable legend (Adolph Rupp) in the process. But doing it at the NBA level in Boston would certainly be a far different matter.

Pitino's first two seasons have not been entirely without highlight moments. There was a shocking debut victory over the defending champion Chicago Bulls with Michael Jordan to set a hopeful tone at the very outset. And there was some late-season impressive play with young stars like Antoine Walker and Paul Pierce down the stretch of the lockout-shortened 1999 second campaign. There were also hopeful newcomers like Walker and Pierce to stimulate sagging hometown interest in the talent-thin rebuilding team. But even with such slight glimmers of hope, Boston's shortcomings were nonetheless being further underscored

Antoine Walker—a collegiate star under Pitino at Kentucky—has been the main hope for renewed franchise glories during the final seasons of the century's last decade.

almost nightly by the simultaneous successes now being enjoyed by hometown icon Larry Bird. Larry Legend had himself now taken over coaching duties for a championship-contending team of Indiana Pacers back in his native Hoosier State.

Most promising for the Celtics faithful were a handful of young stars boasting as much promise as almost any of the league's new Young Turks. Foremost was Antoine Walker, the center piece of Rick Pitino's 1996 national championship team at the University of Kentucky. Walker displays outrageous talents as a leaper and scorer and enjoyed a quality rookie campaign in which he finished fourth in the voting for top rookie honors. A year later he was a fixture in the Eastern Conference All-Star Game lineup. And he was also fast proving one of the league's top ironmen (he didn't miss a game his first two seasons) and most durable performers. If there is a negative to Walker's flashy frontcourt play it is the fact that he seems to play out of control at times and has so far proven a weak free throw shooter. While leading Boston in scoring in each of his first three NBA seasons (peaking at 22.4 in his sophomore campaign), he has also been the team leader in turnovers, commiting 230 during his otherwise glowing rookie campaign.

Ron Mercer is another Kentucky alum who had already played for Pitino at the college level before accompanying the new Boston coach into the pro ranks as a number six overall draft selection. As the team's second most prolific pointmaker (1221 to Walker's 1840) and a versatile performer who shuffled between the forward and guard slots,

Mercer was a heavy contributor to the 21-game improvement by Pitino's first Boston team and was also a rookie first-team selection a mere season after Antoine Walker had earned that honor. Among the league's 1998 rookies Mercer was runner-up in several offensive categories (points, field goals and steals) and third in two others (scoring average and minutes played). And he was especially brilliant in the winter's second half, averaging better than 18 points nightly after the mid-season All-Star break. His hefty scoring (15.3 and 17.0) during two opening pro campaigns was also a solid supplement to Walker's offensive fireworks and promised to badger league opponents for many seasons to come.

Perhaps Ron Mercer's greatest value in Boston is his potential as half of still another sterling Celtics backcourt combo of the future: green-clad fans now cling to the hope that the duo of Mercer and Kenny Anderson can revive old memories of Cousy-Sharman, The Jones Boys, White-Chaney, Archibald-Henderson, and Johnson-Ainge. For that to happen, however, Anderson will have to reverse an unfortunate early-career history of constant injury and Mercer will have to show some rapid improvement as a consistent outside marksmen.

For the third straight season in 1999 the Celtics could boast a top-flight rookie in the person of tenth-overall draft pick Paul Pierce, a slashing athletic forward selected from the powerhouse University of Kansas program. Pierce managed to live up to some wildly optimistic rookie billings during the recent lockout-shortened season, even if his

Boston fans today cling to a hope that Ron Mercer (#5) can team with veteran Kenny Anderson to rekindle memories of such top Boston backcourt tandems as Cousy alongside Sharman, K.C. and Sam Jones, Jo Jo White with Don Chaney, and Dennis Johnson and Danny Ainge.

Boston's franchise future rests in the hands of a trio of top young draft picks who played together for the first time during the strike-shortened 1999 season. Paul Pierce (#34), Antoine Walker (#8) and Ron Mercer pose before the new season's opening game.

numbers were never quite as eye-opening as Walker's and also fell a shade behind those of Mercer. Logging more games in 1999 than either of his pair of rookie-sensation forerunners (48, to Walker's 42 and Mercer's 41), the hefty 6-7 forward scored at a 16.5 rate (the team's third best) but was actually the squad's top pointmaker with 791 and also the club leader (with 50) in blocked shots. Together the trio of Walker, Mercer and Pierce now promises recently depressed Boston boosters a solid young lineup for the opening season of a new millennium. Perhaps the long-awaited resurgence to past-era glories is still well within reach for those unflappable diehards among the Celtics faithful.

Recent seasons have brought a new arena (the physically impressive if nonetheless tradition-thin FleetCenter), a new high-priced and high-profile coach (Rick Pitino), some of the most dismal basement finishes in franchise annals (bottoming out with a galling 15 wins under the disastrous coaching reign of M. L. Carr), a large handful of promising future stars (Kenny Anderson and Walter McCarty, along-

side Walker, Pierce and Mercer), and even the unexpected disappointment of the NBA's first season-shortening labor action during the fall and early winter of 1998-99. It has indeed—for the first time ever—been a rough decade to be a hoops fan up in storied Beantown.

For those born or educated to bleed Boston kelly green it has been necessary of late to feed almost exclusively on whatever bittersweet nostalgia that the Celtics green jerseys alone might still evoke. The topic of choice on Boston's leading sports radio talkshows remains the exploits of Bird, McHale and Parish—as if the sport's greatest frontcourt trio had retired only yesterday. But throughout these lean seasons of the mid and late 1990s— at least for the hopelessly addicted among New England roundball fans—the glory of still another miraculous Celtics rebirth seemed always to lurk somewhere just around the next corner. And if venerable Boston Garden was now merely a dusty memory, Celtic Mystique was nevertheless always still very much alive in the minds and hearts of the true Celtics faithful.

CHAPTER III

Auerbach's Hall of Famers:
Profiles of the Fifteen Celtics Immortals

Cousy was the unparalleled opening act, Russell the featured matinee performance, and Bird the incomparable final encore. No pro team in any sport provides a more impressive gallery of living legends culled from the pages of team history. In the pioneering decade of the '50s Bob Cousy fired schoolyard imaginations just as Air Jordan would a half-century later. Only Mikan had a bigger role in creating the sport than did the man who refined magical ballhandling and invented the point guard position. As the NBA opened its second decade in the late fifties, the most successful basketball player ever invented came suddenly on the scene in Boston. Bill Russell would rule the basketball world throughout all dozen seasons of the sport's true golden age. None to this day have been able to duplicate Russell's winning feats or match his grip on championship rings and none likely ever will.

In the modern NBA era of the '80s-'90s Larry Bird stands firmly in the pantheon alongside Magic and Michael. It is not an exaggeration to claim that the three literally saved the sport from extinction at a time when it seemed about to slip between the cracks as a dull and uninspired entertainment spectacle. As a business as well as a sport professional basketball was in definite need of emergency repair by the closing years of the 1970s. Larry Bird as much as anyone provided the face lift that was so desperately required. And there is almost no argument at all when it comes to claiming that while Russell was the greatest center ever, Bird remains an equally one-sided choice as the greatest forward ever to lace up a pair of high-top sneakers.

Any franchise is lucky to have one or two such stars on its all-time honor roll of past-era legends. With the Boston Celtics these were, of course, only the frontrunners in a full pack of pro basketball immortals. A dozen other overachievers wearing Boston uniforms for all or most of their stellar careers also rank with the greatest ever to dribble, pass or

shoot Naismith's oversized leather ball. And a review of the loftiest stars ever to wear Boston's green jerseys in the end inevitably reads something like a hall of fame tour of the entire sport itself—touching all its epochs, from the stationary set shot to the running jumpshot to the rim-shattering slam dunk.

Larry Bird
(1979-92)

Bird and Magic are names likely to be forever linked throughout the remaining eons of basketball's unfolding epic saga. Their mano-a-mano duel in the last NCAA Finals of the '70s was the undisputed highlight of a college basketball decade that had also boasted the zenith seasons of

---

Larry Bird Career Profile

College Team: Indiana State University
College and Amateur Achievements:
NCAA National Player of the Year (1979)
Naismith Award (1979) and Wooden Award (1979)
Unanimous First-Team All-American (1978, 1979)
Member of 1992 USA Olympic Team
NBA Team: Boston Celtics
NBA Points: 21,791 (24.3 ppg)
NBA Games: 897 (1979-1992, 13 seasons)
NBA Assists: 5,695 (6.3 apg)
NBA Rebounds: 8,974 (10.0 rpg)
NBA Field Goals (Pct): 8,591 (.496)
NBA Free Throws (Pct): 3,960 (.886)
NBA MVP (1984, 1985, 1986)
NBA Finals MVP (1984, 1985)
NBA All-Star Game MVP (1982)
NBA Rookie of the Year (1980)
Three NBA Championships (1981, 1984, 1986)
Naismith Memorial Basketball Hall of Fame (1998)

AP/Wide World Photos

Larry Bird

average at Indiana State remains one of the loftiest in history; he ranks tenth within the tiny circle of a mere dozen college players who have posted 4,000 combined career points and rebounds; he once topped 60 in a single NBA game and averaged better than 25 ppg. on four different occasions; his nearly 22,000 career points ranks second in Boston history (behind only Havlicek). But scoring proficiency aside, Bird did other things even better. He was the best passing forward ever to pick up a basketball: his full-court heaves on the fast break rivalled those of Russell and his over-the-shoulder blind feeds were nearly the equal of Cousy's. He shot the ball from the outside like no towering corner man before him, ranking in the career top ten in 3-point goals and free-throw percentage, and barely missing out on that distinction in career scoring average when his lifetime mark dipped below 25.0 ppg.

Frank P. McGrath

Statistics alone would seem to make Larry Bird an undisputed choice as the greatest forward ever to play the game, but intangibles lift the Boston star even farther above the field.

John Wooden's UCLA dynasty. Together the two 6'9" rookie phenoms effectively rescued pro basketball from near-oblivion at the outset of the 1980s—a time when fan interest had sagged and genuine stars were as scarce as at any point in league history—then carried out their continued personal warfare in three of the most exciting NBA Finals matchups of all-time. Bird in Boston and Johnson in Los Angeles were perfect joint-saviors for the NBA in one of its bleakest hours.

If Bird and Magic were destined to be linked by fate, they were also two of the most differently molded ballplaying heroes in NBA annals. Johnson as a stylish player was the epitome of pure grace personified—a direct descendant of innovative Elgin Baylor, understated Oscar Robertson and acrobatic Julius Erving. He was also the new oversized prototype for perfection at the guard position. Bird, by stark contrast, was a small-town paragon who didn't look quite so cool (he lacked pure foot speed and seemingly couldn't even jump) yet possessed enough hidden proficiencies to ultimately make him arguably the best forward ever to play the game.

Bird's statistical legacy alone seemingly makes him the game's supreme performer at the forward position. While he never won an individual scoring title (no Boston Celtics player ever has), yet he scored with deadly proficiency throughout the full decade of the '80s. His 30.3 collegiate

Bird waves to an adoring downtown Boston crowd during the May 1981 motorcade celebration of his first NBA championship, a six-game blitzing of the Houston Rockets. Bird would twice more ride the same parade route to toast a NBA title.

during his final season. Bird even specialized in three-pointers ("home runs" in the current NBA lingo) as Erving had specialized in rim-rattling dunks. It was Bird, surprisingly, who captured the first three NBA All-Star Saturday Long Distance Shootout trophies. He controlled games like a guard and flaunted an unmatched intelligence and unmatched set of physical reflexes that made him one of the most dangerous all-around offensive performers ever to step onto the court.

And above all else, Larry Bird was a proven winner. With his pinpoint blind passes delivered softly to the open man, and his amazing sense of every movement on the court surrounding him, Bird ran the Boston offense from his forward slot like a true point guard; and like most great players, he always made his teammates better in the process. Perhaps the most deadly outside shooter of all-time (save perhaps Jerry West or Bill Sharman), Bird always wanted the ball when the game was on the line. It was for this reason alone that the greatest of all basketball talent judges, Red Auerbach, annointed Bird as the one player he would choose above all others if he were building a franchise from scratch. "If I had to start a team, the one guy in all of history I would take would be Larry Bird," Auerbach once pronounced at a charity banquet. Auerbach continued: "This is the greatest ballplayer who ever played the game."

Auerbach may well have grown slightly nostalgic and overly effusive in his more senior years. Bird, above Oscar or Wilt or Air Jordan, is perhaps a bit of a stretch; and it was Auerbach himself who built an even greater team on Russell's shoulders than on Bird's. But it is a strong endorsement, nonetheless, and one not to be taken altogether lightly. There is, indeed, a near-endless line of superstars in the annals of the Boston Celtics—one that doubles or trebles that of any rival franchise. But only Russell today remains a brighter star in the Celtics' firmament than does Indiana's Larry Joe Bird.

Celtics Bob Cousy
(1950-63)

Bob Cousy was basketball's first great wizard of ballhandling. He was also one of the most intense and focussed athletes to grace the pages of American sports history. Cousy was driven by an almost maniacal will to succeed and ultimately to win. And once he had shot-swatting Bill Russell at his side, he would indeed win time and again at the controls of the greatest offensive weapon pro basketball has ever known. That weapon was the Boston Celtics fast-breaking attack—conceived on the chalkboard by Red Auerbach, unleashed on the hardwood court by Russell's shot-blocking and rebounding exploits,

and directed down the Boston Garden parquet floor (and those of a couple dozen other NBA arenas) by Cousy's unparalleled ballhandling and dribbling skills.

Few fans today remember precisely what Cousy's original razzle-dazzle showmanship looked like. Today a behind-the-back dribble or snazzy blind pass is commonplace; before Cousy these maneuvers were simply unheard-of and even largely unthinkable. As an All-American at Holy Cross, Cousy had fine-tuned his skills and already earned a reputation as "The Houdini of the Hardwood" from the local New England press. Playing only a minor role as a freshman member of the Holy Cross team that captured the NCAA title in 1947, the Queens, New York,

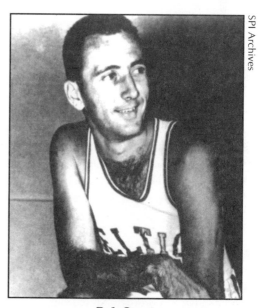

Bob Cousy

SPI Archives

Los Angeles guard Frank Selvy shadows the fabulous Cousy during one of the dozens of postseason 1960s-era Celtics-Lakers matches that were that decade's pro-hoops showcase events.

best-laid plans of Red Auerbach himself—backed into his role as a key ingredient in Auerbach's new style of relentless running and relentlessly winning basketball.

Cousy could do more than merely dribble and pass and stun foes with his bag of ballhandling tricks. He was an effective scorer as well, and often ranked at the top of his team and near the top of the league before the true superscorers (Wilt, Oscar, Baylor, and Jerry West) came along at the end of the '50s and outset of the '60s. For four straight seasons, between 1951 and 1955, he paced the Boston offense, twice averaging a hair over 20 and twice a fraction under; in 1954 he was second in the league behind Philly center Neil Johnston; he once rang up 50 in a playoff outing (admittedly an overtime contest in which he scored 30 on free throw tosses); and his point total reached 17,000 before his 14-year career had closed. But Cousy's true badge was delivering the ball, even in the days before Russell was available to reconstitute Auerbach's fast-break attack: eight times he was the NBA assists champion, and he still ranks seventh lifetime in that category, three full decades after retirement. Cousy was also an intelligent student of the game, one who became a long-time coach after playing days ended and also one who was truly a "coach on the floor" while he ran the versatile Boston offense for more than a dozen seasons.

But Boston's immortal "number 14" was also a ruthless perfectionist who could endure nothing less than 100% effort, total victory, and perfect execution—from himself and all others as well—and in the end excessive intensity sabotaged Cousy's coaching effectiveness with the Boston College team, as well as with the NBA Cincinnati Royals. As a player, however, Cousy's burning intensity (along with a giant assist from Auerbach and Russell) made him a tireless winner as well as one of the game's greatest innovators. None ever delivered a pass better, or with more crowd-pleasing finesse and eye-popping invention—not Magic Johnson or John Stockton, or even Joe Montana or Joe Namath. Cousy was to passing a basketball what Jordan was to dunking it, or Rick Barry and Jerry West were to shooting it. He was the combined Picasso, Rembrandt and Salvador Dali of the ballhandling art.

native was a much-heralded star for a Crusaders team which won 26 straight in 1949-50 before slumping badly during postseason warfare.

Yet despite this lofty status as local legend at the nearby Massachusetts college, a new Celtics coach named Auerbach did not see any particular value in a 6'1" professional player, no matter what his collegiate scoring exploits (19.4 ppg. as a senior) or passing antics might have been. Auerbach stirred considerable local controversy by ignoring the popular Cousy in the college draft, refusing to take the homegrown star under the Celtics' territorial draft option. "Am I supposed to please the local yokels or win ballgames?" Auerbach groused when pressed about not signing Cousy. But fate immediately conspired to put Cousy in a Boston uniform despite Auerbach's unpopular slights; the team originally drafting the tricky guard (Tri-Cities Blackhawks) traded him immediately to the struggling Chicago franchise; when that club folded without playing a game of the new season the ex-Holy Cross ace—behind-the-back passes and between-the-legs dribbles and all—went straight to Boston via a dispersal-draft coin flip. (Boston had chosen seven-footer Charlie Share and Duquesne star Chuck Cooper over Cousy in June and now coveted either Max Zaslofsky or Andy Phillip of the three available Chicago players; but Boston lost the three-way toss and was stuck with Cousy.) Bob Cousy—despite the

Dave Cowens
(1970-80)

It is widely acknowledged that there have been four pivotal oncourt figures in the storied history of the Boston Celtics. Cousy first earned league-wide respect for a team that had usually struggled during its entire first decade of existence. Russell launched Auerbach's dozen-year dynasty with his revolutionary demonstration that defense and not offense wins pro championships. Larry Bird would almost singlehandedly resurrect Boston's lost supremacy as a raw rookie at the outset of the eighties. The fourth figure is of course Dave Cowens, the bridge between the Russell era and the Bird era. Cowens won a pair of championships and earned his share of top individual awards: rookie of the year (1971), league MVP (1973), and All-Star Game MVP (also 1973). He was both the statistical and spiritual leader of one of finest non-Auerbach-coached Boston teams ever. But his tag will most certainly always be that of the supreme NBA overachiever. It was not how big a talent Cowens was that continually raised eyebrows among basketball aficionados of the '70s, but rather the mere fact that the undersized but supercharged center was ever even an impact player in the first place.

Author's Collection

Dave Cowens

Cowens was likely the most unusual star in NBA history. He revolutionized play at the center position as completely as had Russell, though he did so by being as versatile in his talents as Russell had been one dimentional. He shared with Havlicek and later also Bird the unique distinction of leading his team in scoring, rebounding and assists. He also possessed a unique personality that made him not only one of the game's special "characters" but also clearly the most beloved Celtics hero of them all. It was a small miracle that Dave Cowens came as close as he did to filling Russell's giant shoes only a handful of seasons after the big man retired, and personal style—both oncourt and offcourt—

Dave Cowens Career Profile

College Team: Florida State University
NBA Teams: Boston Celtics, Milwaukee Bucks
NBA Points: 13,516 (17.6 ppg)
NBA Games: 766 (1970-1980, 1982-83, 11 seasons)
NBA Assists: 2,910 (3.8 apg)
NBA Rebounds: 10,444 (13.6 rpg)
NBA Field Goals (Pct): 5,744 (.460)
NBA Free Throws (Pct): 2,027 (.783)
NBA MVP (1973)
NBA All-Star Game MVP (1973)
NBA Rookie of the Year (1971, with Geoff Petrie)
Two NBA Championships (1974, 1976)
Naismith Memorial Basketball Hall of Fame (1990)

had as much to do with that miracle as did raw playing talent. While Russell was deadly efficient as a ballplayer he was also personally cold as a human being (at least that was the public perception) and generally aloof from the fandom that adored him. Russell perfected his game in the public limelight but revealed his true face and personality only to his teammates behind closed locker room doors. Cowens was equally relentless—if far less disciplined—and yet always refreshingly accessible. He never polished his offensive game, mainly because he preferred the more manly challenges of rebounding and defense. But there were no deceits about him, on or off the court. He never let up a minute and he was totally ruthless in his oncourt style. The Boston fans unabashedly loved him for it.

Cowens replaced Russell after a brief hiatus in which the Celtics under new coach Tom Heinsohn had almost totally collapsed in the wake of the franchise player's retirement. He came onboard in Boston as almost a complete unknown. Because of NCAA sanctions (and a resulting television ban) his Florida State team had enjoyed almost no national visibility. As he had done with Russell and would later do with Bird, Auerbach had stumbled on this treasure and then ingeniously pulled all the right strings to get him into the fold. The story has been widely circulated about how Auerbach once scouted Cowens in Tallahassee (it was a game versus Dayton) and then stormed out of the arena after only five minutes as if thoroughly disgusted. It was of course all a shameless ploy to deflect possible attention by other NBA bird dogs. Red knew (as he had with Russell) precisely what he needed to rebuild his team for Heinsohn and the Celtics coaching staff, and on draft day—as usually was the case—Auerbach got what he coveted. The Celtics had fourth pick and waited patiently while Detroit plucked Lanier, San Diego collected Tomjanovich, and Atlanta traded Zelmo Beaty for San Francisco's third selection in order to corner LSU scoring

With unique mobility and leaping ability and an unprecedented aggressivness, Boston's second greatest redhead revolutionized the NBA style of play at the showcase center position.

was able to build a new Boston powerhouse around the most mobile and unconventional pivot player the league had ever known and ever would know. When Cowens arrived in camp as an unheralded rookie off the campus of Florida State in the fall of 1970 he immediately revolutionized inside play (aided by the stategy of his coach Tom Heinsohn) by moving the conventional pivot position a full 20 feet from the basket. The strategy soon proved infallible as Cowens utilized his rugged style of play to transform the Celtics from a dull and lifeless outfit (a 1970 record of 34-48, with a sixth-place division finish) into the fast-breaking thoroughbred of old, a team suddenly capable of seizing two more championships (1974 and 1976) and also posting the best regular-season winning mark on the franchise ledgers (68-14, ironically compiled in 1973 when the team failed to bring home a title after Havlicek was injuried during the playoffs). Boston won in the seventies as exclusively because of Cowens as they had won in the sixties because of Russell and would win in the eighties because of Bird.

John "Hondo" Havlicek
(1962-78)

There was never a better sixth man nor a more thoroughly team-oriented player than the Boston Celtics and Ohio State University Hall-of-Famer who opted for a tryout with the NFL Cleveland Browns as a wide receiver before settling on basketball as a permanent athletic vocation. Nor have there been many before or since who might qualify as a more effective clutch scorer, a more tenacious end-to-end

sensation Pete Maravich. When Boston finally grabbed Cowens they had garnered perhaps the greatest number four selection ever made on NBA draft day.

Cowens' uniqueness consisted of three factors. Foremost was his ability to leap. There was also his mobility: Cowens, like Havlicek, simply ran bigger opponents into the ground. He would race around the floor for 45 minutes knowing that in the final three minutes or so he would finally "own" his opponent. The result of this exhausting style, along with his innate intelligence, allowed great success against the other top centers of his era. He was rarely beaten by Jabbar. He dominated future Hall of Famer Bob Lanier. And he held his own with Chamberlain, Nate Thurmond and all others as well. When he couldn't beat them inside he took them outside. The final factor tipping the balance in Cowens' favor was his relish for rough and tumble physical play. He was one of the most aggressive players ever, which made him far bigger than his physical stature. The result of his style was a history of foul trouble. But it was also a history of dominating his opponent regardless of that opponent's size or innate talent level.

In the end Cowens proved one of the greatest Celtics warriors of all—the franchise player of the '70s (an epoch that also housed Havlicek), and undoubtedly the best center in club history after the immortal Russell. Auerbach

John Havlicek

defender, a more versatile athlete at absolutely any spot on the floor, or a more dedicated "winner" than Hondo Havlicek of Red Auerbach's Boston Celtics.

Havlicek is the only man in the game's full history to combine a career of "role playing" and "backup status" with front-line stats that rank with those of the all-time greats. He stands fifth all-time for NBA games played (1,270), fourth in career minutes (46,471), ninth in points scored (26,395), and sixth in field goals made (10,513). And there are only a tiny handful who own more combined NBA and NCAA championship rings. And none can lay claim to a single moment more deeply etched into the sport's mythology—the dramatic closing seconds of an unforgettable 1965 Boston-Philadelphia divisional series when "HAVLICEK STOLE THE BALL!" and thus miraculously kept the dynasty championship string alive.

The greatest "sixth man" of NBA history was also the greatest understudy ever to lace up high-tops in the collegiate game. Havlicek played smack in the shadow of Jerry Lucas, and together they were the most unbeatable combo in Big Ten history (78-6, three conference titles, one NCAA crown, three Final Fours). Despite his role as "second banana," the player called "Hondo" was nonetheless a recognized franchise player from the start and was twice tabbed All-Big Ten and once as a first-team All-American. His outstanding play in his first and third of three national title games also won Havlicek a cherished spot each time on the NCAA's all-tournament team.

But if Hondo Havlicek never quite emerged from Lucas's shadow during college days, he soon dwarfed his

Perpetual motion best defined the playing style of John Havlicek. Here he drives by Knicks defenders Dave DeBusschere and future NBA coaching great Phil Jackson (#18).

teammate's considerable stature when the two reached the professional ranks. Havlicek would first enjoy a near-miss tryout with the NFL Cleveland Browns (despite not playing football in college) and then settle on a career with Auerbach's Celtics which brought eventual accolades as one of the sport's true immortals. Havlicek's reputation in early NBA seasons (he was a rookie in Cousy's final year) was that of the most valued bench player and greatest hustler in all of pro cage history. A decade later he was a mainstay starter and club leader for a two-time championship team coached by Tom Heinsohn and bolstered by Dave Cowens.

The NBA numbers that he would amass in the end (for games played, points, scoring average, minutes played, field goals and a host of other offensive categories) have never been even approached by any other Big Ten Conference alumnus and are equally unmatched among past Celtics greats. Havlicek remains the Boston franchise leader in career games, minutes, points, field goals attempted and made, and free throws attempted and made. He trails only Larry Bird in lifetime scoring average and only Cousy in career assists. And his eight NBA championship rings are also a boast that only Boston Celtics teammates Russell (13), Satch Sanders (8), K.C. Jones (8) and Sam Jones (10) can surpass or share.

John Havlicek Career Profile

College Team: Ohio State University
College and Amateur Achievements:
Concensus Second-Team All-American (1962)
NCAA Championship (1960)
NBA Team: Boston Celtics
NBA Points: 26,395 (20.8 ppg)
NBA Games: 1270 (1962-1978, 16 seasons)
NBA Assists: 6,114 (4.8 apg)
NBA Rebounds: 8,007 (6.3 rpg)
NBA Field Goals (Pct): 10,513 (.439)
NBA Free Throws (Pct): 5,369 (.815)
NBA Finals MVP (1974)
NBA 35th Anniversary All-Time Team (1980)
Eight NBA Championships
(1963, 1964, 1965, 1966, 1968, 1969, 1974, 1976)
Naismith Memorial Basketball Hall of Fame (1983)

Tom Heinsohn
(1956-65)

Heinsohn is one of those giants of the cage sport who deserves equal billing in the history books for each chapter of his tripartite career—first as collegiate All-American for Holy Cross, later as year-in and year-out NBA All-Star with Auerbach's Celtics, and finally as championship-winning professional coach with the post-Russell Boston ballclubs of the mid-1970s. As a head coach Heinsohn's record would nearly approach Auerbach's: he didn't win as many titles—nobody did—but he matched his mentor's two 60-win seasons, one of his teams captured the most club victories in any single season (68 in 1973), and his regular-season and postseason winning percentages were only a faction behind those logged by Auerbach. And despite a limp start and finish—his debut campaign and shortened final season were his only losing outings—he was also the most successful bench coach found anywhere in the league throughout nearly the entire decade of the seventies. As though this 18-year association (nine as player and nine as coach) with the on-court game were not quite enough, Heinsohn today continues his affiliation with the Celtics while completing

Tom Heinsohn (#15) deflects a driving shot by Minneapolis forward Jim Paxson during his 1957 rookie season, a campaign in which he beat out even Bill Russell for top NBA rookie honors.

Tom Heinsohn Career Profile

College Team: Holy Cross College
College and Amateur Achievements:
Concensus First-Team All-American (1956)
NBA Team: Boston Celtics
NBA Points: 12,194 (18.6 ppg)
NBA Games: 654 (1956-1965, 9 seasons)
NBA Assists: 1,318 (2.0 apg)
NBA Rebounds: 5,749 (8.8 rpg)
NBA Field Goals (Pct) : 4,773 (.405)
NBA Free Throws (Pct): 2,648 (.790)
NBA Rookie of the Year (1957)
Eight NBA Championships
(1957, 1959, 1960, 1961, 1962, 1963, 1964, 1965)
Naismith Memorial Basketball Hall of Fame (1985)

his second decade as a popular play-by-play television and radio announcer. In this latter capacity Heinsohn still teams with his former oncourt running mate, Bob Cousy. But it was way back in the late fifties and early sixties that Heinsohn and Cousy first joined forces (they overlapped for seven seasons) to themselves write some of the grandest legends of the early-era NBA saga.

Heinsohn was known foremost as a relentless shooter who earned from teammates the sarcastic nickname "Ack-Ack" for his machine-gun-like firing up of repeated long-range jumpers and running hook shots. Heinsohn's bombs were heaved from any possible angle and almost any time he had the ball in his hands and had gained even a half step advantage on one of his usually overmatched opponents. Putting in a full season with Auerbach's first championship outfit (while Bill Russell only logged a partial campaign, due to his appearance at the 1956 Olympics in Australia), the touted territorial draft pick earned top rookie honors for the regular season (averaging 16.2 points and 9.8 rebounds) and then also poured home 37 points (spiced with 23 rebounds) in the decisive seventh-game championship victory over St. Louis which iced the club's very first NBA banner and thus launched Boston's decade-long dynasty era.

If Heinsohn's playing days were strewn with success they were brief in number; painful knees forced him off the court a year before Auerbach himself stepped down. During his nine-season career as an active player, however, Heinsohn would walk off with an incredible eight championship rings. It was a postseason winning percentage that even outstripped Russell's and (along with K.C. Jones, who was also eight for nine) also bested anyone else in league history who played a half-dozen or more seasons. And Ack-Ack the gunner assuredly contributed as heavily as anyone in Auerbach's stable of studs to each of those year-in and year-out postseason triumphs. Within Auerbach's tightly

Transcendental Graphics

Heinsohn battles Hawks stars Bob Pettit (#9) and Cliff Hagan (#16) for a loose ball during game three of the wild postseason shootout that brought Auerbach and the Celtics a first coveted league championship.

orchestrated scheme Heinsohn was always the designated scorer, while Cousy was the playmaker, Ramsey served as the designated "team spark" and Russell provided the final wall of basket defense.

Heinsohn's stature with Auerbach was so lofty that it had been Tommy—not Cousy, Sharman, Ramsey or Russell—whom Red had actually first approached about succeeding him with the vacant coaching duties upon his pre-announced 1966 retirement. During a reported luncheon meeting in the fall of 1965 (a few month's after Heinsohn's own retirement as a player) the legendary Boston mentor tossed out several names (which also included Cousy who was coaching at Boston College and Ramsey who was farming in his native Kentucky); Heinsohn quickly removed himself from consideration for the post, lamely citing his own new and prosperous insurance business but also more convincingly suggesting that Russell the possible coach was the only plausible solution to the problem of managing Bill Russell the still-active ballplayer.

When he finally did take over the bench duties as successor to both Auerbach and Russell in 1970, Heinsohn would in short order extend his own hero status in Beantown by earning for the proud Celtics two more NBA titles (1974, 1976) and garnering for himself both a coveted NBA coach-of-the-year decoration (1973) and a firm place

in history as perhaps the league's most successful coach for the decade separating Bill Russell from Larry Bird. But for all the bench successes of the 1970s it is still difficult to lionize Tom Heinsohn in the pages of Celtics history without giving true place of prominence to the image of one of the most confident and aggressive offensive stars from the glorious Red Auerbach dynasty epoch. Whether he was firing up ceaseless line-drive jumpers or unleashing his patented running hooks, Heinsohn never shied away from his role as one of the sport's most irrepressible and wide-eyed gunners.

K. C. Jones
(1958-67)

The sparkplug guard who played in the shadows of Bill Russell in both San Francisco as a collegian and Boston as a seasoned professional was indisputably one of the sport's most talented background role players. He was also one of basketball's most enduring winners. Both as collegiate and professional ballplayer and later as an NBA coach, K. C. Jones amassed a collection of championship rings that has been matched by only a mere handful of All-Americans and legendary Hall of Famers. As an NBA star the total for Jones was eight of nine when it came to counting championship trophies (leaving him tied with Heinsohn as the most consistent winner in league annals); in college he garnered two NCAA titles in four outings (not counting an original junior season that was aborted after only one game due to an appendectomy); his single Olympic appearance (1956) also harvested a rare gold medal.

K.C. Jones also built his coveted collection of championship rings (which eventually totalled ten in the NBA, throwing in the two earned as a head coach in Boston) with

---

K. C. Jones Career Profile

College Team: University of San Francisco
College and Amateur Achievements:
Concensus Second-Team All-American (1956)
Two NCAA Championships (1955, 1956)
1956 USA Olympic Team, Gold Medal
NBA Team: Boston Celtics
NBA Points: 5,011 (7.4 ppg)
NBA Games: 676 (1958-1967, 9 seasons)
NBA Assists: 2,908 (4.3 apg)
NBA Rebounds: 2,399 (3.5 rpg)
NBA Field Goals (Pct): 1,919 (.387)
NBA Free Throws (Pct): 1,173 (.647)
Eight NBA Championships
(1959, 1960, 1961, 1962, 1963, 1964, 1965, 1966)
Naismith Memorial Basketball Hall of Fame (1988)

---

legitimate contributions and not just by happening to sit on the right bench for the right team at the right time. More than Russell, it was Jones who shut down phenomenal Tom Gola of La Salle in the 1955 Final Four and in the process earned for USF the first of its back-to-back NCAA titles. Jones not only completely clamped down the hot-shooting Gola in the NCAA title matchup (using his exceptional

K. C. Jones

Rookie point guard K.C. Jones displays his offensive talent during 1959 playoff action.

speed and quick hands to compensate for a five-inch height differential) but also wore out the nets with a game-high 24 points of his own.

A decade later Jones was also contributing heavily to a number of Russell's most hard-earned NBA titles, first as a competent backup to playmaker Bob Cousy and later as himself the playmaking half of a deadly backcourt tandem alongside Sam Jones. It was the "Jones Boys"—K. C. the point guard and Sam the shooting guard—who quickly made Boston partisans forget the once incomparable duo of Cousy and Sharman and who thus also keyed three final 1960s-era Boston banners collected in the wake of Cousy's early retirement.

When K.C. replaced Cousy in 1964 alongside Sam Jones (who had moved into the starting lineup a single season earlier) he also inherited the crucial playmaking role and responded by pacing the ballclub in assists for each of the next three seasons. He also contributed heavily as a ball-hawking defender who pressured opposing quarterbacks relentlessly and whose disruptions at the defensive end were always as vital as any other single element (except perhaps Bill Russell's shot-blocking intimidations) of the vaunted Boston attack. Playing days were followed (when he retired in 1967) by ten years of NBA head coaching spread over two decades which also brought seven division titles and two additional NBA championship rings (both again with Boston, in 1984 and 1986). And as a coach (first within the college ranks at Brandeis, and later as a pro head man with Washington, Boston, Seattle and also the ABA San Diego Conquistadors) his soft-spoken style always guaranteed not only deep respect from all the athletes who played for him, but a continued winning tradition as well. His first NBA head coaching job with the Capital (Washington) Bullets was highlighted by a .630 winning percentage over three seasons and a near-miss of another championship during the 1975 NBA Finals versus Golden State. In five campaigns on the Boston bench at the height of the Larry Bird era he logged regular-season (.751) and playoff (.637) victory percentages that outpaced both Auerbach's and Bill Fitch's as the best in ballclub history.

BOSTON
Sam Jones
(1957-69)

While black stars at large (and thus largely white) colleges were beginning to grab some share of the national headlines in the mid-fifties (viz. Walter Dukes at Seton Hall, Sihugo Green at Duquesne, Bill Russell at USF and Wilt Chamberlain at Kansas), there was another tradition simultaneously being sustained in the backwaters of the college game. This was the tradition of great black teams which often dominated NAIA small college action. Coach John McLendon, for one, had pioneered both fast-break basketball and the small college black powerhouse ballclub during his journeyman career that took him from North Carolina Central to Hampton Institute to Tennessee State and finally on to Kentucky State. McLendon at his height would capture three consecutive NAIA titles with Tennessee State while at the same time recruiting and molding ballplayers like Dick Barnett, Jim Barnhill and Ben Warley.

The first notable individual talent to emerge from this arena and make his lasting mark on the national hoops scene would be Sam Jones, backcourt ace with the Auerbach-coached Bill Russell Celtics of the mid and late 1960s. Jones would first carve out his reputation at North Carolina Central College under McLendon's successor Roy Brown. And he would enter the Celtics lineup as a top June 1957 draft choice already sporting his later reputation as a phenomenal "carom" shooter and (in the words of Boston teammate Bob Cousy) "the fastest thing ever seen" charging

up and down a 90-foot-long hardwood basketball floor.

Of all the memorable superstars to wear the uniform of the Boston Celtics none was more of a surprise find and unpolished gem than was Sam Jones. For one thing, Jones arrived in Boston for his 1958 rookie season as a completely unknown quantity, a player whose college career had transpired in almost total obscurity. In four seasons at North Carolina Central (spread over six years due to military service) Jones averaged nearly 18 points per game after turning down a scholarship at more visible Notre Dame, but in the mid-fifties few scouts and fewer fans were attuned to the small college cage scene. It wasn't long, however, before the lesser of Boston's "Jones Boys" (K.C.

Even as a 12-year veteran, Sam Jones was still hustling for loose balls during his final postseason championship run in April 1969.

Jones joined the squad a year later after his own military stint) had established a personal style and growing list of accomplishments that would rank him right alongside Cousy and Sharman as part of Boston's unforgettable triumvirate of all-time backcourt immortals. Most eye-catching was his shooting style which featured dead-eye bankshots off the backboard, launched from either side of the floor and from a range of between ten and twenty feet from the bucket; equally attention-grabbing was his amazing shooting proficiency which would eventually outstrip even that of the dead-eyed Bill Sharman. After achieving Sharman's spot in the lineup in 1962 the unselfish marksman led the squad in scoring three times during the decade of domination (peaking at 25.9—the league's fourth best—in 1965) and remained in the club's top three for eight seasons in a row.

Bill Russell is today remembered as basketball's all-time

Sam Jones Career Profile

College Team: North Carolina Central College
NBA Team: Boston Celtics
NBA Points: 15,411 (17.7 ppg)
NBA Games: 871 (1957-1969, 12 seasons)
NBA Assists: 2,209 (2.5 apg)
NBA Rebounds: 4,305 (4.9 rpg)
NBA Field Goals (Pct): 6,271 (.456)
NBA Free Throws (Pct): 2,869 (.803)
NBA Silver Anniversary All-Time Team (1971)
Ten NBA Championships
(1959, 1960, 1961, 1962, 1963, 1964, 1965, 1966, 1968, 1969)
Naismith Memorial Basketball Hall of Fame (1983)

biggest winner with a miraculous 11 world titles in his 13 NBA seasons. It is rarely mentioned that Sam Jones (who arrived on the scene a single season after Russell) was an equally big winner, logging 10 for 12 across his own victory-strewn career. With a key spot on ten Boston championship teams Sam Jones compiled enough outstanding postseason playing time to eventually rank second in total NBA playoff games (at the time of his 1969 retirement), fourth in playoff points, and third in Celtics career scoring. More significant still, the rangy 6-4 marksman who once collected a club record 51 against Detroit in 1965 was an early prototype of the tall shooting guard which would become an NBA staple a full quarter-century later. With Sam Jones and K.C. Jones inheriting the backcourt in the early-sixties from Cousy and Sharman, Auerbach's dynasty was destined to steamroll on for several more seasons without so much as a single missed step.

Ed Macauley poses with owner Walter Brown and backcourt ace Bob Cousy before the debut NBA All-Star Game at Boston Garden in March 1951. Macauley would score 20 points that night and carry off the first-ever All-Star Game MVP trophy.

"Easy Ed" Macauley
(1950-56)

Today Ed Macauley is the stuff of numerous trivia questions. Who was the first Boston Celtic to average 20 points for a season? What Celtics immortal has his retired uniform draped on the rafters in Boston yet never earned a championship ring with the green-clad occupants of Boston Garden? Who was the forgotten "other" player featured in the most significant trade in NBA history? But during his heyday Macauley was a talent awesome enough to merit every ounce of his Naismith Hall-of-Fame plaque now hanging in Springfield. Despite a brilliant All-American collegiate career at St. Louis University—AP national player

of the year recognition in 1949, as well as 1948 NIT MVP honors and a 1947 national field goal percentage leadership—Macauley gained his greatest renown in the early '50s with the Boston Celtics, when he teamed with Cousy and Sharman to produce one of the greatest scoring cominations in league history (theirs was the first team to average better than 100 per game for a full season). Nonetheless it was destined to be Macauley's departure from Boston and not his debut there that would clinch his true measure of lasting fame.

Boston had acquired Macauley only after the sudden folding of the St. Louis Bombers franchise for which he debuted, and also only after the New York Knicks offered unsuccessfully to purchase the entire defunct midwest franchise just to obtain Macauley's stellar offensive talents. But the athlete popularly known as "Easy Ed" for his smooth-as-silk playing style was—for all his point-making skills—something of a liability as a post-position player, since he stood only 6-8 and weighed in well under 200 pounds. Once Auerbach arrived in Beantown with his vision of a fast-breaking offense fuelled by aggressive frontcourt rebounding it was clear that Macauley's Boston tenure would be severely limited. This despite the fact that he was such a personal favorite of owner Walter Brown that Brown offered to block Auerbach's scheme to use Macauley as trade bait for luring Russell, until Macauley himself okayed the deal. (Macauley wished to return to his native city where he could find better care for his severely ill child).

The end for Macauley in Boston came in spectacular fashion when one of the league's most versatile scorers (along with draft property Cliff Hagan) was peddled back to his home town of St. Louis in 1956 for the draft rights to coveted USF All-American Bill Russell. Macauley for all his

Ed Macauley Career Profile

College Team: St. Louis University
College and Amateur Achievements:
Unanimous First-Team All-American (1949)
Consensus First-Team All-American (1948)
National Field Goal Percentage Leader (1949)
NIT Most Valuable Player (1948)
NBA Teams:
St. Louis Bombers, Boston Celtics, St. Louis Hawks
NBA Points: 11,234 (17.5 ppg)
NBA Games: 641 (1949-1959, 10 seasons)
NBA Assists: 2,079 (3.2 apg)
NBA Rebounds: 4,325 (7.5 rpg)
NBA Field Goals (Pct): 3,742 (.436)
NBA Free Throws (Pct): 3,750 (.761)
NBA All-Star Game MVP (1951)
NBA Championships (1957)
Naismith Memorial Basketball Hall of Fame (1960)

talent was not even a small approximation of Russell, and in future years the Hawks for all their victories and postseason title challenges were never quite the Celtics either. But Macauley did play well enough in the remainder of the decade to wrap up Hall-of-Fame certification nonetheless. And when he was tabbed for enshrinement by the Naismith Memorial Basketball Hall of Fame in 1960 (merely two years into retirement and still only 32 years of age) Ed Macauley earned yet another special distinction by becoming the youngest man or woman ever elected for permanent residence in Springfield.

BOSTON
Kevin McHale
(1980-93)

My own vote would probably still fall to Mikan, Mikkelsen and Pollard when it comes to selecting the best-ever NBA front line trio. The "Tall Timbers" outfit in Minneapolis at the dawn of league history did after all win six championships in their seven seasons together and also revolutionized the way the game was played (by forcing legislations that widened the foul lanes, introduced the 24-second shot clock, and barred defensive goal tending—all aimed at neutralizing Mikan and his sidekicks). New England-based pundits like *Boston Globe* beat writer Peter May, who have more tunnelized vision when its comes to anything involving Red Auerbach and the Boston Celtics, would dismiss the oldtimers in Minneapolis in favor of the Boston "Big Three" crew of the 1980s-epoch—Larry Bird, Robert Parish and Kevin McHale. And it must be admitted that sportswriter May (in his book appropraitely entitled *The Big Three*) states an awfully convincing case for such a choice.

McHale's part of the argument (whether he is compared to Mikkelsen or Pollard—Hall of Famers both) is difficult to discount. As a 6-10 tower of strength with one of the longest pair of arms seen in the NBA since seven-footer Walter Dukes of the Mikan era, McHale is without

Kevin McHale

doubt one of the premier low-post scorers (20,517 combined regular season and postseason career points) in NBA annals. He possessed a turnaround jumper that was practically impossible to block; his long legs and arms allowed pivot moves that left any defender confused and overmatched; and his work ethic was so strong that he even eventually turned himself into one of the league's lankiest adequate three-point shooters (he heaved up 69 long-range bombs in 1990) anywhere on record.

And then there was Kevin McHale the unsurpassed low-post defender to talk about. The long tree-limb arms that made him one of the surest upclose scorers in the league also contributed to rare defensive skills—especially shot blocking. Across his full career McHale was one of the best rejectors ever among forwards, posting an average for six straight seasons that stretched across the early part of his career of better that two defensive stuffs per game. Three times running (1986, 1987, 1988) he was elected to the All-NBA defensive first team, and another three times (1983, 1989, 1990) he also took second team honors as a defender.

While he was slow of foot and often prone to nagging injury, McHale always made up for any such deficiencies with an iron will and razor-sharp intelligence that were matched nowhere in the league except by the two giants (Bird and Parish) playing alongside him. And of course he could flat out shoot the basketball like few front court stalwarts before or after. Longtime Boston beat writer Bob Ryan is hardly alone in his repeated claim that McHale was

Kevin McHale Career Profile

College Team: University of Minnesota
NBA Team: Boston Celtics
NBA Points: 17,335 (17.9 ppg)
NBA Games: 971 (1980-1992, 13 seasons)
NBA Assists: 1,670 (1.7 apg)
NBA Rebounds: 7,122 (7.3 rpg)
NBA Field Goals (Pct): 6,830 (.554)—
(Tenth Best in NBA History)
NBA Free Throws (Pct): 3,634 (.798)
Three NBA Championships (1981, 1984, 1986)
Naismith Memorial Basketball Hall of Fame (1999)

Robert Parish
(1980-94)

Frank P. McGrath, Jr.

Before Kevin McHale's career was closed out in 1993 the towering offensive threat would boast over 17,000 career points, nearly 1,000 games, and above 7,000 career rebounds.

"Ironman" is a label traditionally attached to Ron Boone or Randy Smith, or more recently to Kareem Abdul-Jabbar and A.C. Green. But perhaps it now best fits long-time Boston Celtics tower of strength Robert Parish. The Parish career resume features records for most NBA seasons played (21) and most games played (1,611), a pair of milestones recently captured from Kareem. That kind of rugged longevity has also allowed "The Chief" (a reference to his Native American heritage) to garner an additional "official" NBA standard for defensive rebounds (10,117), to log 23,334 career points and 14,715 total rebounds, to play in nine NBA All-Star Games (all packed into his fourteen Boston seasons), to garner the NBA playoff record for career offensive rebounds (571), and to collect three NBA championship rings in Boston (all earned while playing in the potent mid-eighties lineup featuring Bird and McHale) and one in Chicago (alongside all-everything Michael Jordan).

The rebounding records—though impressive—are a bit tainted, since past-era greats like Russell, Chamberlain, Abdul-Jabbar, and even Elvin Hayes and Moses Malone unquestionably collected more, before the the NBA separated out defensive caroms as a separate statistical category in 1974. A further blemish perhaps is the fact that Robert Parish does not hold a single league record that is not in some fashion related to his amazing longevity. But indistructability is, after all, a virtue not to be lightly scoffed at. And only one other past great—Abdul Jabbar—can boast of similar milestone numbers: 1500 games, 23,000 career points, 14,000 rebounds, and 2,000 blocked shots.

As an offensive force Parish relied largely on finesse over raw power, a surprising fact, perhaps, given his towering physique and solid 230-pound frame. His arching turn-

perhaps the surest two points in the history of basketball once he was fed the ball down in the low post. He is after all the only 60-80 man in the game's long annals, hitting above 60% (.604) of his field goal tries and 80% (.836) of his free throws efforts during his hot-shooting 1987 campaign, only his second after relinquishing his touted sixth-man role for an equally productive starting assignment. Twice while still filling the former role he would collect the league's prestigious NBA Sixth Man Award, while at the same time posting scoring and minutes-played totals in both compaigns which compared favorably with almost any of the league's top-flight front court starters. Five straight seasons he also averaged above 20 points (1986-1990, barely missing the mark the season before the string started) and his career .554 field goal shooting percentage remains the tenth highest on record. With the most durable center of all-time (Parish), the best all-around "point-forward" ever invented (Bird), and the last in the patented Boston line of great sixth-man subs turned into frontline superstars (Ramsey, Havlicek, Silas and finally McHale), it is not surprising that Boston fought Magic Johnson's Lakers tooth and nail across the 1980s for domination of perhaps the NBA's strongest decade ever.

Robert Parish Career Profile

College Team: Centenary College
College and Amateur Achievements:
National Rebounding Leader (1975, 1976)
NBA Teams: Golden State Warriors, Boston Celtics,
Charlotte Hornets, Chicago Bulls
NBA Points: 23,334 (14.5 ppg)
NBA Games: 1,611 (1976-1997, 21 seasons) (NBA Record)
NBA Assists: 2,180 (1.4 apg)
NBA Rebounds: 14,715 (9.1 rpg)
NBA Field Goals (Pct): 9,614 (.537)
NBA Free Throws (Pct): 4,106 (.721)
NBA Championships: 1981, 1984, 1986, 1997

around jump shot—his weapon of choice a dozen feet from the hoop—had such a pronounced arc that it seemed to scrape the rafters before tickling the net. He held his favorite shot so far aloft before launching it that it was virtually unblockable even by comparably-sized giants. And along the baseline especially, it was usually heaved up with near-uncanny accuracy by a talented marksman sporting a lofty 20-year career .537 mark for field goal accuracy.

When it comes to simple aesthetic assessment rather than raw numbers, many longtime NBA watchers have also concluded that the decade-long Boston front line of Parish, Bird and McHale was—simply put—the best front-wall combination ever to play the game at any level and in any era. There was only one apparent drawback to

"The Chief"—Robert Parish—would topple nearly all NBA longevity records during his 21-year professional career.

Parish's hanging around the NBA until he was nearly 44 years old; his feats of stubborn longevity moved back by a few seasons his inevitable first-ballot election into basketball's top shrine at the Naismith Memorial Hall of Fame.

Robert Parish's career was reborn in 1980 when he was acquired by Boston from Golden State for a pair of top draft picks in what would soon prove to be one of Auerbach's shrewdest bargaining-table moves.

Frank Ramsey
(1954-55, 1956-64)

Today the "sixth man" is a basketball staple, especially in the play-for-pay ranks. This is the talented non-starter who enters the game as an early reinforcement, usually (but not always) is at home as both a backcourt and frontcourt replacement, and inspires his team with bursts of offensive firepower and defensive intensity aimed against already worn-down opponents. European import Toni Kukoc—a brilliant outside shooter and inside rebounder—has most recently filled the role admirably with the Jordan-led Chicago Bulls; more renowned exemplars were Boston stalwarts John Havlicek in the late sixties and Kevin McHale in the early eighties. For the past decade and a half (since 1983) NBA writers and broadcasters have even selected a yearly recipient for an officially sanctioned league award in this category. The prototype, however, was actually invented four long decades ago—of course by Red Auerbach in Boston—and Auerbach's first near-perfect experimental model was former Kentucky All-American Frank Ramsey, the progenitor of a long line of such super-

Frank Ramsey was rarely a starter in his best NBA seasons but he nonetheless resides in the Naismith Hall of Fame, his #23 hung among the rafters, and he claimed 7 NBA championship rings.

Kentucky All-American Frank Ramsey was Auerbach's prototype for what would evolve into the famed sixth-man role of the vital all-purpose bench player.

versatile bench players that have resided in Boston (most memorably in the guises of Paul Silas and Bill Walton) and elsewhere over the subsequent near half-century.

Ramsey had of course been anything but a bench player for Adolph Rupp at Kentucky. As a sophomore sensation in 1951 Ramsey teamed with Cliff Hagan to spark Rupp's 32-2 national championship squad; as the quarterback of that team (from his forward slot) the 6-4 Madisonville native was the squad's second leading rebounder. When Kentucky's basketball program fell on difficult times over the next three seasons (sitting out the 1953 season because of recruiting violations and missing the 1954 NCAA postseason by choice despite the school's first undefeated record) things only got better for Ramsey on the personal level. He averaged nearly 16 a game in scoring for a 1952 squad that was stunned by St. John's in the NCAA regional finals, then earned second team All-American honors and scored a shade under 20 for the 25-0 team that followed on the heels of 1953's probation year. Kentucky lost a shot at another national championship in 1954 when it voluntarily bypassed postseason play when seniors Ramsey, Hagan, and Lou Tsioropoulos (who had all been given an extra season of eligibility because of the 1953 suspension) were rulled ineligible for March tournament competitions.

Ramsey (first overall pick) and Hagan (third selection) were both plucked by Auerbach in a surprise move during the 1953 NBA draft, though it was already apparent that both would enjoy another year of NCAA eligibility. It was only the first of several ingenious lottery moves that would eventually mark Auerbach's resume and also the one that is today least remembered in the wake of his later fortuitous selections of Russell and Bird and his draft-day-connected trades for McHale and Parish. While Hagan was traded for the rights to Russell before he ever put on a Boston uniform, Ramsey launched a Hall-of-Fame career with Cousy and company that was interrupted briefly for a one-year military stint after his rookie campaign, but then extended for eight more seasons that were all championship campaigns except one. While he only once failed to score in double figures (in his final season of 1964), he excelled off the bench as a sparkplug at the forward slot, where despite his limited height (6-3) he was consistently able to outrun and outthink all of his bulkier and more offense-minded opponents.

Ramsey's career pinnacle came early in his pro tenure (during his second season) when his closing-seconds off-balance 20-footer helped clinch a game-seven double-overtime victory against Hagan's St. Louis Hawks and hand Auerbach and Boston their inaugural long-sought-after NBA title. It was Ramsey's biggest single shot and one which played a huge role (along with Jim Loscutoff's two vital free-throws which iced the game) in launching what was about to blossom into the basketball's longest-lasting championship tenure.

Celtics
Bill Russell
(1956-69)

More than any other imposing figure among basketball's true superstars, Bill Russell has always had his numerous doubters and detractors, naysayers and negators. Perhaps it goes with the territory for a franchise player whose game was effective defense and not crowd-pleasing offense. In sum: Jordan was the most entertaining player ever while Russell was simple the best by any measure that involves either winning or controlling ballgames rather than displaying individual flash. Larry Bird likely struck the most perfect balance between unparalleled entertainment (Jordan) and total domination (Russell).

As both a high school and college recruit Russell was

hardly outstanding and struggled to make the varsity squad; he was cut from tryouts for his junior high school team in Oakland and barely made the junior varsity while a high school sophomore. Once he began to dominate opponents at the University of San Francisco he was nonetheless still viewed as one-dimensional and thus a huge gamble as pro prospect. And after establishing his hold over the NBA as the driving engine of Auerbach's Boston dynasty, Russell was nonetheless never an extremely popular icon either among Boston fans or league fans as a whole.

A mixed reaction to Bill Russell is all the more surprising when set against the backdrop of his simply unrivalled impact upon the sport of basketball. On the occasion of the NBA's 35-year anniversary in 1980 it was Russell and not Chamberlain, Mikan or Oscar Robertson whom members of the Professional Basketball Writers Association tabbed by a wide margin as "the greatest player in the history of the NBA." Russell was among that truly rare handful of athletes—Babe Ruth comes immediately to mind in baseball—who dominate their sport so thoroughly that they actually change the way the game is played and perceived by future generations. Russell's dominance was of course of a far different order from Wilt's or Oscar's or Air Jordan's. Russell set few individual records (none for offense) and spent remarkably little time holding onto the basketball. Yet in thirteen NBA seasons his Boston team won the league championship on eleven occasions (it would have been twelve of thirteen if an ankle injury hadn't sidelined Russell for the final three games of the 1958 postseason); his USF college team was two for three in winning NCAA tourna-

---

Bill Russell Career Profile

College Team: University of San Francisco
College and Amateur Achievements:
UPI National Player of the Year (1956)
Unanimous First-Team All-American (1956)
Concensus First-Team All-American (1955)
NCAA Final Four Most Outstanding Player (1955)
Member of 1956 USA Olympic Team
NBA Team: Boston Celtics
NBA Points: 14,522 (15.1 ppg)
NBA Games: 963 (1956-1969, 13 seasons)
NBA Assists: 4,100 (4.3 apg)
NBA Rebounds: 21,620 (22.5 rpg)
NBA Field Goals (Pct): 5,687 (.440)
NBA Free Throws (Pct): 3,148 (.561)
NBA MVP (1958, 1961, 1962, 1963, 1965)
NBA All-Star Game MVP (1963)
NBA Silver Anniversary Team (1971)
NBA 35th Anniversary All-Time Team (1980)
Eleven NBA Championships (1957, 1959, 1960, 1961, 1962, 1963, 1964, 1965, 1966, 1968, 1969)
Naismith Memorial Basketball Hall of Fame (1974)

Bill Russell was not only the first-ever black coach of a major US pro sports franchise, but he was also the only NBA star ever who could thoroughly dominate games without having to score a single point.

seven-year NBA winning streak in 1965, for example, even though Wilt outplayed Russell in game seven of the Eastern Division Finals and Russell's errant inbounds heave in the closing seconds handed Philadelphia a rare chance to capture the series and scuttle the streak; Boston and Russell were miraculously saved on this occasion by Havlicek's memorable last-second pilfering of Hal Greer's own misguided inbounds toss.

It was also Russell's personality which forever got in the way of unconditional acceptance. Bill Russell was from the start a proud and private man, and that pride—both in his oncourt play and in his oppressed black race—was also key to his championship successes while at the same time fuel to his unpopular image. Boston's most dominating cage star was also the first black superstar in professional basketball, and he occupied this role during a decade when racial segregation was still the law of the land

ment championships and won 55 straight between the outset of his junior season and the close of his career. He was also one-for-one in Olympic gold medal triumphs. It was not at all surprising that while Wilt Chamberlain captured seven straight individual scoring titles in the '60s and obliterated nearly every NBA offensive record along the way it was Russell whom sportswrters picked as "Player of the Decade" by nearly a three-to-one landslide margin.

Yet if Russell was a nonpareil he was never an unconditionally beloved icon, even among hometown boosters. Part of the problem of course is that while dominating defense wins games and even wins championships it hardly ever wins over a majority of the fans. Russell's style could inspire admiration and even awe, but it did not attract legions of worshippers and imitators. As a college and pro star Russell never dominated when it came to numbers: even in college where he carried more of the offensive burden he nonetheless barely averaged 20 a game (though he does remain one of only seven in history to average 20 points and 20 rebounds for a full career); his lofty totals for NBA rebounds still fell short of numbers posted in the same seasons by Chamberlain; a search of the NBA career top-ten lists reveals his name only in the total rebounds (second) and minutes played (eighth) categories. The areas in which he did prove matchless—blocked shots and defensive rebounds—were not even acknowledged in the stats columns of his era. And when he went head-to-head with Chamberlain he would usually lose the individual battle yet gain the war of team victory. The Celtics maintained their

Bill Russell supporters point to only one set of numbers in arguments about the greatest NBA hero of all time—Russell owned 11 NBA titles in his mere 13 seasons in the league.

in nearly a quarter of the nation, as well as an unspoken custom in other areas, including Boston itself. More importantly, like Jackie Robinson in Brooklyn, Russell was always outspoken and thus controversial, unwilling to repress or conceal his rage about racial injustice. In Boston of the '60s Russell was thus destined to be a figure who personified unpopular and distasteful racial rebellion, despite all his athletic heroism. Boston's greatest star on the city's greatest-ever team (even the NBA's greatest-ever team) was thus also a painfully controversial figure who robbed that very team of far greater audiences than the surprisingly slim ones it enjoyed. The Celtics with Russell owned the entire NBA in their heyday, but they were only a backstage act in Boston—poor cousins to the ever-popular Red Sox and NHL Bruins with whom they shared the spotlight.

The same mixed review also clouded stage two of Bill Russell's basketball life, the one that came after his playing days had ceased at the end of the sixties. As a coach in Boston he accomplished what perhaps no other figure could possibly have accomplished. He successfully replaced the legend that was Red Auerbach and stretched out Boston's winning grip on the NBA through the end of the decade. (Cynics contended at the time that Russell was Auerbach's only possible choice as coaching replacement simply because Bill Russell the coach was the only man who could possibly control and motivate Bill Russell the player.) Yet when he took his act to Seattle a few seasons later he was to be victim of his own growing disrespect for modern-age players and the modern-era game. As coach and general manager with Seattle from 1974 through 1977 Russell posted losing records in both regular-season (162-166) and postseason (6-9) action before wearing out his welcome with players, management and fans alike. Returning to a similar role with the Sacramento Kings a decade later Russell again bombed on the bench and was relieved early in his second campaign with the Kings owning the league's fourth worst record at the time. Whatever magic Russell exerted in Boston Garden throughout the sixties was clearly not still part of his act out on the west coast in either the

late seventies or late eighties.

Russell had one more public role to play and that was behind the microphone. As a pro basketball television analyst—first with ABC Sports "NBA Game of the Week" and later with NBA broadcasts on Ted Turner's WTBS cable network—he would prove to be one of the most honest and insightful color commentators the business has ever known. But the broadcast career was shortlived as the private Russell withdrew even further from the public limelight. Over the past decade he has remained largely detached from his own towering legend, making few appearances at NBA functions and shunning fans in the process. Russell has never signed autographs, for one thing, viewing the popular practice cynically as a bothersome symbol of the American sportsfan's misplaced values. Given this history of unpopularity and standoffishness with fans, both during his playing days and after, and the somewhat one-dimensional nature of his on-court presence, it is truly remarkable that Bill Russell's star still looms today as large as it does in the basketball firmament. But then, eight straight NBA championship—all attributed in lion's share to Russell's presence on the court—is a monument beside which even the individual achievements of Jordan, Oscar, Baylor, Chamberlain and all the game's greatest offensive stars seem somewhat palid. Add on 55 straight college victories and the first-ever undefeated NCAA championship team with the University of San Francisco and Bill Russell remains a monument as large as any in the game's century-long history.

All Michael Jordan had left to be accomplish at career's end was the winning of six more NBA crowns without interruption and he would have finally stood in the same league with Bill Russell. Except, of course, for the reasonable argument that Russell played during an era when winning league titles was a far more challenging accomplishment. One has to remember that year after year Russell and his Boston teammates had to climb the postseason hurdle of Warriors and Sixers teams built around Chamberlain and Lakers outfits anchored by West and Baylor—rival

Red Auerbach—in what soon became a most familiar scene—celebrates yet another NBA championship victory with his star center and franchise player, Bill Russell. This time it was Auerbach's ninth and final league title in 1966.

teams that boasted rosters that looked something like modern-era NBA All-Star squads. In the 1960s there were no NBA lineups fleshed out with a string of CBA refugees, or with collegiate hardship cases (sometimes even fresh high school grads) still learning how to play the game. And there is also the issue of individual statistics to be debated: if Russell seems to be overwhelmed by Jordan in the area of career numbers, there are numerous extenuating circumstances demanding full consideration.

When Bill Russell played in the NBA blocked shots were neither counted as an "official statistic" nor kept anywhere in the record books. This is about the same as not counting home runs when Babe Ruth played or not tracking batting averages for Ted Williams, Stan Musial and Tony Gwynn. Or perhaps ignoring steals as an official category in the deadball age of Ty Cobb or the astroturf era of Rickey Henderson. But while there are no official numbers on Bill Russell's blocked shots there are indeed plenty of eye-witness accounts from fans, writers and opposing players themselves. And all agree that Russell used the blocked shot to totally dominate games and even to revamp the sport as no one had ever revamped it before him. Cincinnati star Jack Twyman spoke for a decade-worth of Russell opponents: "Russell was the greatest impact player in any sport. He couldn't throw the ball in the ocean, but he allowed his teammates to press and gamble. You knew that if you got by Cousy or Heinsohn, that SOB Russell was back there waiting to block your shot. No one ever dominated a sport the way Russell did with the Celtics."

Of course it was something of a pure distortion to suggest that Russell couldn't even heave the ball into the ocean. Cousy set the record straight on that matter: "If we needed him to, Russ could have averaged 20 points for us. For God's sake he got 15 a game and we only had one play for him to shoot the ball. When we were clicking, he'd get a half dozen slams a game on lob passes off the fast break. Even though he didn't have a shooting touch, he arranged his game so he never had to take a bad shot."

Perhaps much of the credit for creating Bill Russell as a superstar can be laid squarely at the doorstep of Red Auerbach. It is likely that no other coach would have made the gangly shot-blocker a top draft pick, traded away his star player (Ed Macauley) and top newcomer (Cliff Hagan) to obtain such a one-dimensional prospect, and then built a complete team around his shot-blocking style. More likely, other NBA coaches inheriting big Bill's physical talents would have labored to turn him into an effective scorer and in the process would have lost most of his unique contribution to the game. Red Auerbach saw from the beginning that here was a special and rare player who didn't have to score points to be remarkably effective at both ends of the floor.

Nor was his defensive prowess the run-of-the-mill sort of stuff. Russell didn't block shots simply to intimidate an opponent or to make personal statements based on ego-battles like today's trash-talking rim defenders. His game was controlled and oriented entirely to fit into Auerbach's scheme for fashioning an invincible champion. Russell used his defense to launch the Boston constant-motion offense. He would defend the goal in order to open up the inevitable fast-break that would be ignited after each shot. Russell would never knock an opponent's missile into the third row of courtside seats; instead he would guide the ball (either a shot he blocked or a rebound he had corralled) to a fast-breaking guard (usually Cousy) who would propel it ahead to a streaking Heinsohn or Frank Ramsey or Bill Sharman for an instant score. Russell was thus the ultimate defensive weapon. And as such he dominated games, sometimes entire seasons, even a whole decade, without having to score a single basket along the way.

There were other unique facets of Bill Russell the basketball player. He was quietly efficient on the floor yet burned with a competitive fire perhaps never matched in any other player—certainly not another post-position player of his size and his awesome talent. Here was the ultimate advantage that Russell always owned over Wilt and any of his other rivals in the trenches. And Russell was also one of the smartest men ever to play the game—a meticulous student of defensive positioning and of shooting and rebounding angles, ball movements, and other nearly invisible elements of the game.

He was also his own man and thus not always popular with a working press or with Boston fans. He shunned signing autographs (maintaining a strong distaste for hero worship), spoke out angrily on civil rights and racial intolerance, openly criticized the city of Boston for its treatment of black athletes, bypassed his own induction ceremony at the Naismith Memorial Hall of Fame, and attended the retirement ceremony for his number "6" at the Boston Garden only on the condition that it be held before the arena gates were opened to the public. Grace and composure on the playing court were an effective mask for inner turmoil and seething hidden anger; Russell usually vomited in the locker room before any important game, a surefire signal to his teammates that Big Bill was more than ready for the heat of battle.

The true legacy of Bill Russell, of course, is not uncovered by perusing his statistical line in the *Basketball Encyclopedia*. But it is found in the record books nonetheless—over on the page devoted to yearly NBA championship results. No other player in hoopdom's history owns 11 world titles and none likely ever will; no one else (outside of teammates like Heinsohn and the Jones Boys who were carried on his coattails) even comes close. Teammate Cousy was around for the raising of six of those banners; Tom Heinsohn survived long enough to share eight of those rings. Neither one might have ever tasted the victory champaign even a single time without Russell as a teammate.

Auerbach's Celtics (while the Redhead was first coach and then later GM) won 11 titles in but 13 seasons in what still stands unchallenged as the greatest winning legacy in all of American professional sports. And they didn't win a single one of those titles without their big man at the post—Bill Russell. In fact, it seems quite evident that they won every one of those titles only because they had Bill Russell hovering around the basket, providing the most relentless intimidating force basketball has ever known.

Tom "Satch" Sanders
(1960-73)

NYU All-American Tom Sanders was seemingly the designated "quiet man" of the dynasty Red Auerbach Boston Celtics. He was also the top defensive forward of his era and thus another player perfectly cut to fit the mold of the ideal (that is, totally selfless) Red Auerbach athlete. On top of his easily perceivable willingness to sacrifice personal heroics for team values, "Satch" was also one of the most underrated contributors to the regular Boston championships that stretched from one end of the sixties to the other. He had a well-defined role—that of clamping the lid on the opposition's star frontcourt scorers—from which he rarely ever strayed and at which he rarely ever failed. His own offensive numbers were always minimal—consistently scoring close to ten a game and religiously corralling a half dozen rebounds nightly.

On a series of Boston teams noted for their defensive prowess, it was Sanders who was the most effective all-around defender, even while the headlines in that department always went to Russell and K.C. Jones. Russell was the more dramatic, with his well-timed blocks and bushels of board-cleansing rebounds, and K. C. the more relentless, with his ceaseless shadowing of opposing playmakers; Satch was always ruthlessly efficient as he quietly hounded the top

Tom Sanders ably assisted Russell on the boards and always drew the assignment of guarding the opponent's toughest frontcourt threat.

opposing marksman. Sanders' "dirty work" usually involved attempting to shut down the scoring floodtide from the likes of Elgin Baylor, Bob Pettit, Dolph Schayes or Rick Barry, and it was a task he was usually up for as well as anyone else on the circuit. It was not a labor that went very often unrewarded either, since in the end Sanders owned more NBA championship rings than any man save Russell and Sam Jones—a total of eight (which tied him with Heinsohn and K. C. Jones). And there were a few other personal tropies as well, including a well-earned spot on the NBA All-Defensive squad (second team) in the very year (1968-69) that award category was introduced.

After his playing days Satch also blazed new trails as the first African-American coach at an Ivy League institution, in this case Harvard University. His coaching success was muted both in collegiate circles and back in Boston, where a brief stint as Heinsohn's mid-season replacement left him with the third worst winning percentage (.371) among all Boston mentors (edging out only Doggie Julian and recent bust M. L. Carr). "Satch" Sanders also has another special if not trivial distinction to boast of: he likely is the only NBA star who picked up his colorful nickname from a Negro leagues baseball legend. As a youth Sanders had first loved baseball above all sports, and his physical characteristics by teen years reminded his friends of the legendary Satchel Paige. Sanders' own favorite player was never the immortal

"Satch" Sanders Career Profile

College Team: New York University
NBA Team: Boston Celtics
NBA Points: 8,766 (9.6 ppg)
NBA Games: 916 (1960-1973, 13 seasons)
NBA Assists: 1,026 (1.1 apg)
NBA Rebounds: 5,798 (6.3 rpg)
NBA Field Goals (Pct): 3,416 (.428)
NBA Free Throws (Pct): 1,934 (.767)
Eight NBA Championships
(1961, 1962, 1963, 1964, 1965, 1966, 1968, 1969)

Paige but instead the equally immortal Jackie Robinson. It was clearly a more fitting choice of hero and certainly one more intimately connected down the road with his own eventual post-playing-days role—that of a pioneering black head coach in what was still largely a white man's coaching world.

Celtics
Bill Sharman
(1951-61)

Bill Sharman was unquestionably one of basketball's greatest pure shooters of all-time. He was also one of the most adept athletes at making foul shots (he led the NBA seven times in this category, five times consecutively), one of the game's most relentless winners (four NBA championships as a player and three pro titles as a head coach),

basketball's most fanatic proponent of relentless physical conditioning, and also one the sport's cleverest and most fate-charmed bench coaches.

As a player Sharman rained his deadly jumpers first at Southern California (twice Pacific Coast Conference MVP) and then in the Boston Garden during the earliest seasons of Red Auerbach's fledgling Boston Celtics dynasty. He teamed with the Hardwood Houdini, Bob Cousy, as half of the finest NBA backcourt of the league's first decade. It is even arguable that basketball at any level has never displayed a better combo of adept playmaker and unerring shotmaker. Sharman's free throw shooting numbers during those Boston years were nothing short of spectacular (never dipping below 84% for a season and thrice soaring above 90%), especially when considering the conditions which prevailed in early NBA seasons. Balls were not always perfectly round, playing floors were often wharped and rarely allowed for true bounces, and arena temperatures in Rochester, Syracuse, Fort Wayne and elsewhere were often in the low forties (since windows were left open to filter smoke-filled gymnasiums) and shooters' hands often nearly turned blue as a result of the drafty indoor environment.

Throughout his playing days Bill Sharman maintained a physical conditioning regime that crossed the boundries of the obsessive. The eight-time league all-star ran opponents into the ground as Havlicek would do a decade later, exhausting defenders and thus freeing himself for open jumpers that regularly (by the day's standards) found their mark. When it came to coaching, Sharman also had a knack for being in the right place at the right time. He first enjoyed a championship team in the ABL (with Cleveland in 1962) and later another in the ABA (with Utah in 1971). His best stroke of fortune, however, involved taking over the 1972 Los Angeles Lakers team which featured Wilt Chamberlain, Gail Goodrich, and Jerry West and won a still-record 33 straight games. That same Sharman-coached outfit (with a starting lineup of Wilt, Goodrich, West, Jim McMillian and Happy Hairston) collected a league mark for victories (69) which stood until Jordan's Bulls won 72 of 82 a quarter-century later. Sharman thus stands as the only coach to win titles in three pro leagues (NBA, ABA, ABL) during the second half of the century—the half which contains the bulk of the sport's history.

And this knack for timely positioning also

Tom "Satch" Sanders was a defensive workhouse similar to the likes of Russell and Jones, who contributed mightily to eight championship banners.

Bill Sharman Career Profile

College Team: University of Southern California
College and Amateur Achievements:
Concensus First-Team All-American (1950)
NBA Teams: Washington Capitols, Boston Celtics
NBA Points: 12,665 (17.8 ppg)
NBA Games: 711 (1950-1961, 11 seasons)
NBA Assists: 2,101 (3.0 apg)
NBA Rebounds: 2,779 (3.9 rpg)
NBA Field Goals (Pct): 4,761 (.426)
NBA Free Throws (Pct): 3,143 (.883)
NBA All-Star Game MVP (1955)
NBA Silver Anniversary All-Time Team (1971)
Four NBA Championships (1957, 1959, 1960, 1961)
Naismith Memorial Basketball Hall of Fame (1975)

A top baseball prospect in the Brooklyn Dodgers chain, Sharman never played a big league game but did sit in uniform on the Brooklyn bench on the fateful day of Bobby Thomson's pennant-winning 1951 homer.

showed up on the baseball diamond where Bill Sharman also starred as a promising late-1940s outfield prospect with the Brooklyn Dodgers organization. Called to the big leagues for the final month of the 1951 season (his last month in pro baseball), the future basketball Hall-of-Famer would be in uniform on the Brooklyn bench when Bobby Thomson cracked the most famous homer in baseball

history to win a renowned pennant playoff for the Giants at New York's Polo Grounds. Weeks earlier the same Bill Sharman—who would never appear in a big league game—was tossed from the Dodgers bench for umpire baiting, thus making him the answer to one of the most famous among baseball trivia questions. Bill Sharman is perhaps the only ballplayer ever ejected by umpires from a major league game while at the same time never having "officially" appeared in a big league boxscore.

B O S T O N

Jo Jo White
(1969-79)

Revival of the Boston Celtics NBA dynasty in the mid-seventies headlined three franchise immortals—Dave Cowens, John Havlicek and Jo Jo White—who together share almost equal billing with Cousy, Russell, Sam Jones, Larry Bird and Kevin McHale in the expansive pantheon of all-time Celtics greats. This is the second tier of Boston immortals, to be sure. But what a matchless tier it nonetheless is, after all is said and done. Cowens was the next great Boston center after Russell and handled that near-impossible task with enough unorthodox flair to become one of the all-time Boston Garden fan favorites. Havlicek was the club's all-time scorer before he was done and the only

If Cousy was the slickest ballhandler of the NBA's first decade, Bill Sharman was the circuit's deadliest shooter, both from long range and from the charity free throw stripe.

Celtics great to span both the Auerbach and Heinsohn coaching eras. And White, for his part, was one of the best-kept secrets of an NBA era featuring flashier playmakers like Pete Maravich, Walt Frazier and Earl Monroe, a trio who thrilled more crowds and grabbed more headlines but were never any more proficient than Boston's point guard of the same epoch at guiding good solid teams to top-flight championship performances.

Like other indelible Boston legends from the four decades stretching between Red Auerbach and Rick Pitino, White was rarely found atop any of the NBA indivdual

White evolved into his role as a top Boston backcourt leader, eventually becoming both a reliable playmaker and a ruthlessly efficient scorer, a most versatile player capable of complementing both a defensive wizard like Don Chaney and a relentless scorer like Charlie Scott.

Jo Jo White was never one of the NBA's flashier playmakers, but he nonetheless extended the Boston backcourt tradition of stellar shooters started by Bob Cousy and Bill Sharman and continued by Sam Jones.

Jo Jo White Career Profile

College Team: University of Kansas
College and Amateur Achievements:
Concensus Second-Team All-American (1968, 1969)
Member of 1968 USA Olympic Team
NBA Teams: Boston Celtics, Golden State Warriors, Kansas City Kings
NBA Points: 14,399 (17.2 ppg)
NBA Games: 837 (1969-1981, 12 seasons)
NBA Assists: 4,095 (4.9 apg)
NBA Rebounds: 3,345 (4.0 rpg)
NBA Field Goals (Pct.): 6,169 (.444)
NBA Free Throws (Pct): 2,060 (.834)
NBA Finals MVP (1976)
Two NBA Championships (1974, 1976)

statistical categories. But he was nonetheless a regular fixture on league All-Star teams (seven selections in all, and all with Boston) and also a frequent visitor to postseason NBA winners' circles (two NBA championships and five divisional titles). Among the myriad Boston heroes, White was (like Satch Sanders) a ubiquitous "quiet man" who tended always to fade from the limelight and perform his on-court deeds of scoring and ballhandling magic some-what in the shadows; not only was the former Kansas All-American doomed to play second fiddle to flashier NBA backcourt stars of the era like Monroe, Frazier, Austin Carr and Maravich, but he was also overlooked in his own backyard due to more attention-grabbing Boston team-mates like the frenetic Cowens and the tireless Havlicek.

Nonetheless the University of Kansas All-American was a major contributor to two NBA championships in the mid-seventies (1974, 1976) as both a reliable playmaker and a dependable scorer, and he was also the NBA Finals MVP on the second of those winning ballclubs. A mark of his versatility and adaptability was that he teamed with defensive backcourt whiz Don Chaney on one of those title outfits (thus assuming the shooter's assignment for himself) and then lined up with crack shooter Charlie Scott on the other (necessitating his switch to the playmaking role). Continuing a tradition of noteworthy Boston shooting guards that had debuted with Sharman and was extended with Sam Jones, White combined the gunner's role with much more extensive playmaking duties. He still averaged above 18 ppg. in all but his first and last of nine Boston campaigns, and he led both championship teams in steals and assists while simultaneously also ranking among the team leaders in scoring. There were more colorful and charismatic Boston cage heroes down through the years, but rarely if ever was there a more efficient backcourt assassin than Jo Jo White.

BOSTON *Celtics*

B OSTON *Celtics*

CHAPTER IV

Sixth Men, Role Players and Memorable Auerbach Steals:

Profiles of 50 Memorable Boston Celtics

I t is perhaps the most remarkable fact of Boston Celtics history that in more than a half-century of NBA domination no Boston player has ever reigned as an NBA individual scoring champion. No basketball team in pro or college history has ever paid such careful attention to "role players" as have the five decades worth of teams coached or administered by Red Auerbach and his many able assistants. The very concept of "the sixth man"—now an NBA staple—was originally an Auerbach/Celtics invention and the greatest prototypes from Frank Ramsey to John "Hondo" Havlicek down to Kevin McHale all wore Boston uniforms. If there is indeed magic in the green and white Boston Celtics jersey the potency of that magic has been most consistently demonstrated by the honor roll of sagging veterans, overlooked draft picks and underappreciated journeymen who over the years have been transformed from hapless has-beens to hefty hometown heroes simply by signing on with Auerbach's forces.

Danny Ainge
(1981-89)

The baby-faced Ainge sported a youthful expression of innocence that worked to belie his fiery competitve spirit and near-violent intensity as one of the sport's most com-bative warriors. And the versatile athlete who was also talented enough to play major league baseball for three seasons with the Toronto Blue Jays displayed throughout his tenure a savvy knowledge of the game that also earmarked him for potential coaching successes at the end of his whirlwind playing career. Over the past three seasons on the bench with the Phoenix Suns Ainge has built that team into a solid year-end title contender and proved that his surprise

Across eight seasons of the Larry Bird epoch Danny Ainge proved one of the most fiesty competitors in Boston basketball annals.

hiring in November 1996 to replace Cotton Fitzsimmons was a major coup for owner Jerry Colangelo. As a 14-year NBA player in four cities Ainge was universally disliked by opposing ballplayers and fans; trading a uniform for a suit and tie in Phoenix he has emerged as a coach universally liked and respected by his own players (as he clearly always was by his playing-days teammates).

Ainge played baseball for three years with the big league Toronto Blue Jays while still starring on the hardwood as an All-American at BYU, where he averaged above 20 across four seasons and was the Wooden Award winner for 1981. But a not rare inability to hit consistently in the baseball big-time (Ainge sported a .220 career BA in 220 games) soon caused a reassessment of his professional career goals. Struggles on the diamond were weighed against quite excellent odds for successes on the hardwood court, where Red Auerbach's Celtics had demonstrated their faith in the four-year 20-ppg. scorer with a 31st overall draft selection.

Joining the Boston Celtics in time for the 1981-82 season (Larry Bird's third year) proved quickly to be a solid career-advancing decision. Overnight a baseball bust (relatively speaking) transformed into a basketball bright spot as Ainge became a valued role player and provided solid backcourt bench strength. With the strong Boston teams of the mid-'80s Ainge became a key element in the always-balanced Celtics team mix and rode behind Bird's leadership to a pair of NBA titles (1984, 1986). And a half-dozen post-Boston NBA years hardly spelled obscurity either. There was modest success in Portland (on teams that reached the Conference Finals in 1991 and the NBA Finals versus the Bulls in '92) followed by a late-career peak in Phoenix (where Ainge again played in the championship round versus Chicago in 1993). As a coach with the Phoenix Suns in the late 1990s Ainge was a most pleasant surprise right from the start by directing colorful, well-drilled and contending teams in each of his first three winters on the bench.

Kenny Anderson
(1998-99)

Rick Pitino's first earthshaking move as a general manager in Boston was the attention-getting six-player transaction with Toronto in February 1998 which shipped away promising rookie Chauncey Billups and brought on board always-promising but still unfulfilled point-guard ace Kenny Anderson. Anderson brought considerable baggage to Boston including a reputation for underachievement, a pair of much-traveled recent seasons split between New Jersey, Charlotte, Portland and Toronto (where he had been traded in exchange for Damon Stoudamire), and a penchant for nagging injuries which have allowed him to log

Despite a checkered start to his promising NBA career in New Jersey, Charlotte, Portland and Toronto, Kenny Anderson still holds the immediate key to an anticipated Celtics backcourt revival.

only two full seasons during a seven-year pro career. But a revived and healthy Anderson as complement to youthful Ron Mercer in the Boston backcourt could provide the revival that will vault Pitino into the genius status of his predecessors Red Auerbach and Jan Volk.

Anderson is one of the showcase examples of that new breed of athlete who shines brilliantly on the college court for only a season or two before cashing in his immense talents for an early NBA paycheck. And like the majority of the new breed, Kenny Anderson's NBA career has never managed to reach anticipated heights or even imitate the heady achievements of shortlived college days. The lefty-shooting point guard peaked early as a freshman member of the 1990 Georgia Tech "Lethal Weapons III" offense, when he was perhaps the finest of a long line of Yellow Jacket backcourt aces (a list which includes Mark Price in the '80s, Rick Yunkus in the '70s, and Roger Kaiser in the '60s). The triple-threat offense of Dennis Scott (27.7), Brian Oliver (21.3) and national freshman-of-the-year Anderson (20.6) rewrote record books as the first trio of teammates ever to all average above 20 in a full year's ACC league play. That winter Anderson also became the school's sixth top ACC rookie in only eight winters. And the playground legend from New York City's Archbishop Malloy High School also paced the ACC in assists, for all his own scoring efforts. A season later the 6-1 speedster upped his scoring output to 25.9, repeated second-team honors on *The Sporting News*

All-American squad, and carried the Yellow Jackets on his back almost singlehandedly after Scott and Oliver departed for the NBA.

But as a highly touted pro (2nd overall NBA pick after his sophomore season) Anderson has remained little more than a high-price journeyman, putting in stints with New Jersey, Charlotte, Portland, and finally Boston and never matching the offensive production which made him a phenomenal 23 ppg. career scorer in the nation's best collegiate circuit. A contract holdout and feud with New Jersey coach Bill Fitch largely scuttled his promising rookie season; bouncing back under coach Chuck Daly as a second-year mainstay with the Nets he was again waylaid with a season-shortening injury when flagrantly fouled by New York's John Starks. Anderson's best year was his third when he played a full schedule, scored almost 19 per game, and dished out nearly ten assists nightly. Over recent seasons, however, his apparent weaknesses (playing out of control, a scrawny build, and inconsistent perimeter shooting) have always overshadowed his many strengths (classic point guard makeup with an eye toward scoring; excellent ballhandling, passing and penetrating skills). Anderson was only a half-dozen seasons back perhaps the most naturally gifted young point guard in the pro game; by the start of his seventh NBA campaign he was already one of basketball's most overpaid normal achievers.

Nate "Tiny" Archibald
(1978-83)

Nate Archibald was hardly a one-season wonder, yet his single peak campaign of 1973 so far outstripped the rest of his 13-season pro sojourn and so heavily contributed to his Hall-of-Fame status as to almost make it seem that way. In just his third NBA season and his first with the Kansas City Kings (after the Cincinnati Royals relocated to the midwest), the 6-1 backcourt flash would become the first and only performer to pace the pro circuit in both points (34.0 ppg) and assists (11.4 apg) in the same season. Archibald's incredible offensive performance that season was not enough to earn him league MVP honors, with the nod going to Boston's versatile center Dave Cowens. It was enough, however, to earn a place in the record books and also lasting immortality for the rail-thin guard who was durable enough to also play a league-leading 46 minutes during his remarkable career campaign. Archibald would post scoring averages above 20 in four other campaigns and also serve as an important bench player for Boston in the early Larry Bird years at the outset of the 1980s, yet never again would he control the entire league as he had from end-to-end of one incomparable dream season in Kansas City.

Tiny Archibald once posted perhaps the most remarkable all-around offensive season in NBA history, then later played an important bench role for the Bill Fitch-coached Celtics.

Jim Ard
(1974-78)

Except for one clutch performance in the memorable 1976 NBA Finals which featured Boston's triple-overtime dogfight with the Phoenix Suns, 6-9 forward Jim Ard would have boasted only a highly forgettable journeyman's

Jim Ard might have remained a forgotten NBA journeyman except for his one shining postseason moment during one of playoff basketball's most truly unforgettable games.

career which spanned four ABA seasons in New York and four NBA campaigns in Boston and briefly Chicago. Acquired as a free agent in October 1974, the University of Cincinnati veteran proved a strong rebounder and valuable bench role player but only occasional scorer on three powerful Heinsohn-coached teams that reached two conference finals and one NBA title series. It was during the title round verus Phoenix in 1976, however, that Ard joined forces with Kevin Stacom and Glenn McDonald to provide some heroic reinforcement work that contributed mightily to NBA championship number thirteen. It was Ard, filling in on an emergency basis for Cowens and McDonald subbing for Paul Silas that together eventually turned the tide in the final five exhausting minutes of one of the most famous games in NBA history. Ard controlled a vital tip in the third overtime session of memorable game five and canned two clutch free throws that also weighed in heavily as the Celtics desperately hung on by the slimmest of margins in a game that may well have been Boston's most miraculous postseason triumph of them all.

BOSTON
Don Barksdale
(1953-55)

Chuck Cooper of the Boston Celtics may have received too much credit as a pioneer of basketball's integration. Don Barksdale, also a Boston Celtic, has never received quite enough. It has recently been clarified in the better histories of early NBA play that Cooper may have made headlines as the NBA's first draft selection from his race, but he did not earn a unique niche as the league's first-ever black man to step upon the court (Earl Lloyd was there first, and Dolly King pioneered even earlier in one of the two NBA forerunner leagues, the NBL). What has remained buried in the backpages of history is the list of pioneering achievements accomplished by UCLA's earliest basketball All-American, Don Barksdale. The 6-6 collegiate center and pro forward would cross the racial barriers of his sport first on several different occasions. In 1947 (ironically the same year that ex-UCLA basketballer Jackie Robinson integrated major league baseball) he became the first African-American named to an NCAA consensus All-American squad. His appearance on the 1948 Olympic Basketball roster alongside Bob Kurland of Oklahoma A&M and the "Fabulous Five" contingent from Kentucky earned him distinction as the first black US Olympic basketballer. And Barksdale was also the first black in an NBA All-Star Game when he suited up for the third classic played in 1953 at Fort Wayne. The sum total of Don Barksdale's pro career was two seasons with Baltimore and two more in the uniform of the pre-Bill Russell Boston

Two of pro basketball's long-forgotten racial pioneers—Don Barksdale of the Boston Celtics and Nat "Sweetwater" Clifton of the New York Knicks—battle for a 1954 rebound in Madison Square Garden.

Celtics. He scored less than 3,000 points, but he left a ground-breaking legacy that deserves far more recognition and credit than its has so far ever spawned.

Celtics
Quinn Buckner
(1982-85)

Only a handful of players have ever matched Buckner's feat of collecting championships on all three major levels of competition—Olympic Games, NCAA Tournament and NBA Finals. Only a couple dozen NBA veterans have topped his career steals total of 1337. But Quinn Buckner's reputation—built most solidly on his six seasons in Milwaukee—was largely based on tenacious ballhawking, skillful ballhandling, and four selections to the NBA all-defensive team. The former Indiana All-American and a starter on the last undefeated NCAA championship squad, Buckner arrived in Boston just in time to pick up a single NBA championship ring as a key backcourt sub on the 1984 Celtics edition, the first outfit coached by K. C. Jones. It was that season that Buckner teamed with Danny Ainge, M. L. Carr and Carlos Clark to provide plenty of second-line relief for starting guards Dennis Johnson and

Guard Quinn Buckner had a special talent for stealing basketballs, as well as a remarkable penchant for collecting championship rings.

If M.L. Carr was not always popular with Hub fans during his brief coaching tenure, he was always a crowd-pleaser during his half-dozen seasons as a Boston role player.

Gerald Henderson. At the time of his retirement to the broadcast booth in 1986 Buckner had climbed to sixth on the all-time career steals list. But the fleeting distinction hardly meant as much as the one piece of championship jewerly garnered during a second late-career season wearing the proud green jersey of the legendary Boston Celtics.

M.L. Carr
(1979-85)

Among great Boston sixth men the name of M. L. Carr is rarely if ever raised. Part of the reason is that Carr's long Boston sojourn on both ends of the bench (as player for six seasons and coach for two) has other far more memorable highlights and lowlights. And part of the reason is also that Carr never distinguished the position with quite the same flair as Ramsey, Havlicek, Silas or McHale. Yet for five

seasons of the early eighties—before career-shortening injuries set in—Carr nonetheless made some very significant contributions in the highly specialized sixth-man role. His aggressive defense caused problems around the league, and he even contributed double-figure scoring during Bird's rookie season. Carr's greatest asset, however, was his role as clubhouse emotional leader for teams coached by Bill Fitch and K. C. Jones. And he was also a special fan favorite in Boston Garden where he often served as a bench-riding cheerleader whose sideline waving of a victory towel during Boston rallies could always be counted on to whip the partisans into near frenzy.

Don Chaney
(1968-75, 1977-80)

If Frank Ramsey was the consummate role player on the dynasty-era Boston ballclubs of the sixties, Don Chaney claimed that role for the rebuilding-era Heinsohn-coached teams of the early seventies. "Duck" Chaney was Boston's top draft selection out of Houston (where he played with Elvin Hayes) in 1968 and seemed at first destined to be the legitimate heir to K. C. Jones's role as defensive stopper. Long spider-like arms and unmatched upper-body strength

Long arms and a powerful upper body fitted Don Chaney for his role as a rugged defender and an heir to K.C. Jones' valued role as the backcourt defensive stopper.

seemed to fit the 6-5 guard ideally to the role of applying ceaseless pressure to the opposition's toughest backcourt offensive weapons. But Chaney also worked endlessly on his own offensive game during his earliest pro seasons and by his third season on the circuit (1971) he was contributing double-figure scoring as well as solid backcourt generalship. After skipping town for the ABA on the heels of the 1974 championship victory over Milwaukee (during which he teamed with Jo Jo White in the backcourt), Chaney eventually returned via the trade route to finish out the decade and his own 12-season career as a valuable bench contributor in Boston at the dawn of the Larry Bird era.

Like Danny Ainge three decades later, Gene Conley traded in his big-league baseball togs during winter months for an important role in the Boston Celtics' always potent supporting cast.

Gene Conley
(1952-53, 1958-61)

Gene Conley stands alongside Dave DeBusschere, Dick Groat, Bill Sharman and Danny Ainge as one of the handful of accomplished baseball professionals to make an equal or even larger mark on the indoor game of basketball. Among NBA two-sport stars, perhaps only DeBusschere can surpass Conley when it comes to a player's impact on postseason championship play. Yet even here Conley seems to hold the upper hand: of the numerous talented athletes who have reached the big time as both cagers and baseballers, it is only Gene Conley who can boast of playing in both sports on world championship teams. As a lanky major league fastballer Conley was able to keep his head above water (91-96, 3.82 ERA) over eleven seasons (1952-1963) with the Braves, Phillies and Red Sox, pitch in three All-Star Games, and make one ineffective World Series appearance with the 1957 World Champion Milwaukee Braves. During a half-dozen NBA seasons with the Celtics (1953, 1959-61) and Knicks (1963-64) he earned three championship rings as a backup forward and center, occasionally giving the great Bill Russell a few moments of bench rest. But for all the fastballs he lobbed and rebounds he wrestled, Gene Conley was destined to be remembered by sportsfans more for his flaky diamond behavior than for

any athletic prowess. Conley's moment of greatest infamy would come when he and reserve infielder Pumpsie Green left a Red Sox team bus stalled in Manhattan traffic after a loss at Yankee Stadium and hailed a cab for LaGuardia Airport with the plan of boarding a flight to Israel. Lack of passports foiled the plot immediately and the wayward athletes returned to the team only after several days of AWOL Manhattan bar hopping.

Chuck Cooper
(1950-54)

Jackie Robinson's singular and universally acknowledged credit for integrating major league baseball is improperly attributed only on a technically—or at worst a small string of such technicalities. Robinson was indeed the first 20th-century African-American black to set foot in the majors; he was not, of course—despite popular mythology—the first-ever big league black man (Fleetwood Walker and several others had already been there in the 19th-century), nor for that matter the first present-century major league man of color (numerous Cubans, Venezuelans and Puerto Ricans can lay claim to this latter distinction).

When it comes to NBA integration, however, one man has wrongly received all the credit, albeit credit that has had little popular hold on the consciousness of even the most rabid sports fans. What happened in the NBA in the early

Red Auerbach and Walter Brown made racial history in June 1950 when they settled on Duquesne's Chuck Cooper as the first African-American to be chosen in the NBA's college draft.

fifties was about as noteworthy as peasant uprisings in Outer Mongolia. Most formal and informal NBA histories point to Chuck Cooper of Duquesne University as the first black to set foot inside the NBA, based on the bold move of Boston owner Walter Brown in plucking Cooper out of the June 1950 college draft. The actual facts are that Cooper was indeed the first man of his race to be formally drafted by an NBA team, followed closely by Earl Lloyd of West Viriginia State on the same day. What weakens Cooper's case as the true first NBA black, however, are all of the following related events and circumstances.

First and foremost, the NBA had already had black players several seasons earlier, even if it wasn't yet calling itself the NBA. In at least one of the two leagues that were to become the NBA after the 1950 merger, blacks had already appeared on several rosters. Dolly King (Rochester Royals) and Pop Gates (Tri-Cities Blackhawks) together broke racial boundaries in the NBL as early as 1947, the exact year that baseball welcomed Robinson and basketball experienced its first "Negro" collegiate All-American in Don Barksdale of UCLA. The same league had also already had a contingent of other blacks (on the 1943 roster of the Chicago Studebackers), but this was well before the 1947 season, usually considered the launching year for the NBA (thus allowing a Golden Anniversay season in 1997). Also a whole team of blacks would play under the banner of the Dayton Rens in the NBL season of 1949, that league's final year before NBA merger. Finally, while Cooper was first to be drafted, minutes ahead of Lloyd, Lloyd was the first

actually to play in an NBA regular-season game. And Sweetwater Clifton of the Harlem Globetrotters had signed a contract with the New York Knicks before either Lloyd or Cooper had "officially" joined the league with their own contract signings. These latter two players—Earl Lloyd and Nat Clifton—thus deserve equal credit alongside Chuck Cooper as the NBA's recognized troika of earliest black pioneers.

BOSTON

Mel Counts
(1964-66)

The top Celtics draft choice of 1964 never lived up to expectations, either in Boston or anywhere else. In fact Mel Counts may have been one of the biggest draft day busts of all time. But for all the career-long disappointment Counts was nonetheless a player who earned a lasting footnote in basketball history. As a number seven overall draft day choice the Oregon State seven-footer was grabbed that year ahead of such second-rounders as Willis Reed and Paul Silas, and such third-rounders as Wally Jones and Jerry Sloan (there were only nine teams in the league at the time). He wore out his welcome after only two seasons of under-achievement in Boston but did provide some return on the investment when he was dealt off to Baltimore for Bailey Howell. As a seven-footer with some mobility Mel Counts did hang on for a dozen seasons and did post double-figure season's scoring averages for three campaigns in Los Angeles and one in Phoenix. But he was hardly a Russell, a Cham-

Transcendental Graphics

Mel Counts first disappointed as a top draft choice, then later proved his true value as important trade bait in the Bailey Howell transaction. Yet he is best remembered as the NBA's first jump-shooting seven-footer.

berlain, or even a Darrall Imhoff or Clyde Lovellette. Nonetheless Counts did leave his mark and it was more a matter of style points than anything else. It was Counts who was the first seven-footer to employ the standing jump shot as a basic offensive weapon, opting to pop ten footers from the lane rather than launch sweeping hooks or drop down easy lay-ins. While never overly impressive with his scoring touch, Mel Counts was nonetheless a forerunner of a tradition of soft-shooting behemoths that would eventually include far more effective modern-era post players like Patrick Ewing and Hakeem Olajuwon.

Pervis Ellison
(1994-99)

A tiny handful of freshman have made major impacts on the NCAA Final Four weekend which is still college basketball's biggest showcase event, and "Never-Nervous Pervis" Ellison of Louisville's 1986 national champions stands among the most successful of the lot. Arnie Ferrin had paced Utah's all-freshman lineup of NCAA champions way back in 1944; later Michael Jordan launched a career of seemingly endless heroics with a championship-winning last-second heave in 1982; and Patrick Ewing had almost as large an impact on the 1982 title shootout contest as did North Carolina's Jordan. MJ's jumphot with 16 ticks remaining decided the affair, but Ewing with 23 points (and a game-best 11 rebounds) battled Carolina scoring star James Worthy to a draw and kept the game close to the wire. Ellison would shine every bit as brightly during his own freshman moment in the NCAA limelight. His 25 points (after averaging only 13 for the season) and 11 boards overwhelmed the more balanced Duke attack and authored a tight 72-69 win over the favored Blue Devils. The ice-water-veined frosh sank the crucial free throws with 27 seconds remaining and the national championship squarely on the line. As reward he was named the first freshman Final Four MVP since Ferrin. But unfortunately for Ellison, for Louisville, and for the NBA teams (Sacramento, Washington, Boston) that would later employ him, the freshman heroics of more than a decade ago provided the apex of an otherwise disappointing career. A season's average of 20 for Washington in his third campaign earned NBA most-improved-player accolades. But his scoring, rebounding and playing-time numbers have all dipped radically since then and in recent campaigns the journeyman role player has known only a handful of individual nights when he has been able to crack double figures as a scorer or attract even passing notice with his brief trips off the Boston bench.

Wayne Embry
(1966-68)

Wayne Embry's lasting place in the pages of hoops history will assuredly be attached to his role as the NBA's first black general manager. Yet as a player Embry was also a significant pioneering figure, first in Cincinnati with the Royals, later briefly in Boston with Red Auerbach's dynasty Celtics, and also in Milwaukee with the expansion pre-Alcindor Bucks. It was in Boston that the burly center was destined to play his most memorable role as one of Auerbach's most successful reclamation projects.

As a muscular 6-8 center-forward Embry launched his pro career in Cincinnati where he played alongside Oscar Robertson, Jack Twyman and Jerry Lucas, logged seven of eight seasons as a double-figures scorer, and was team captain between 1962 and 1966. His two seasons in Boston (1967-1968) included his only NBA championship, earned during a brief tenure as a front wall reinforcement alongside Russell, Bailey Howell, Satch Sanders and Don Nelson. Embry will perhaps be remembered as much as anything else in his career for his role as one of the long list of great Boston short-term "pick-ups"—a list which also includes Clyde Lovellette, Andy Phillip, Willie Naulls, Don Nelson and Bill Walton. Taken by Milwaukee in the 1968 expansion draft he concluded his playing career as the Bucks' inaugural team captain and expansion-season second leading rebounder. It was three seasons after his retirement that Wayne Embry broke new ground (in 1972) when named vice president and general manager for the still-young Milwaukee franchise. In June 1986 Embry became vice president and general manager of the Cleveland Cavaliers, a position which again underscored the ex-player's exceptional administrative talents. Cleveland would make six playoff appearances in the first eight seasons of Embry's tenure, a string of successes which led to the honoring of Cleveland's top front office figure as *The Sporting News* 1991-92 NBA Executive of the Year.

Henry "Hank" Finkel
(1969-75)

Henry Finkel is not a household basketball name and he was hardly a player with either exceptional skills or any particularly memorable feature to his workman-like game. But he still boasts a rare distinction, nonetheless—that of the toughest season-opening assignment in all of professional cage history. When the three-year veteran center was picked up from the Houston Rockets for cash in November 1969 he was handed the starting Boston post position and the task of replacing just-retired legend Bill Russell. These were shoes that perhaps even Lew Alcindor or Bill Walton or Wilt Chamberlain could not have adequately filled. For the seven-footer who had performed only a notch above adequately in collegiate circles with Dayton and on pro courts with the Lakers and San Diego Rockets, it was an altogether hopeless assignment.

"High Henry" predictably endured considerable wrath and much derision during a short spell in Boston Garden until Dave Cowens fortunately came along and he could settle out of the limelight and into the backup role he was far more suited for. As a reserve Finkel could contribute his modest arsenal of soft hooks and stationary pump shots and do yeoman's work in the trenches blocking opponents off the boards with his wide body and setting picks that were always jarring if rarely artistic. He also proved something of a favorite among his teammates as a clubhouse jester, and while Boston fans eventually softened a bit in their rough treatment of the inadequate Russell clone, they never fully appreciated the steady if unspectacular Finkel quite the way that Boston players and coaches universally did.

BOSTON
Chris Ford
(1978-82)

Chris Ford's biggest chunk of Boston lore admittedly came with three seasons of solid coaching (two divisional titles and one second), followed by two final desperate campaigns when the team under him came apart at the seams (mainly due to Bird's career-ending injuries, the aging of McHale and Parish, and Reggie Lewis's heart ailment). His tenure thus earned distinction as the unluckiest of all Boston coaches. But exceptional court savvy and a deadly outside shooting eye also made the 6-5 Villanova guard a considerable contributor during the years he wore an NBA player's uniform. The outside shooting proficiency would keep Ford in the league for a decade in Detroit (six-plus seasons) and Boston (his final three-plus campaigns). It would also earn him a trivial niche in history as the gunner who collected the league's first-ever three-point field goal.

The historic moment came in Boston Garden on Columbus Day of 1979, during the season's lidlifter in which the home team edged the visiting Houston Rockets 114-108, and at the outset of a year in which the league had decided to spice its game with a new rule adopted from the once-popular red-white-and-blue ABA circuit. This particular game drew little attention for the new scoring legislation, however, or for Chris Ford's historic toss, since another debut that very night grabbed all the fan and media interest. It was also the game which marked the official Boston coming out party for a celebrated rookie phenom named Larry Bird.

Dickie Hemric
(1955-57)

Dickie Hemric's NBA career was both modest and disappointing, yet as a collegian he was a ture colossus. With Hemric, Wake Forest unquestionnably owned the Atlantic Coast Conference's first legitimate superstar and they already had him on board for the 1954 launching of the newly constituted league. Dickie Hemric would rule the ACC during its two maiden seasons, pacing Wake to first-division finishes both winters, topping all league rebounders, ranking second (1954) and then third (1955) among conference scorers, and engraving his name on the first two league MVP trophies. The only true rivals to Wake's powerful 6-6 pivotman were Virginia's hot-shooting Buzz Wilkinson (owner of the league's first two scoring titles) and Clemson's talented backcourt ace Bill Yarborough. Len Rosenbluth and Ronnie Shavlik were waiting in the wings at North Carolina and North Carolina State repectively during Hemric's senior season but both were still a year away from glory.

Hemric's dominance sprang in part from his uniqueness: as an aggressive board-crasher who could also shoot with a soft touch he was a rare phenomenon for his era. But the rules then governing play also added a strong assist for a hard-nosed player of his size. The foul lane was still at six-feet and not twelve, thus allowing the mobile but not exceptionally large Hemric to take up a spot next to the hoop without fear of drawing three-second violations. Another rule aberration allowed each team an inside foul-line position on free throws (today both go to the defense); Hemric thus had plenty of extra opportunity to score off tap-ins of missed free throws by his teammates. A special 1954 provision also allowed players a second bonus free throw after a first miss; thus teams with strong offensive rebounders like Hemric would often intentionally miss the second charity toss by aiming it toward their own rebounder's side of the bucket.

With these considerable assists from the rules makers plus his own superior talents Hemric posted outstanding numbers during the first two league seasons and he still owns several pages in the Wake Forest basketball record book. He is not only the school's first great scorer—still holding the career four-year records for total points and overall scoring average—but also the greatest rebounder in Wake Forest history. In the final two seasons of his career Hemric would altogether dominate statistical play in the new Tobacco Road conference with combined rebound and point totals that outdistanced the rest of the league field by a country mile. And very few have matched his numbers in the four full decades that have since followed.

Gerald Henderson
(1979-84)

Three remarkable and crucial steals are etched forever into Boston basketball lore—Bird's against Detroit (1987) in the fifth game of the Eastern Conference Finals, Havlicek's which kept the dynasty string alive against Philadelphia (1965) during yet another Eastern Conference title showdown, and Henderson's that saved game two of the 1984 NBA Finals versus Los Angeles. The defining moment for the role-playing guard came within the series better known for its first head-to-head matchup of the NBA's two biggest marquee names of the '80s—Magic Johnson and Larry Bird. But it was nonetheless Henderson's one marvelous play as much as Larry Bird's nightly feats that in the end saved the day and thus also the championship series for an emotion-driven Boston ballclub.

Magic's Lakers had established both their brimming confidence and seeming superiority at the outset of the 1984 championships series. They stole game one in Boston

Gerald Henderson's game-saving steal and bucket in the 1984 NBA Finals will always rank right alongside similar pilferings by Havlicek and Bird as a cherished moment in Boston's sporting annals.

Garden on the strength of a 32-point performance by veteran Kareem Abdul-Jabbar and then rode the hot offensive hand of James Worthy (11 of 12 from the floor and 29 points) through much of game two to stand on the doorstep of a potentially devastating (to Boston hopes) Boston sweep with only moments remaining in the second contest. Two missed free throws by McHale seemed to seal the deal for Los Angeles, but than an ill-called timeout with 18 seconds on the clock allowed Boston and Henderson to step up big. Magic's wayward inbounds pass to Byron Scott was snatched by the Boston guard who raced downcourt unmolested for a game-tying hoop that turned the tide. In the overtime period that followed another key Boston role-player, Scott Wedman, hit the bucket that tied the series, but only after Henderson had fed him with an exceptional pass. When Boston rolled to a 15th world title in game seven back in Boston Garden Bird was the celebrated Finals MVP with a 27.4 series scoring average and 14-rebound average. But few would forget that in this dramatic series it was Gerald Henderson who had been the unexpected and unsung savior.

It was not only a highlight moment but also a swan song moment for Henderson's brief Boston career. At the dawn of the new season he was shipped off to Seattle for a first-round 1986 draft spot later used for the ill-fated selection of Len Bias. Danny Ainge after three seasons had matured into a starting role alongside Dennis Johnson and thus—with still more than half his NBA career before him—Henderson had already become very expendible in Boston. But Henderson's five-year Boston stint of course featured far more than one isolated and surprising heads-up postseason play. He had filled in at both point guard and shooting guard alongside Tiny Archibald and M. L. Carr, and for one season alongside Dennis Johnson, and thus was an integral cog in the versatile Boston backcourt of the early Bird seasons. Equally crucial was his nightly contribution of always-tenacious defensive play. And it was that tenacious defense that once saved both the day and another Boston championship—in the moment that now seems to crystalize Gerald Henderson's entire Boston career.

Bailey Howell
(1966-70)

Had the ugly specter of racism not surrounded the Mississippi State University basketball program in the two decades following World War II, Bailey Howell's glorious Southeastern Conference cage career might have boasted even a good deal more glitter on the national scene than it did. As it turned out Howell seemed to make a career out of being second best (which is not always bad, especially when it comes to the star-studded worlds of college and profes-

In the annals of other ballclubs Hall-of-Famer Bailey Howell would rank as a true immortal. If he is overshadowed in Boston by more colorful role players like Nelson, Walton and Silas, he was nonetheless one of Auerbach's greatest late-career pickups.

sional basketball). This penchant for being an overlooked runner-up began with the 6-7 forward's stellar senior season at Mississippi State, when the SEC's premier player finished second in the land among major college players in both rebounding (15.2) and scoring (27.5 behind Oscar Robertson). It was all to little avail, however, as Howell's 24-1 SEC championship squad withdrew from the NCAA postseason chase due to the presence of black players. As a sophomore he rebounded at nearly 20 per game and also paced the nation in field goal percentage. By the time of his graduation Bailey Howell ranked among the all-time all-around collegiate greats, joining Tom Gola and Elgin Baylor as the only players up to that time to log as many as 2,000 career points and 1,000 career rebounds. It was a sterling enough record to earn top-draft-pick status with the NBA's Detroit Pistons.

Howell's grip on second-best status continued through much of his considerable NBA career, which spread over a dozen seasons split between Detroit (5 years), Baltimore (2 years), Boston (4 years), and a final swan song season in Philadelphia. While he managed to pace the Pistons in scoring four times and rebounding three times, he later occupied his familiar runner-up spot for those team categories while with Baltimore in 1965 and 1966. Traded to the champion Celtics for Mel Counts, Howell trailed only John Havlicek in scoring and Bill Russell in rebounding for three straight Boston campaigns (the three that Russell served as head coach). It was also in Boston that Bailey Howell finally reached championship status when the Dynasty Celtics won

their final two NBA banners of the Auerbach-Cousy-Russell era.

Bailey Howell's route to Boston was one demonstration of actually how highly thought of this bruising forward/center actually was as an invaluable team-oriented performer. Between the 1956 maneuverings to acquire Russell's draft rights from St. Louis and the 1972 swap with Phoenix that relinquished Charlie Scott's NBA rights for Paul Silas, Auerbach engineered exactly one significant player trade to resupply his aging Boston championship forces. And that was the deal with Baltimore that handed over strapping Mel Counts (a disappointing backup to Russell) for the rugged Howell (who immediately became the club's top scorer after Havlicek). And if Bailey Howell was often only second-best when it came to league or team statistical categories, nonetheless his long-term consistency was sufficient to eventually make a deep impact on the NBA record book. Mississippi State's most productive NBA performer retired in 1971 with top-ten rankings in eleven different career statistical categories. It is not surprising, given his reputation as a punishing rebounder and bruising defensive player, that the highest of these rankings fell in the area of personal fouls committed, a dubious category in which Howell once stood entrenched as the fifth most notorious hacker in NBA league annals.

Dennis "DJ" Johnson
(1983-90)

One of the finest defensive players in league history (a nine-time member of the NBA All-Defensive squad) was also a talented playmaker and a dependable clutch scorer for a trio of the most memorable NBA championship teams of the modern era. Dennis Johnson (popularly known as simply DJ) was the second leading scorer and third leading assists man with the 1979 Seattle SuperSonics, a team which captured that city's only franchise title by blitzing Washington in five games. And as a backcourt mainstay on both the 1984 and 1986 Boston playoff winners, DJ trailed only Bird as the assists leader on teams that boasted perhaps the finest front wall— Bird, Parish and McHale—of the modern era or any other NBA era.

The summer 1983 deal which moved DJ from Phoenix to Boston in exchange for center Rick Robey was destined to surprise was one of the most successful front office moves in ballclub history. A player who reportedly had a reputation as a selfish malcontent with the Phoenix Suns transformed overnight into one of the sport's consummate team players once he pulled on a Celtics jersey and immersed himself in Celtics tradition. But there had already been pleasant surprises and sudden transformations marking Johnson's cage career. He never played high school basket-

No lesser critic than Larry Bird once referred to Dennis Johnson as the most intelligent performer he ever played with. It was appropriate praise indeed for one of the best defensive guards ever to don an NBA jersey.

ball and logged only one college season at unheralded Pepperdine (after two years of junior college ball at Los Angeles Harbor JC); it was nonetheless enough to earn a second-round hardship draft nod from Seattle. A 14-year pro career (seven seasons in Boston) turned out illustrious enough to include All-NBA first (1981) and second team (1982) selections and nine straight seasons on the NBA All-Defensive first or second teams. The latter was a mark surpassed only by Kareem Abdul-Jabbar and matched only by Bobby Jones. For more than a half-decade of unrivalled overall hustle and defensive prowess Johnson was also honored in Boston with a retired uniform number.

Dennis Johnson topped 15,000 career points and 5,000 career assists (only the eleventh player to do so at the time of his retirement), was NBA Finals MVP with Seattle (1979), and shares an NBA Finals record for free throw shooting (most made in one half). But it was as a relentless defender that he made his lasting reputation. Long arms, quick hands and feet, and an aggressive ball-pressuring style made him as tough and relentless a straight-up man-to-man defender as found anywhere. An when it comes to endorsements that carry the weight of unquestionned authority, none other than Larry Bird once labelled Dennis Johnson as simply the best he ever played with.

Steve Kuberski
(1969-74, 1975-78)

No NBA franchise has boasted such a rich supply of faceless blue-collar ballplayers who quitely and faithfully performed their backup duties with flawless professionalism for years—going almost unnoticed in the process—and then burst out for one rare fleeting moment of stardom when their services were most vitally needed. Glenn McDonald, Jim Ard, Gerald Henderson, Chris Ford and

Steve Kuberski's Boston career peaked with the 1972 Eastern Conference semifinals versus Atlanta, but it also included more than a half-dozen campaigns as steady bench performer.

Henry Finkel all fit the prototype. But Steve Kuberski is the shining exemplar. A 6-8 forward out of Bradley was an afterthought round-four pick in the 1969 collegiate draft. His bench play over the next several seasons (where his average contribution was 15 minutes and 6 quiet points per game) was all sweat and consistency and little that resembled finesse. Then during the 1972 Eastern Conference semifinals with Atlanta Kuberski suddenly came to life with the six-game string of a lifetime, putting up not one but three 20-point games over that brief stretch. He had never played like that before and would never play like that again. Yet he hung around for seven seasons (both before and after a pair of brief trials with Milwaukee and Buffalo) and could always be counted on for some quality bench minutes whenever they were most needed.

Tony Lavelli
(1949-50)

A local New England favorite, Lavelli came out of Yale University in 1949 with an All-American reputation for a deadly and artistic hook shot and equal billing as a talented accordion player. Basketball skills alone earned a draft pick, but the vaunted hook never paid many dividends in the new pro professional league just renamed the National Basketball Association. One season with Boston witnessed an 8.8 scoring average in a backup forward's role; a second and final campaign with reduced playing time was less productive in New York. The musical skills were enough, however, to provide a small niche in pro basketball lore as Lavelli negotiated a second contract with the young league as a half-time entertainment act. Always on the lookout for features to spice the evening's entertainment, even in its earliest winters, the NBA was willing to pay Lavelli $125 for each of 25 intermission accordion concerts, some coming during his own Boston games. The ex-All-American whose cousin (Dante Lavelli) was a pro football standout with the Cleveland Browns thus earned a unique niche in American sporting lore, becoming the only basketballer whose halftime exploits drew bigger notice than his game-time performances.

Jim Loscutoff
(1955-64)

Basketball has had few "enforcers" whose singular role on the floor seemed to be physical intimidation of more talented opponents. Unlike hockey, basketball is not structured to allow for such a role or such a style of knock-down, drag-out play. Yet with the talent-rich Boston Celtics of the Russell-Cousy era, nonetheless, "Jungle Jim" Loscutoff provided the NBA's closest-ever model for such a muscle-bound prototype. The Oregon graduate debuted with Auerbach's crew in 1956, a year before the championship run began, and lasted through nine campaigns until 1964, a year after Cousy bowed out. Through more than 500 NBA games and more than a decade of action he only once averaged double figures (10.6, 1957) and most often scored at only half that rate. While a ferocious rebounder who played more than 1100 minutes five different seasons, his rebounding average also reached double figures on one occasion (the same 1957 season). Loscutoff was on the floor most of the time simply to wear down opposing centers and forwards and to protect the rest of the Boston front line that consisted over the years of Heinsohn, Frank Ramsey, Lou Tsioropoulos, Jack Nichols, Gene Conley, Clyde Lovellette, and Gene Guarilia. It was a job he did profi-

"Jungle Jim" Loscutoff's #18 jersey hangs from the Boston rafters with Dave Cowens' name attached, but his "nickname" was nonetheless retired in honor of his role as rebounder and enforcer on Auerbach's first seven world championships.

ciently enough to have his number eventually retired, though since that same number (18) was later worn more distinctively by Dave Cowens it was actually Loscutoff's nickname ("Loscy") and not his numeral that was eventually hoisted into the Boston Garden rafters.

Clyde Lovellette
(1962-64)

Clyde Lovellette owns one of the rarest of collegiate basketball bragging rights. To date, after almost six decades of postseason championship play, Lovellette remains the only man ever to win a national scoring title and simultaneously lead his team to an NCAA Tournament championship. The two-time consensus Kansas All-American and future journeyman NBA center-forward would accomplish this rarest of feats during the 1952 season—his senior campaign—while filling a role as marquee player on Phog Allen's only tournament-era national championship team.

As a somewhat disappointing NBA journeyman Lovellette would be most noted for his "second-fiddle roles" as backup to several of the game's most memorable starting centers—first George Mikan in Minneapolis, later Bob Pettit on St. Louis, and finally Bill Russell in Boston. The two-season backup role as Russell's understudy was tinged with a bit of irony, since Lovellette himself had been the target of Russell's rage two seasons earlier in one of the only melees the Boston star ever engaged in. When he was forced to step in as Mikan's permanent replacement in 1955, however, it became clear that Lovellette possessed neither the quickness nor requisite ruggedness to stand on his own as a full-fledged NBA star. The gentle giant never held down an NBA starting role long enough to continue his prodigious collegiate scoring with Kansas. Yet he did log enough seasons and enough minutes to compile nearly 12,000 points as a pro and to register an 11-year 17.0 regular-season scoring average.

In Boston the journeyman center who Johnny Most once labelled as "Wide Clyde" would join the ranks of other fortune-kissed veterans like Andy Phillip, Willie Naulls, Wayne Embry and Paul Silas—all journeymen castoffs who successfully and often miraculously extended their careers with Auerbach and company and happily picked up championship hardware in the process.

AP/Wide World Photos

There is not a more tragic saga in Boston Celtics or NBA annals than the premature end to the life and playing career of inspirational team captain and stellar forward Reggie Lewis.

Reggie Lewis
(1987-93)

Reggie Lewis was not only the most tragic figure in Boston Celtics annals but may well qualify for that dark distinction across the entire history of the NBA. Perhaps only fifties-era stalwart Maurice Stokes—unaccountably struck down by deadly encephalitis in the prime of his own all-star career—ranks in the same category when it comes to potential athletic stardom sadly cancelled out by fatal circumstance. Circumstances surrounding Lewis's final campaign constituted certainly the most deadly and painful blow in a string of endless catastrophes that plagued the Boston ballclub in the final Larry Bird years, beginning with the shocking 1986 drug-overdose of prize recruit Len Bias, ending with Lewis's fatal heart disease, and including a rash of devastating injuries that hobbled Bird himself and also plagued a number of his teammates across nearly a half-dozen years.

Lewis came on board in Boston as the most promising draft day recruit since the equally ill-fated Len Bias and also the most promising new talent in a Celtics lineup since Bird. Plucked from the local Northeastern University campus with the 1987 22nd overall draft choice, Lewis had been a Boston area standout as Northeastern's all-time scoring leader and shot-blocker (as a 6-7 forward), and also as the first three-time East Coast Athletic Conference player of the year. Playing only 400 minutes as a little-used but highly touted Boston rookie, he had steadily improved his offensive game in three subsequent seasons (twice averaging above 18). By his fifth and sixth seasons (his final two campaigns) he had already inherited the club's main offensive burden from a fading and oft-injured Bird. In the processes he had also become one of the most feared scorers in the entire league. But all that was changed overnight with the unfolding events of the 1993 postseason, and what now remains of the Reggie Lewis heritage is largely only the disturbing details of his final months.

First came the surprising ailment that felled the Boston star during the playoff series with Charlotte. No one at the time suspected the seriousness of the situation when Boston's ace player collapsed to the floor late in the first quarter of an opening round playoff game in Charlotte. The news that followed was more shocking still and raised immediate fears about far more than an early postseason ouster for the team: three days after the incident in Charlotte a team of a dozen top cardiac specialists at New England Baptist Hospital diagnosed cardiac abnormalities. But Lewis was nonetheless allowed to continue on a program of limited exercise after a period of rest, a medical decision which would years later bring a medical malpractice suit against some of the doctors who alledgedly misdiagnosed and mistreated the player's condition. At the time of Lewis's extensive examination in early May 1993 Dr. Gilbert Mudge had pronounced that "there was no damage to the heart muscle" and further pronounced the star athlete fit to resume his basketball career without limitation; but there was a desenting opinion from Celtics' team doctor Arnold Scheller that Lewis's heart appeared to be susceptible to a potentially lethal condition (ventricular arrhythmia) that had earlier led to the 1990 fatal collapse of collegiate star Hank Gathers. Both the team and the player's family at the time seemed to be in a state of denial about pessimistic assessments of Lewis's chances to resume an

NBA career.

But for all the doubt and fear, nothing could quite prepare the Boston faithful and the club front office for the sudden developments occurring only a few months after Lewis's original collapse and treatment. In July, at the age of 27, Lewis collapsed again while shooting baskets in a Boston gymnasium and died almost instantly. Almost without warning one of the league's most promising future stars was suddenly gone. And the shockwaves throughout the Celtics family were ones from which the once-mighty Boston franchise has seemingly never yet completely recovered.

"Pistol" Pete Maravich
(1979-80)

Maravich rarely is mentioned in serious discussions of basketball's greatest individual players. Perhaps this has most to do with his reputation as an outrageous "gunner" or perhaps it is simply the result of his failures to prop up any of the teams he ever played for. But when the issue is showmanship Pete Maravich of LSU is rarely assigned anywhere except at the top of the list. And in the NCAA record books Maravich—after more than a quarter of a century of challengers—still merits nearly an entire page of his own. Maravich was a true '60s phenomenon if there ever was one. He wore floppy socks that dusted his shoe tops, featured a rock n' roller's floppy hair style and was the hardwood court's supreme individualist. He was a player who was truly the stuff of mind-stretching myth and larger-than-life legend.

One of hoopdom's greatest showmen—Pistol Pete Maravich—made a brief and colorful 26-game stopover in Boston at career's end.

In the same colorful package hoops fans here had not only the most prolific college scorer ever, but also the most flamboyant ball handler to boot. "Pistol Pete" could do things with a basketball that no one else had ever done— not even Bob Davies at Seton Hall with his behind-the-back dribbling or Bob Cousy at Holy Cross with his behind-the-back no-look passing. But most of all Pete could flat-out shoot the pill. If Julius Erving (whose sophomore year at Massachusetts overlapped Maravich's senior season at LSU) would by the mid-'70s redefine the game played above the rim, Maravich would at the outset of the '70s already have redefined the game being played below the rim.

Pete Maravich left a scoring legacy in his wake that has never yet been matched. While other schools boast their select lists of career 1,000-point scorers, with Maravich LSU had a shooter who would top the four-digit figure in each of his three individual varsity seasons. He scored more than 50 points in 28 different games and registered high games of 66 and 69. Three straight times he reigned as national scoring champ, something that only Oscar Robertson accomplished before him and no one has duplicated since. He would average a phenomenal 44.2 for an entire three-year career and do this not against phony competition, like Bevo Francis had at tiny Rio Grande, or inconsistent competition like Furmans' Frank Selvy faced, but instead against defenses from one of the premier conferences (SEC) in the land. No one except Francis and Selvy had ever before scored quite like this. And neither Bevo Francis nor Frank Selvy ever had to face nightly opponents from conference rivals named Kentucky, Tennessee, Vanderbilt, Georgia or Mississippi State, or intersectional rivals named Southern Cal (against them Pete scored 50), UCLA, or St. John's (Pete once outscored the entire St. John's opposing team in the second half of a Rainbow Classic tournament matchup).

The one thing Maravich did not do was win championships—in either the college or pro ranks (where he did capture one individual scoring title but never a league MVP or even rookie of the year)—and it was at LSU that the surrounding overall team ineptitudes were most glaring and inexplicable. LSU with Maravich was barely an above-average team, posting two .500 campaigns before finally going 22-10 in 1970 and enjoying a third-place NIT finish. The reason was quite obvious—Maravich did nothing to make his teammates better and perhaps quite a bit to make them worse. He played over their heads, bounced spectacular passes off their legs and shoulders, gambled and freelanced on defense, and soloed in search of big-scoring nights rather than hard-earned team victories. It was a style that would eventually earn a seven-figure pro contract at the end of the line but few team triumphs along the way. And for all his individual brilliance, Pete Maravich was never enough of a team player to earn himself or his supporting crew even a single visit to the college sport's main event, postseason NCAA tournament play.

Cedric "Cornbread" Maxwell
(1977-85)

There was nothing overly impressive about Cedric Maxwell's 11-year NBA career, unless it was the consistency of nine straight seasons as a double-figure scorer. His career scoring average was a shade over twelve, his rebound totals never reached double figures, he was only once (his second season in Boston) the team's top scorer, and as a starter he never qualified either for the honored lists of memorable Celtics sixth men or honored role players. But Maxwell was linchpin of two championship teams, nonetheless, and his place is secure when it comes to recounting remarkable Boston postseason perfomances.

Maxwell specialized in playoff heroics, especially during his two trips to the championship round in 1981 (against Houston) and 1984 (versus Los Angeles). The 1981 NBA Finals series was deadlocked at two when Maxwell—inspired by taunting from rival center Moses Malone—exploded for a 28-point and 15-rebound performance in a crucial series game five. Bird took over as the Celtics coasted in a final sixth game back in Boston. Bird's 27 points were underscored by Maxwell's 19 in the 102-91

A workhorse mainstay of the Larry Bird era, Cornbread Maxwell never made his presence more indispensable than during the 1981 and 1984 postseason championship derbies.

game that clinched Larry's first title and the club's four-teenth. But Maxwell had been the deciding factor and his efforts earned a niche of immortality with the Finals MVP trophy that some thought might have been Bird's.

Maxwell was again a deciding factor in championship play when the Celtics returned to the NBA Finals three seasons later. The team that battled Los Angeles in the first Bird-Magic title showdown was a very different squad, coached by K. C. Jones and now featuring a new backcourt of Dennis Johnson and Danny Ainge and the up-front help of veteran center Bill Walton. Kevin McHale had now also matured into a starter and also a key component in the "Big Three" front wall that also featured Bird and Parish. Maxwell's own role had been reduced to bench support for the Bird-Parish-McHale tandem, but once more the veteran forward was more than ready for the postseason call to battle. His moment came in the deciding seventh game of a see-saw series when the team's clubhouse leader uttered a memorable challenge to his teammates. As Bird later remembered it, Maxwell jumped to his feet in the pre-game locker room and yelled, "Get on my back tonight boys, this is my game."

It was not an idle boast, as Maxwell that night went to work on LA forward James Worthy for 24 points, 14 from the foul line. Maxwell, Bird and Parish outrebounded the entire Lakers squad with 36 boards between them. Bird with 20 points and 12 rebounds was the Finals MVP this time around, but once more Maxwell had perhaps been the deciding factor in the series' most crucial game. A year later Boston would fall in the return match, dropping a championship on their home court for the first time in club history. When asked about the differences between the '84 and '85 Boston squads Bird would later be quick to point to Maxwell as the deciding factor. Cornbread had injured a knee and undergone an operation during what would prove to be his last Boston season. He missed 25 regular-season games and scored at a weak 3.8 clip in postseason. Without a healthy and tenacious Maxwell—Parish, McHale and Bird aside—the Celtics simply couldn't match the Lakers' rebounding and offensive frontline firepower the second time around and went down to defeat in six games.

Bob McAdoo
(1979)

Bob McAdoo is a monument to the individual star who piled up reams of impressive statistics but never seemed to make any of the teams he occasionally carried on his shoulders any better or more competitive for all his heavy-scoring presence. If there is a unique niche for the 6-9 pivotman out of North Carolina (where he played a single 1972 All-American season as leading scorer on the NCAA third-place team) it is the fact that probably no one playing the post position ever shot the ball any better than this second overall NBA draft pick of the Buffalo Braves. His pro career (Buffalo, New York, Boston, Detroit, New Jersey, Los Angeles Lakers, Philadelphia) spread over 14 seasons and it boasted three-consecutive scoring crowns early on (in his first three seasons, all with Buffalo) and two NBA team titles in his twilight years (with Los Angeles in 1982 and 1985). While he logged the bulk of his playing time in the pivot, McAdoo launched most of his frequent missiles as medium-range jumpers, a fact that underscores the brilliance of his career-long .503 shooting percentage. Most memorable about Bob McAdoo in the NBA was his inside quickness and deft shooting touch which allowed him to constantly outmaneuver and outscore much rangier inside players he matched up against. Most overlooked about his stellar career was his "second life" in Europe where between the ages of 35 and 41 he logged seven remarkable seasons as a scoring star in the high-quality Italian professional league.

But for all the impressive numbers and considerable renown that surrounded Bob McAdoo's decade and a half in the NBA, his stopover in Boston was hardly more than a blip when in comes to oncourt efforts. The prolific scorer pulled on a Boston jersey for only 20 games in the second half of the 1979 season, for which he averaged his customary 20-plus points. As a player McAdoo was far more memorable as a formidable Boston antagonist than he was as a Celtics protagonist. McAdoo provided most of the singlehanded opposition in a dramatic and hard-fought 1974 first-round playoff series in which Heinsohn's ballclub barely survived a scare from the upstart Buffalo Braves on their way to a first post-Auerbach championship.

But if Bob McAdoo's tenure with the Celtics was indeed brief it was nonetheless significant. Indeed no other player logged so brief a Boston career yet figured so prominently in the ballclub's future fortunes. And all of that impact involved McAdoo's strange comings and goings into and out of Boston. One of the league's biggest gate attractions had wound up in Boston during an arduous period of disastrous ballclub ownership shuffles which had left Red Auerbach near the point of exasperation. The fabled GM had stood by helplessly as owner Irv Levin had conducted a revolving-door policy of player moves that left the team in shambles during the wasteland seasons of 1977 and 1978. Then when Levin swapped franchises with Buffalo owner John Y. Brown the whole mess seemed to worsen. The new owner traded away three first round picks that Red had stockpiled as a means of rebuilding the club for the new decade. The picks went to New York and were later used to acquire Bill Cartwright, Larry Demic and Sly Williams. The return for the three prime draft slots was none other than McAdoo—hardly a player cut in the Auerbach mold but one the new club owner's wife (former Miss America Phyllis George) enjoyed watching and thus wanted in the Boston stable.

But the last laugh would nonetheless belong to the shrewd redhead. After abandoning his plans to flee Boston and Brown for a similar post with the New York Knicks, Auerbach welcomed a new ownership group headed by Harry Mangurian and committed to let Red run the operation without further interference. One of the GM's first maneuvers in pursuit of that goal was to hire on Bill Fitch as coach. Another was a complicated series of player moves that involved the same Bob McAdoo. Detroit veteran M. L. Carr was signed at the outset of the 1979-80 season (Bird's rookie year) and McAdoo was sent over to the Pistons as compensation. Two 1980 first-round picks also came Boston's way in the transaction. These were soon peddled to Golden State (who used one to grab Joe Barry Carroll) in exchange for Robert Parish and yet another draft slot, the one then used by Boston (3rd overall) to pluck Kevin McHale from the college ranks. To state it all simply, the unwanted McAdoo was quickly unloaded for Parish and McHale, with valuable role player M. L. Carr casually thrown into the bargain.

Xavier McDaniel
(1992-95)

Owner of some stellar collegiate credentials, "The X-Man" of Wichita State was the first NCAA performer ever to pace the nation in both scoring (27.2) and rebounding (14.8) when he pulled off the stunt in 1985. Since then the double has been repeated by only Hank Gathers of Loyola Marymount (1989) and Kurt Thomas of Texas Tech (1995), leaving McDaniel as part owner of one of the rarest among NCAA achievements. The number four overall pick of the 1985 NBA draft (by Seattle), McDaniel also paced the country's college rebounders as a junior, twice averaged above 20 as a scorer, and posted 2152 points in his four-year All-American career.

As a twelve-year NBA mainstay the achievements have been a bit more muted but nonetheless eye-catching. For eight straight seasons at the outset of his career McDaniel posted double-figure scoring and four times topped the 20-point barrier in Seattle. Coming to Boston in 1992 as a free agent he quickly proved a solid starter (1992-93) and later a valuable bench performer (1993-94 and 1994-95) for a trio of seasons that spanned the bulk of Chris Ford's coaching tenure. During his first Boston season he was the club's second leading scorer (behind Reggie Lewis) and also the second leading rebounder (trailing Robert Parish). When his playing time dipped and his starting role evaporated after Dino Radja's arrival, the veteran continued to contribute in a backup role. After a season in the Greek pro league in 1996 McDaniel would return to the New Jersey Nets for a final chapter in his long and consistent NBA tenure.

Xavier McDaniel's NBA sojourn was never as spectacular as a sterling collegiate career.

McDaniel never matched earlier glories during his brief Boston sojourn. But his big-name presence in the Celtics lineup alongside Dominique Wilkins in the final season at historic Boston Garden would provide a small measure of crediability during one of the darkest epochs of ballclub history.

Glenn McDonald
(1974-76)

Glenn McDonald like Jim Ard had one shining moment in the spotlight, and like Ard that moment came with the 1976 postseason, during an epic championship struggle with the spunky Phoenix Suns which turned into one of the bright chapters of franchise history. And it was McDonald's own heroics that wrote one of the crucial segments of that most unforgettable chapter. The setting was the first three-overtime game in NBA Finals history and the upstart Suns were on the verge of grabbing command of the title series that Boston had entered as an overwhelming favorite. With the game knotted at 112 after Gar Heard's miraculous buzzer-beating shot in the second extra session, Heinsohn's Celtics found their backs truly to the wall. With the bulk of his starting lineup already on the bench with six personal fouls Heinsohn had to turn to an unlikely source for some season-saving heroics. Little-used

forward Glenn McDonald had come to Boston as a number one draft pick out of Long Beach State two seasons earlier but had made little contribution to the Celtics cause in the intervening pair of campaigns. While no one knew it at the time, he was in his final days on the Boston roster and would begin the new season in Milwaukee. He would in fact play only nine more NBA games after his moment of unexpected heroics that finally turned the tide against Phoenix.

In that single overtime frame McDonald would step up big, however, performing for those few brief moments in

Glenn McDonald was a number one draft pick whose entire NBA legacy boiled down to one single overachieving postseason moment.

the finest championship tradition of the uniform he briefly wore. He would drop in six vital points, the final two a short-range jumper that sealed the affair in Boston's favor at 128-126. It was the briefest moment of glory among a long series of stellar Boston postseason performances. But it was enough nonetheless to earn Glenn McDonald a permanent niche alongside more recognizable names like Havlicek, Jones, Nelson, Heinsohn, Russell, Cowens, Maxwell, Cousy and Bird in the almost endless list of remarkable Boston Celtics postseason heroes.

Ron Mercer
(1997-99)

One of the keys to Boston's future at the turn of the new century is first round 1997 draft pick Ron Mercer, a two-year Kentucky star under Rick Pitino and an early entry to the NBA after his stellar sophomore season in which he averaged 18 points per game and carried the Wildcats to an NCAA Finals showdown with Arizona. Mercer didn't waste much time displaying his pro potential, enjoying a spectacular rookie NBA campaign by finishing near the top of the heap among first-year players in every major offensive category (including second in points with 1221, made field goals with 515, and steals with 125). He was also the league's number three rookie in scoring average (15.3 ppg.) and minutes played (33.3 mpg.). He especially gained momentum in the season's second half, when he averaged 18.1 ppg. and reached double figures in 31 of 35 games after the mid-season All-Star Game break.

Mercer's second campaign with Boston also seemed to demonstrate beyond doubt that this youngster was anything but a one-year wonder or a temporary flash in the pan. As a second-year player he averaged 16.8 as a scorer to split the team offensive burden with Antoine Walker (18.8) and rookie Paul Pierce (16.2), trailed only Pierce in steals, and continued to prove as spectacularly athletic as any young backcourt performer in the league. If there was a disappointing area of play in Mercer's rookie campaign it was a dismal 3 for 28 performance in launching shots from behind the three-point arc; and he hadn't improved all that much (5 for 27) as a second-year performer. Perhaps only an improvement in outside shooting is now needed to make Ron Mercer one of the NBA's most talented backcourt performers for years to come.

Willie Naulls
(1963-66)

The Celtics experienced a solid dose of good fortune when they picked up veteran Willie Naulls from the San Francisco Warriors at the outset of the 1963-64 season in a minor cash transaction. Naulls—a 6-6 forward who starred for John Wooden at UCLA a decade before the Bruins were regular NCAA tournament winners—would pay big dividends over the next three seasons as a solid 10-point scorer and key reserve who shot 80% from the free throw stripe and above 40% from the floor. In his middle year in Boston (1964-65) he even served a spell as a frontcourt starter alongside Heinsohn. But the payoff was far greater for Naulls himself. After a very successful but unrewarded stint with some exceptionally poor New York Knicks teams

at the outset of his career, Naulls would suddenly become the right man in the right place, as three Boston seasons turned into three easy championship rings.

From 1960 to 1962 Naulls regularly scored above 20 (seventh in the league two years running) for New York teams that wallowed in the Eastern Division basement with victory totals that largely corresponded to his own personal nightly point scoring: Naulls averaged 23 points for the stretch

Willie Naulls arrived in Boston in the twilight of a solid pro career and walked off with championship rings—to which he himself contributed mightily—in each of his final three league seasons.

while Knicks teams coached by Fuzzy Levane, Carl Braun and Eddie Donovan averaged but 25 wins. Earlier at UCLA he had been Wooden's first genuine star on teams that won 18, 21 and 22 games yet only once made the NCAA postseason party, and then was immediately eliminated by the championship-bound USF Dons with Bill Russell. Willie Naulls had played at both UCLA for Wooden and at Madison Square Garden with the Knicks a handful of seasons too early to enjoy the emotional highs of being with a big-time winner. But in Boston at the end of his career his timing was impeccable. While ending his career on the last three Auerbach-coached Boston rosters, the record for Naulls was a perfect three world titles in but three tries. Basketball doesn't boast a better poster boy anywhere in its long history for the Pollyanna motto that all good things eventually come to those who patiently wait.

Don Nelson
(1965-76)

Don Nelson was Red Auerbach's biggest bargain, picked up off the waiver wires for a few bucks in 1965 (after a mediocre debut with the Chicago Zephyrs and Los Angeles Lakers) and hanging around for eleven productive seasons as one of the most reliable clutch performers on the league's yearly best all-around team. Auerbach made a fistful of player moves over the years that had "genius" written all over them. Perhaps only those involving Russell, Bird, Parish and McHale were any more astute or profitable than the one involving Nelson.

Nelson might have never coached an NBA game (he

The perpetual bridesmaid Los Angeles Lakers earned part of the blame for their own fate in the mid-sixties when they let rugged Don Nelson escape to Boston by placing the future playoff hero on unconditional waivers.

ranks 7th in all-time victories, sandwiched between Larry Brown and Jack Ramsay) and he would still stand among the pro game's most memorable figures. As a player with Auerbach's Boston Celtics the Iowa All-American never won many individual distinctions. He was never among the league's leaders in scoring or rebounding or shot blocking, he only averaged double figures as a scorer once in his first five seasons, he was only occasionally a starter, and he never made a league all-star team or All-NBA selection list. His one record-book distinction is that of leading the circuit in field goal percentage in his 13th and penultimate season. But there have not been many in league annals who were better role players and who contributed in one fashion or another to the winning of more championship banners. Nelson boasts five NBA championship rings as a player (1966, 1968, 1969, 1974, 1976) and he contributed heavily to every one of those Boston glory seasons. He was a deadly jump shooter and one of the most unflappable performers under the pressures of postseason play. Of the few individual distinctions Nelson did earn, one has overbearing significance—his number "19" is one of the 13 retired jerseys that long graced the rafters of legendary Boston Garden.

BOSTON

Andy Phillip
(1956-58)

When it comes to selecting ultimate examples of the perfect "team player" World War II-era collegiate All-American and early NBA journeyman Andy Phillip may have to stand at the top of almost any list. Phillip's earliest fame came as floor leader of the legendary University of Illinois "Whiz Kids" club which was the best in the nation at 17-1 in 1943 but disbanded before postseason tournament action so that all five starters could volunteer for military duty. The 6-3 versatile guard and forward set a Western Conference (Big Ten) scoring record for the first-place Illini as a sophomore, erased his own mark during the repeat championship year of 1943, and repeated his previous two All-American honors after returning from the war for his senior season in 1947. But his eleven pro seasons in the BAA and NBA with Chicago, Philadelphia, Fort Wayne and Boston were known more for quick defensive hands, agile passing, and fiery play as a tireless competitor than for big time scoring or individual stardom. He was twice a league leader in assists (with Philadelphia) and for times the league runner-up (twice with Chicago and twice with Fort Wayne). And it was Phillip and not Bob Cousy who in 1952 became the first NBA player to register more than 500 assists in a single season.

Two incidents in Phillip's career, however, are far better yardsticks of his esteemed value than any raw statistics. When the Chicago Stags franchise folded on the eve of the 1951 season three top Chicago players—Phillip, Max Zaslofsky and Bob Cousy—were placed in a special dispersal lottery involving New York, Philadelphia and Boston. All three clubs coveted Phillip and Boston was especially disappointed when Cousy's name rather than Phillip's came up under their banner. Five seasons later Auerbach talked Andy Phillip out of retirement, and when the aging playmaker joined the Celtics lineup as a top substitute his presence would have almost as much to do as anything else (including the arrival of rookies Bill Russell and Tom Heinsohn) with Boston winning its first NBA crown.

Celtics

Paul Pierce
(1999)

The current Boston braintrust is banking on Paul Pierce as a crucial piece of the puzzle in rebuilding the saging team fortunes that have characterized recent seasons. As the club's fourth overall top-ten draft pick of the past three seasons—alongside Antoine Walker (#6 in 1996),

Ron Mercer (#6 in 1997), and Chauncey Billips (#3 in 1997) who was shipped off to Toronto for point guard Kenny Anderson—Pierce was also Rick Pitino's second important draft day move, a not-so-risky follow-up to the 1997 choice of Ron Mercer. Pierce, like Mercer, demonstrated with a solid rookie campaign that the gamble to go with a potential-laden youngster leaving college early would quickly return huge dividends. As a raw rookie he was already the club's number three offensive weapon (Walker and Mercer shared the spotlight) and made the league's all-rookie first team despite being blitzed by Toronto's Vince Carter for coveted top-newcomer recognition. Pierce's demonstration that he was indeed as good as most scouts thought he was has provided the youth-laden Celtics with a frontcourt manned by Antoine Walker (already one of the best power forwards in the league), Pierce, and backup Walter McCarty, another Kentucky product who served his college apprenticeship under Pitino. It is a front wall that lacks the vital contributions of a potent center and it is a combo hardly likely to soon make Boston fans forget The Big Three of a few seasons back. Nonetheless Pierce and Walker are as potent a duo already as any young frontline tandem in the league.

BOSTON
Dino Radja
(1993-97)

Radja represented Boston's short-lived investment in the new-found European market which has become a fruitful font of raw talent for the 1990s-era NBA. The lanky forward-center out of Split, Croatia, peaked in his third campaign as the club's leading scorer, as well as the team pacesetter in minutes, blocks and rebounds. But this all came in the first of two seasons under M. L. Carr which marked the lowpoint in a half-century of franchise history. Radja had been drafted by Jan Volk and the Boston braintrust on the heels of his performances with the 1988 Olympic silver-medal-winning Yugoslavian national team. His original Celtics contract (signed in August 1989) allowed further play with the powerhouse Yugoslav national squad with Boston retaining his NBA rights. In 1992 he starred for the Croatian Olympic contingent in Barcelona alongside NBAers Drazen Petrovic, Stojko Vrankovic and Toni Kukoc, earning a second silver medal. After several campaigns in the Italian pro circuit he was resigned by Boston for a 1993-94 rookie NBA season that saw him averaging above 15 points and garnering second-team all-rookie honors.

The Celtics rebuilding plans under Rick Pitino did not hold a role for the 30-year-old veteran and Radja was eventually traded to Philadelphia in July 1997 for another veteran pair, Michael Cage and Clarence Weatherspoon. The deal quickly came apart, however, when Radja failed a

Philadelphia physical examination and Cage and Weatherspoon never joined the Boston ballclub. Radja eventually returned to Europe after signing on for the 1997-98 campaign with a club in the Greek professional league.

Celtics
Arnie Risen
(1955-58)

Today Arnie Risen is a forgotten figure, but in the early fifties he was a highly recognizable fixture for the first generation of NBA followers. He was also a constant thorn in the side of some of the 1940s and 1950s more prominent big men like George Mikan, Alex Grosa and Larry Foust. In thirteen seasons with the Indianapolis Jets (NBL), Rochester Royals and Boston Celtics the slim but extremely agile 6-9 pivotman collected two NBA titles (1951, Rochester and 1957, Boston), tallied 9,000 points and 5,000 rebounds (the true figure was likely one-third higher, since no rebounding numbers were recorded during his first five pro seasons), ranked high among league scorers and rebounders in his earliest seasons, and also proved an able bench player with Boston during his final three campaigns.

Perhaps only Mikan, Neil Johnston, Ed Macauley and Alex Groza were more polished at the bucket position during the NBA's first half-dozen seasons than was the one-time Ohio State star. Risen's undisputed career season came with Rochester in the final winter of the BAA (1949) when the rock-solid if wiry beanpole paced the circuit in field goal percentage, trailed only Mikan, Fulks and Max Zaslofsky in overall scoring, shouldered much of his team's rebounding responsibilities (though no official league statistics were yet being kept in this category), and was voted second-team all-league center behind the incomparable George Mikan. Risen's scoring average dipped below double figures for the first time in eleven pro campaigns during his first season with Boston, yet he nonetheless played a crucial role in the season's early weeks by holding down the center post (along with fellow veteran Jack Nichols and versatile rookie Tom Heinsohn) until Auerbach's prize recruit, Bill Russell, belatedly returned from a leave of absence for Olympic duty. It was that same season that the recent Naismith Hall of Fame inductee would also earn his second NBA championship ring.

BOSTON
Rick Robey
(1978-83)

If Rick Robey made no other contribution to the Boston Celtics cause he might still be remembered as the tempting trade bait that pried future hall-of-famer Dennis Johnson away from the Phoenix Suns. But of course 6-10

Rick Robey's career strangley paralleled that of Ed Macauley decades earlier, first as a solid frontcourt performer and then as the player indirectly responsible for an upswing in ballclub fortunes when he was traded away for the invaluable Dennis Johnson.

widebodied Robey did contribute in Boston in other ways as well, logging five productive seasons with occasional flashes of almost-brilliant pivot play. The muscular giant out of Kentucky averaged double figures (12.4 and 11.5) in two initial campaigns as backup to a fading Dave Cowens, and those two seasons remain the zenith of his NBA journey.

Robey continued as a solid role player during Larry Bird's earliest years on the scene and even became Bird's closest confidant on the ballclub. But his games and minutes dropped significantly by his final Celtics season in 1983 and the handwriting was on the wall that the Kentucky All-American's days in Beantown were limited. As a durable post player Robey displayed two rare features to his game: he was ambidextrous and shot equally well with either hand, and he loved to run the floor, displaying surprising alacrity for his size. Once McHale arrived on the scene Robey's value (and thus related playing time) slid and his stock tumbled accordingly. But he was still enough of a prize in 1983 for Phoenix to pull the trigger on a deal that brought the remarkable Dennis Johnson into the Boston fold and nudged Bird and company closer to yet another world championship.

Ed Sadowski
(1947-48)

When underscoring the relentless emphasis on team play that has always characterized Boston teams from the earliest Red Auerbach seasons down to the final campaigns of the Larry Bird era, it is often repeated that the Celtics have never boasted an individual NBA scoring champion. While this is true enough, there have been some tantalizing near misses that have threatened to nullify the boasting point, and most of them (despite a couple of high finishes by Bird) came in the early franchise years. Cousy was third thrice (1952, 1953 1955) and runnerup on a fourth occasion (1954); in 1953 the Boston playmaker trailed league pacesetter Neil Johnston of Philadelphia by only 2.5 ppg. But the closest Boston sharpshooter to the top of the pack was one-year center Ed Sadowski way back in the ballclub's second season. During that 1947-48 BAA campaign the bulky 6-5 center (a giant in his day) trailed Max Zaslofsky of Chicago by a mere 1.6 per game.

Sadowski enjoyed several productive offensive campaigns during a seven-year pre- and post-war pro career that covered both the BAA and the National Basketball League. His 16.5 average with Toronto and Cleveland in the inaugural BAA campaign was again the second loftiest mark in the circuit. Two years later with the Philadelphia Warriors the much-traveled center outpointed everyone in the league except Mikan, Zaslofsky, Arnie Risen and his own teammate Joe Fulks. And these averages in the mid and upper teens were earned in an era when entire ballclubs usually averaged in the mid or low seventies.

Charlie Scott
(1975-78)

As an eleven-year pro star in two leagues Charlie Scott rang up five seasons of 25 ppg. (or better) scoring and also earned one significant record-book niche with the highest-ever single-season ABA mark (34.8 ppg. in 1972 with the Virginia Squires). But the pro achievements of this sweet-shooting guard never outdid the college legacy already on the ledgers. Charlie Scott was, for one thing, the final noteworthy link of a '50s and '60s tradition of North Carolina-bound New York City playground imports—a potent pipline that stretched from Lennie Rosenbluth to Larry Brown to Billy Cunningham and beyond.

This particular 6-5 leaper from the Big Apple was a heavy-duty scorer who paced the ACC (27.1ppg.) during his senior season, after working his way up from eighth slot (17.6) as a sophomore to fifth (22.3) as a junior. But he was also an anchor on the Larry Miller-led Carolina team which stretched its string of NCAA Final Four appearances to

Charlie Scott contributed heavily to a 1976 NBA title in Boston, yet it was a final triumph largely overshadowed by the brilliance of his earlier play as a collegian at North Carolina and a high-scoring pro in the rival ABA.

three straight during Scott's first two seasons on the squad. While it was Scott's senior season that posted the biggest individual numbers, it was his junior year that brought the most memorable team results: 12-2 in the ACC, fourth in the year-end AP national poll and an appearance in the Final Four, a 27-5 overall record during Dean Smith's eighth season on the job. It was the postseason ACC shootout of that year, in fact, which brought Charlie Scott's supreme hour as a collegiate cager. In one of Carolina's best-ever comebacks, Scott poured home 40 points against Duke, rallying the Dean Smith forces from a nine-point halftime deficit to an 11-point championship victory.

Charlie Scott's high-firepower ABA debut was a hard act to follow, and one he chased without equal success for the remaining nine seasons of his pro career. There were another three seasons of potent offense in Phoenix but by the time he came to Boston his value had been reshaped as a role player, a switch in assignments that he for the most part handled with great professional poise and skill. In Boston he will most likely be best remembered for the two blockbuster trades in which he was involved, the one that brought Paul Silas to Boston in 1972 (for the NBA rights to Scott who was still playing in the ABA), and the one in which he himself was acquired for a young Paul Westphal. The Scott-Westphal deal was a less clearcut gain in Boston. But Charlie Scott did contribute mightily to a 1976 Boston championship that culminated in a hard fought victory over the very team that had only recently shipped him over the Auerbach's crew.

Brian Shaw
(1988-91)

A Pacific Coast Athletic Association 1988 player of the year for the University of California at Santa Barbara, 6-6 guard Brian Shaw was the last of three straight ill-fated top Boston draft picks (Len Bias in 1986, Reggie Lewis in 1987, Shaw in 1988) that were intended to revive sagging franchise fortunes but seemed in the long haul only to

further compound the endless spate of 1990s Boston ballclub woes. While Bias's wrecked pro career was immediate in its impact and Reggie Lewis's heart-break a bit longer in coming, Shaw's failures in Boston were a rapid but not overnight affair. He was a second-team All-Rookie performer in his debut season, and after his acrimonious departure to the Italian League for his second pro season, he did return to rank in the NBA's top fifteen in assists during his second and best Boston year. After a hamstring injury kept him on the sideline for the first month of his third NBA campaign, however, the Boston braintrust had already decided to cut their losses on a backcourt performer who

Both on and off the court, Brian Shaw may have been Boston's biggest disappointment of the past dozen seasons. The top draft pick was outspokenly unhappy in Boston Garden and contributed only sporadically in his two brief Boston sojourns.

never seemed to be cut in the old-style "team-first" Boston Celtics mold.

Shaw's potential was not hard to assess at the time he was drafted into the pro ranks: he provided size and rebounding skills in the backcourt and was versatile enough to play three positions—point guard, off-guard and forward. But it didn't take long for his weakness to show up in the Boston lineup. Jan Volk and company had speculated that Shaw's physical talents would show up in much-needed defensive play, but he quickly proved both incapable and unwilling as a pro defender. The problem was seemingly compounded when Brian Shaw's value on offense also sagged when he proved an inconsistent shooter (a glaring weakness in any half-court game) and one of the least creative among the league's ballhandling guards.

Brian Shaw will inevitably be remembered as a malcontent in Boston—at the worst—and an exemplary case of unfulfilled potential—at the best. Plucked as the top franchise pick in the 1988 draft (number 24 overall), expected to team for years in the backcourt with the previous year's draft plum Reggie Lewis, valued as a key piece of the franchise rebuilding puzzle, and thought highly enough of to trigger the peddling of star guard Danny Ainge, Shaw played only a single season before bailing out of his contract and escaping to the Italian League after an acrimonious dispute about higher compensation. Though forced by a Boston law court to return to his Celtics contract a season later, Shaw would log only another season and a half in Boston before being dealt off to Miami for yet another guard with a reputation for sometimes moody play, Sherman Douglas.

BOSTON
Jerry Sichting
(1985-88)

Red Auerbach has not been the only one making bold and productive front office moves to constantly retool the Boston championship machine. GM Jan Volk engineered a pair of off-season deals in the summer of 1985 which paid rich dividends in the pursuit of a 16th (and so-far final) NBA title banner. The first was the free-agent signing of a veteran Bill Walton, who many had thought was already at career's end, a move coupled with a deal that peddled an aging Cornbread Maxwell to the Los Angeles Clippers.

Solid playmaker and hustling defender Jerry Sichting was one of the prize acquisitions brought on board during the mid-eighties by new GM Jan Volk.

Then in a less-heralded but almost as vital deal Volk also inked sharpshooting and icewater-veined free-agent guard Jerry Sichting as added bench insurance. Both Auerbach-like moves would contribute mightly to assembling a perfect cast of characters for still another anticipated championship run.

While Bird and McHale received valuable relief from both Walton (who also spelled Parish in the center slot) and Scott Wedman, Sichting played a similar backcourt role in spelling Dennis Johnson and Danny Ainge as the number three guard. Sichting would have one memorable moment etched in the public eye when he scuffled with giant Ralph Sampson during championship postseason action with Houston. But during the entire campaign and two that followed Jerry Sichting also provided dependable bench heroics that were molded squarely in the proud Celtics tradition.

Celtics
Larry Siegfried
(1963-70)

Almost completely lost in the dust bin of hoops history is the remarkable collegiate career of rock-steady understudy Larry Siegfried. Ohio State's Siegfried made a career out of playing in the shadows of John Havlicek and Jerry Lucas, and a handful of other Buckeye stars. He then repeated the stint at the professional level. Among basketball's endless list of important role players, however, none boasted any more awesome individual talents than did the guard who pocketed an NCAA championship with Ohio State and also collected several NBA rings with the Boston Celtics.

Siegfried had launched his schoolboy and collegiate hoops career as a rising star of the brightest magnitude; then suddenly this can't-miss prime-time player was relegated to an unfamiliar and uncomfortable slot as backstage role player. Unlike most spoiled superstars of the modern era, however, Siegfried adjusted quite admirably to his new diminished stature. An immensely talented Ohio schoolboy star, Siegfried had averaged a thunderous 38 per game during his final high school season; as a Buckeye sophomore he maintained his spot as scoring front-runner pacing the 11-11 1958-59 OSU team with a 19.6 average. Then sophomores Lucas and Havlicek suddenly arrived on the scene, and while the OSU team soared, Siegfried was just as suddenly forced out of the limelight.

It was a far different era, of course, and there was no whining from Siegfried about lost scoring chances and also no threats of transfer to another program. He would later admit that the new role as caddy to Lucas and Havlicek did not suit him at all well. Yet through it all he would nonetheless quietly accept his fate and continue to contribute more than adequately to the endless (and undoubtedly

During seven productive seasons Ohio State alumnus Larry Siegfried came to personify the very essence of the dedicated Boston Celtics role player—sacrificing his body for loose balls and his substantial offensive skills for more valued defensive tenacity.

Rebounding paragon Paul Silas followed Frank Ramsey and John Havlicek and preceded Kevin McHale and Bill Walton in perfecting a unique Boston phenomenon known as the Celtics' sixth man weapon.

consoling) team victories. Siegfried was the second leading pointmaker (13.3) in the balanced championship lineup of 1960; as a senior he was again the number two scorer (15.2) behind Lucas. And down the road there would still be a credible pro career, though one that also extended Siegfried's destined role in the supporting cast (as a member of seven editions of the "dynasty" Boston Celtics teams of the 1960s) and deep in the shadow of teammate John Havlicek.

Larry Siegfried was destined to be that type of semi-important player who always remains a key cog in the team wheel yet nonetheless never quite manages to emerge as the blustery hero who can enjoy center stage. His career might thus seem laced with underachievement by some—especially by today's NBA fans and players nurtured on the notion of front row celebrity—but one NCAA championship trophy and five NBA championship rings were hardly insignificant compensations.

BOSTON
Paul Silas
(1972-76)

Paul Silas earned his lasting place in NBA annals as one of the sport's most tenacious rebounders. He also etched his name forever in the collective memories of Boston partisans as one of the Celtics' most innovative sixth men. In fact, when Silas inherited the position under Tom Heinsohn in 1972 he put a distinctively new spin on the role already immortalized by Ramsey and Havlicek. The former pair were scorers in their top-sub roles; Silas came off the bench to control the backboards and pick up vital caroms rather than precious points.

Long before Dennis Rodman made a professional career out of monomaniacal focus on pursuing rebounds to the exclusion of more celebrated offensive (i.e. scoring) play, Paul Silas had built a solid league-wide reputation for precisely the same one-dimensional talent. Over sixteen seasons the Phoenix, Boston and Seattle star (he also played in St. Louis, Atlanta and Denver) logged 1,250 games and 12,000 points, but also posted almost an identical number of rebounds. Silas was in fact one of the few pros in history actually to accumulate more rebounds snagged (12,357, 9.9 rpg) than points scored (11,782, 9.4 ppg). Silas's rebounding totals of course do not stack up with the giants of the art like Chamberlain, Russell, Abdul-Jabbar or Elvin Hayes, to mention but four of the dozen or so who far outdistanced his career totals. He never paced the league in this category, though he did crack the top five in 1976 and did average double figures seven years running in the decade of the 1970s. But there was never much doubt what Silas's roll on the floor was, especially in Boston (1973-76) where he converted the team's famed sixth-man slot from that of heavy-artillery scorer (Frank Ramsey and John Havlicek) to efficient board sweeper. Silas's most memorable niche as a rebounder, however, had already been earned as a collegian, where at Creighton in the early sixties (1962-63) he earned special stature as one of but seven athletes ever to complete a collegiate career with both scoring and rebounding averages lodged above twenty.

Tom Thacker
(1967-68)

One of basketball's best-known trivia questions features the journeyman who collected championships with remarkable ease as both a collegiate and pro player and yet rarely grabbed any frontpage headlines on his own. Tom Thacker was a versatile 6-2 guard who managed to hang around for seven pro seasons, three in Cincinnati, one with the Boston Celtics, and three more with the ABA Indiana Pacers. In only one of those campaigns, however—with Indiana in 1970—did Thacker manage to log as many as 70 games and post as many as 1000 minutes of floor time. Only once—during only 18 games with Indiana the previous season—did his scoring average soar above five points per game.

Yet if Tom Thacker was never the recipient of much playing time, he was nonetheless a genius when it came to impeccable timing. Thacker's most active season in Indianapolis coincided with the Pacer's first ABA championship victory. One year in Boston also translated into a spot on an NBA championship roster as part of the penultimate chapter of the Celtics' thirteen-year dynasty run. As a starting forward and double-figure scorer on all three Cincinnati Bearcat Final Four teams of the early sixties the fortune-blessed cager also picked up a pair of NCAA title trophies. This remarkable string of improbable victories would make Tom Thacker the sole player in history who could boast NBA, ABA and NCAA championship credentials.

John Thompson
(1964-66)

A one-time NBA backup center for the mid-sixties Boston Celtics lost in the shadows of Bill Russell, John Thompson has emerged from those shadows in recent decades to build one of the country's most successful college cage programs and also to construct one of its largest individual collegiate coaching legends. It is a legend and a ledger which includes 600-plus victories, 18 seasons of 20-plus victories, three national coach-of-the-year selections, one NCAA championship and two additional heartbreaking near-misses, a half-dozen Big East Conference tournament championships, and even an Olympic Games head coaching assignment.

In the process Thompson has followed in Russell's footsteps, always mixing basketball achievement with outspoken racial crusading which has impressed a majority of fans (as did Russell's) as being unnecessarily devisive and unwisely confrontational. Thompson's Georgetown Univer-

John Thompson once lived in the shadows of Bill Russell as a journeyman professional ballplayer before he stepped fully into the limelight as a trailblazing collegiate coach at Georgetown University.

sity teams (especially those featuring superstar centers Patrick Ewing, Dikembe Mutombo, and Alonzo Mourning) have often won games at record levels; have usually stood near the top of one of the nation's powerhouse conferences; have produced a bevy of NBA players including superstars Ewing, Mutombo and Mourning; and have featured four Final Four appearances and one thrilling national championship. Yet Thompson's most notorious moments—the one's burned in the public eye—involve either boycotts or protests or tirades in the name of battling perceived racism. And there are also the inconsistencies of a coach who often rails at others for exploiting black athletes while at the same time accepting a hefty $200,000 fee from Nike in exchange for the company's logo on Georgetown uniforms, or who boasts of the graduation rate (98%) of his ballpayers while at the same time admitting academically unprepared athletes (like Michael Graham or John Turner in recent seasons) and then bouncing them from his program at the first hint of classroom difficulties. If there is any difference in the often brusque behavior of John Thompson and the parallel performances of Indiana's legendary Bobby Knight it has seemingly been only that the self-serving actions of the former are usually mollified by a better (or at least more identifiable) external social or political cause.

But Thompson's playing career was not all shadows and bouts of playing second fiddle; and his coaching career has contained much that is positive and unparalleled, despite the sometimes thick veneer of controversy. His final two seasons at Providence College under Coach Joe Mullaney brought an NIT title (junior year), a pair of top-twenty rankings and 20-win campaigns, and also a measure of individual stardom as one of the nation's field goal percentage leaders (seventh, senior year). The 6-10, 230-pound pivot man was highly enough regarded to be plucked by Boston in the third round of the college draft (25th overall), on the heels of selections of Mel Counts (7th) and Ron Bonham (16th). Two years as Russell's backup resulted in limited NBA playing time (64 games one season and 10 the next) and miniscule scoring and rebounding (less than four per game in each category). But two years on the Boston bench did mean a perfect two-for-two when it came to collecting championship rings.

As a coach at Georgetown (he stepped down early in his 27th campaign in December 1998) Thompson won at one of the most proficient rates of all time (above 70% for his first 25 seasons) and was three times a national coach of the year (USBWA in 1982, NABC in 1985, UPI in 1987). But his biggest contribution may well have been his molding of all-time Georgetown great Patrick Ewing in the early eighties, eventually one of the closest approximations to Thompson's Boston teammate Russell at the defensive end of the floor during the modern-era NBA. Not only was Ewing John Thompson's most successful project but also his central key to coaching fame. All three of the supercoach's NCAA Final Fours came with Ewing in his lineup, as did his one national championship and two of his three national coach-of-the-year trophies. Thompson the coach rode the coattails of Patrick Ewing during the pinnacle of his long mentoring career just as he had earlier ridden the coattails of Bill Russell during his brief NBA playing career.

Antoine Walker
(1996-99)

An immensely talented Antoine Walker was the centerpiece for Rick Pitino's first national championship team at Kentucky back in 1996, and a handful of seasons later Pitino harbors hopes that the same phenom will play a similar role in a revived lineup of long-dormant Boston Celtics. At 6-9 and 250 pounds Walker is perhaps as physically talented as any man his size in today's NBA, a player so gifted that at times it appears that the pro game's many individual oncourt demands are hardly a serious challenge for him. But given the ardor of Boston partisans and the long drought they have suffered since The Big Three of Bird, Parish and McHale hoisted the final NBA banner in Beantown, Walker is also the young superstar with the NBA's largest and most persistent monkey on his back. In short, Bostonians are expecting Antoine Walker to

perform miracles and they are not willing to wait very long to see results that are spelled out with a return to postseason championship play. Without a highpowered NBA center of the type that Bird and McHale played alongside of, the expectations of course remain shockingly unrealistic.

Pitino nonetheless holds out hope that Walker will indeed be able to work a miraculous transformation in Boston. In the coach's estimation, it is just a matter of going about business in the correct fashion. "He doesn't always use the right methods right now," his college and current pro coach has claimed in recent interviews, "but he has great leadership qualities." In Pitino's view Walker's emotion-laden game needs only the proper touch of discipline. Walker of course faces perhaps the most severe test ever laid before a budding Celtics star. He arrived at the lowest possible moment in franchise history when he was drafted on the heels of the worst season record-wise in ballclub annals. And he plainly has far less supporting cast than a Cousy, Russell, Havlicek, Cowens or Bird ever had to work with in the rebuilding and re-energizing effort.

Walker did nonetheless achieve immediate rapport with Boston fans, despite the runaway expectations of his rookie season. Quite a rookie season it was, one that displayed enough talent and achievement to keep at least part of the old guard glued to their seats in the new Fleet Center. And it was the presence of Walker as a foundation to build a team upon that had more than just a little to do with landing Pitino for the coaching job the following season. Slowly the pieces are now being put around the athletic and high-scoring forward, especially with the additions of Paul Pierce and Ron Mercer to supplement the Boston front wall. So if the jury is still out on Antoine Walker in Boston and elsewhere around the NBA, at least it is a jury that is still in the main favorably disposed toward remaining patient with a budding superstar, as least for a small handful of additional unfolding and potential-laden seasons.

Bill Walton
(1985-87)

If there is not widespread accord concerning the two or three greatest players of college basketball history (my own vote would be cast for either Oscar Robertson, Lew Alcindor or Tom Gola, or perhaps even Bill Russell) there is nevertheless fairly wide agreement about the two or three best-ever teams. Two invincible outfits in Westwood built around Lew Alcindor and Bill Walton, plus the San Francisco University juggernaut anchored by Russell and directed from the backcourt by K. C. Jones.

Walton's team didn't quite live up to impossible expectations as well as the other two, capturing but two NCAA titles instead of the universally anticipated three,

If Bill Walton's brilliant collegiate career at UCLA turned largely to unfulfilled promise in the professional ranks, there were nonetheless numerous highlight moments and sufficient championship glories to be savored in both Portland and Boston.

also hauled down 13 rebounds in UCLA's almost effortless 87-66 championship romp.

While Walton and his team stumbled for a rare moment at the end of his final UCLA season, it was on the pro circuit that the often eccentric redhead's career seemed to come apart at the seams. Foot injuries that would plague the remainder of his uneven career would ruin a much-anticipated rookie season in Portland by limiting the top draft pick to 35 games and a 12.8 scoring average. An alternative lifestyle and anti-establishment attitude, both carried over from UCLA years, added to the aura of disappointment. Yet despite the slow start there were several marvelous seasons with the Portland Trail Blazers that displayed the brief domination that had been expected from Bill Walton. That honeymoon period lasted long enough for a spectacular championship season in 1977, in which the versatile Portland center topped the league in both rebounding and shotblocking. As a hub of Jack Ramsay's patterned offense Walton also logged one of his two 18-plus scoring averages (the other coming during an MVP campaign which followed in 1978). Then renewed injuries once more intervened and wiped out the brilliant future that might well have been.

There would be a few lesser milestones left along the way and the biggest of these was the 1986 season in which Boston won a championship largely because a veteran Bill Walton provided invaluable bench strength to supplement the powerful Celtics front line of McHale, Parish and Bird. But Walton's NBA career in the end would largely remain a painful legacy of unfilled promise and vacuous dreams of championships unwon and individual milestones unclaimed. So large was the legend surrounding the 1977 championship season in Portland, however, and so weighty was the image of Wooden's former problem child at his occasional best, that Bill Walton was found among the privileged honorees when the league's "50 Greatest" were nominated to commemorate the NBA Golden Anniversary season.

The college phenom who was once apparently destined to emerge as one of the best two or three centers in NBA history in the end had to settle for far less during his limited seasons on the pro circuit—one marvelous championship campaign and a follow-up award-studded curtain-call season in Portland during 1977 and 1978, and an equally productive one-year sixth-man stint in tradition-rich Boston a decade later.

and winning only 86 of 90 games, two worse than Alcindor's talented group (at 88-2). But the second great Wooden dynasty ballclub built around a single dominant player did post the longest winning skein (88 games) in college history, and if Walton was not the most dominant collegiate center ever to dunk basketballs then he misses the mark by preciously little. Walton was a three-time national player of the year while Alcindor only reigned twice (being edged out one season by Elvin Hayes); this seems adequately to balance the fact that Alcindor captured three NCAA Final Four MVPs while Walton garnered only two (losing both the individual trophy and the national title to David Thompson in 1974). And as dominant as Alcindor was for three seasons and Russell was for two, no one ever put on a championship performance that could rank with the one Walton authored as a curtain call to his junior season. It was in that memorable game against Memphis State that Walton dominated from opening tap to final horn, drilling 21 of his 22 field-goal attempts (most from close range) and adding a pair of free throws for a championship-game record 44 points. The incomparable redhead

Paul Westphal
(1972-75)

At one point in his career Paul Westphal was considered the best at his backcourt playmaking position to be found anywhere in the entire NBA. An electrifying guard out of the University of Southern California, Westphal had dulled campus memories of former Trojan great Bill Sharman and had also become a career 1,000-point scorer, although he never earned All-American honors or broke any important school offensive records. Entering the pros as a 1972 first-round pick of the Boston Celtics, Westphal quickly launched a red-letter NBA career that easily outstripped his moderate collegiate credentials.

Sharman's USC protégé was not destined to remain in Boston long, however, even if a solid rookie campaign off the bench in 1972-73 contributed heavily to the league's best regular-season record and a still-standing franchise mark of 68 victories. Contract squabbles arose on the heals of the team's 1974 NBA title and Westphal was sent

Paul Westphal's single indelible moment in Boston Celtics history ironically came while wearing the uniform of the Phoenix Suns. And it was a moment that almost turned to nightmare for legions of Celtics fans.

packing to Phoenix in exchange for Charlie Scott (who himself had earlier been dealt to the Suns for Paul Silas, in one of Auerbach's most astute front office moves). The stage was thus set with the Westphal-Scott trade for a single great irony coloring the remainder of Paul Westphal's NBA career. Despite an early and unhappy departure from Boston Garden, Westphal would nonetheless now be fated to become a featured player in what may well be the most storied moment of Boston Celtics postseason history.

That moment came in 1976, during the three-overtime Boston Garden NBA Finals thriller which saw the Celtics outlast a never-say-die Phoenix ballclub (128-126) and thus turn the tide irrevocably toward a second league title in three years. The pivotal game five hung in the balance when

Westphal suddenly rose to the occasion to haunt his former team by scoring 9 of the Suns' final 11 points and fashioning a 95-all tie at the end of regulation play. Curtis Perry's jumper off a Westphal steal also gave the Suns a one-point lead in the final minute of the second overtime session. John Havlicek's own desperation shot next put the hometown team back in the driver's seat with only seconds left on the game clock. Amidst the pandemonium that followed Havlicek's successful heave, it was again the pesky Westphal who managed to call a time out which Phoenix no longer had, a brilliant ploy since although it permitted Jo Jo White to sink a technical free throw for a 112-110 Boston lead, it also allowed Phoenix one last half-court possession which would result in a memorable game-extending desperation bucket by Garfield Heard. Westphal's heroics were not enough in the end to salvage the series or even to rescue the crucial see-saw game. (Boston socked the game away on the strength of exceptional substitute play from little-used Glenn McDonald during the final extra session.) His brilliant time-out call would nonetheless be sufficient to secure his own lasting spot among the most memorable architects of indelible NBA postseason heroics.

BOSTON
Sidney Wicks
(1976-78)

Among the endless stream of star players graduated from John Wooden's UCLA dynasty teams of the sixties and early seventies, only Lew Alcindor can boast a more productive long-term NBA career than the one fashioned by 1970 Bruins stalwart Sidney Wicks. A starring role on three successive NCAA champions, two All-American selections, and national player-of-the-year and NCAA Final Four MVP honors might have been an impossible act to follow for most collegiate headliners. But the second overall 1971 draft pick of the Portland Trail Blazers maintained only a slightly diminished pace during ten NBA campaigns split between Portland, Boston (two seasons, 163 games, 14.2 scoring average) and San Diego.

The NBA ledger for Wicks included four 20-plus scoring averages (and a fifth only a shade below), 1972 rookie-of-the-year plaudits, and four All-Star Game selections, plus one of the highest NBA career scoring averages among graduates of John Wooden's all-star training grounds. Former Wooden-coached UCLA greats and their lifetime pro league scoring averages are as follows: Abdul-Jabbar (24.6), Marquis Johnson (20.1), Gail Goodrich (18.6), Keith Wilkes (17.7), **Sidney Wicks** (16.8), Willie Naulls (15.8), Lucius Allen (13.4), Bill Walton (13.3), Walt Hazzard (12.6), Curtis Rowe (11.6) Dave Meyers (11.2), Richard Washington (9.8), and Henry Bibby (8.6). On that august list are four former All-Americans who eventually

Four 20-plus scoring seasons in the NBA were never quite enough to remove the label of unfulfilled potential from the solid NBA career of UCLA All-American Sidney Wicks.

put on Boston Celtics uniforms for at least part of a productive NBA career. On this shorter list of Wooden trainees who also doubled as Boston alumni Sydney Wicks was the most productive pointmaker of the lot.

Dominique Wilkins
(1994-95)

Dominique Wilkins—one of basketball's biggest showpieces from the mid-eighties to mid-nineties—will hardly be remembered for his single late-career season in a Boston uniform. As the NBA's highest-scoring non-US-born athlete of all-time (he was born in Paris during his father's early-sixties military stint there) Wilkins added some further footnotes to his lengthy pro career during his temporary Boston stopover: the first Celtic since Ed Sadowski back in BAA days to lead the club in scoring during his only year on the roster, the hometown player who scored the final points in hallowed Boston Garden, and the loftest career scorer ever to pull on (however briefly) a Boston Celtics jersey. But 99.9% of Wilkins' overflowing resume of achievements were nonetheless logged while wearing rival colors.

Basketball's "Human Highlight Film" eventually evolved from the NBA's top-ranking acrobatic slam-

dunking sideshow into one of the premier offensive players of the modern epoch. Overcoming a severe late-career Achilles tendon injury which nearly ended his playing days back in 1992, Wilkins stormed back in altogether spectacular fashion. His burgeoning scoring totals eventually placed him tenth in career average (25.3) and also left him in the top ten for cumulative points (counting NBA games only), and with one or two more semi-productive seasons perhaps remaining, a 30,000-point career still seems within the realm of possibility. Wilkins' ironic legacy, nonetheless, seems more than anything to be the fact that he was the last NBA scoring champion (1986) before Michael Jordan took personal charge of the title throughout the remainder of the '80s and most of the '90s. But as with the cases of Oscar Robertson and Jerry West—both stuck playing alongside Wilt Chamberlain—had it not been for the presence of the NBA's most awesome point-maker ever, Wilkins himself today might well rank high up on the list for most individual scoring titles won.

For the better part of the 1980s the name Dominique Wilkins was synonymous with the Atlanta Hawks franchise; in more recent seasons "Nique" has been transformed into one of basketball's highest-priced journeymen. His career as franchise player in Atlanta ended suddenly in February of 1994 with a shocking trade to the lowly LA Clippers (for Danny Manning), an exchange which came immediately after he had arduously worked his way back to stardom from the severe Achilles rupture which had seriously threatened his career. Brief stops with the Clippers (where

While Dominique Wilkins made a major impact on the NBA record books during his decade in Atlanta, his single noteworthy Boston achievement was scoring the final historic basket in hallowed Boston Garden.

he played for less than two months) as well as the Celtics (where he signed on as a free agent the following July) were followed by a brief stopover in Europe. On the European circuit with Club Panathinaikos (Greece) he would win his first team championship—the men's European Cup—while also capturing tournament MVP honors.

And then it was back to the NBA for a near-final fling in San Antonio (1997) where an 18.2 scoring average at age 37 indicated that neither injury nor biological clock had yet altogether slowed the game's highest flyer. There was ultimately a brief stopover alongside brother Gerald Wilkins in Orlando (1999), where he added the final 100-plus points of his career and courted personal embarrassment by barely averaging five a game in limited duty. Through all this gypsy existence Wilkins continued his steady climb to higher and still higher levels in the record books, passing 26,000 career points and 1,000 games played, and approaching 10,000 field goals made.

Unfortunately much of this final handful of seasons was played in relative obscurity with basement NBA teams and thus only served to dull some of the luster of one of the most individually productive careers in league history. Eighties fans will long cherish an indelible image of Wilkins as a power-packed slam dunker (he twice won the All-Star Weekend Gatorade dunking contest) on equal par with Air Jordan and Julius Erving. Yet for all his flash and fame Wilkins was likely the most overlooked superstar of his own generation or any other. When the NBA announced its annointed list of fifty greatest all-time players in time for the Golden Anniversary season of 1997, it was arguably the name of Dominique Wilkins that was the most glaring omission from that august mythical roster. Shaquille O'Neal was there in the NBA's "big fifty" and so was Scottie Pippen, even though the former was equally without championship boasts and the later was more than 12,000 career points in the rears of the greatest Hawks offensive force since Bob Pettit.

Art "Hambone" Williams
(1970-74)

Among the quite considerable honor roll of Boston unsung heroes over the past four-plus decades, double-barreled threat Art "Hambone" Williams was one of the most productive and most memorable. Coach Heinsohn relished Williams running his up-tempo offense and forcing the ball down the throats of enemy defenders, and John Havlicek loved to run the floor with the one-time San Diego Rockets castoff who delivered the ball to the open man as well as any sure-passing guard in the league.

Williams never scored much (only once topping 5

For a brief span of seasons "Hambone" Williams knew few peers among the NBA's flashiest ballhandling playmakers.

ppg. for a full season) during his four Boston campaigns, and his assist numbers were never overwhelming either, only once reaching four per game during part-time play. Yet the 6-1 speedster out of Cal Poly proved an ideal third guard (1971-1974) behind the frontline duo of Jo Jo White and Don Chaney. Williams sandwiched his Boston stint (which included one championship ring) between two sojourns in San Diego, consisting of three seasons with the NBA Rockets and one swan song year with the ABA Conquistadores. And if he didn't stick around long he nonetheless left a glowing reputation in his wake, built as much as anything on his dependable defensive play as a hardnosed scrapper who could handle the opposition's toughest offensive backcourt threats and could also box considerably bigger frontcourt opponents off both the offensive and defensive boards. Hambone Williams ranked for a short span of five or six winters among the flashiest playmakers in the league, and he even developed into a pesky shooter for a spell while playing under Tommy Heinsohn's "if you have a shot, never be embarrassed to heave it up" philosophy.

BOSTON Celtics
B OSTON *Celtics*

CHAPTER V ────────────

Greatest Dynasty in American Sports History:
The Russell Era

"I still hear people talk about the Celtics system. The Celtics system was Bill Russell." - Tom Heinsohn

Any case supporting Red Auerbach's top-ranking genius can almost certainly be built upon his acquisition of Bill Russell alone. With a single pre-season draft choice—one that most other coaches or general managers would never have made—Boston's Auerbach instantaneously changed the entire face of modern basketball history.

Pro basketball before Bill Russell's arrival in the NBA was a painfully slow and plodding affair that was played strictly on a horizontal plane. The sport's reigning prototypes were the long-range-shooting "outside" men (mostly diminutive guards) who lived by the two-handed set shot, and the rugged behemoths (centers) who camped under the hoop and launched short-ranged lobs or hooks. The jumpshot was still a truly novel weapon in the hands of a few agile forwards like Philadelphia Warriors teammates Paul Arizin and "Jumpin' Joe" Fulks and an occasional mobile guard like Boston's own Bill Sharman or journeyman Kenny Sailors. Almost all the emphasis of the George Mikan era was on raw power, particularly within a dozen feet of the bucket. But Bill Russell in his final college seasons had pioneered a revolutionary strategy based on agility and quickness, and Russell's game was always played exclusively up in the air.

And there was another feature of Bill Russell's style of basketball play that had first the college coaches and later his pro opponents scratching their heads in pure wonderment. Russell's approach was strictly defensive in emphasis. His specialty was blocking shots, not making them, and his very style of shot-blocking had never been practiced before. Russell stuffed opponents heaves back in their faces just

often enough to make them constantly wary of where he might be lurking somewhere behind on the floor. Russell knew that blocking every shot or even most shots by skilled pro gunners was nearly impossible, and so he picked his spots for maximum efficiency and impact—blocking an opponent's heave when the other team most need a bucket, or his own club could benefit from an emotional lift. He was the first true defensive intimidator the sport had ever seen.

And his blocks were not the showoff kind— grandstanding swats that sent balls careening into the seats—but rather a more pragmatic kind which kept the ball always in play, often directed it to teammates, and launched fast breaks in the opposite direction toward the enemy basket. Russell almost always blocked shots the instant after they left opponents' hands and

Red Auerbach

were still on the way up, thus avoiding any costly goaltending infractions. Often he recovered and controlled the blocked shot himself. With his new and infuriating method of defending, Russell actually ended (or at least shortened) several previously productive careers among opposing NBA pivot men—especially those immobile hook-shot specialists like Philadelphia's high-scoring Neil Johnston, a three-time NBA scoring champion (1953, 1954, 1955) who was never close to the same player after

Red Auerbach's former George Washington University coach Bill Reinhart had originally alerted the Boston coach to the potential greatness of San Francisco University All-American Bill Russell. Russel was not a talented scorer but he was the best rebounder and defender Reinhart had ever seen.

Russell entered the league. In the process he also rendered completely obsolete—almost overnight—the reigning textbook notion of what a pro center was supposed to be like.

One of the most familiar stories in NBA annals is of course the oft-told tale of how Auerbach pulled the several strings that allowed him to draft the stringbean University of San Francisco star in April of 1956. (Auerbach's previous top draft picks—with the exceptions of Frank Ramsey in 1953 and Jim Loscutoff in 1955—had hardly been noteworthy: Charlie Share rather than Bob Cousy in 1950, Ernie Barrett in 1951, Bill Stauffer in 1952, and Togo Palazzi in 1954. Only Share became an NBA starter—in St. Louis.) Boston already owned the third overall selection in the upcoming draft but would have to give up that pick in exchange for the territorial choice they were also guaranteed and which Auerbach was bent on using to select local Holy Cross All-American center Tom Heinsohn.

Auerbach had early on been alerted to Russell's potential greatness by his own former George Washington University mentor Bill Reinhart, godfather of the fast-break style of offensive attack which Auerbach had been slowly adapting to his own needs. It would be Russell's rebounding, shotblocking and overall defending—Auerbach had immediately grasped—that would make the fast-break strategy work to its fullest potential. But after leading USF to back-to-back national titles in 1955 and 1956 Bill Russell was hardly any longer much of a secret around NBA circles. The top two picks in the draft belonged to Rochester and St. Louis and it was rumored that the first ballclub could not afford Russell's probable contract demands (reported to be $25,000) while the latter was not likely to gamble on bringing him to a racist city like St. Louis. But without a high draft choice of his own Auerbach couldn't count on even being in the running for the services of such a unique ballplayer. Once Auerbach relinquished the number three draft slot for the privilege of taking Heinsohn, that selection would be handed over to the rebuilding Minneapolis Lakers, and the Lakers would certainly not let Russell escape their clutches.

The true mark of Auerbach's prevailing wisdom was not just the shrewd machinations to land Russell on draft day, but rather it was his acute interest in the seemingly one-dimensional player in the first place. No one is quite sure exactly when Auerbach first saw Russell perform, but whenever he did witness the phenom firsthand he apparently knew immediately that this future rookie was something very special. (It is documented that Red was on hand in Madison Square Garden in December 1955 when Russell's USF Dons dismantled Heinsohn's Holy Cross Crusaders during a Holiday Festival matchup; Auerbach had attended that game to scout the local phenom, Heinsohn, who was outpointed 24-12 by Russell, who also

garnered 22 rebounds. But the Boston mentor had also already been receiving numerous tips and scouting reports on the 6-9 west coast wunderkind two years earlier, not only from Reinhart but also from other friends and associates who numbered among them Cal coach Pete Newell and ex-Celtics Fred Scolari and Don Barksdale.) Boston was a high-scoring but nonetheless run-of-the-mill team that had suffered in Auerbach's first half-dozen seasons from an obvious lack of brute force in the middle that could shut down opponents when a key stop or a key rebound was needed. Boston's center was the slick-scoring 6-8 Ed Macauley who was a respectable pointmaker but an anemic defender and even weaker rebounder; even point-guard Bob Cousy had outdistanced Macauley in the rebounding department (by 70) the previous season. Watching Russell quickly convinced Auerbach that a ball retriever and defensive intimidator was essential, even if he played little or no offense himself. It was indeed a radical idea and it took a radical coaching mind to appreciate it fully.

Russell was a truly remarkable college player, but he was indisputably a college player who differed drastically from the accepted model of the day. Even Phil Woolpert who had launched Russell on the collegiate scene hadn't quite known what to make of him at first. The spindly and awkward converted lefthander showed little athletic promise in his first season or two at McClymonds High School in Oakland (alma mater of '50s-era baseball stars Frank Robinson, Vada Pinson and Curt Flood). Russell was even cut by the junior varsity football squad and later taken on only as a charity case by JV basketball coach George Powles. But along the way the youngster had already acquired a sound piece of early coaching advice. An uncle who had once failed a Negro league baseball tryout had convinced young William Felton Russell to develop left-handed shooting for versatility's sake, and also as a hedge against the athletic failures that he himself attributed to his exclusive righthandedness during his own shortlived baseball-playing past. It soon proved a chunk of advice very well-heeded.

Under the patient tutelage of Powles, Russell was able to mature quietly into a third-string backup as a junior and then a 6-6 unpolished starting center as a schoolboy senior. Few colleges took much notice, however, and only a lukewarm scouting report delivered to Woolpert by Hal DeJulio (an alumnus who kept track of local high school talent) over at the hometown Jesuit college induced even a modest scholarship offer. Russell would later be quoted as recalling that coach Woolpert didn't think much of his game at first, simply because he had never seen anyone block shots before. To Woolpert's undying credit, however, remains the startling fact that he didn't rush headlong into trying to convert his unorthodox recruit into just another oversized jumpshooter or hookshooter.

Woolpert learned fast (as did Russell) and soon figured

Auerbach, Cousy and Heinsohn somberly contemplate the road loss in St. Louis which tied the 1960 NBA Finals series at three apiece and thus forced a deciding game to determine the league title. Boston would successfully defend their championship banner two nights later back in Boston.

out how to polish his rare jewel. Here indeed was the perfect coach to exploit and unleash Russell's rare and novel talents. While defense was this coach's passion and his true forte, he also drilled his charges for hour upon hour on precise set offensive plays which had been fine-tuned to achieve perfection. More importantly, however, Woolpert recognized the unprecedented impact Russell might have if he were simply allowed to develop his native inclinations to camp near the bucket, ward off any and all rivals for missed shots, and reject enemy missiles by the dozens.

So special were Russell's talents that even conspiracies by collegiate rule-makers only seemed to widen his advantage over hapless opponents. NCAA legislators made one serious attempt to neutralize Woolpert's colossus at the outset of his senior campaign (on the eve of the first unblemished championship season in NCAA history) with a new rule widening the foul lane from 6 to 12 feet. It was a change aimed directly at Russell himself and yet one that

only seemed to give the imposing Dons center an extra advantage in the long haul. Celtics teammate Tom Heinsohn (quoted by Nelson George in *Elevating the Game*) would observe a few winters later that Russell's athletic skills were so immense that the super-talented pivotman had an effective rebounding range of 18 feet—nine feet on either side of the rim. "If he was nine feet off to one side of the basket," Heinsohn noted, "he could race over to pull down a rebound nine feet to the other side."

Yet for all the dominating play at USF during the winters of 1954-55 and 1955-56, the jury was still out on Russell among the pro scouts. Owner Ben Kerner in St. Louis wasn't alone in thinking that up against players like Pettit, Lovellette or Schayes the gangly collegiate star simply wouldn't be all that effective. (This may also in part have been rationalization, since Kerner was apparently fearful of the response a black superstar might garner in a racist town like St. Louis.) The new NBA emphasis on running and shooting and scoring once the 24-second shot clock came along seemed to mandate more versatile offensive players as the single desired model for pro-style success. Shot blockers who were not also talented shot makers seemed an unwarranted luxury.

Yet Auerbach clearly saw things differently. By the mid-fifties the Boston Celtics already had all the pieces of a contending ballclub firmly in place, save one. And that missing element was painfully proving, season-after-season, to be easily the most vital piece. Boston already had a solid and entertaining team and with their potent running game they were indisputably the most enjoyable bunch of NBAers for fans to watch. Cousy was a revolutionary impact player in his own right and had been busy during the past several years in inventing the prototype model for the modern-era point guard. Sharman was the best pull-up jump shooter in the circuit as well as the most efficient free-throw shooter. Ed Macauley was the most mobile and best-shooting pivot man in the business. With this triple threat offense Auerbach had fine-tuned the running style he had learned years earlier from Reinhart. In 1955, with an assist from the new shot clock rule, Boston had become the first team to average above the century mark (101.4 ppg.) for the entire 72-game season. Cousy, who had once been the league's best at utilizing his dribbling and ball handling skills for stalling and protecting leads in the "stall ball" pre-shot-clock era had now also become the best anywhere at pushing the ball up the floor relentlessly.

Cousy and Sharman were indisputably the league's best backcourt tandem (perhaps the best ever, before or since) and when they could get control of the ball Boston already ran the most devastating run-and-gun offense that anyone had yet seen. Remember here that the NBA in 1955 was just emerging from the pre-shot-clock-epoch dominated by George Mikan, a time when the essence of the game was a painfully slow attack based on plenty of pushing and shoving in the effort to get the biggest man on the floor as close to the bucket as possible. Within the new playing style Boston could outscore anyone, as they proved with their 101-plus scoring average in 1955. The trouble was that Boston was not only the first club ever to average triple figures on offense, but also the first to give up a like amount to its opponents. Even with their lofty point totals Boston was thus actually outscored for the season, yielding 101.5 per contest. And if Cousy and company could run like the wind toward the opposite hoop once they retrived the ball, the sad fact was that, with slender Ed Macauley manning the center slot, Auerbach's crew just didn't get hold of the ball anywhere near often enough.

"Easy Ed" Macauley is today a forgotten figure of Boston Celtics history. But there was a time early on when Macauley was as good an offensive player as there was to be found anywhere in the league. He often ran past his

counterparts as Boston pushed the ball down the floor and was frequently on the receiving end of Cousy's pinpoint fast-break passes. Macauley was one of the most talented scorers of the league's first decade and his talent was large enough to earn eventual hall-of-fame status. And of course there is also the vital role that Macauley would eventually play as the trade bait that soon sprung the blockbuster deal for Bill Russell.

Knowing how much Red Auerbach coveted Russell—though perhaps not quite sure precisely why—Hawks' owner Ben Kerner drove a hard deal during April's pre-draft maneuverings. Kerner and Auerbach were barely on speaking terms since Auerbach had quit as Kerner's Tri-Cities coach a half-dozen years earlier, after Kerner had pulled the triger on a trade not at all to his volatile coach's liking. Macauley was offered to Kerner in exchange for the St. Louis number two draft slot, one that might guarantee Russell for Boston. Macauley wished to return to his hometown (where his seriously ill son might receive expert medical care) and Kerner wished to have him as a team contributor and box office drawing card. After all, he would complement the rugged Bob Pettit perhaps better than Russell, who would most likely also not be well-received in St. Louis as a black athlete. Yet Kerner was no fool to be tricked out of maximizing his advantage. Sensing Auerbach's anxiousness to nab Russell, he demanded former Kentucky star Cliff Hagan as well, a star collegian of several seasons back whose rights Boston had held while he served out his military commitment. The price for Russell was thus to be coated with considerable irony. If the deal made Boston an immediate powerhouse outfit, it also cemented Kerner's own future teams. It would be Macauley (as both player and later head coach) and Hagan—as much as Pettit—who together carried St. Louis into year-end championship matches with Auerbach's team in four of the next five seasons.

More intriguing still were Boston's related dealings with owner Lester Harrison—himself a Naismith Hall of Famer—over in Rochester. Harrison likely could not have afforded Russell even if he drafted him. He also already had the league's best rebounder in a youngster named Maurice Stokes, 1955's top NBA rookie sensation. He was thus content to settle for Sihugo Green, a talented guard out of Duquesne, with his top pick in the upcoming college lottery. But there was still always the danger that Auerbach might unload his top scorer and one of his most promising rookies to Kerner and then see the whole scheme go up in smoke with Harrison's drafting of Bill Russell. Thus to sew things up in Boston's favor it would also be necessary for Walter Brown to intervene on Auerbach's behalf with his fellow owner and fellow league founder. Harrison clearly coveted a visit from the touring Ice Capades as an important annual revenue producer for his smalltown arena and

Whatever credit may be due Red Auerbach's innate coaching genius, it always seemed axiomatic that Boston won year-in and year-out largely because they owned the league's most unmatchable defensive force in Bill Russell.

had been having trouble landing the big money-making show. Brown, an original organizer of the touring event, thus hastily arranged to make certain that Harrison got his profitable ice show. In exchange Lester Harrison promised to leave Russell untouched for Auerbach.

The Boston draft day haul on April 30, 1956, turned out to be the most remarkable one-day bonanza in American sports history. Rome may not have been built in a single day, but Auerbach's Boston dynasty indisputably was. Heinsohn first joined the club as a bonus territorial choice. In addition to the traded St. Louis pick which guaranteed them Russell, Boston still had their own first-round selection to be utilized for Russell's USF teammate K. C. Jones. No other pro team has ever garnered three future hall of famers with the same day's drafting lottery. Russell, of course, was commited to an Olympic appearance in Australia, as was teammate Jones; and the latter athlete also faced a two-year army stint before he would be available to join Boston's roster. But Boston's and the league's fate had now been suddenly all but sealed.

Auerbach had to wait a brief spell to get his prize player into the fold. But once Russell joined the Boston Celtics he did so with an immediate and more than merely noticeable bang. While the prize recruit had been busy in Melbourne, Australia, leading the USA forces (a team that included teammate K. C. Jones from USF, Carl Cain from Iowa, and a remaining lineup of military and AAU stars) to a gold medal romp (their smallest victory margin was 30 points),

Boston had jumped out to a quick lead in the NBA race, even without their top draft choice in the lineup. The number two rookie, Heinsohn, had filled in some at center, along with veterans Arnie Risen and Jack Nichols, and the team had raced out to a 16-8 mark by mid-December. Russell's noteworthy debut came finally on December 22, ironically against Kerner's Hawks in a nationally televised weekend game, and featured 16 rebounds in 21 minutes of play, as well as a trio of blocks against all-star Bob Pettit during tight fourth-quarter action. Thus it took Bill Russell only one game to demonstrate that Auerbach had apparently been right on target in assessing the new rookie's unmatched defensive and rebounding potential. Even the players knew after that first outing that they had something special in their midst: Cousy remembers coming away from that St. Louis game flushed with the thought that the team was now finally on the verge of doing something big.

The first Boston run to a league title wasn't only a matter of having Russell in the center post, of course, though Russell was the main difference between this Boston club and the ones that had always worn bridesmaid's gear. But there was also potent rookie Tom Heinsohn to renovate Boston's on-court fortunes. Heinsohn duplicated Macauley's offensive production, was the club's best rebounder after Russell and Loscutoff, and earned league top-rookie honors. The improvement by year's end was only five games over a season earlier, but that meant a jump from

Rookie Tom Heinsohn battles Nats forward Dolph Schayes for a rebound in early-season 1957 action, while pioneering black star Earl Lloyd (#11) also awaits the carom.

six games behind (trailing Philadelphia in 1956) to six ahead (leading Syracuse in 1957) in the annual Eastern Division regular-season wars. Cousy (20.6, 8th in the league) and Sharman (21.1, 7th) were the big pointmakers as usual, but Heinsohn (16.2 ppg.) adequately filled the third slot in place of the departed Macauley. And in the postseason Heinsohn elevated his game yet another notch and then some and was—as much as Russell—the difference in turning a perennial also-ran into the new belle of the championship ball.

Boston's first NBA title victory was one of the most gut-wrenching of any of the championship runs that would soon become a regular Boston springtime fixture. Of the fifteen banners that eventually followed, few if any were earned with a more heart-stopping final game performance. The series with St. Louis—now itself bolstered in the starting lineup with Macauley and Hagan to supplement Pettit—plowed through a rugged seven games, with Hagan tipping in the clutch basket at the end of game 6 which sent the see-saw affair back to Boston for one final tense shootout. In Game 7 the usually reliable Cousy and Sharman both strangely went silent, hitting a dismal combined 5-for-40 between them from the floor. But rookie Russell dominated the boards with 32 caroms and 19 vital points. And above all it was the other rookie, Heinsohn, who carried the title-starved Celtics on his back most of the way. The league's top freshman netted 37 (and pulled in 23 boards) before fouling out in the final two minutes of a second heated overtime session.

Bob Cousy remains the only Celtic to twice capture MVP honors at the NBA mid-season All-Star Game. In 1958, Cousy would have to settle for the MVP runner-up slot and thus found himself congratulating Bob Pettit after the Hawks star forward walked off with the prestigious trophy.

AP/Wide World Photos

The tension near game's end almost reached the breaking point. Hawks forward Jack Coleman drove to the hoop for a pivotal score with less than a minute still on the clock when Russell not only blocked Coleman's heave but then sprinted the length of the floor for a basket of his own that put Boston on top by one. Heinsohn years later would still refer to Russell's game-saving play as the greatest single effort he had ever witnessed on a basketball court. Gloom then quickly settled over the Boston Garden crowd as Cousy uncharacteristically missed a key foul toss and

Sharman misfired on two close-range jumpers that could have overcome Pettit's game-tying free throws. The contest headed into an extra session deadlocked at 113 apiece.

Before heading to the bench with his fifth foul in the second overtime session, Heinsohn had continued his hero's role with three key buckets, including a twenty-foot jumper that left Boston nursing a 121-120 eyelash margin. A Frank Ramsey basket kept Boston on top at 124-123 with a half-minute remaining, and Loscutoff then seemingly iced the game 125-123 with a vital free throw when only one second remained on the clock. But in what would soon become a pattern to be repeated numerous times in the coming decade, a Boston championship victory seemingly required a final heart-stopping moment to be fully sanctioned. Player-coach Alex Hannum put the ball in play with a floorlength heave that careened off the Celtics backboard, a designed play which transpired perfectly with a carom into Pettit's waiting hands. Pettit's shot had to be rushed and slid off the front rim as uncontrolled bedlam finally broke loose for the first of many times in rapture-filled Boston Garden.

The rivalry with Kerner's Hawks would continue to simmer and at times even boil over during the subsequent half-dozen seasons. The Hawks would return for full revenge only a season later, during a campaign which temporaily (but only temporarily) disabused the notion of any budding Red Auerbach-led dynasty. The two powerhouse teams originally involved in the Russell draft deal might well have met five times running for the NBA title had it not been for the marvelous 1958-59 rookie season of nonpareil forward Elgin Baylor, who lead a rebuilding Lakers ballclub at the twilight of their Minneapolis years to a shocking upset of Pettit's vaunted Hawks in that year's Western Division finals. Then Pettit and company roared back for two more cracks at the suddenly invincible Boston team, which by the first seasons of the new decade was well launched on its already storybook dynasty run.

Two factors blocked the best efforts of Auerbach and Russell and Cousy and company to earn a second set of rings the first winter following their initial breakthrough NBA title. The sportworld's most worn cliché contends that the hardest task for any champion is to repeat, and it was a lesson quickly learned (but then as quickly discarded) up in Boston. Russell's injury in the playoff rematch with St. Louis a season later would be a prime factor in tipping the scales in another direction. Russell severely sprained an ankle while blocking a Pettit shot in the fateful third minute of the third championship series game; Boston's franchise player sat out the next two games (a nip-and-tuck victory for each side) and then contributed only eight points while hobbling around the court for twenty minutes of the finale. Loscutoff also went down with a severe knee injury only five games into the regular season and never suited up for postseason action. But equally crucial to the failed title defense would be Bob Pettit's own unmatched performance in the deciding game-six 1958 championship shootout.

Pettit's postseason encore in 1958 was one of the most memorable ever. And it was more than just the final game heroics, even if that outing was itself altogether without parallel. In regular season play the Hawks' powerful forward was runnerup to only Russell in rebounds (his third straight campaign ranking either first or second in that department) and trailed only Yardley and Schayes in scoring. (A season later Pettit easily outpaced the league's other scorers, picking up his second and final individual scoring crown in the final season before Wilt Chamberlain would take permanent possession of that role.) And throughout that entire long winter and springtime postseason which followed, Bob Pettit demonstrated time and again the dominance which made him perhaps the best forward of all-time, save only Larry Bird (who outdid him only in versatility) and Elgin Baylor (who was admittedly more athletic, even if not that much more potent as scorer and rebounder). While averaging nearly five and a half points less than the previous year during the first ten postseason contests, it suddenly all came together for Pettit in the final contest of the six-game championship series. With Russell absent for two games and hobbled and ineffective in the finale, the Boston frontline forces (also without Loscutoff) were no match for Bob Pettit, no matter what backcourt superiority Boston might have owned. And yet it took perhaps the most dominant final game individual display in NBA history for St. Louis to finally turn the trick against their Boston rivals.

The indefatigible Pettit was a two-time league MVP who was selected All-NBA first team ten times and second team once during his eleven-year career. But in the deciding Game 6 of the 1958 championship round Bob Pettit seemed—in retrospect from today's vantage point—to have been Chamberlain and Baylor and Michael Jordan all rolled into one. In the deciding game a season earlier, Pettit had played 56 of a possible 58 minutes, scored 39 points and

gathered 19 rebounds (tying Russell for game high), and also shot 14 for 34 in the losing double-overtime effort. But given another chance a season later Pettit would not be overmatched a second time. With Boston leading in the final quarter—despite the injury to Russell which limited him to playing less than half the contest on a still badly sprained ankle—Pettit exploded for 19 fourth-period points (including the 15-footer that clinched victory with 15 second remaining) to settle the issue. It was a record-breaking performance that topped Mikan's earlier standard of 47 points in a regulation-length postseason contest. And while the 50-point total was later surpassed on several occasions as a playoff highwater mark, never since has a more scintillating performance been turned in during a deciding NBA Finals game.

On the heels of the Hawks' revival and Pettit's new-found dominance, few could guess at the outset of the new decade just how potent the team up in Boston Garden was about to become. Especially given the appearance in the league of a new and unprecedented rookie named Wilt Chamberlain playing for arch-rival Philadelphia. And also the simultaneous arrival of a pair of hotshot guards named Robertson and West the following fall. Wilt and Oscar immediately began rewriting all the record books—the former with his first-year explosion of 37.6 ppg. to outdistance runnerup Jack Twyman by a half-dozen and Pettit's previous league record by even more, and the latter by consistently posting averages in the thirties while also ringing up double figures in both rebounding and assists. Jerry West also soon revived the transplanted Minneapolis Lakers out on the West Coast when the potent Elgin Baylor was slowed by endless injuries. But none of these new young turks could find the means to convert their teams into serious rivals for the constantly self-renewing Celtics juggernaut up in Boston.

A quiet addition to the Celtics roll call had arrived in the person of Sam Jones, acquired on the heels of the first championship with yet another shrewd Auerbach draft move. Jones was a slick-shooting but unheralded guard from tiny North Carolina College (a hot tip from former Celtic "Bones" McKinney), a player that seven other teams ignored in the April 1957 college lottery before Boston plucked him out of the pack as future backcourt insurance to supplement the aging Cousy and Sharman. The acquisition of K. C. Jones to fill out the backcourt contingent a season later (after his two-year military stint and a brief preseason flirtation with the NFL Los Angeles Rams as a linebacker) would mean that all the pieces of Auerbach's puzzle were finally firmly set in place. At least for the next handful of seasons at any rate—before the arduous business of constant replacement and replenishing would finally be inevitably at hand.

The Boston teams that took the floor between 1958

and 1963—with Cousy, Heinsohn, Ramsey and Russell always in the lineup, and Sharman, Sanders, The Jones Boys and Hondo Havlicek also contributing heavily—were perhaps the most dominant among the numerous power-house Boston units. This seems evident despite Bob Ryan's reasoned arguments for the 1985 and 1986 Bird-McHale-Parish squad as the best NBA unit ever. The won-lost record alone seems unequivo-cal here. Over the half-dozen year span the regular season mark for Cousy's gang was 286 wins out of 386 matches. And the champion-ships were uninterrupted, with the exception of Pettit's single dominant outing back in 1958, a lost opportunity that represents the only postseason party where Dame Fate (in the shape of Russell's postseason injury) was clearly sitting in the opponent's corner.

With the start of the 1958-59 campaign Auerbach and his troops were driven by the challenge to regain their lost throne. (There always seemed to be an external motivation: revenge and wounded pride in 1959, Cousy's recent retirement in 1964, Walter Brown's death in 1965, Auerbach's an-nounced upcoming retire-ment in 1966.) The result by year's end would be the first Finals sweep in league history. Baylor's stellar rookie performance—the best on record at that time—had garnered most of the year's headlines. Boston, back East, was so potent that they came out of the gates at 23-9 over the first two-and-a-half months and scored 173 in one game against Baylor's overmatched club. And as the playoffs heated up the big story was the shocking loss by the rival Hawks—clearly the best team out West—to the surprising Baylor-led Lakers, who had themselves finished the regular-season circuit six games under the breakeven point and 16 games off the Hawks' division-leading pace. The Celtics themselves barely escaped an unforeseen upset at the hands of an equally tough upstart team up in Syracuse: they trailed by 16 in the

APWide World Photos

Next to Bob Pettit, the biggest thorn in Boston's side throughout the 1960s was Minneapolis and LA Lakers nonpareil forward Elgin Baylor, and a more injury-free Baylor might well have spelled disaster for Auerbach's team during several sixties-era postseason shootouts.

final period of game 7 on their own floor, Russell fouled out in the final period of the deciding game, and only the fourth-quarter heroics of unheralded backup Gene Conley eventually saved the day and the season. But after the pair of semifinals matches (Boston-Syracuse, Minneapolis-St. Louis) involving rousing underdog performances, the NBA Finals were quite anticlimactic. Minneapolis, even with Baylor, had little firepower to match Boston's superb Cousy-and-Russell-led running game. Only one of the four Boston victories came by double figures, yet none of the four games was ever in serious doubt.

The plot thickened considerably a year later when giant Wilt Chamber-lain joined the league from the Harlem Globetrotters as a territorial pick for Eddie Gottlieb down in Philly. Wilt's immediate individual impact buried the still-fresh memories of Russell's earlier debut, as well as Baylor's only a season before. Chamberlain rewrote virtually all the scoring records in his first trip around the league and had every team scrambling to cope with the offensive force he now represented. And Boston and Russell now suddenly had a new serious challenger for bragging rights planted right smack in the middle of their own Eastern Division backyard.

For all Wilt's awesome numbers the best teams were still those built around Russell and Pettit and a championship rematch seemed almost inevitable as the postseason reopened. Boston had already picked up two key new additions in the final two seasons of the fifties to supplement the backcourt corps. With the arrival of Sam Jones (1958) and K. C. Jones (1959) Boston now had a pair of backups that could outstrip any other *starting* guard tandem in the league. It was this Boston team balance that paid huge dividends in the postseason which ended Chamberlain's rookie year. While Wilt concentrated all year on individual scoring to please an owner who

Graceful UCLA seven-footer Lew Alcindor was arguably the greatest college big man ever, and when Alcindor took his act to Milwaukee as the NBA's Kareem Abdul-Jabbar he would inherit Chamberlain's role as Boston's biggest championship obstacle.

the NBA scene—Oscar Roberton, Jerry West and the newly situated Los Angeles Lakers. But little had changed by year's end. Boston was once again easily the best of the pack. And for the second time in his career Russell was the league MVP, an honor he would now hold for the next three years running.

If Wilt had been largely unstoppable for his first two seasons—at least until playoff time rolled around—he would now seemingly enter another separate universe. Chamberlain's 1962 campaign was so spectacular in terms of its individual numbers as to literally defy proper description. Nothing had ever been seen like this before and nothing ever again would. And it was not just Wilt who rewrote the existing record books during this magical season. For 1961-62 was also the winter when professional basketball seemingly decided to throw the record books and even the definition of merely mortal performance straight out the window. Wilt averaged above 50 (fifty!) and even managed a previously unthinkable 100 in a single March 2nd game. Eight times he crossed the 56-point plateau and twelve more times he logged over 60. Twice he scored 70 or more. Oscar in turn averaged a triple-double (double figures in all three major offensive categories) and the feat went almost unnoticed in an era which paid small heed to rebounding and assists totals. Baylor played only on weekends (while completing his military obligations) but his 38.3 season's average (48 games) has since never been surpassed by anyone not named Wilt. And Chicago Zephyrs rookie center Walt Bellamy (31.6 ppg. and 19.0 rpg.) also enjoyed the most sensational debut-year ever, outside, of course, of Wilt's own rookie breakout two winters earlier.

But championships were then as now won by teams and not individuals, and Wilt and Oscar would thus have to once again take a back seat to Russell and Cousy when playoff action rolled around. The 1962 NBA Finals would mark the historic first-ever meeting of the greatest postseason rivals in league history. That series also set the tone for how the Boston-Los Angeles rivalry would inevitably always play itself out over the next couple of decades. It all came down to a dramatic final showdown game with two nearly even forces squaring off with everything on the line during a dramatic "one-game" season. And the deciding moment would unfold with one of the most memorable missed-shots in championship history. Frank Selvy, the man who was often unstoppable as a collegian at Furman, would unfortunately now etch his name into NBA history by missing the most crucial single shot of his entire basketball career. With West and Hundley tightly guarded in the final

wanted to fill empty seats in Philadelphia, his rookie campaign only proved in the end that basketball was still essentially a team-oriented game. (Cousy loved to comment in later years that Wilt never did figure out why there were four other guys out there on the floor with him.) At year's end Philadelphia's one-man gang couldn't match Boston's superior team play. And neither could the revived Hawks still featuring the potent and highly motivated Bob Pettit. Philadelphia offered little challenge to Russell's crew in the division finals series that was highlighted by Wilt injuring his hand during a scuffle with Heinsohn. Chamberlain's MVP season was only an afterthought by the time Boston repeated their title claim against St. Louis with a seventh-game blowout on the Boston Garden home floor.

The next goal was matching Mikan's Lakers with a three-peat and that was accomplished with relative ease by a 1961 team that Auerbach would one day call the best squad ever assembled. That team rolled to 57 wins in the division, then waltzed past Syracuse in the East and St. Louis in the West, losing only one contest in each postseason series. It was a season that brought three spectacular new names onto

Bob Cousy's final NBA season would prove to be one of the most memorable championship campaigns of the Auerbach coaching tenure.

became a colossal disappointment. The club won 18 fewer games than a season earlier and slumped to fourth in the five-team Western Division, leaving Chamberlain (for the only time in his 14-year career) on the sidelines at playoff time. It would all create a competitive void which took several more seasons to straighten out.

Bob Cousy's farewell season was one of the more memorable in Boston annals. Yet on the surface it was merely business as usual for Auerbach and his crew. Sharman had already departed a season earlier, and with The Jones Boys now shoring up the backcourt, Satch Sanders on hand with several seasons under his belt as a defense-minded front court reinforcement, and John Havlicek in camp as the latest crack rookie sensation, the first Auerbach-Russell team was beginning to segue into a new and largely transformed edition.

This was of course bad news for the league's other franchises which were apparently still doomed to keep chasing Boston for most of the remainder of the decade. Oscar Robertson and his Cincinnati Royals almost upset the apple cart when they replaced departed Philadelphia as Boston's substitute rival in the Eastern Division Finals. But once the Celtics climbed over that hurdle—winning in seven after trailing 2-1 early in the series—there was little to slow the championship momentum in still another anticlimactic final round. Cousy seized upon the rematch against Jerry West's Lakers as one final stage to celebrate the last glorious hurrah of a marvelous victory-strewn career. The season's finale was Game 6 in the Los Angeles Sports Arena, and Cousy returned from an early-game ankle sprain to quarterback the team down the stretch and dribble out the

seconds of a tie game, Selvy launched a jumper which rolled off the rim and allowed the Boston crew to escape into an overtime session in which Russell (with 30 points and 40 rebounds on the afternoon) again proved the decisive difference.

After the offensive explosions of 1961-62 the NBA landscape would be forever changed. If Wilt and Oscar had taken the sport and its statistical output straight into the stratosphere, Wilt's owners in Philadelphia would now take the game coast-to-coast as well. Gottlieb sold out to West Coast interests and his Warriors (charter league members back in 1946) were relocated to San Francisco with Wilt in tow. An immediate impact was the temporary suspension of the lusty Chamberlain-Russell Eastern Division rivalry over the course of the regular season. And with Wilt and the Warriors relocated to the opposite coast, what had been one of the league's most outstanding outfits now suddenly

Cousy and Russell celebrate a championship for the final time in the wake of the fifth NBA banner that capped Cousy's swan song 1963 season.

final seconds of a 112-109 thriller which extended the championship string to five straight.

After Cousy (in 1963) and Sharman (in 1961) had retired, Auerbach would waste little time in coming up with a new sage formula for keeping the championship fires burning annually. He still had Russell, of course, and that made it easy to tinker rather than contemplate anything resembling a complete overhaul. The gimmick now became finding veteran discards from around the league who still had serviceable mileage on their legs and who were hungry for the chance at a championship ring before career twilight and retirement inevitably set in. Baseballer Gene Conley had been the prototype when he had returned after a brief 1953 trial with the team and a subsequent half-dozen years away from basketball to provide a valued backup for Russell from 1959 through 1961. Then in the '60s it would be first Clyde Lovellette (1962-64), Willie Naulls (1963-66) and Don Nelson (1965-76) and later Wayne Embry (1966-68) and Bailey Howell (1966-70) who filled in heroically. Lovellette replaced Conley as primary reinforcement for Russell; Naulls started briefly in 1966, thus giving Boston the league's first all-black starting five; Nelson was the biggest catch of all when plucked from the wavier wires after being dropped by Los Angeles; and Howell was acquired from Baltimore for Mel Counts in Auerbach's only important player-for-player trade of the entire decade. And Havlicek's former Ohio State teammate Larry Siegfried would be another valuable cog in the well-oiled and constantly refueled Celtics machine. The super-energetic (sometimes frenetic) Siegfried played briefly in the short-lived American Basketball League before becoming a key role player who usually got the job done by harassing opponents, diving wildly for loose balls, and flying chaotically all over the floor on both offense and defense.

One of Auerbach's earlier transactions now came to bear full fruit. The 1964 season—the first without Cousy—marked the first full flowering of a new Boston hero named John "Hondo" Havlicek. Havlicek had first followed Ramsey in that novel Auerbach invention known as the "sixth man" and designed to expose opponents' weaknesses by exploiting the depth of the Boston bench. The team's number four point producer as a rookie, Hondo was already the team's top scorer in his second NBA season, even though he was still coming off the bench as the first line of reinforcement and thus never started a single game. Before long it was apparent that Havlicek was possibly the greatest two-position player ever to come along, equally as comfortable and valuable as a ball-handling guard or a board-crashing and bucket-pounding forward. What was most remarkable about Havlicek from the opening bell, however, was an inexhaustible stamina which quickly wore down any and all opponents assigned to cover him on defense or cope with him on offense. Learning the sixth-man role to perfection from Ramsey, Havlicek would eventually graduate (during the first round of the 1968 postseason) to a lengthy tenure as one of the league's most formidable starters. His career would span much of Boston's proud cage history: he came on the scene (the seventh overall draft pick of 1962) in time for Cousy's final season and didn't hang up his famed number "17" jersey until a mere year before Larry Bird's arrival. By the time he retired in 1978 he was not only Boston's career scoring leader but also the career club pacesetter in every imaginable offensive category outside of rebounds, assists and field goal percentage. He was also—way back in 1978—the greatest career pointmaker in NBA history outside of Wilt Chamberlain and Oscar Robertson.

The combination of "The Jones Boys" which now supplanted Sharman and Cousy in the backcourt guaranteed a smooth transition from The Russell Celtics I championship unit to The Russell Celtics II championship unit. In the finest tradition of the tight family atmosphere which Auerbach had fostered, both Joneses had quitely waited on the bench for their turn eventually to come. There had been no squabbling about playing time which might have plagued modern-era teams. Everyone wearing a green jersey had one single focus—winning NBA championships. And the lengthy apprenticeships served by Sam Jones and K. C. Jones now assured that more championships would almost certainly be in the immediate offering.

Yet it was not always as easy to maintain dynasty status as it sometimes appears to have been from our own distant vantage point of several decades. The NBA of the sixties was always a highly competitive affair. Thus there were certain moments along the way when whimsical Fate was perhaps the biggest player in the ongoing Celtics saga. It was in those special moments that the notion of a "Celtics Mystique" was continuously being fueled.

Boston's dynasty never came quite so close to total collapse as it did during the 1965 divisional championship series with arch-rival Philadelphia. Wilt—first with the Warriors and later the Sixers (after returning to Philadelphia in a whopper January 1965 trade)—long remained a huge obstacle to be surmounted during every spring's renewed

The first post-Cousy Boston season also would mark the first full flowering of a new Boston hero named John Havlicek.

championship plans. And on at least one occasion (the one in which Philadelphia was unaccountably handed a golden chance to score the winning bucket in the closing seconds of the deciding 1965 divisional playoff game) it was Wilt by all reasonable measures who should have gone home a winner. But the team in green seemed at times to have overriding luck as well as overriding talent squarely on its side. Such was clearly the case on Tax Day in 1965 when John Havlicek anticipated an inbounds pass from Hal Greer to Chet Walker and stole a game-seven victory—a victory which once more put Boston back in the championship round for another almost laughably easy title defense against ill-fated Los Angeles.

Havlicek's steal which squelched a desperate 76ers challenge in the closing seconds of the 1965 Eastern Division Finals looms as a special moment in club mythology—almost obliterating similar dramatic moments orchestrated years later by Bird, Henderson and Parish. Even casual basketball fans around the land have likely heard of Havlicek's clutch pilfering that once saved the Boston club and its string of six-straight titles, though the details may today be altogether fuzzy for anyone residing very far outside of Boston. The event also served the role of cementing in the popular imagination what has always been apparent to anyone closely following Boston's year-in and year-out postseason fortunes. For all of Havlicek's contributions as a scorer and rebounder over the years, it was as a clutch defender that he was truly without parallel.

The focus for Boston during the 1965-66 campaign was inevitably set on Red Auerbach's planned swan song season. Red had most nobly announced at the outset of his 16th league tour that he would not depart from the coaching ranks without giving everyone around the circuit at least one last shot at dethroning him. Auerbach was aging quickly of late and the physical strain of an increased work load after Walter Brown's unexpected death a year earlier had been taking an increased toll. More than likely, of

Author's Collection

Havlicek inherited the sixth-man role from Frank Ramsey in 1964 but would eventually log enough time as a starter to rank first in virtually every important ballclub offensive category.

course, there was more arrogance than sportsmanship in the nearly exhausted coach's noble gesture. Auerbach's real craving, undoubtly, was to experience what he was almost certain would be yet one final delectable victory cigar.

That final cigar almost never happened. The regular season was rough enough in its own right, despite another 50-win ledger, as was most of the postseason, despite a record eighth-straight world title. For the first time since Russell's arrival the Celtics would not win the divisional crown that was the rationale for regular-season play. Philadelphia finally edged out the Auerbach forces by winning 18 of their final 21 games, though only by the narrowest possible margin of a single game. Then in the opening playoff rounds a still-gritty Cincinnati ballclub with Oscar Robertson at the controls grabbed a 2-1 lead before an aging Boston contingent rebounded to take two straight against the Royals and then overwhelm another Chamberlain-led outfit that again didn't seem to show up in the proper mindset for postseason warfare. The Lakers did come prepared to battle all out in the finals, of course, and unlike the previous three seasons the Celtics were now finally pushed all the way to the wall. There were several moments in the championship series—especially an opening overtime loss at home and a pair of defeats after going up 3-1—that seemed even to suggest the Celtics were finally not up to the task of yet another draining title defense.

But it was Auerbach's final game, in particular, that nearly transformed itself into an unmitigated Boston Garden disaster. Game 7 seemed to be well in hand for Boston by the time the final quarter rolled around. A ten-point lead with a half-minute to play was signal enough for Auerbach to savour one final tasty victory-pronouncing stogie. For a moment the usually wily coach seemed somehow to forget all those recent moments when championships had hung on a final few seconds in which his fate-kissed team somehow only managed to survive with a

Red Auerbach puffs a cigar on January 13, 1966, in celebration of his 1,000 NBA career win—a tally which included Red's postseason victories.

strong assist from Lady Luck. There had been Selvy's near-miss, and Havlicek's steal, and also a life-saving bucket by Sam Jones in the final two seconds of the 1962 division finals, among other recent last-gasp miracles. Now Los Angeles nearly pulled off a rare miracle of their own. West dropped in two buckets to cut the lead to six in the seconds immediately before Red took his first symbolic puff. A delirious Boston crowd inspired by the coach's gesture—Red's cigar had actually been lit by Governor John Volpe who was standing alongside the Boston bench—next engulfed the playing floor and there was near chaos before space could be cleared for Havlicek to inbounds the ball after West's second bucket. An unraveling Boston ballclub would then turn the ball over four times in the final ten seconds. With six seconds left the dwindling victory margin was down to two. K. C. Jones finally saved the day by dribbling out the final tense seconds in front of a suddenly stunned crowd and an equally stunned home team bench.

At age forty-eight, and still in the prime of life, Auerbach would be walking away from his prized seat on the Celtics bench. But he would not be walking away from either the sport or the Boston organization he had so long served. In fact he would now potentially be facing his biggest basketball challenge of his illustrious career—that of somehow effectively replacing a coach like Red Auerbach. There appeared to be several options available and former

star Tom Heinsohn seemed to be the most obvious among them.

Heinsohn, who himself had retired a season earlier to launch a successful insurance business, had another suggestion, one that immediately caught Red's ear. It seemed self-evident that the biggest challenge for Red's successor was not the Auerbach legend or legacy itself. With Russell still on the floor it was apparent to most that no imminent team collapse was likely. But the problem would be finding a coach who could manage to control and inspire Bill Russell. And when it came to that, it seemed like only one option presented itself. Russell could likely be managed and directed only by Russell himself.

Russell's appearance on the Boston bench as head coach was a truly historic moment. It would mark the first time that an African-American would coach a major professional sports team. And it would happen in a city not known for any exceptional air of racial tolerance. Down through the years Boston's Celtics would at times be justifiably criticized as something of a lily white organization, such as when a December 1985 *Time* magazine article by Tom Callahan referred to the Celtics (with eight whites on a twelve man roster at a time when the league was already 75% black) as "South Africa's team." This was also the city that had once dragged its heals on baseball integration, with the Red Sox

Player-coach Russell battles Elgin Baylor (#22) and Darrall Imhoff (#14) of the Lakers during game five of the 1968 championship series, another crucial Boston overtime victory.

of the American League being the final big league club (in 1959) to cross the racial barrier. And a city, as well, that had not always treated Russell particularly well. Russell's suburban home was once broken into at the height of his playing career and excrement and racial epithets were smeared upon the walls.

Of course, Walter Brown's Celtics had always "officially" followed a dictum which the owner had early on handed down to coach Auerbach: "I don't care if they're green, white, black or yellow, as long as they can play!" Brown had drafted the first black player (Chuck Cooper in 1950) into the league. Boston boasted the first contingent of five blacks simultaneously on the floor (Russell, Sanders, Sam and K. C. Jones, and Willie Naulls in 1964) and also the first all-black starting five (the same five, once Naulls replaced Heinsohn as a starter in 1966), and now Boston pioneered with a black head coach. But the lily white Boston Garden always sold out in the '80s during the Bird years and during most of the '70s in the Cowens-Havlicek years, but never in the '60s during the Russell years, and the suspicion remains that this went beyond the sport's general popularity in respective eras. And Russell's own mid-career cynical observations about NBA quotas—"The general rule is you're allowed to play two blacks at home, three on the road, and five when you're behind"—had a certain eerie ring of truth about it when first uttered.

Finally it would be Wilt's turn during this first season played out in Auerbach's wake. Philadelphia's team was now one of the strongest in league history, boasting an imposing starting five that included a revamped Wilt Chamberlain at center, Hal Greer and Wally Jones in the backcourt, and Luke Jackson and Chet Walker as athletic forwards. Coach Alex Hannum (a previous thorn in Auerbach's side when he played for and coached Pettit's Hawks earlier in the decade) also had the league's heftiest bench—previously always a Boston luxury—with veteran Larry Costello and youngsters Bill Melchioni, Matt Guokas and Bob Weiss lending further backcourt strength; Dave Gambee shoring up the front line; and Billy "the Kangaroo Kid" Cunningham suddenly rivaling Havlicek as the circuit's most potent sixth man. It was a club that had already outpaced Boston in the division race a year earlier and now seemed to simply have more horses than the team Auerbach left behind for Russell. Philadelphia's season-long performance would certainly justify this analysis: a new league record for victories (68), 45 wins in the first 49 games, and a comfortable eight-game division lead at season's end. And if Russell had now been transformed into something never heretofore anticipated— a head coach, even if one of the playing variety—Wilt had also undergone a miraculous and unanticipated transformation of his own. Wilt was now a team player, not a one-man show. The "new" Chamberlain averaged only 24.1 ppg., still third in the circuit but low enough to finally yield the league scoring crown (picked up by Warriors' second-year

phenom Rick Barry). But five 76ers teammates also posted double figures and the huge center passed off frequently enough (for the first time in his career) to actually place third in the assists category.

But before Wilt and his Sixers could take their bow there was a regular season in which the Russell-coached Celtics also won 60 contests and lapped at their heels from late December to March and even managed a 5-4 advantage in the head-to-head matches against Wilt's potent ballclub. The postseason showdown for the Eastern Division banner was enough, however, to demonstrate that a new order had now risen—at least temporarily. The Eastern Division title matchup was an absolute reversal this time around with Wilt's team now coasting home free in only five games. After Philly swept the first three with ease a clean sweep was avoided with a nationally televised 121-117 Boston face-saving victory at Boston Garden. Two days later long-suffering 76ers fans were gleefully chanting "Boston is dead, Boston is dead!" during the final period of a lopsided 140-116 wrap-up.

The only two times Bill Russell ever lost a championship the circumstances were special if not entirely unique. There had been the ankle injury that had punctuated Pettit's Paul Bunyan-like playoff performance at the end of Russell's sophomore campaign. This time Russell and his crew had to face arguably the strongest lineup in league history, and one with Chamberlain actually playing Russell-type defense. Add the advanced ages of four-fifths of the Boston starting lineup in 1967—K. C. Jones 34, Sam Jones 33, Russell 33, Bailey Howell 29—and the postseason debacle was almost a foregone conclusion.

Yet there was still one final glorious act in the unfolding drama. An argument can be made that for pure thrills and inspired story line there is nothing else in Celtics lore that quite matches Russell's final two campaigns on the hardwood. Certainly these were the most unlikely of all the exciting Boston championship runs. K. C. Jones had now stepped aside (as had Sharman in '61, Cousy in '63, Ramsey and Loscutoff in '64, and Heinsohn in '65) yet the rotation of quality players continued with Larry Siegfried now stepping to the fore as a double-figure scorer and versatile ball-hawking backcourt defender cut squarely in K.C.'s own mold. And Bailey Howell was now a solid fixture in the starting lineup, adequately filling the shooter's role that had long belonged to Heinsohn. In the three years that Russell coached Howell posted scoring marks of 20-even, 19.8, and 19.7 (runner-up to Havlicek in each of these campaigns). This was a very different-looking Boston team, except of course for Russell solidly anchoring the middle as always. Thus the charge back to the top started with a 1968 campaign and postseason that at the outset looked every bit like the one that had gone before.

After once more winning 50-plus, finishing as division runner-up a third straight time, and again trailing Philly by

Philadelphia 76ers coach Alex Hannum offers congratulations to his exhausted counterpart, Bill Russell, after Boston had staged a miraculous comeback to clinch the hard-fought 1968 Eastern Division title series. Russell was of course also Boston's top player during the memorable championship battle.

somehow was largely a matter of a revived Boston defensive effort. In the crucial fifth game on an enemy court 34-year-old veteran Sam Jones sparked the club with 37 points and Havlicek (adapting to his new starter's role) also canned 29. The deciding seventh game—also played in Philadelphia—was a tense thriller in which Bill Russell seemed to recapture lost youth by blocking one last-second shot from Chet Walker and rebounding another by Hal Greer to preserve the 100-96 victory. For the first time ever a team came back from a 3-1 series deficit on the way to an NBA championship. And most significant in the scenario was Wilt Chamberlain's complete disappearance from the scene in the final game of the surprising series (also his final contest with Philadelphia). Chamberlain shot only twice in the entire second half—both tip-ins—scored only 14 overall, and stood around helplessly as teammates failed to get him the ball. He touched the ball just four times in the game's crucial last quarter. It was truly Wilt's darkest hour and truly one of Russell's brightest.

Boston's sudden revival meant a renewal of hostilities with their longtime rivals out west. The Lakers still had West and Baylor, but they were still weak in the post position. They had a new owner, Jack Kent Cooke, who removed their blue and white uniforms and substituted the now familiar gold and purple togs. They also now played in a new palacial structure known as the "Fabulous" Los Angeles Forum, having abandoned the familiar Los Angeles Sports Arena after lease-related squabbles with local government officials. And they had a new coach in Butch Van Breda Kolff. Van Breda Kolff was a former successful Princeton coach who attempted to bring a new playing style and work ethic to the proud Lakers club when he replaced Fred Schaus; but the new mentor would quickly find that treating seasoned pros like college kids (he even tried to institute a team bed-check) was a sure recipe for dissention and disaster. Over the course of a rugged six-game championship series Van Breda Kolff was clearly outcoached by Russell while the Lakers' veteran players (especially Mel Counts and Darrall Imhoff in the post) were also ultimately outplayed by Russell.

Despite Jerry West's hefty scoring (38 in Game 4 and 35 on a sprained ankle in Game 5) Boston maintained full control throughout a series in which they never trailed (LA winning only Games 2 and 4 to gain a pair of short-lived ties). The wrap-up in Game 6 was an LA disaster from the opening bell, with Johnny Mathis confusing words from "God Bless America" and "The Star Spangled Banner" in pre-game ceremonies, Russell shifting Sam Jones to the forward slot and thus disrupting Van Breda Kolff's defensive alignments, and team captain Havlicek erupting for 40 and "garbage man" Bailey Howell for an additional 30 to

an identical eight games, Boston was most anxious for the postseason to roll around and provide another shot at Chamberlain and his hencemen. And also, of course, at the irksome Philadelphia fans. Havlicek later remembered how the chants of Philly fans late in the previous postseason and throughout the 1968 campaign to boot had remained ever-so-fresh in his mind. "The Celtics are dead, Boston's dead! The dynasty is dead!" had been a taunting chant ringing out almost everywhere around the league that year, but it was especially galling when endured in Philadelphia. And it is was the best type of motivation for revenge that any team could ever find. Especially one coached and led into action by ultimate-competitor Bill Russell. Bailey Howell noted that "it's tough, playing as often as you do, to be emotionally ready every night … when you get some help like that from opposing fans, it's really a lift." Boston clubs led by Russell had always found a cause to pysch them up for title defenses; now it was even easier when revenge and lost pride were the motivators.

The Boston-Philly rematch at the end of the 1968 season was one of history-making proportions. Philly had gotten there by surviving a surprising first-round challenge from a New York team inspired by new coach Red Holzman; Boston had met a challenge from Detroit in a series where Russell finally made Havlicek into a starter. Brimming with confidence the Sixers raced to a seemingly insurmountable led, taken three of four against the reeling Celtics, two in Boston Garden. A second blowout suddenly seemed in the offering for the supercharged Philly faithful. And then the tide somehow miraculously turned—and that seal the Lakers' fate.

Even Bill Russell knew it would be tough to stay on top much longer. When the final campaign of the decade opened, Russell and Auerbach seemed to have plotted a new strategy to compensate for the anticipated difficulties in momentum. The regular season no longer meant much in Boston where only championships during April or May carried much currency. The idea now was to coast through the long winter and win just enough games to gain a necessary playoff spot, then to peak with a roster of veterans in time for the annual postseason wars. Russell was now 35, Sam Jones 36, Howell 32 and Sanders 30. Havlicek was the

and Philadelphia now altogether exasperated. Coach Alex Hannum abandoned the Sixers to take charge of the Oakland Oaks in the new rival ABA, and Chamberlain escaped as well, settling for a quarter of a million dollars a year to provide Jack Kent Cooke with the apparent missing piece in his own championship puzzle. Wilt's Philadelphia departure was thus part of the Lakers' own plans to finally acquire the inside force that would compliment Baylor and West and allow them a decent chance against an aging and somewhat diminished Bill Russell. LA had now put together a superteam that finally seemed invincible—Mr. Inside (Baylor), Mr. Outside (West) and Mr. Giant (Wilt).

The setting is game three of surprising 1968 NBA Finals series between Boston and Los Angeles. Larry Siegfried (with the ball) maneuvers for a pass to Bailey Howell (#18) with Elgin Baylor (#22) and Archie Clark (#21) providing the Lakers defense.

key to the veteran lineup, with Siegfried now running the offense and Don Nelson anchoring the front line. They were seasoned veterans all.

The strategy seemed brilliantly conceived during the first two postseason rounds with Philadelphia and New York. The first was a laugher since Chamberlain was no longer in the Sixers lineup and a depleted Philadelphia team that relied on Cunningham and aging Hal Greer for most of its scoring mustered only a Game 4 victory to avert the sweep. New York was perhaps a tad overconfident after demolishing regular-season pacesetter Baltimore in round one and soon was stunned by the still-dangerous Celtics. Boston's pair of one-point homecourt victories in Games 4 and 6 unhinged the Knicks, who were still a full season away from the championship promised land.

The previous season's unexpected return to prominence by Russell and Boston had left Los Angeles again frustrated

Arguably owner Cooke and coach Van Breda Kolff now had in their lineup the greatest center, guard and forward of this or any other era. And it all came about at a time when the league's talent surrounding the Lakers was further diluted by ABA expansion. The rival league was now plucking off some of the best college talent and the NBA itself had two new rosters to fill with expansion teams now placed in Phoenix and Milwaukee.

What transpired by season's end, however, was truly a tale for the ages. If Boston had a surprisingly easy time in opening playoff rounds (thanks to New York's second-round collapse) and LA a surprisingly rough one (they needed six games to get by opening-round foe San Francisco), nonetheless LA was stocked with sufficient powerhouse talent and Boston was glaringly old and tired. LA's big three had posted big numbers all season as expected: Baylor remained injury-free long enough to average

24.8ppg.; West scored at an even higher clip (25.9) but missed 21 games; and Wilt also averaged 20-plus and was the circuit's field-goal-percentage leader. For the first time ever the Lakers actually entered the final playoff round against Boston as an overwhelming favorite. Yet that was all that would be novel about the renewal of the annual Boston-Los Angeles springtime feuding. Once more Russell would outplay Wilt, and once more (and more significantly) he would also outcoach Van Breda Kolff.

The final Russell-Chamberlain showdown was doomed to end in a disappointing fizzle. But the doom was all on the LA side of the ledger. The Lakers shot out of the gate well enough, with 53 points from West in the opener and a quick 2-0 series lead; the blue-glad Lakers were determined not to be humiliated with a seventh-straight Finals loss (starting with the one back in Minneapolis) to Boston. Boston was also motivated by a more recent humiliation, a 35-point drubbing by the Lakers on national television a week before the regular season ended. Spurred perhaps by an awareness that no team had ever lost the opening pair in an NBA title series and rebounded to win, Jack Kent Cooke shipped cases of champaign to Boston Garden for what he hoped was a now-imminent victory party. That party was first delayed went Siegfried came off the bench to score 28 in Game 3 and then put in some jeopardy when Sam Jones (playing his final postseason) tied the series with a off-balance buzzer-beater in decisive game 4. Over the next two high-spirited contests the desperate opponents courageously maintained their respective homecourt advantages and thus Cooke's still-unopened cases of champaign were doomed to make one final cross-country trip back to Los Angeles.

Cooke next decorated his Fabulous Forum for game seven, still expecting a huge victory party: the rafters were

Oft-injured Jerry West playfully dons some appropriate protection before entering another rugged title slugfest with his perennial Boston rivals.

filled with colorful balloons to be released for the anticipated post-game celebration and even the USC marching band was on hand for expected festivities. Yet again a careless opponent had gone out of its way to provide the sagging Boston ballclub with its annual much-needed extra emotional lift—a huge dose of motivation for facing the arduous challenge at hand. Boston would of course spoil the celebration once more, this time with another huge unexpected assist from Wilt himself, as well as from Wilt's demoralized coach. Boston owned a 17-point fourth-quarter cushion when Wilt banged his shin and removed himself to the sidelines. When an late LA comeback was mounted Wilt finally decided to re-enter the fray, but his steamed coach would have no part of it and left replacement Mel Counts out on the floor.

Boston held on for a 108-107 victory on the strength of a near-miracle shot by Don Nelson which bounced high off the back rim before crashing through the net. It was the Boston team and not the home forces that quietly sipped champaign in an orderly locker room celebration. Auerbach gloated as he blew cigar smoke at the still-trapped bags of rafter balloons. Heroic Jerry West found little consolation in the Finals MVP award as he swallowed his most bitter defeat at the hands of Russell's charges. And even Bill Russell was subdued in the afterglow of victory, miffed that his arch rival Chamberlain had not been out on the floor for a legitimate last-ditch showdown.

Wilt Chamberlain was the number one antagonist of the 13-season Boston dynasty run. And the rivalry between Chamberlain and Russell was the greatest head-to-head conflict of basketball history. Over a full decade beginning in November 1959 and ending in May 1969 the two squared off 142 times during regular-season action and those titanic events were usually earthshaking if not always artistic. The NBA—perhaps every other sport played on North American soil—has never known another such rivalry. Wilt seemed to always hold the slight edge when it came to tallying the stat sheets alone: Wilt racked up 4077 points and averaged 28.7 against Russell; Russell's numbers for the same games were 2060 and 14.5. The margin here was almost two to one. When rebounds are the measure—Russell's forte—Chamberlain still comes out on top by a wide margin: 4072-3373, or 28.7-23.7 in game average. The pair also met 49 times in postseason battles and here the old standby line that Russell energized and Wilt wilted at playoff time just doesn't seem to withstand scrutiny. Wilt held the advantage 1260 (25.7) to 730 (14.9) in pointmaking and 1393 (28.4) to 1243 (25.4) in rebounding. There is of course one category in which Bill Russell overwhelms Wilt Chamberlain on a statistical scale; Russell holds an most decisive 7-1 series advantage when the measure is head-to-head divisional and NBA team championship matches.

Jerry West was almost as big a rival for Boston over the years as Wilt was. West was one of the sport's all-time great pure shooters, one of its most proficient all-out scorers (he remains fourth in career average behind Jordan, Chamberlain and Baylor), and certainly one of its most fearless and gritty all-around competitors. The all-star Lakers guard held the playoff career scoring record (4,457 points) until Kareem Abdul-Jabbar and Michael Jordan came along, and West was always at his best when postseason play was at hand. He is still second behind Jordan in career playoff average (29.1 ppg.). Of course West never won a championship ring until after Russell was gone from the scene, making seven trips to the Finals (one against the Knicks in 1970) before finally tasting champaign in 1972, two seasons before retirement. But the career-long head-to-head duals between West and Havlicek from the mid-'60s to mid-'70s may well have been the most titanic square-offs ever witnessed been a pair of mid-sized players.

Pettit and Oscar also proved to be grand enemies, especially Pettit during the several championship-round matchups during Russell's earliest seasons. Today's fans have lost out on appreciating Pettit's one-time stature as the sport's most durable and versatile scoring and rebounding forward; perhaps only Larry Bird and Elgin Baylor have ever been better at the frontcourt position. And with a 20-point average and three MVPs in 11 appearances Pettit was also arguably the greatest All-Star Game performer in NBA annals. Bob Ryan's assessment that Charles Barkley is a new and improved version of Bob Pettit is likely an anathema to anyone whose perspective on the NBA reaches back to a time before Russell's retirement. Pettit was the only man ever to singlehandedly beat the dynasty Boston Celtics at the very height of their postseason game (Wilt had tons of help from an all-star lineup when Philadelphia won all the

marbles in 1967). And his overall hall-of-fame stature even outstrips that single salient fact.

But despite these great players in other ports, in the end it was always Boston's unmatchable depth that won out when championships were on the line. The role players were always at the very heart of Boston's greatest triumphs, even back when Cousy and Russell were still on the scene. Ramsey and Havlicek fine-tuned the sixth man role to a true sportsworld art form. Paul Silas would carry on that tradition of super-sub in a new decade, as would Kevin McHale in the one that followed. But there were hordes of other role players who didn't wear the official "sixth man" mantle. Gene Conley earned a niche in Celtics history as a vital backup for Russell and a versatile frontcourt performer. Jim Loscutoff was one of pro basketball's earliest effective enforcers. Clyde Lovellette, Andy Phillip, Willie Naulls, Don Nelson, and Bailey Howell were all castoffs from other teams who resurrected their own careers while reinforcing numerous Boston charges down to the postseason wire.

Certainly Boston didn't win its endless championships in the era between Sputnik and Woodstock with Bill Russell alone, although his presence under the bucket always removed most doubt from the issue. Especially on defense. While "switch" was also the popular cry in the middle of the court for other teams' defensive schemes, in Boston the plea was never more than "Russ" whenever defensive help was needed anywhere on the floor.

But an argument can certainly be made that Russell was the greatest basketballer of all-time. Not the flashiest like Jordan, and not the most perfectly molded like Ocsar, or the most statistically dominant like Wilt Chamberlain. And certainly not the most diversified like Larry Bird. But when talk turns to the sport's greatest figures there seems to be only one statistic that remains important in the end. Russell's championship stats are 11 for 13, and perhaps nothing more needs ever to be said.

An inescapable irony surrounding the Celtics of the Bill Russell era is of course the fact that the team was never a top drawing card in Boston at the time of their greatest on-court glories. Boston was still first and foremost a baseball town devoted exclusively to the beloved Red Sox, and also secondarily a hockey town devoted in winter months to the colorful NHL Bruins. Pro basketball in its earliest Boston days—in the shadows of World War II—had drawn its sparse following largely from the city's Jewish sector, and thereafter—despite the dozen-year presence of local college hero Bob Cousy—the team's popularity never quite kept pace with its outrageous on-court successes. During the glory-run of the '60s sellouts were reserved for a handful of playoff games (usually game seven) and the team never managed to sell out a single season's home opener. Russell was black, and an outspoken black at that, and this didn't endear him to hometown faithful as an unqualified local

Year-by-Year Boston Garden Attendance

Year	Games Played	Attendance Totals	Average per Game
1946-47	30 (including Boston Arena)	108,240	3,608
1947-48	24 (including Boston Arena)	90,264	3,761
1948-49	29 (including Boston Arena)	144,275	4,975
1949-50	26 (including Boston Arena)	110,552	4,252
1950-51	32 (including Boston Arena)	197,888	6,184
1951-52	29 (including Boston Arena)	160,167	5,523
1952-53	24	161,808	6,742
1953-54	21	156,912	7,472
1954-55	25	175,675	7,027
1955-56	26	209,645	8,064
1956-57	25 (NBA Champions)	262,918	10,517
1957-58	29	240,943	8,308
1958-59	30 **(NBA Champions)**	244,642	8,165
1959-60	27 **(NBA Champions)**	209,374	7,755
1960-61	28 **(NBA Champions)**	201,569	7,199
1961-62	28 **(NBA Champions)**	191,855	6,852
1962-63	30 **(NBA Champions)**	262,581	8,753
1963-64	30 **(NBA Champions)**	223,347	7,445
1964-65	30 **(NBA Champions)**	246,529	8,318
1965-66	31 **(NBA Champions)**	246,189	7,941
1966-67	31	322,690	10,409
1967-68	37 **(NBA Champions)**	320.788	8,670
1968-69	36 **(NBA Champions)**	322,130	8,948
1969-70	37	277,632	7,504
1970-71	39	313,768	8,045
1971-72	41	346,701	8,456
1972-73	39	423,234	10,852
1973-74	32 (NBA Champions)	355,261	11,102
1974-75	34	452,421	13,307
1975-76	36 (NBA Champions)	484,039	13,446
1976-77	35	453,672	12,962
1977-78	36	437,937	12,165
1978-79	41	407,926	10,193
1979-80	39	565,105	14,490
1980-81	36 (NBA Champions)	536,883	14,913
1981-82	38	582,160	15,320 (all sellouts)
1982-83	38	582,160	15,320 (sellouts)
1983-84	38 (NBA Champions)	565,820	14,890 (sellouts)
1984-85	38	565,820	14,890 (sellouts)
1985-86	38 (NBA Champions)	565,820	14,890 (sellouts)
1986-87	38	565,820	14,890 (sellouts)
1987-88	38	565,820	14,890 (sellouts)
1988-89	38	565,820	14,890 (sellouts)
1989-90	38	565,820	14,890 (sellouts)
1990-91	38	565,820	14,890 (sellouts)
1991-92	38	565,820	14,890 (sellouts)
1992-93	38	565,820	14,890 (sellouts)
1993-94	38	565,820	14,890 (sellouts)
1994-95	38	565,820	14,890 (sellouts)

Boston Garden was closed at end of the 1994-95 season and replaced by a new Fleet Center arena.

hero to compare with baseball's Ted Williams or hockey's Bobby Orr (or even his own teammate, Bob Cousy). Boston cage fans wouldn't turn out in large numbers until the Cowens-Havlicek team of 1974 reclaimed lost championship glories and Celtics rooters thus became nostalgic about a lost era they had largely ignored while it was upon them. In short, the Boston Celtics dynasty was built against a backdrop of box office indifference and constant financial instability. And this was seemingly largely because the Boston partisans never truly appreciated what they had sitting smack before them—for the span of an entire decade—until well after it was over and gone.

Auerbach was usually right in his intuitions, especially when it came to spotting and drafting top talent. But on at least one occasion the famed redhead was flat dead wrong. In his renown opening press conference before the Boston media—the one in which he denounced the "local yokels" for being more interested in Bob Cousy than a winning program—the new coach had assured all who would listen that the key to fan interest (read "attendance" here) was a winning team, pure and simple. Of course it didn't happen quite that way.

An irony shadowing Bill Russell's incomparable NBA career is the fact that the dynasty ballclubs featuring the unparalleled defensive star never drew exceptionally well in Beantown. There was no solid basketball tradition in Boston in the fifties to build upon, Russell was himself unpopular for his outspoken stance on racial matters, and the city may even have been essentially racist in its attitudes. The team did pack in its first string of 10,000-plus crowds with Russell and Heinsohn as newly minted rookies in 1957 and the first-ever serious run at a championship season underway; that figure was reached only once more during the Russell epoch—ironically in the one year that the Celtics lost out to a better team from Philadelphia. Crowds didn't come in any impressive numbers until the mid-70s, when a new climate surrounded both the team and the city. A ballclub headlining Cowens and Havlicek was one that white fans (the bulk of the ticket buyers) could fully identify with; basketball was on the rise in popularity in New England as elsewhere after 1970; and perhaps Boston fans only began to appreciate the Celtics once they had fallen off their pedestal and then courageously climbed back on.

Another irony was the fact that the greatest of all NBA teams also performed in relative obscurity on the national scene. Basketball—especially pro basketball—was still sport for purists during the '60s, a very distant third among the big three sports in terms of overall fan popularity. There was little television coverage before the mid-'70s and therefore most fans around the land never caught more than a rare glimpse of stars like Russell and Wilt and Pettit and Oscar Robertson. When Russell won his first championship there

were only eight cities that boasted NBA teams, and when he captured his last the number had only expanded to fourteen. In the 1990s era of instant video exposure, when even journeymen role players are common faces and ubiquitous celebrity endorsers, one can hardly fathom the phenomon that a Russell or Chamberlain or Oscar Robertson would have been in today's marketplace. Just imagine the hoopla surrounding a player who averaged fifty points for a season (like Wilt in 1962), or posted a year-long triple-double (like Oscar did during the same season). Conceive if you can—in light of the celebrity status surrounding either one of the Chicago Bulls three-peat ballclubs—what a marketing tool a team would have been that captured a near decade's worth of world titles without a single championship defeat. In a world where a single night's forty-point explosion by a journeyman pro hoopster brings an endless glut of highlight replays, what would Bill Russell have wrought in today's marketplace? The imagined answers actually threaten to stretch our credulity beyond the breaking point.

At the end of the millennium perhaps Bill Russell's immense stature in the sport of basketball will now finally receive some of the credit so long overdue. *Sports Illustrated* with its edition of May 1999—published on the thirtieth anniversary of Russell's last championship team—would reopen the case with a cover-story tribute designed to set the record straight. The editors of America's top sports monthly released their choices for the top dynasty teams of the past full century—literally the entire span of major American professional sports. The choice for the supreme dynasty team—not in basketball alone but in all sports—was Russell's Boston Celtics of the 1960s. And the cover of that *SI* collectors' issue also fittingly carried the magazine's obvious choice for the greatest "team player" of the entire century in any team sport—again Boston's Bill Russell.

There will likely never be another dynasty like the Boston Celtics of the Bill Russell and Bob Cousy era. In Russell's long 13 seasons his NBA teams won 70.5% of their regular-season games, and 63.9 percent of their playoff games. In the NBA Finals he was eleven for 12 (add to that the two for three in NCAA titles during collegiate years, and also the one for one in Olympic crowns). Only Magic Johnson with a 74.2 regular-season winning ledger (one admittedly compiled against far more watered-down competition) can boast comparable domination. Today's celebrity athletic careers with the emphasis squarely on individual stardom and not team achievement will simply not allow such relentless group winning; nor will the free-agent marketplace which has top players shifting uniforms with each new bi-annual contract renewal. And in a watered-down era of diluted competitive balance, the sport will perhaps always be much the poorer for the change.

BOSTON Celtics

BOSTON Celtics

CHAPTER VI ———————————

Rebirth of
Celtics Pride:
The Bird Era

*"If I had to start a team, the one guy in all of history
I would take would be Larry Bird."*
- Red Auerbach

There seemed to be little doubt in Red Auerbach's mind that Larry Joe Bird was the best player he had ever seen. His assessment making that claim came in a ceremonial banquet at the end of Bird's hall-of-fame career and not in a hype-filled press conference at the time when he first signed on his franchise-building player. The judgment may have been colored by old-age forgetfulness (what about Cousy or Russell?) and some home-team prejudice (what about Michael Jordan or Oscar Robertson?)—with maybe even a slight note of racism thrown into the mix. Bill Russell never was fully appreciated, even by his own teammates or by the coach he dragged into the hall of fame with him. Yet Russell was only a vital component in building the Celtics dynasty, whereas Larry Bird was the complete package.

It is not difficult to build the argument that Larry Bird was the best forward ever to play the game, if not indeed the best all-around player ever to step onto the court. No front court operative ever combined rebounding, passing and perimeter shooting the way Bird did. Not in the same full doses at any rate. Despite a bad back which limited his late-career mobility, as well as the need to concentrate on offense and the fact that he was sharing rebounds on his own team with McHale and Parish, Bird still outrebounded such stellar front line **centers** as Patrick Ewing, Brad Daugherty and Jack Sikma during two seasons in the late '80s. And then there were the intangibles not found in any statistical summaries—the team leadership, the unmatched work ethic, and the unsurpassed will to win. Larry Joe Bird always raised the level of each and every other Boston player

out on the floor with him. Name another NBA star who improved the won-lost record of his team by 32 games his first winter in the league.

Bird and his alter ego Magic Johnson also saved the entire league when they arrived on the scene together in 1979 as the most anticipated pro rookies since Kareem Abdul-Jabbar earlier in the same decade. The NBA had undeniably fallen on hard times in the late seventies. Here was a league with sagging television ratings and a major public-image crisis. There were no superstars left of the ilk of Russell, Pettit, Chamberlain, Oscar Robertson or Bob Cousy to fire national or even regional interest. But a much-hyped Bird-Magic rivalry from the previous collegiate season was just the thing to put the league squarely back in business.

Only on rare occasion has the American sportsworld been privileged to receive the perfect savior at precisely the perfect hour. Earvin "Magic" Johnson and Larry Bird—two 6-9 phenoms, one a stellar oversized guard and the other an agile if earth-bound forward, one a black man from the urban sprawl of metropolitan Detroit and the other a white man from small-town Indiana—single-handedly rescued pro basketball from near oblivion when they took their polished play from the collegiate courts of East Lansing (Michigan State) and Terre Haute (Indiana State) to the professional venues of the glitsy Los Angeles Forum and the storied Boston Garden. And never were two novice marquee players blessed with more symbolic and appropriate names to spice their rescue missions.

As a business as well as a sport, professional basketball was in definite need of emergency repair by the closing years of the 1970s. In an age when big-time professional sport was now counting on a lucrative television connection to achieve economic solvency, the league remained the only

Larry Bird is most experts' clearcut choice as the best-ever NBA forward, and he was also Red Auerbach's easy selection as the one player around whom he would most like to build any mythical team from scratch.

Celtics never completely dominated league play in that decade: Milwaukee with Jabbar grabbed as many headlines, New York's Knicks were the media darlings of the early '70s and captured as many world titles, and upstart expansion clubs in Seattle and Portland were the biggest story by decade's end. The word "dynasty" was hardly applicable until the final season of the '70s, when GM Auerbach pulled off his second stunning and far-reaching draft-day coup and again set events in motion that would once more make Boston a scourge of the entire league.

Bird's instantaneous impact can reasonably compare to Russell's. Admittedly there was no immediate NBA championship ring to decorate Larry's rookie season—that would have to wait for an equally brilliant sophomore campaign—but there was nonetheless the biggest overnight turnaround in league history. Russell's arrival (combined with that of Tom Heinsohn) had only meant a regular-season improvement of five games. Three of the previous four pre-Russell campaigns had already witnessed Auerbach's team making it into the postseason conference finals (which was only the second playoff round at the time). Bird's arrival brought a leap of mindbending proportions—an improvement from 29 wins to 61 and a jump all the way from last place to first in the Atlantic Division. And the team that hadn't reached

This unforgettable NCAA championship duel between Larry Bird and Magic Johnson would merely set the stage for a subsequent decade of battles which revived the entire NBA.

one of the nation's three major spectator sports spectacles without a major television contract. At the threshold of the new decade, 16 of the league's 23 teams would actually lose money during 1980-81. There had already been serious talk of abandoning small market franchises like those in Indianapolis, Kansas City and San Antonio and shrinking the circuit to a 12-team league. NBA revenue certainly could not compare with that for football or baseball, and yet franchise survival often depended on meeting escalating salary demands of a limited number of superstar players.

Boston was hardly a pro basketball backwater in the ten seasons that separated Russell's retirement from Larry Bird's rookie debut. There were two Boston championships in the decade of the 1970s and the Celtics did break the franchise single-season victory record (with 68 in 1973) and twice led the entire league in regular-season wins. And there were memorable stars on the scene like Havlicek, Cowens, Satch Sanders, Jo Jo White, Paul Silas and Charlie Scott. The revamping of the franchise in the early '70's with Tom Heinsohn as head coach may indeed have been Auerbach's greatest (certainly his most complex) rebuilding job. But the

Bird's college credentials were so impressive that Auerbach and the Celtics' braintrust were willing to gamble a top draft choice on a future franchise player who would certainly eschew a pro contract for another year.

postseason play in either of the previous two campaigns—despite veteran lineups featuring Havlicek, Cowens, McAdoo, Charlie Scott, Jo Jo White, Dave Bing, Cedric Maxwell and Nate Archibald—also jumped straight to the conference finals (again the second round for a division winner) with Bird now ensconced in the lineup.

In terms of playing styles it is perhaps better to compare Bird to Cousy than to Russell. Bird ran Boston's offense from what he himself established as the newly created "point-forward" position. He upped the tempo of every game and every practice session and ran the floor ceaselessly like Havlicek and Cowens had always done during the previous decade. Bird was a physical animal who ran his opponents at the forward position into the ground in the same manner as Havlicek. And at the same time he was one of the great passers of all-time. Certainly he was the greatest passer ever to come along at the forward position, outstripping even Rick Barry in that capacity.

Bird was indeed like Cousy and also like his own rival Magic Johnson when it came to utterly controlling the game on the court around him. His numbers of assists were always most impressive, especially given his forward position and his simultaneous scoring numbers. His career average of 6.3 in that department (6.5 in the playoffs) has no close rival among the game's top scoring forwards: Havlicek is next best at 4.8 for career average, while Julius Erving checks in at 3.9 and Elgin Baylor at a shade over four. But assists counts by themselves were always a most inadequate measure with Bird, as they were with Magic Johnson, in gaging the true impact and obvious genius of Larry Bird's sensational floor generalship. Like Magic and Cousy, he seemed to actually see the game developing at all points on the floor as if it were actually happening all around him in slow motion.

The drafting of Larry Bird was nearly as remarkable in its details as was the saga of Russell's acquisition back in the mid-fifties. Auerbach was seemingly convinced early on that Bird was an absolute necessity when it came to plans to rebuild his team around a single draft choice. It was always Auerbach's stated philosophy to take the very best athlete available in the college lottery and worry about the details later. But this time—in June of 1978—the best player was a junior-eligible phenom playing at Indiana State who not only had a year of college eligibility remaining but had made it clear he intended to complete his NCAA career. It was a huge gamble to spend the number six overall selection on a player who would certainly be the number one choice a year later and thus eligible for big bucks if he waited and re-entered the lottery rather than hastily signing with Boston. Minnesota's two-year All-American center Mychal Thompson, stellar North Carolina guard Phil Ford, and Kentucky's rugged Rick Robey were also eligible for selection, and Boston and Auerbach would look silly if they squandered their highest pick in years on a player who would not be immediately available and then would likely opt to sign elsewhere.

While no one doubts Auerbach's earlier solo role in Russell's recruitment, questions have often been raised about his initial assessments of (and his enthusiasms about) Bird. Outspoken Auerbach critics Harvey Araton and Filip Bondy (in their book *The Selling of the Green*) suggest that Red took unjustified credit for Bird only after he was painfully persuaded by an unheralded Boston scout of the rare value of the pick. The same pair also argue that Bill Fitch and not Auerbach engineered the important dealings a year later that locked up both Parish and McHale. In the case of Bird, Auerbach himself had seen little of him in the college ranks and later admitted on several occasions that at the time he was not aware of how truly great a find the Sycamore star was. Bird had been called to Auerbach's attention by his single overworked scout, John Killilea, who had only seen the phenom on limited occasions (especially one outstanding game his sophomore year in Cincinnati versus Arkansas and Sidney Mongrief). Shabby Boston scouting throughout the '70s had led to numerous draft day gaffs, including the forgettable selections of such highly overestimated "talents" as Steve Downing and Phil Hankinson in 1973, and then Glenn McDonald, Tom Boswell and Norm Cook the following three years. In 1978

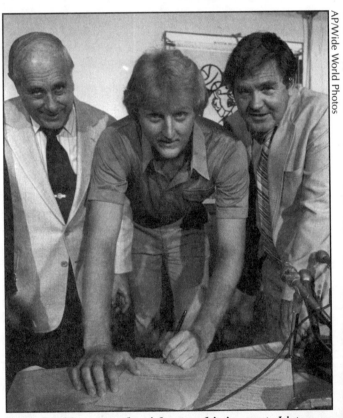

Larry Bird becomes the richest rookie in sports history on June 9, 1979, when he inks his $3.25 million five-year contract in the presence of club president Red Auerbach and new Boston head coach Bill Fitch.

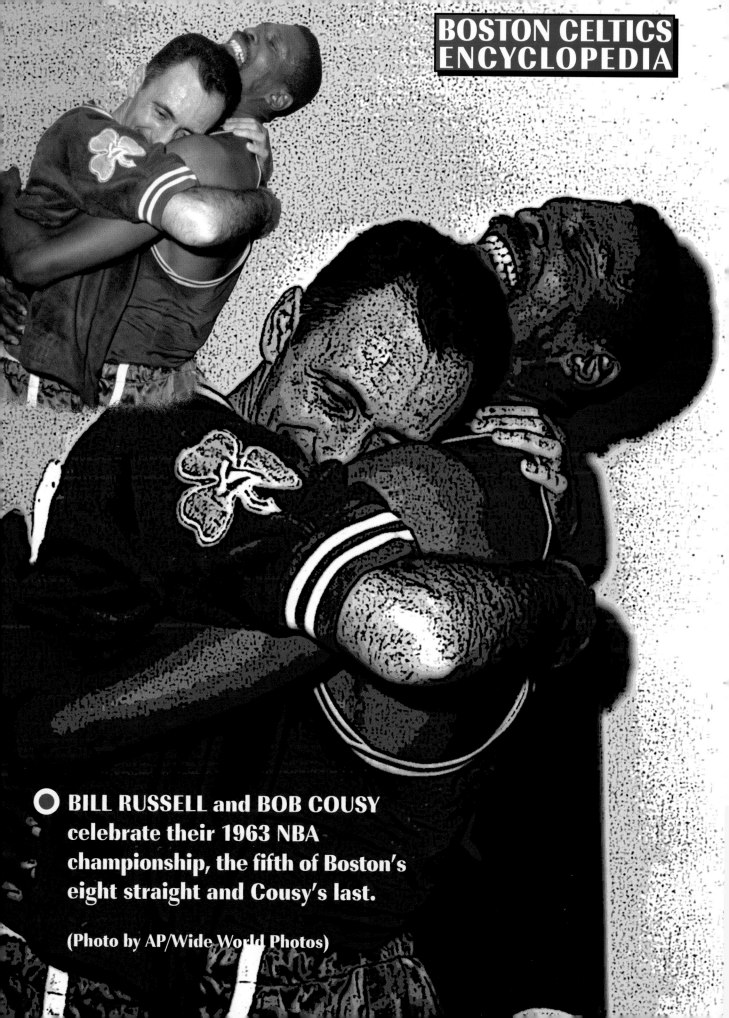

○ **BILL RUSSELL and BOB COUSY** celebrate their 1963 NBA championship, the fifth of Boston's eight straight and Cousy's last.

(Photo by AP/Wide World Photos)

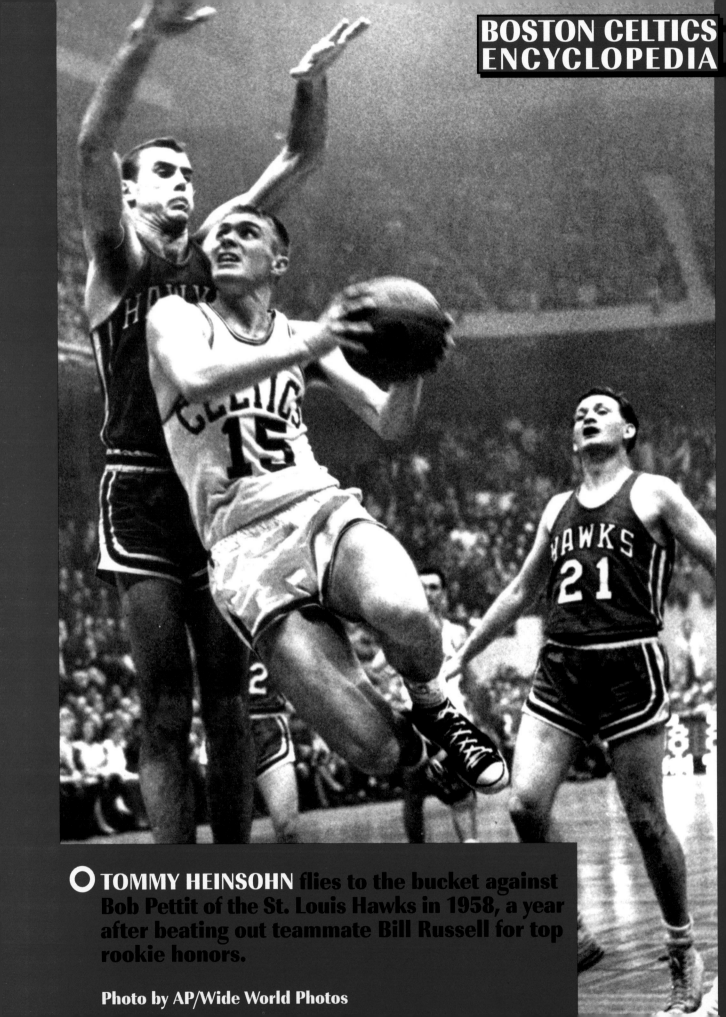

⭘ **TOMMY HEINSOHN** flies to the bucket against Bob Pettit of the St. Louis Hawks in 1958, a year after beating out teammate Bill Russell for top rookie honors.

Photo by AP/Wide World Photos

○ **JOHN HAVLICEK** douses **TOM HEINSOHN** while celebrating the 1974 NBA title, Heinsohn's first as head coach.

Photo by AP/Wide World Photos

○ **"THE BIG THREE"** frontcourt of the 1980s Celtics is considered one of the best in history. Here **ROBERT PARISH, LARRY BIRD** and **KEVIN McHALE** enjoy a break on the bench as teammates mop up another opponent.

Photo by AP/Wide World Photos

Still dominating opponents late in his career, LARRY BIRD is considered the game's best all-around forward.

○ **BILL WALTON** continued a Celtics tradition of late-career heroics when he helped Boston to the 1986 NBA championship.

Photo by AP/Wide World Photos

Basketball's two great ironmen meet head to head in 1984.
ROBERT PARISH would overhaul **KAREEM ABDUL-JABBAR'S**
records for seasons and games played.

Photo by AP/Wide World Photos

⭕ **The tragically short career of REGGIE LEWIS, shown here in 1992, marked the beginning of a Celtics downslide in the 1990s.**

Photo by AP/Wide World Photos

Killilea was able to hold sway with Auerbach regarding Bird, but he never got much credit for the effort since by draft day he had already moved on to a better playing assistant's slot with coach Don Nelson over at Milwaukee.

But whatever first motivated Auerbach to go after Bird (his own intuitions or his scout's arm-bending) there is one indisputable fact connected to the entire affair. It was Red Auerbach who in the end believed that Bird could be convinced that joining the Boston Celtics instead of re-entering the lottery a year later for bigger bucks as a top overall pick would be a wise career move. It was Auerbach who persuaded Bird and his agent Bob Woolf to come on board with the Celtics family. Before Draft Day of 1979 Bird had already happily inked a $650,000 deal, making him the best paid rookie in NBA history. It would turn out, of course, to be a solid investment for Boston, and also for Larry Bird. And when Auerbach saw Bird in action for the first time in that summer's rookie camp in Marshfield, Massachusetts—shooting, passing, crashing the boards with abandon, and running everyone else off the floor—the penny-pinching GM was instantly convinced that the club had not spent a single dollar too much on their prized rookie investment.

The Boston team that Bird joined still featured big names from the past decade and there were already a bevy of stars wearing the traditional Celtics green. Cowens, Jo Jo White (traded away to Golden State in the middle of the 1978-79 season), Archibald, and Maxwell were all in the fold the previous year, and Chris Ford (from Detroit) and Rick Robey (from Indiana) had recently been acquired via the trade route. But the 1979 edition had not been a winner, despite all the high-profile names and past franchise legends. And in the brief coaching tenures of both Satch Sanders and Dave Cowens the ballclub had most often played in utter disarray.

There was also an additional new piece to the Boston puzzle during Bird's first season. After a blitz of constantly rotating owners (eight different ownership groups since Lou Pieri had thrown in the towel in 1965) and a succession of egotistic meddling bosses who didn't appreciate his special talents or fire-tested savvy, Red Auerbach had finally regained command of the front office under new owner Harry Manguarian. One of his first moves was to sign on Bill Fitch as his head coach. Cowens had begun to doubt his fading skills on the playing floor, and his coaching skills in one partial season on the job had

also been a casualty of his new self-doubts. Fitch had already demonstrated his touch with the expansion Cleveland Cavaliers (where he had made that young club a postseason threat after only six years) and seemed just the kind of wise-cracking control freak and rebuilding genius that Auerbach like to have on board. The start that Fitch would now enjoy in Boston with Larry Bird in the fold would only further convince Auerbach of the wisdom of his decision to bring in a new coach at the outset of the new decade.

In his first year on the Boston bench—with a huge assist from his stellar rookie who immediately demonstrated that labels such as "too slow" or "can't jump" were huge misassessments of his unrivalled game—Fitch's team won more regular-season games than any Auerbach-coached squad save one. The huge turnaround in Boston's on-court fortunes brought top honors to the three principle figures in the franchise resurrection. Auerbach was NBA executive of the year for the first time (the award was instituted in 1973), Fitch gained the league's best-coach honors, and Bird was of course the league's top rookie, edging Magic Johnson by a comfortable margin in the balloting for that most prestigious honor.

An abortive 1980 postseason title chase proved that

CAPSULE HISTORY OF BOSTON CELTICS OWNERSHIP AND MANAGEMENT

Years	Owners	General Managers
1946-48	Walter Brown/ Boston Garden Arena Corp.	Walter Brown
1948-50	Walter Brown	Walter Brown
1950-64	Walter Brown	Walter Brown and Lou Pieri (Business)/Red Auerbach
1964-65	Lou Pieri and Majorie Brown	Red Auerbach
1965-68	Marvin Kratter/ National Equities	Red Auerbach
1968-69	Ballantine Brewery	Red Auerbach
1969-71	Woody Erdman/ Trans-National Comm.	Red Auerbach
1971-72	Investors' Funding Corp.	Red Auerbach
1972-74	Bob Schmertz/ Leisure Technology	Red Auerbach
1974-75	Bob Schmertz and Irv Levin	Red Auerbach
1975-78	Irv Levin	Red Auerbach
1978-79	John Y. Brown and Harry Mangurian Jr.	Red Auerbach
1979-83	Harry Mangurian Jr.	Red Auerbach
1983-92	Don Gaston, Paul Dupee Jr. and Alan Cohen	Jan Volk (1984-94)
1992-99	Boston Celtics Limited Partnership (Paul E. Gaston)	M.L. Carr (1994-97)/ Rick Pitino (1997-99)

Rookie standout Kevin McHale—the first newcomer since John Havlicek 18 seasons earlier to be handed the vaunted Boston sixth-man role—takes some practice pointers from head coach Bill Fitch on the eve of the 1981 championship series with Houston.

while Bird may have been the biggest element in the revitalization plan, he was nonetheless by himself not quite the final piece to the rebuilding puzzle. The leadership mantle had passed smoothly from Cowens to Bird, just as it had once passed from from Havlicek to Cowens. Boston behind Bird's scoring and all-around stellar play (he even led the team in rebounds) and Cedric Maxwell's steady performance (he was the league's leader in field goal accuracy and the team's number two scorer and rebounder) had finished two games better than Philadelphia in the regular-season Atlantic Division race. But the NBA second season always was a far different adventure and the Celtics were not yet playoff tough. A perhaps too-easy four-game sweep of Houston was followed by a five-game slaughter at the hands of the more experienced Sixers team that could boast a lineup of veterans like Julius Erving and Bobby Jones up front with Doug Collins and Moe Cheeks on the perimeter. After two nip-and-tuck games at home (96-93 loss and 96-90 victory), two down-to-the-wire road losses (99-97 and 102-90) would turn the tide. Philadelphia just had too much strength up front for Boston, despite the consistently heroic efforts of Bird and Maxwell. Board work was a definite shortcoming in the Boston playoff run: Bird was again Boston's top postseason rebounder but Cowens in his final go-around could not dominate even a journeyman center like Darryl Dawkins.

Bird was a phenomenal rebounder despite his deficits in height, foot-speed and leaping prowess, and from his rookie campaign on he always carried part of the club lead in that vital department. As a rookie he ranked tenth in the league overall and third among all forwards. For the next half-dozen seasons—before back ailments eventually set in—he would never be out of the top ten in the former category or the top five in the latter. But Larry was also too great a shooter to concentrate heavily on board work alone. Before long Parish and McHale would be hovering around the basket to corral a large portion of the loose caroms while Larry often ranged far from the hoop with his deadly jump-shooting arsenal. Nonetheless, rebounding remained perhaps the most underappreciated part of Larry Bird's phenomenal impact.

The problem of reinforcements for Bird was soon solved. Auerbach's earlier coups in seizing Russell, Cowens and finally Bird from under the noses of his jealous rivals were now about to be duplicated, this time with an apparent large assist from coach Bill Fitch. Fitch apparently played a far bigger role in landing the two desperately needed frontcourt stalwarts than has sometimes been previously reported. It is again Araton and Bondy who emphasize that while Auerbach was the chief architect of Celtics' fortunes down through the years he wasn't always

Robert Parish played an all-time record 1600-plus NBA games and more than 1100 were logged while wearing a Boston Celtics jersey.

the one who deserved credit for the most valuable purchases of the furniture. When Auerbach was able to solve the problem of an unwanted Bob McAdoo in 1979 by shipping him to Detroit coach Dick Vitale as compensation for Boston's free-agent signing of M. L. Carr, he was also able to snatch two Pistons' 1980 top draft picks. Red certainly deserves a full tip of the cap for at least that first stage of the deal. But when Detroit then unwittingly set the Celtics up with the top overall selection by finishing dead last, it was Coach Fitch who orchestrated the deal to grab Parish from Golden State (who wanted the first pick to use on Purdue 7-footer Joe Barry Carroll). Auerbach had to be convinced by much lobbying from his trusted head coach that it was Parish not Carroll that held the key to the club's future. When a Golden State first round pick was also part of the exchange (Golden State got the two original Detroit picks) the Celtics were able to jump on Kevin McHale to complete the draft day windfall.

McHale became part of the transaction only because in their haste to garner Joe Barry Carroll the Warriors front office not only parted with Parish—a far better player than Carroll as it would turn out—but forked over a valuable draft selection as well. After Carroll went to Golden State and Darrell Griffith was plucked by Utah, McHale was there for Auerbach and Fitch to latch onto the final piece of their puzzle. This 1980 draft day bungling by Golden State may not in hindsight have been quite as goofy as the one by Portland four years later— when the Trail Blazers opted for Kentucky's often-injured seven-footer Sam Bowie over a North Carolina guard named Michael Jordan. But it was nevertheless remarkably close.

Boston's wheelings and dealings to get Parish via a draft-related transaction with the Golden State Warriors now ranks as one of the biggest heists of NBA history. What had originally been an unwanted (from Auerbach's viewpoint at least) and unproductive (in the win column certainly) acquisition of Bob McAdoo by owner John Y. Brown a year earlier was now fully transformed into the followup deal which would put in place in Boston Garden the most potent forward wall in basketball history. Fitch would later seeth over Auerbach getting credit for the string of transactions and probably even left Boston a few years

After twice winning the NBA's prestigious Sixth Man Award, Kevin McHale moved into Boston's starting lineup and continued to flourish with All-Star team selections the next six years in a row.

SPI Archives

down the road due to his lingering resentment. But the fact remains that without Fitch's insistance on Parish (and the spinoff bonanza of Kevin McHale) Boston might not have won much of anything at all in the '80s, for all the individual talents that Larry Bird brought to the table.

Across the sixties the Celtics had slugged it out season after season with three great rivals—Pettit's St. Louis Hawks, a pair of Wilt-led ballclubs with different logos but always the same rowdy fans in Philadelphia, and Jerry West's West-Coast-based Los Angeles Lakers. In the 1980s the pattern would now be repeated, this time with Philly, LA and Detroit playing the villains' roles. And as with the '60s, once again the bulk of the sternest tests came in conference matchups before the Celtics could ever reach the championship round.

While the 1980s are rightfully remembered for the legendary Bird-Magic rivalry—both on the court and in the marketplace—the two marquee stars would remarkably only meet head-to-head three times for much-anticipated title showdowns. The first of these clashes was delayed all the way until their fifth season in the league, although one or the other would make it into the NBA Finals in each of the four preceding campaigns—Bird once and Magic on three occasions. In fact, there wasn't a single season in the entire decade of the eighties when one or the other didn't have a direct shot at the championship ring, Magic tasting the excitement of eight NBA Finals (winning five) and Bird five (with three victories). No wonder that the two put their indelible stamp on the decade the same way Russell had twenty years earlier.

During Bird's first three seasons his team had to do annual battle with some ever-tough Philadelphia Sixers teams anchored by Julius Erving (and eventually also by Moses Malone, who brought his dominating act from Houston to Philly in time for Bird's fourth campaign) before they could ever think about the NBA Finals and Magic's Lakers or Malone's Rockets. For three years running the Eastern Conference Finals involved the same two teams, and only once—when Bird was a rookie—was the matchup one sided. The other two encounters stretched to the maximum seven games and the arch rivals split the pair of nail-biting series.

Bird's first playoff frustrations would come in the encounter with Dr. J and the Sixers at the end of his debut season. The series was a runaway from the start and it was clear almost from the opening tip that the "made-for-television" rematch of 1979 NCAA heroes would have to wait for at least another year. Given Erving's quick dispatching of Bird and company and Magic's eventual heroics against the same Sixers team that had just drubbed the Celtics, it was a blessing for Larry Bird that rookie-of-the-year balloting had already taken place before the ball was ever thrown into the air for postseason play.

Reinforcements in the guise of Parish and McHale paid huge and immediate dividends during the following winter and spring. Parish and McHale between them added 29 points and 14 rebounds, along with 4.5 blocks, to the nightly Boston totals in 1980-81 alone. Both Boston newcomers, like Bird himself, were soon on a fast track bound for the game's top shrine in Springfield. And when linked up with Bird to form Boston's "Big Three" (after 1986, when McHale became a starter) the whole became even greater than the sum of the parts. Meanwhile Joe Barry Carroll lasted but six seasons in San Francisco, never averaged as much as 25 points or 10 rebounds in a single NBA campaign, and never brought championship-style play to any of the five cities in which he eventually displayed his usually lackluster game.

But even with Parish and McHale in the fold, Boston only made it to the Big Series of the NBA Finals once in the trio of seasons that marked Bird's earliest outings, and that time around Magic himself wasn't fated to be there. In Bird's second season the newcomers Parish and McHale had been enough to tip the balance against Erving's Sixers in a series that went the full distance and then was decided by only a single point. But there was more to Bill Fitch's retooled lineup than the two "towers of power" stolen from Golden State. Nate Archibald was now physically sound and in full control of the offense. Chris Ford and M. L. Carr also provided enough backcourt depth that this Boston team could return to the fast-breaking style that had always been a key to victory in the past. But even with all the plusses the season had started slowly when newcomer McHale along with Nate Archibald and Cedric Maxwell were all disgruntled over contracts and thus all reported late.

Magic Johnson was not quite so lucky in escaping the proverbial sophomore jinx. An early-season injury sidelined the Los Angeles phenom for much of the long season, restricting him to just 37 games. When Magic returned for the playoffs his team seemingly hadn't had sufficient time to regain its full stride of a year earlier. LA dropped two home games to fall flat in the opening round against a Houston Rockets club led by Moses Malone which had played under .500 for the long winter and thus had barely qualified for the "second season" playoffs.

The Eastern Conference Finals showdown that season provided yet another round in the on-going tradition of

Joined by their stellar backcourt support team of Dennis Johnson and Danny Ainge, the greatest front wall in NBA history enjoys a rare relaxing late-game moment together on the Boston bench.

epic matchups against teams representing Philadelphia. As they had already done several times during the Wilt-Russell confrontations back in the '60s, the Sixers jumped out to a quick 3-1 lead and seemed about to dispatch their Boston rivals with surprising ease and alacrity. Parish, McHale, Maxwell and Bird then took turns playing the hero's role in yet another amazing Boston comeback played out in the best Russell-era tradition. Trailing 109-103 with less than two minutes left in Game 5 the desperate Celtics scored eight straight and sealed the issue on two final foul shots by Carr. Parish truly saved the day, however, intercepting a final pass that could have meant a game-winning shot for Philadelphia. In game six the Sixers again seemed to have the upper hand before a wild melee broke out when Philly fans roughed up Maxwell during an end-court scramble for a loose ball. The 17-point rally which followed allowed the embattled Celtics to knot the series, but only after another game-saving steal—this time by McHale—cut off Andrew Toney's potential game-tying heave.

Back in Boston the final pitched battle of the series turned on defense as the home club climbed out of an 89-82 hole by holding Sixers gunners without a bucket from the field over the final five minutes. Boston won by a single point, 91-90, with Bird stealing the ball and charging the length of the court for the final basket. Maurice Cheeks had a chance to tie at the charity line in the waning seconds but made only one of two as Boston enjoyed yet another miraculous escape of the kind synonymous with Celtics mystique.

Maxwell was once again inspired by on-court confrontation during the NBA Finals versus Malone and Houston. The Rockets themselves were inspired enough at season's end, despite their dismal year-long record, to push Boston hard in the championship round. With the first four games split down the middle, Moses Malone mistakenly taunted the emotional Maxwell at the outset of Game 5 and Cornbread responded with an explosive 28-point and 15-

NBA Finals MVP Cedric Maxwell scores over powerful Houston center Moses Malone during the sixth game of the 1981 title matchup.

rebound performance during a 109-80 Boston Garden thrashing that all but settled the issue. Boston rolled in the finale, Bird icing the 102-91 game with seven points in the final two minutes. Bird had been big as usual throughout the entire series; despite being blanketed defensively by Houston's Robert Reid he had compensated for frosty shooting with nearly 16 rebounds and 8 assists across the series. But is was Cedric Maxwell who had ignited the vital game-five charge, and it was thus unsung Maxwell who walked off with series MVP honors.

The unlikely—even the unthinkable—occurred a year later, at the end of Larry Bird's third season. Once more—in what was becoming a disturbing pattern—the Celtics started slowly against Philadelphia in the conference finals and slipped dangerously far behind with only a single victory in the first four contests. Boston had actually gotten out of the gate with a blowout in Game 1 but then seemed to come unaccountably unglued. A contributing factor in the slide had certainly been an injury to floor general Tiny Archibald, who separated his shoulder in the Game 2-loss that seemingly ignited the Sixers. Yet history seemed about to repeat itself when the always-dangerous-when-wounded Celtics roared back with a pair of wins at home and on the road to deadlock the see-saw affair. But even the charm of the shamrock eventually runs out of storybook finishes, and in 1983 Boston's Game 7 luck ran completely dry. The deciding match was a stunning 120-107 Sixers romp in Boston Garden of all places. Andrew Toney's 34 and Dr. J's 29 put exclamation points on the one-sided affair. It was the first time that any Philadelphia team had captured a Game-7 match on the charmed parquet floor and also only the second time a Boston team had ever lost a seventh game in either the conference finals or NBA Finals.

Defeat in the conference showdown of 1982 had been a painful affair for a Boston ballclub that had improved in the victory column during each of Bird's seasons (logging 61,

62 and 63 victories) and yet had only once made it to the season's final series. The Bill Fitch coaching saga had now taken a distinct turn for the worse. The drill-sergeant coach's non-stop intensity seemed to be wearing thin on his veteran team. The lowpoint would come in next season's second postseason round, a four-game sweep at the hands of a Central Division champion Milwaukee Bucks team that had won five less regular-season games than Fitch's runner-up Atlantic Division outfit. None of the games were even exceptionally close, although the game2 margin was only four points at the final buzzer. The Boston team was clearly no longer playing with much enthusiasm and had only seemed to be going through the motions against a hungrier Milwaukee contingent.

Bird took the Milwaukee drubbing seriously and even personally. He would later call it the most painful moment of his life. And in his autobiography entitled *Drive* he would tell veteran Boston writer Bob Ryan that "it was the worst feeling I've ever had playing basketball" and one that even seemed at the time like the end of the world. Bird vowed to spend the winter relentlessly working alone to prepare himself for a strong comeback season. For Bird, the supreme competitor, only a truly marvelous upcoming year and a resulting championship ring could hope to erase the nightmare of that embarrassing Milwaukee debacle.

A new era dawned with Bird's fifth year in the form of two crucial personnel changes. Former backcourt great K. C. Jones now replaced a disillusioned Bill Fitch on the bench in what was seemingly the most significant move. On the roster front, Rick Robey—Bird's best pal off-court —was shipped off to Phoenix for veteran guard Dennis Johnson in what was quickly to prove another stroke of Boston front office genius. Tiny Archibald also departed via the wavier wire, where he was claimed by the very Milwaukee Bucks who had provided last season's humiliation. But with all the shakeups it was nonetheless business as usual in Beantown and the Celtics once again systematically put 62 victories and an Atlantic Divi-

sion title on the board.

Jones would prove to be a breath of fresh air on the beleaguered Boston bench. He allowed his players far more freedom to freelance on the court and then to relax off the court. Where Fitch was sometimes overbearing in his maniacal approach to game-day preparations, Jones was laconic and almost detached in his soft-sell approach to winning. Under Jones a player's individual creativity was no longer being stifled. But the switch from Archibald to Dennis Johnson in the backcourt was equally vital. DJ would soon be labelled by no lesser figure than Larry Bird as the most intelligent defender he had ever played with.

There were also other changes for the new-look Boston Celtics, and they were in every case more than merely cosmetic tinkerings. Danny Ainge was a second round 1981 draft pick who was highly enough considered by Auerbach for the Boston front office to hand out $800,000 in compensation to the American League Toronto Blue Jays to terminate the BYU All-American's brief major league baseball career. Quinn Buckner had been added to the backcourt mix a season before Dennis Johnson in exchange for the rights (shipped to Milwaukee) to "retired" superstar Dave Cowens. Scott Wedman was added in midseason of 1982-83 and promised to shore up the frontcourt offense. Jerry Sichting became a more permanent backcourt fixture at the outset of the 1985-86 season when picked up from Indiana, and injury-weakened Cedric Maxwell was unloaded at the same time to the Los Angeles Clippers for equally injury-riddled legend Bill Walton.

Also by the 1984 season Kevin McHale had fully matured in his familiar sixth-man post and later (after the trade of Maxwell) also in his newfound starter's role. The 1984 campaign which marked K. C. Jones's takeover of the ballclub would be McHale's best outing as the team's frontline substitute. His scoring output jumped to above 18 per game and he was the team's third rebounder and blocked shots leader. And when Maxwell was peddled for Walton in 1985 McHale stepped into the everyday lineup, with Walton in

Frank P. McGrath, Jr.

Kevin McHale—once he got the ball—was the most difficult low post player to defend in the entire half-century history of the NBA.

turn inheriting McHale's former role. For the first time "The Big Three" lineup of Bird, Parish and McHale was a fixture for opening tip-offs.

It would be in the 1984 postseason that the Celtics and Lakers would finally renew their storied championship rivalry after a remarkable fifteen-year hiatus. The last head-to-head title confrontation had been the altogether memorable one featuring Russell's final curtain call, as well as Chamberlain's famed AWOL fourth-quarter non-performance and sideline spat with Coach Van Breda Kolff, and Jack Kent Cook's ruined post-game celebration party. There had been six previous title shootouts between the two (plus a seventh when Elgin Baylor was a rookie and the Lakers were still in Minneapolis) and Boston had won them all, though rarely very easily. This time promised the same intense competition from start to finish. But Boston didn't arrive at that showdown without a titanic struggle in earlier rounds. First they had to contend with the spunky New York Knicks and the feisty Bernard King in an Eastern Conference semifinals matchup that went down to the wire.

The renewed Los Angeles-Boston title shootout started out as a most one-sided affair. But the momentum suddenly reversed with Gerald Henderson's perfectly timed steal of a lazy James Worthy to Byron Scott pass in the closing moments of Game 2. Henderson's resulting bucket tied the game, which Scott Wedman eventually won in overtime. After an LA rout in Game 3 Boston somehow dodged another bullet in the next outing by coming back from a five-point deficit in the final minute, then again winning in overtime when Magic and Worthy missed crucial free throws and M. L. Carr settled the issue with a final breakaway dunk.

Boston would finally take command of the hard-fought series with two of the most memorable clashes ever staged in the rickety but home-team-friendly Boston Garden. Los Angeles could easily have won in four straight but instead Magic's forces now fell behind 3-2 when Boston coasted

Larry Bird displays the personal hardware he won—a sporty new Trans Am automobile and the highly coveted NBA Finals MVP trophy—while leading the Celtics to the 1984 league title over Los Angeles and Magic Johnson.

121-103 in a fifth game contested in near 100-degree courtside temperatures inside a crammed and cramped Boston building. A deciding Game 7 in the same locale also fell Boston's way when Maxwell made good on his pre-game locker room boasts (that he would carry the entire team on his back) by carving up James Worthy, while Parish and McHale overpowered the rest of LA's suddenly helpless inside forces.

Maxwell unfortunately would not be around for much of the following season and the impact of that fact was considerable. Surgery for a nagging knee injury wiped out 25 regular-season games, and he wasn't much of a force when he returned, short on physical stamina, at year's end. Bird would later attribute the observable difference between the 1984 championship club and the 1985 title loser to Maxwell's midseason debilitating knee injury, one that forced an operation, limited him to 57 regular-season games, and rendered his postseason performance nearly useless.

Maxwell's injuries didn't slow the second Jones-coached club during regular season wars as they actually improved by a single game and bested everyone else in either conference from November to April with 63 victories. They also breezed in early playoff rounds against Cleveland (3-1), Detroit (4-2) and Philadelphia (4-1). But the rematch with the Lakers would take on a far different tone with a crippled Maxwell averaging less than four per game throughout postseason action. Things started well enough when the hot-handed Celtics shot 61 percent from the floor in the lidlifter and romped 148-114. But 38-year-old Kareem Abdul-Jabbar survived that humiliation to outplay Parish in the next two outings. Jabbar would in the end stand as the series MVP and was the obvious difference between the two ballclubs, with an able assist from James Worthy. When LA captured Game 6 on the strength of 29 each from Jabbar and Worthy the victory would not only even the ledger between Bird and Magic but also provide a pair of historical "firsts" which were both exceedingly painful to all Beantown fans. The Lakers had at long last—after eight futile tries—won an NBA title against their ancient foes. And for the first time ever the Celtics had also witnessed an opponent steal a championship from them on their very own legendary Boston Garden parquet floor.

As so often happened on the heels of embarrassing defeat, the Celtics would now retool with still another prize castoff veteran about to experience a Boston-based career revival. Injury-slowed Bill Walton was destined to be the surprising prized supporting actor of the 1986 championship season which brought Boston a 16th world championship banner. With the often-hobbled but once incomparable redhead now providing much-needed relief for Parish, McHale and even Bird, the team claimed a record 67 regular-season games. The total was the second best in franchise history, and the homecourt 41-1 record was the best of any team in league history. Walton was without parallel as a dominating low-post player during his days at UCLA, and therefore the most brilliant of NBA futures seemed all but

Boston's Bill Walton grapples for the ball with Houston Rockets star Akeem Olajuwon during Game 2 of the 1986 NBA Finals.

assured. There was a bright start with an NBA ring earned in Portland back in 1977, but then an endless string of recurring foot ailments had robbed Walton of most of his promised brilliance. Now he was merely hanging on with the dream of one final title, yet healthy enough finally to play a key role in bringing that dream to life.

For the second time of the decade there would be an unanticipated title showdown with spunky Houston. The Rockets seemed to have a knack for grabbing the final postseason spot in June that was conceded by all the expert prognosticators to Los Angeles back in November. Malone was now residing in Philadelphia, but the Rockets were still surviving with rugged frontline play, this time around from the vaunted Twin Towers duo of Hakeem Olajuwon and Ralph Sampson. They dropped an opening game to the Lakers in the conference finals out West and then rolled off four straight, one coming on a miraculous final shot by Sampson. The six-game series with Boston was perhaps most memorable for the image of diminutive Jerry Sichting scuffling with the towering Ralph Sampson and the latter being ejected from the floor for his indiscretions. And also of course for the image of Walton joyously celebrating at

the end of the series in which he had been a major and unlikely contributor for one final time in his often ill-starred career.

Long-time *Boston Globe* columnist Bob Ryan appears to be basketball's version of baseball chronicler and filmmaker Ken Burns. And this goes far beyond the immense observational talents usually displayed by both. While Burns in his award-winning public television documentary seems to have operated largely from an assumption that little in baseball's illustrious history ever transpired very far from the nation's eastern seaboard and the two-league cities of New York and Boston, so too has Ryan also approached the cage sport with the thickest possible set of kelly green blinders. In penning an essay on the ongoing Boston-Auerbach dynasty for a 1994 edition of *The Official NBA Basketball Encyclopedia* Ryan proposes as non-negotiable his claim that Parish and Walton in 1986 constituted the best one-two center punch in NBA history, and furthermore that Walton in 1985-86 was the greatest backup center ever seen anywhere on the planet. This is a bit much to swallow when one remembers that the Golden State Warriors had so potent a reserve pivot man in Nate Thurmond that they were once forced into trading Wilt Chamberlain. On the other hand, Ryan's exaggerations on behalf of his favored Boston team are nowhere near as far askew as Burns's own ignoring of crack players like Musial, Banks and Killebrew (since none played in New York or Boston) on the major league diamonds of the '50s and '60s.

The three marvelous seasons between 1984 and 1986 would thus be the pinnacle of Larry Bird's unmatched career. Three straight times he walked away as the league's most valuable performer, and also unquestionably its most dominating single force. It was only the third time in history that an individual was the league's MVP three years running, and the first time that the trick was accomplished by a non-center. Bird thus joined Russell and Chamberlain not only in this singular honor but also in stature as one of the game's true immortals. The final of the three miraculous campaigns was indeed one of the most dominating one-man performances in pro cage annals. Not only had Bird carried his team to the fourth best winning percentage (67-

Bird holds the 1986 NBA Championship trophy aloft for thousands of fans gathered at Boston City Hall Plaza. It was Bird's third and final league title and also number 16 in franchise history.

Boston Celtics are the only franchise with four different MVPs down through the years.

Another corner was now about to be turned, and this one certainly wouldn't be at all pleasant or fortune-blessed. What would soon become an unparalleled track record for unexpected misfortune and franchise misery would all start with the tragic circumstances surrounding the drafting of top prospect Len Bias a mere two weeks after the club had claimed a 16th world title by drubbing Houston and the Twin Towers. For a period of a few short hours it seemed as though Auerbach had once more worked his magic, getting a player in the draft who would inherit the ongoing tradition of Boston sixth-man standouts and then provide the key to team successes for the next decade or perhaps more. But Bias would never make it into a Boston uniform and his shocking death two days after the draft-day celebrations of 1986 would send the franchise reeling for the next several years. Given the circumstances that would follow, it might be claimed that a dozen years later the Boston ballclub has not yet fully recovered from the chain of bad breaks and dark clouds that trailed after the Len Bias catastrophe.

The death of Len Bias at first seemed to be only a temporary setback and nothing more than a rare aberration of extraordinary bad luck. But it soon didn't seem quite that way after a few additional ill-fated seasons had also passed. The team was on the surface strong enough the following winter, during K. C. Jones's fourth campaign at the con-

15) over the league's forty-year span, but he also himself finished in the top ten in five statistical categories: scoring average (25.8, fourth), rebounds (9.8, seventh), steals (2.02, ninth), free throw percentage (.896, first), and three-point shooting percentage (.423, fourth). As an afterthought, Larry also was the Celtics' top assists man at 6.8 per game.

It is a worn-out observation that Boston teams have never enjoyed a league scoring champion in the lineup. But scoring champions rarely win rings, something that has happened, in fact, on only 9 occasions and with three different players (Mikan, Abdul-Jabbar and Michael Jordan). When it comes to a truer measure of star players, Boston is more clearly in the lead. Only four NBA franchises can boast more than a single MVP winner (multiple claims on the honor by a single player, such as Chicago's Michael Jordan or Milwaukee's Kareem Abdul-Jabbar or Utah's Karl Malone are not considered here), and the

NBA Teams With Multiple MVPs

Boston Celtics

Bob Cousy (1957)
Bill Russell (1958, 1961, 1962, 1963, 1965)
Dave Cowens (1973)
Larry Bird (1984, 1985, 1986)

Philadelphia Sixers

Wilt Chamberlain (1966, 1967, 1968)
Julius Erving (1981)
Moses Malone (1983)

Los Angeles Lakers

Kareem Abdul-Jabbar (1976, 1977)
Magic Johnson (1987, 1989, 1990)

Houston Rockets

Moses Malone (1979, 1982)
Hakeem Olajuwon (1994)

Within a week of the 1986 championship victory storm clouds were about to gather on the horizon for the NBA's proudest franchise, and they would first arrive with the tragic circumstances surrounding the draft choice and sudden death of Maryland star Len Bias.

AP/Wide World Photos

trols. Both the divisional and conference crowns were defended in timely fashion and there was another date in the Finals with the traditional rivals from Los Angeles. The magic of Bill Walton's performance came to a sudden end, however, with a recurrence of the foot injuries that had seemingly always plagued the great center. Without Walton the Boston powerhouse front court rotation was significantly diminished. That wasn't the end to the events which transformed the Celtics from an amazingly deep team to a surprisingly thin one. Scott Wedman was soon eliminated with a heel injury and Jerry Sichting was also slowed by a persistent virus.

And thus the road to the Finals rematch with LA was significantly rougher to negotiate. There was still Bird at the top of his game and the conference finals with Detroit even provided one of Bird's most spectacular individual moments. The steal on an inbounds pass from Isiah Thomas (and subsequent toss to Dennis Johnson for the game-winning score) in the closing seconds of the fifth game saved the hour and also perhaps the entire series. Yet two seven-game series with Milwaukee and Detroit had left the defending champions dragging and in no condition to do proper battle with the once-again geared up Magic Johnson Lakers.

All the luck ran out of the Celtics' coffers when the final series opened against Los Angeles. Magic was now at the top of his game, as Larry had been during the several previous seasons. With Abdul-Jabbar now near retirement, LA coach Pat Riley was calling on Magic to carry most of the offensive load. He had done so with a balanced season that had brought his own first MVP trophy. Now his 29 points, 13 assists and 8 rebounds—without even a single turnover—launched a blistering running game which

soundly thrashed the weary Celtics in the championship opener. Boston could slow the momentum only in games three and five and thus fell without putting up much of an expected fight. McHale who had broken his foot earlier in the season was further hobbled as the one-sided finale wore on. The merciful end came in the Forum in Game 6 with Kareem and Worthy doing the big scoring and Magic applying the final icing with another all-around brilliant display: he averaged 26 points and 13 assists in the Finals and hit 54% from the field and 96% on charity tosses. Magic had also won Game 4 in the closing seconds with a memorable shot he would later label as "my junior, junior, junior sky hook." There was little surprise that Magic Johnson added the Finals MVP award to his earlier regular-season trophy.

No one could have guessed it at the time, but an era had now suddenly ended. Magic and Bird had met in a championship series for a final time, with the count standing 2-1 in Johnson's favor. The Lakers would be back to defend their title a year later with the first NBA "repeat" in the twenty seasons since Russell's retirement. And they would appear twice more in the Finals in losing roles before Magic's career shockingly ended with the Fall 1991 pre-season announcement of his infection with HIV. For Birds' part, this had been the last championship dance. It would be all downhill in Boston from here on out.

With the 1988 campaign—the last for K. C. Jones on the Boston bench—began also the long, slow decline of Larry Bird. The end was in sight almost from the earliest days of the 1988 season, but Bird was far too much of a ruthless competitor to throw in the towel immediately. He would battle on gamely against his deteriorating physical condition—acute back pain despite corrective surgery in the summer of 1991. The decline was anything but apparent during that final Jones-led season as Bird actually posted his highest scoring totals (loftiest average and second highest point total) of his career. The margin of divisional domination was the widest ever (19 games over Washington) and the first two rounds of the postseason seemed to augur yet another showdown with Magic and the Lakers. This time the Pistons with their new "Bad Boy" image would not be pushovers, however. The tarnish that was beginning to adhere to the "Celtics mystique" now revealed itself in the form of several near misses in the kinds of games in which past Boston squads always managed somehow to escape. When it appeared that Bird and company were again about the evade the bullet with a game-five victory in the Garden, Isiah's troops worked a big second half comeback and prevailed in overtime. The issue was settled a single game later back in Detroit. Luck and time were beginning to run out for Larry Bird and his teammates.

The bad luck that had begun for the team as a whole

Celtics coach Jimmy Rodgers speaks with reporters about the injuries which have slowed franchise star Larry Bird early in the 1989 season. Bird meanwhile hones his shooting touch in the background.

as a shameless trash talker. One incident in the locker room moments before Bird captured his third long distance title underscored a mastery of the art of psychological warfare. "Which one of you is planning to finish second?" Larry inquired while sizing up his competition.

Bird's final four seasons—two under Rodgers and two under Chris Ford—saw the team still posting some remarkably good numbers. In the three campaigns when Larry played a half-season or more there were fifty or more victories and also two divisional titles and one runner-up finish. Larry carried the team's scoring load twice more, though he finally dipped below a 20-point average for the first near-full-season of his career during his penultimate NBA winter. But the famed and dreaded Boston drive seemed gone from the postseason wars. The embarrassing collapse against the Knicks in the opening round in 1990 cost Jimmy Rodgers his coaching job. A year later, under Ford, the backsliding Celtics again struggled mightily in the first round just to get by the usually lowly Indiana Pacers. And against the defending champion Pistons they managed a 2-1 lead before falling so far behind in each of the final three games that even marvelous fourth-quarter comebacks could not salvage even a single victory. Parish missed the final game with a badly sprained pair of ankles. And Bird's back pain was now so severe that he spent spells off the

also reached flood-like proportions in the final seasons of the eighties, especially during postseason competitions. Walton's foot injury had robbed the team of vital bench strength for the 1987 playoff run, as had Wedman's and Sichting's ailments. Foot problems had also begun to bedevil the sturdy McHale. But the biggest blow came with Bird himself, when Larry went down after only six games of the 1989 season. Heel surgery meant the end of Bird for the year and the end of the Celtics as a serious challenger as well, although Jimmy Rodgers' first-edition team did manage to hang on for a .500 season (42-40) and a first-round playoff appearance. With no Bird in the lineup, however, the ascending Pistons made quick fodder out of the once-proud Celtics on the way to their own first championship flag.

On the heels of three consecutive MVP seasons came some lesser landmarks along the Larry Bird trek directly toward the Naismith Hall of Fame in Springfield. There would be three consecutive triumphs in the All-Star Weekend Long Distance Shootout competition that had become a midseason showcase event for the league. It was a competition that showed off an element of Bird's game often buried under all the other brilliance. And it was an event that also revealed another side of Larry Bird—his reputation

Reggie Lewis already seemed the franchise star of the future in 1990, but he would enjoy only three more seasons before tragedy once again struck the Boston Celtics family.

court lying on the floor in front of the team bench, since sitting was all but impossible. Back surgery followed in the off-season and the end seemed frightfully near.

And there were now new kids on the block for the NBA's annual title hunt. The Detroit Pistons had become the league's dominant team by the late 80s when they finally overtook Boston in the East and posted their own pair of titles to match the earlier repeat performance by Magic's Los Angeles Lakers. Then Jordan's Chicago Bulls began constructing their own mini-dynasty as the new decade opened. A few seasons earlier Jordan had been a virtual one-man-team against the Celtics in a magical Boston Garden solo performance. Now he had players like Scottie Pippen and Bill Cartwright and Horace Grant in the lineup alongside him and the old order in Boston and LA had suddenly been supplanted by a new order in Chicago.

There were also new faces in the Boston lineup at the twilight of Bird's career. Some of these new teammates were truly exciting athletes, and a couple were even awe-inspiring with their eye-catching displays of raw future potential. Top draft picks Reggie Lewis and Brian Shaw provided a promising backcourt tandem that dredged up shadows of Sam Jones and K. C. Jones if not of Cousy and Sharman. Lewis, in particular, was a most special talent who quickly inherited the club's top scoring role as Bird wilted under his bouts with back pain. Dee Brown also produced speed and a good deal of flash and drew attention with his slam dunk contest showing on All-Star Weekend in Miami.

The old guard was now changing rapidly in Boston Garden. And there was even talk that the famed Garden itself would not survive many more winters. Danny Ainge had left along with Brad Lohas for Sacramento in a February 1989 trade that brought Joe Kleine and Ed Pinckney on board and was designed to alievate pressure on the aging Parish and McHale up front. Lewis and Shaw had quickly made an aging Ainge expendable. Parish and McHale didn't seem to have much time left as each was hounded by injuries almost as much as Bird. With Bird on the sideline for virtually the entire 1989 campaign the nightly lineup hardly looked like that of the Boston Celtics anymore.

Each new decade in the past had always managed to bring with it amazing revitalization of franchise fortunes. Auerbach himself first arrived on the scene in 1950 as the team poised to lead the young league in integration with Chuck Cooper and in fastbreak offense with Bob Cousy. The Russell-Cousy dynasty had first reached high speed with the team's first repeat title in 1960. Heinsohn assumed the coaching chores in 1970 and then Fitch and Bird arrived jointly exactly one decade later.

The coaching debut of Chris Ford in 1990 had at first looked like a bright continuation of this noble decade-opening tradition. But every professional sports franchise is bound to have its bad decade somewhere along the line. For the Boston Celtics who had never yet known a truly bad stretch of more than a handful of seasons the time was now finally at hand. The last Bird-Magic championship showdown began to look more and more with the passage of time like the final hurrah for a once proud but now laughingstock franchise.

It all wound down in the summer of 1992 when the pain finally became too much even for Larry Bird. There was a token and perhaps even merely "honorary" appearance with the fabulous USA "Dream Team" at the Barcelona Olympics, but Larry didn't play much and suffered physically through most of the experience, which was far more like an ordeal. Finally came the long-dreaded retirement announcement at the close of the 1992 season. It was one of the darkest days ever for Boston, New England, and even the NBA itself.

Verbal tributes for Bird at career's end were seemingly endless and at times seemingly unmatched in the post-career celebratory tours for any previous NBA stars. Old-rival Magic Johnson paid perhaps the greatest single tribute on the day they retired famous jersey number thirty-three in Boston. "You lied," Magic gently and playfully chastized in response to Bird's own earlier self-effacing comments, because "there never will be another Larry Bird."

Sudden loss by the NBA of both Bird and Magic had left, seemingly overnight, a huge void, despite the endless hype and adoration surrounding the career of their league-anointed heir, Michael Jordan. Many would later claim that the Bulls' championship run against watered down competition—despite the ceaseless hype it engendered—never quite matched the achievement of the two tradition-draped teams in Los Angeles and Boston during the heyday of Magic and Bird. Bird and Magic were the last of the great team-oriented players. Michael Jordan—for all his athleticism and shooting skills—launched an era of selfish superstars which are now being replicated at dizzying speed with the likes of Allen Iverson, Kevin Garnett and Kobe Bryant. And basketball as a fan spectacle has been in a downward spiral ever since.

Bird ended his magical career—despite a handful of subpar seasons near the end—with a statistical line that reads 24.3 points, 10 rebounds, and 6.3 assists for 13 years of regular-season play. The postseason totals were nearly identical: 23.8, 10.3, 6.3. No other forward in the game's history boasts a line anything like this. But like the case of Bill Russell, the numbers are only the flip side of the story. Russell launched a dynasty and then steadfastly maintained it. Bird resurrected a franchise and an entire league along the way.

CHAPTER VII

A Dozen-Plus Games for the Ages

In baseball it is the slowly unfolding season—spread across five languid summer months—that is the true measure of the game's internal pulse. Baseball is the one sport played without a ticking time clock. It is thus a game which unfolds to its own innate rhythms—pitched balls, the ebb and flow of elastic innings, ritual heaves and tosses or arching fly balls and sizzling liners—and at its own unhurried step-by-step pace. Earl Weaver once brilliantly pegged the very essence of the diamond game when he reminded a pestering sportswriter that "this ain't football, we do this every day." A standby cliché of the sport after any tough loss or during any prolonged player or team slump is that "it is a long season" yet to be unfolded, one where the best teams and best performers always somehow eventually rise to the top like enriched cream. The unfolding summer-long pennant race—the measure of the full day-by-day season—capsulizes the essential flavor of the game.

In pro basketball, however, it is the frenetic ebb and flow of each individual game that better mirrors the true essence of the sport. Basketball's rhythm is indeed the rhythm of a beating time clock, which in the modern era marks not only the duration of each 48-minute game but the pace and strategies of each trip down the floor. A shot clock means that each possession of the ball is a race against a clicking sideline time piece. The nature and speed of play makes the action most difficult to segment in our memories—we may remember a crucial play at the game's end—or even a handful of them—but we are hard pressed to recreate the details or pinpoint the exact place of the event in the game's ebb-and-flow actions. Did that breathtaking drive to the bucket by Jordan come in the third or fourth quarter? With two minutes left or two and a half? With the score tied or the home team still trailing? Such memories are usually a hopeless blur.

Basketball remains a short race to a frenzied conclusion, especially as it is played in the top professional league. The notion correctly exists that seemingly endless regular-season marathon schedules to decide playoff qualifiers are almost meaningless and the sport's true rationale—in the NBA at least—is a "second-season" of playoff contests—a short string of highly significant individual games with elimination staring squarely at the losers. Indeed, it is the individual game and not the drawn-out full season which is basketball's most significant measurable time period.

And the Boston Celtics' annals are jammed with some (perhaps most) of the truly memorable games comprising the sport's half-century history. Often the cynic will observe that the unfolding course of Boston Celtics history has been littered with a remarkable collection of lucky breaks. It is the miraculous survival of the team's championship record in so many breath-stopping moments over the years (especially throughout the decade of the '60s) that many have in mind when they refer to something called a Celtics mystique. Time and again during the Russell Era and again across the Bird Era a series of championship seasons always seemed to turn on a lucky bounce or surprise happenstance (perhaps an injury like Wilt's tender knee, or a bad coaching decision like Van Breda Kolff's choice of Mel Counts over Wilt down the stretch run) which kept the green-clad team alive and barely breathing.

If it were not for so many key baskets or rebounds or steals with last-second victory hanging in the balance, Boston's unbeaten string in the sixties would have been broken on a number of occasions. There was Havlicek's steal, remarkable desperation shots by Sam Jones and Don Nelson and Frank Ramsey, key misses by opponents like Pettit and Selvy—lucky bounces all, unaccountable gifts that somehow always seemed to keep the Celtics juggernaut straight on course toward hanging another banner in the rafters.

But of course it is the most obvious truism of the sportsworld that all championship teams in the end make their own luck, and that seeming "good breaks" are nearly always the clear result in one fashion or another of mere preparation, hardwork, and overriding skill. On one level, at least, the essence of Boston Celtics history lies in the stories of so many individual games in which it was demonstrated on the hardwood time after time that the best and not just the luckiest team always managed to find the wherewithal to win. Here are the capsule portraits of a dozen of those most memorable games. Any one or two taken out of context might appear to demonstrate that Lady Luck and Dame Fortune were annually riding the Boston bench. But taken together these landmark contests are the living testimony to the Boston team's hard-earned if inexorable winning tradition.

Cousy's Record-Breaking Fifty Points
(March 21, 1953)

Celtics 111, Syracuse 105 (4OT)
(Eastern Division Semifinals)

On the surface of it this was one of the ugliest games of early NBA history, one of a string of plodding postseason sideshows that did the league near irreparable harm and one that league officials in subsequent years would have loved to strike from memory. It was also the game which clinched Bob Cousy's credentials as a league star and demonstrated his rare abilities to dominate any game under existing league rules. However you choose to look at it, one of Boston's ugliest-ever postseason wins was also one of the most historically significant games of early pro basketball history.

The context for this memorable contest was the postseason of the NBA's fourth season after the BAA-NBL merger, a time when fouling was the game's chief strategy, and an era when each new season was bringing a host of desperate rule adjustments to stem the plague of hacking and grabbing that slowed every tightly contested battle. There was still another full season to be played before two truly earthshaking adjustments in playing rules would change the sport forever—Danny Biasone's shot-clock and the sanctions on the number of fouls a team (not a player) could commit in any one quarter without penalties. When Boston and Syracuse squared off in Beantown in the second game of the best-of-three Eastern Division semifinals (Boston up 1-0) with the Celtics anticipating their first trip ever past the first playoff round, rampant fouling was still the rage (and the sane strategy, given the league's operating rules) and fouls would indeed play a major role in the outcome. And so would Bob Cousy.

But with regulation time running out and the Nats nursing a one-point advantage, the flashy Boston backcourt ace was nearly the game's designated goat rather than its gallant hero. Cousy's crisp pass to an open teammate in the closing seconds fooled everyone on the floor and sailed out of bounds. Only a Boston steal on the inbounds pass handed Cousy a second chance to shine—one he took advantage of. Cooz was hacked intentionally driving to the hoop with two seconds showing and was awarded a single shot, which he calmly canned to send the contest into an extra session. The teams continued to jockey for position in the overtime with Syracuse out-pointing the Celtics 9-8 (5 by their backcourt ace) into the final seconds. Again Cousy was fouled savagely to prevent a final shot and again he proved to have ice-water in his veins by sinking the tying charity toss.

Cousy was not done. In a second overtime period he again provided the heroics, this time with a running hook (as he avoided another attempt at fouling) which knotted the count once more only seconds before the clock again expired. In the third overtime, with tension reaching the breaking point and the home crowd in a frenzy, the Dolph Schayes-led Nats edged out to a seemingly safe five-point advantage with only thirteen ticks remaining. But no lead seemed safe on this night with Bob Cousy hitting on all cylinders and with everything the "Hardwood Houdini" tossed toward the hoop seemingly guided by radar. First the Cooz drove the lane, canned a bucket, and was fouled in the process. His three-point-play sliced the margin to a single bucket with the clock down to five seconds. A turnover and another wild heave from near midcourt by the charmed Boston guard spelled a fourth overtime and convinced drained patrons (and probably also exhausted opponents) that they were on this rare night witnessing pure magic.

With Cousy canning six of his team's nine in the first overtime and then eight of nine in the third it might have appeared that the evening's heroics had been pushed to the limit. But Cousy was still not done. Syracuse again built a five-point advantage and then again wilted under Boston's backcourt pressure as the remarkable Cousy accounted for nine more tallies in the final frame and the home club at last pulled out to a series-ending 111-105 advantage. Those who witnessed the game and those who read press accounts the next day had little doubt they had seen the most miraculous single effort ever witnessed in a game of professional basketball. (Frank Selvy's collegiate 100-point game was still a year away and Wilt's similar NBA effort was still nearly a decade down the road.) Cousy had canned 50 points by himself, but more remarkable still, half of them had come in four pressure-packed overtimes. He had drilled 30 of 32 charity throws under the most arduous of circumstances, killing single-handedly the fouling tactics of the enemy team. And he had dominated a postseason game as no guard had ever dominated one before, and as few would ever dominate one in all the many seasons that have followed. It would be a handful of seasons more before Boston would be regarded as one of the league's elite teams; the following week they would quickly be eliminated in the division finals by a less-than-stellar New York team. But after this one heroic performance Boston's Bob Cousy was already universally accepted as the best backcourt man to be found anywhere on the pro hardwood circuit.

Boston's First Championship Banner (April 13, 1957)

Celtics 125, St. Louis 123 (2OT) (NBA Finals Game 7)

The difference between the dynasty that Auerbach would eventually build around Russell, Cousy, Sharman, The Jones Boys, and an endless cast of reinforcements and the dynasties that might have been for other teams like the St. Louis Hawks with Bob Pettit or the Los Angeles Lakers of West and Baylor would often in the end come down to but a single game—most often even a single buzzer-beating shot. The Celtics' very first championship was certainly that way. And the game that decided that inaugural title is still

Hawks superstar Bob Pettit drives around Bill Russell (hidden) for a score in the opening game of the exciting 1957 St. Louis-Boston championship shootout. Tom Heinsohn (#15) and Bill Sharman (far left) also watch the action in Boston Garden.

considered—four decades latter—to be one that not only launched a budding dynasty but also solidified an entire infant NBA as a big-time national sport. With the new high-speed action and high-octane scoring brought on by the radical 1954 24-second shooting legislation the circuit had steadily been gaining fans and respectability nationwide. With an increased television audience tuned in for the Saturday afternoon finale and with a huge press contingent in town for the opening of a new baseball season at Fenway Park, pro basketball was primed to benefit from a nail-biting and emotion-packed contest that featured some of the sport's greatest athletes. And that was precisely what the league and its newfound audience got. Few subsequent NBA championship showdowns have ever been better played or more laced with unbearable excitement.

For any franchise the first world championship is always perhaps the very sweetest. This was especially true for Walter Brown's and Red Auerbach's Boston Celtics, a barely respectable team during the NBA's first dozen of so seasons and an outfit which had endured a long decade of frustration trying to crack the small circle of the league's elite teams. Only a few seasons earlier owner Walter Brown had been forced to mortgage his home and sell off furniture to keep the struggling franchise afloat. The City of Boston had not owned a world champion in any sport since the 1941 NHL Bruins, and the beloved baseball Red Sox had not worn a postseason crown in almost four decades. For all his innovations with fast-break basketball Auerbach had been tolerated in most league circles as colorful but annoying; and he had at first been widely second-guessed at home for only begrudgingly accepting local hero Bob Cousy on his roster. Now Brown and Auerbach finally had their hour to gloat, and although it would be far from the last it had to be one of the most savory.

The victory that locked up the first Boston title did not come easily or without its own gigantic portion of apparent luck. This despite the fact that Boston with veterans Cousy and Sharman in the backcourt and rookies Russell and Heinsohn up front had dominated the regular season (winning six more games that the next best club, Syracuse) and were heavily favored in the finals against the Western Division survivor from St. Louis. Yet the underrated Hawks, with former Celtics Ed Macauley and Cliff Hagan now in the front court alongside superstar Bob Pettit, were much better than their sub-.500 regular-season ledger. The teams split the first six games and battled to a draw through almost the entire rubber match. There were few heroics this time around from Bob Cousy; in fact the Boston backcourt duo of Cousy and Sharman picked the first legitimate shot at a championship in club history to simultaneously suffer their worst postseason performances ever. Together they canned only five of forty shots; Cousy missed a foul shot that might have iced the game with 13 seconds remaining;

Sharman drew iron on two of his patented jumpers that might have sunk St. Louis in the final seconds of regulation play. But there were other heroes to fill the void on both sides of the floor. Rookie Russell blocked a shot by the Hawks' Jack Coleman that would have put the visitors up by three in the final minute, then sprinted to the other end for a bucket of his own. (Heinsohn later called Russell's block on Coleman the greatest single play he ever witnessed on a basketball court.) Fellow rookie Heinsohn nailed three vital shots in the second overtime before fouling out and was the offensive standout with 37 points and 23 rebounds. On the Hawks side, Pettit canned two pressure free throws with three seconds left to force an overtime.

The final outcome wasn't settled until the waning seconds of the second extra frame. Heinsohn's final bucket at the two minute mark had edged Boston in front 121-120. Ramsey's wild jumper which somehow found the mark and Loscutoff's pressure free throw keep to Celts on top by a pair with one second left. And then fate played its last trump card. After a final time out Hawks' player-coach Alex Hannum put the ball in play by heaving it the length of the court off the Boston backboard in an unorthodox but carefully designed play. The strategum nearly paid championship dividiends as the ball bounced into Pettit's hands before the final horn. Pettit's last shot was necessarily rushed and from just inside the foul line and skidded off the rim as a jammed Boston Garden held its collective breath. As would so often in the future be the case around Boston Garden, the difference between championship joy and also-ran dejection was in the end a single clock tick and barely the width of a basket's iron rim.

Pettit's Marvelous Fifty-Point Show
(April 12, 1958)

St. Louis 110, Celtics 109
(NBA Finals Game 6)

Only twice in Russell's thirteen years in a Boston uniform did the invincible Celtics fail to hoist a championship banner into the Boston Garden rafters, and on both occasions it took some exceptionally bad breaks alongside some incredible individual performances by opposition players to block Russell's path to the winner's circle. The first time was not long in coming and involved a fitting piece of revenge for the very man who had missed by a mere hair's breadth of stealing the NBA title which had punctuated Bill Russell's rookie stellar season.

There was little indication throughout most of Russell's sophomore pro season that the results would be any different from those enjoyed during his first trip around the league. Boston had little trouble repeating its regular season domination, breezing to the league's top won-lost mark (49-

Pettit defends in Boston Garden versus a driving Tommy Heinsohn in game five of the 1958 NBA title series. Three nights later Pettit would take over the series with his marvelous 50-point performance.

23) and an eight-game bulge over Syracuse in the Eastern Division. And St. Louis with the ever-dangerous Pettit was waiting in the wings once more for a replay postseason showdown. But things turned bad for Boston in the third game of the final series when Russell badly damaged an ankle with the issue knotted at a single game apiece. Yet even with Russell's injury (removing him from games four, five and six) changing the odds drastically, Auerbach and company nearly pulled off a gutsy title defense. They might well have done so if Pettit had not chosen to have the most stellar postseason of his spectacular career. Boston evened the series in the fourth contest and nearly walked off with the next game as well, even though their weakened front court (Loscutoff also missed the entire season due to injury) was no match for the Hawks' inside power game spurred by Pettit and Hagan. Pettit's final heroics came in the turning-point sixth game which spelled ultimate doom for Boston.

But even here, the margin between defeat and victory was as almost as fine as a slim silk thread.

Pettit replaced Mikan as the game's greatest offensive center and retired in 1965 at the top of the career lists in scoring (20,880) and rebounding (12,849), although Wilt Chamberlain (at the end of only his sixth season) was already nipping savagely at his heels in both categories. While a dozen players have now passed Pettit's career rebounding numbers, his legacy remains intact as the first ever to score 20,000 NBA points and also as the most talented rebounding forward of the league's first half-century. In the first ten of his eleven pro campaigns this rugged clutch player never finished lower than fifth among league leaders in rebounding or scoring, a claim no other NBA player can make to this day. Such accomplishments would be remarkable enough for even the most gifted of athletes; they were simply overwhelming for a basketballer who was first cut twice from his high school squad and later considered too frail physically to succeed in the NBA ranks, despite two All-American seasons and a 27.4 career scoring average at LSU.

There was far more to Bob Pettit and his brilliant career, of course, than mere numbers. He was for one thing the most relentlessly driven and highly competitive star of his era, and also as much a champion of the model work ethic as he was of indivual point-producing and rebounding. In fact, Bob Pettit was arguably the greatest "second-effort player" in all of basketball history. No one worked harder than the 1955 NBA rookie of the year, two-time NBA MVP, and eleven-time league all-star. And no one could be more devastating to the opposition when it came to crunch time—in either crucial postseason games or less vital nightly regular-season games. No example of this outshines one memorable 50-point performance delivered in the deciding sixth game of the 1958 league championship series. Revenging a previous-year's defeat by the Celtics, Pettit put Boston away with a torrid shooting display that featured 19 of his team's final 21 fourth-quarter points, including the game-deciding tip-in with 15 seconds left on the clock. Pettit's 50 only tied the league single-game playoff mark by Cousy (which had been achieved with the help of 30 points from the foul line and four overtimes of extra clock time); but it was nonetheless the most stunning offensive display before or since in a postseason NBA game with the league title sitting squarely on the line.

With that one performance this exceptional franchise player delivered the Hawks their only NBA title banner. But night-in and night-out for a full decade stretching from the mid-fifties through mid-sixties Bob Pettit almost singlehandedly made the Milwaukee and St. Louis Hawks one of the league's most rugged challengers to an early reign of Boston Celtics mastery.

Selvy's Infamous Misfire
(April 18, 1962)

Celtics 110, Los Angeles Lakers 107 (OT)
(NBA Finals Game 7)

No major college star has ever scored more proficiently than Furman's Frank Selvy. Selvy's 100 points in a single game (versus Newberry College on February 13, 1954) has never been matched (or even approximated) in Division I NCAA play; the 6-4 forward was the first two-time national scoring champion (after "official" NCAA record-keeping began in 1948); and he was also first to register a single-season 40-plus scoring average (41.7, 1954). It is therefore a grand piece of unmatched irony that no NBA star is more narrowly remembered or more often vilified for a single important shot which he failed to make. Frank Selvy unfairly remains to this day the Bill Buckner of NBA championship play. Such are the rare twists of fickle fortune.

Frank Selvy (left) enjoys a happier postseason moment with Minneapolis Lakers teammates Rod Hundley (center) and Elgin Baylor (right). The occasion was a clinching victory over Detroit in the 1960 Western Division semifinals.

The 1961-62 season was so outrageous in its achievement that the Boston postseason triumph is today almost buried in the season's other details. It was in this campaign that Wilt averaged 50 a night in scoring, posted better than 4000 individual points for the only time in league history, and outpaced all other league marksman by an unheard of margin of nearly 40 per cent. This also was the season when Elgin Baylor averaged 38.3 (the best ever by anyone other than Wilt) in a shortened campaign (he was playing only weekends due to military service), while a rookie named Walt Bellamy averaged over 30 and was still outdistanced by Chamberlain by almost 20 points a night; it was also a campaign that witnessed the incomparably versatile Oscar Robertson average a triple-double (double figures in scoring, rebounding and assists) for an entire 80-game campaign. But by the time the Lakers and Celtics squared off for a championship the season's individual stars—Chamberlain and Robertson and Bellamy—had already long retired from the scene.

This set the stage for Selvy's unfortunate moment in the postseason spotlight. The NBA championship series itself turned on many crucial moments which might have brought ultimate victory or defeat to either team long before the two equal combatants reached a dramatic seventh-game showdown. The Lakers grabbed an early 2-1 series lead which also handed them a homecourt advantage they would fail to protect. West's buzzer-beating drive to the bucket in Game 3 might well have benefitted from the favorable control of the scoreboard clock by a zealous hometown official. In Games 4 and 6 Boston's gritty road victories blocked the inconsistent Lakers from riding the momentum of memorable outings by West (his Game 3 last-second heroics) and Baylor (a record 61 in Game 5) to ultimate victory.

Frank Selvy's unaccountable moment of rare ignominy unfolded in the waning seconds of a remarkable season's finale. It was a game that in the end (and the ending) truly rivalled the 1957 deciding match between Boston and St. Louis for its rare moments of raw drama and bone-crunching intensity. With some last-second heroics by Jerry West in Game 3, and Elgin Baylor's 61-point explosion in Game 5, the ill-starred Lakers had climbed within a single victory of their first-ever West Coast title. But as always, Red Auerbach's Celtics were simply invincible (and also more than a little lucky) in the final stretch run and thus roared back for a pair of crucial victories of their own, clutch wins which made them the first four-time back-to-back champions in NBA history.

The true turning point of the memorable series came in the final seconds of the closing game, a matchup that is rivalled perhaps only by the 1957 finale for its final-second heroics. As they had in Game 3, LA charged from four points back during the final minute of play on two clutch goals by none other than Frank Selvy. Aiming to duplicate West's last-minute performance of several nights earlier, Selvy also unleashed one final dramatic shot which glanced off the rim just as the regulation horn sounded. Had Selvy's missle connected with the game knotted at 100 the title would have been finally owned by the upstart Lakers, but it was simply not meant to be; an overtime session which followed would be all Boston, to the final tune of 110-107.

As painful as the 1962 championship loss was, it took on even further symbolic dimensions for West, Baylor, Selvy and company. The LA defeat allowed Boston to extend its own championship streak to four, besting the

Lakers' own record earlier set (1952-1954) when the franchise still resided in Minneapolis. Also continued was Boston's unbroken mastery over the Lakers during postseason play that would eventually continue on for another full decade. And in a final touch of irony, Selvy's fateful miss came at the end of the very season in which Wilt Chamberlain had scored 100 in a single game (March 2, 1962), a feat which had duplicated on the professional level Selvy's own unprecedented collegiate effort of eight short years earlier.

Cousy's Last Loud Roar
(April 24, 1963)

BOSTON

Celtics 112, Los Angeles Lakers 109
(NBA Finals Game 6)

At the time it seemed like the end of an era and more than likely the end of a remarkable dynasty run, but from the perspective later lent by history it would prove to be nothing more than a mere midpoint in the saga of basketball's most relentless winners. But for Bob Cousy and his many fans there could not have been a more perfect final curtain call—unless, of course, it had been one played out on the parquet floor of storied Boston Garden rather than thousands of miles away in the dingy environs of the Los Angeles Sports Arena.

It was not a surprise when Cousy announced at season's outset that his 13th NBA campaign would be his last. But it did of course add a special luster to the season, since one of the league's primary fixtures of its first two decades was now making his last trip around the circuit. And it also gave a special incentive to the team to send Mr. Basketball out as a winner yet one final time. Of course the Celtics already had plenty of motivation in the form of an opportunity to match the baseball Yankees and hockey Canadiens as the greatest consistent winners in pro sports history. At stake as the 1962-63 season raced toward its close was an unprecedented fifth straight NBA title and only the previous year's final opponents—the Lakers—stood in the way of the record-setting victory skeen.

The road to Cousy's final championship proved surprisingly rough, however. First there was a titanic struggle with Cincinnati and Oscar Robertson, the nonpareil guard who was about to inherit Cousy's personal crown as the league's supreme all-around backcourt performer. It was a tough and extraordinary series from end to end. Oscar proved up to the occasion when he led the challengers to a pair of narrow Boston Garden victories early in the series; the first four contests all uncharacteristically fell to the visitors and in the second Cincinnati win every player in the Royals' lineup cracked double figures. Game 4 was not only Cousy's one hundredth postseason appearance but

AP/Wide World Photos

AP/Wide World Photos

Auerbach storms the sidelines with his usual intensity during the Celtics tense 1963 title-clinching victory, which was also Bob Cousy's final game.

Cousy enjoys one of his numerous playoff highlight moments in Los Angeles as he drives for a bucket during the 1962 championship matchup. Lakers defenders are Jim Krebs and Frank Selvy (#11).

also the crucial match of the series with Boston finally drawing even on the strength of a lopsided 128-110 count. While the championship round versus LA started out as an easier road there were also difficult moments there, such as the ankle injury which slowed Cousy in the final quarter of game six and which thus threatened to prevent the Celtics from closing out the series and avoiding a risky "for all the marbles" finale.

The finals matchup with Los Angeles would at last gasp prove to be another in what would soon become a long line of frustrating matchups for the team led by Jerry West and Elgin Baylor. A year earlier a championship had squirted out of their hands when Selvy's shot rolled harmlessly off the rim in the deciding match. This time around the pill they had to swallow would be almost as bitter. Cousy's injury allowed the home team to shave a substantial Boston lead (built largely on the strength of first-half hot scoring by

rookie John Havlicek) to a mere bucket with the final period expiring. Only Cousy's limping return to action with five minutes left seemed to stem the LA tide and preserve Boston's slim advantage.

In fitting and almost poetic fashion, the final moments of the season found Robert Cousy once more at center stage, where he had been throughout most of his brilliant career. The game ended just as it should have, with Boston in front on the scoreboard and Bob Cousy in final possession of the basketball. A key steal and bucket by Heinsohn just under the three-minute mark provided a 106-102 bulge and Cousy took over the game by working the clock with his adroit ballhandling. Cooz dribbled out the final seconds of a 112-109 game and threw the ball high into the air seconds before the final buzzer. A final hug with cigar-puffing Red Auerbach at the edge of the playing court then put the ultimate seal on Bob Cousy's final championship victory.

"Havlicek Stole the Ball!" (April 15, 1965)

Celtics 110, Philadelphia Sixers 109 (Eastern Division Finals Game 7)

If there is a single candidate ranking above all others when it comes to selecting the most unforgettable single play or single moment of Boston franchise history it would

Transcendental Graphics

Hondo (center) and his teammates celebrate an Eastern Division championship with Coach Auerbach and Massachusetts Governor John Volpe. The locker room scene came moments after the most famous "steal" in NBA history.

likely have to be the one involving Havlicek's defensive heroics and Johnny Most's broadcast histrionics early in the 1965 postseason. And the irony of course is that while Havlicek's famed steal of Hal Greer's inbounds pass indeed kept a championship string alive, in reality it didn't even occur during a true championship series. Such is the power of the electronic media in shaping fans' most cherished memories.

Havlicek's legendary steal is in many respects, then, basketball's equivalent of Bobby Thomson's famed "shot heard 'round the world" which won a 1951 National League pennant for the comeback New York Giants. Thomson's homer was a moment immortalized forever in the nation's consciousness by a radio call, a call which made the broadcaster (Russ Hodges) who reported the action almost as memorable as the ballplayer who authored it. It was also a moment which came not in the final championship round but earlier on the road toward a world championship (the National League tie-breaker playoff). It was the kind of event that made championship play which followed—in this case a World Series with the crosstown Yankees—largely anticlimactic.

The 1965 postseason which resulted in Boston's record seventh straight championship might have been remembered merely for another frustrating year-end collapse by the Los Angeles Lakers in the title showdown captured by Auerbach's crew in five easy games. But instead—in no small part thanks to Havlicek—it is everywhere recalled primarily for perhaps the most hard fought Russell-Chamberlain showdown of the dynasty decade. Wilt had returned to Philadelphia in a shocking midseason trade that sent three top players and $300,000 to San Francisco. When his Warriors faced off with Boston in the second playoff round the Celtics were reeling in the aftermath of the recent death of team owner Walter Brown and a knee operation which had slowed Havlicek. The two big men played to a standstill in the series lidlifter won by Boston, but Wilt had the upper hand in the second contest by a wide margin and the series was knotted. It was still knotted for the seventh-game rubber match.

The excitement of the Philadelphia-Boston semifinals collision finally came to a peak in the final five seconds of the deciding shootout. And it was Russell who for perhaps the only time in his career came within inches (quite literally) of being the season's ultimate goat. Bill attempted an inbounds pass under his own bucket, with the Celtics nursing a one-point lead and owning the opportunity to run out the game's final precious seconds. Trying to loft the ball over the wagging arms of Chamberlain, however, Russell somehow misfired and the sphere bounded harmlessly back in his direction after striking a low guide wire supporting the Boston backboard. It was suddenly Philadelphia's ball in front of the hoop with the game still hanging in the balance.

But while Russell pleaded in the timeout huddle for someone to step up big and rectify his mistake, the 76ers were planning an inbounds strategy for moving the ball from Greer to Chet Walker—rather than Chamberlain, as expected—which would next backfire just as resoundingly as Russell's own errant pass. When Greer released the ball toward the waiting Walker, Havlicek suddenly streaked out of nowhere to make the needed game-saving deflection to Sam Jones. It was over in a flash, and miraculously Boston's lengthy postseason string had barely survived intact for yet another year.

Red Auerbach's Last Victory Cigar (April 28, 1966)

Celtics 95, Los Angeles Lakers 93 (NBA Finals Game 7)

What ended up as one of the most emotional of all Celtics victory parties came within an eyelash—or more appropriately a cigar-stub's length—of outright disaster for the usually invincible home team. The occasion was Red Auerbach's last postseason game, and the showboating sideline antics of the volatile Boston mentor almost in the end caught up with him during his final night on the Boston bench.

Red had given his team its annual dose of inspiration early in the year by announcing that this would be his final

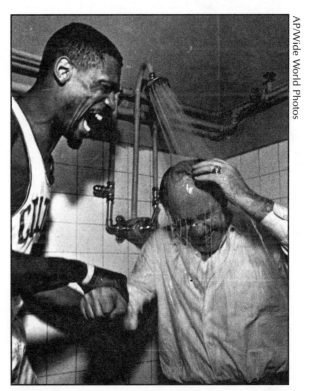

In what had become a New England ritual by the mid-sixties, Auerbach enjoys another championship "victory shower" to the delight of Bill Russell. This one in 1965, Boston's seventh consecutive NBA title.

Player-coach Bill Russell swats away a shot from Tom Hawkins during the 1968 Boston-LA title showdown. This hard-fought series would result in the first of Russell's two championships as coach.

campaign as Celtics head coach. Everyone around the circuit would thus enjoy a final shot at dislodging the seven-time champion before he faded into the Boston front office with his consecutive championship string yet untarnished. For most of the season it seemed that someone—most likely the 76ers with Wilt, who wrested the regular-season division title from Auerbach's grasp—would finally be able to take full advantage of the opportunity. Then when things got tense in the postseason warfare, Auerbach provided another final dose of vital team inspiration with his startling announcement that Bill Russell and not Heinsohn or Ramsey or Cousy would be his successor as the team's next coach.

The motivational ploys (along with the always-strong Boston roster) had seemingly been enough to keep the championship machine well on track toward one final Auerbach title. As the final game with Los Angeles wound down the victory seemed well in hand. Boston led the deciding match by a comortable ten points with only a half-minute of playing time remaining. That was when the usually canny Auerbach almost made the biggest mistake of his coaching career by handing the biggest motivational lift of all to the opposition's side. Two clutch baskets by Jerry West had sliced the margin to six with 14 ticks remaining when Auerbach's traditional victory cigar was lit in full view of the throngs jamming the endlines under both baskets. Seeing Auerbach's false vistory signal the fans swarmed onto the floor with playing time still unexpired. Order was quickly restored, but several additional Boston turnovers trimmed the final count to a mere bucket before K.C. Jones finally dribbled away the last few clock ticks. Years later the retired Auerbach would repeatedly admit that he never came quite so close to total disaster anywhere in his long tenure as he did during his final few seconds on the Boston Celtics bench.

Russell Bows Out with a Final NBA Title (May 5, 1969)

Celtics 108, Los Angeles Lakers 106 (NBA Finals Game 7)

Red Auerbach's final victory lap was almost ruined by his team's premature sideline celebrations. In similar fashion Bill Russell's own curtain call—sweet as it was in the end—was somewhat diminished in Big Bill's own eyes by the shameless sideline behaviors of his longtime rival, Wilt Chamberlain. It the last-ever meeting between the two epic rivals Wilt failed, as he almost always did, to gain the ultimate victory over Russell. But he did nonetheless seemingly find—whether by chance or by sinister design—a perverse way of tarnishing that final meeting much to Russell's evident displeasure. And in doing so Wilt had gained a huge unwitting assist from his despised coach—

Butch van Breda Kolff—who also played a not insignificant role in the unfolding final-period drama.

Van Breda Kolff coached some of the sport's biggest pro stars as the 1968 and 1969 mentor of the talent-rich Los Angeles Lakers and also directed the fortunes of two of the NBA's most successful teams, but he will always be remembered above all else for his destructive relationship during that brief LA stint with one of basketball's biggest icons. A season-long war of personalities in Los Angeles between the control-conscious Butch Van Breda Kolff and giant Wilt Chamberlain reached a crucial nadir during the 1969 game-seven championship matchup which tarnished the final head-to-head confrontation between Wilt and his long-time foil, Bill Russell.

The Lakers were rallying desperately to narrow a hefty Boston fourth-quarter lead which threatened once more to crush the Lakers' oft-frustrated championship hopes. When Chamberlain sustained what appeared to be only a minor leg injury he removed himself from the game in a surprise action that shocked the Lakers faithful as well as the entire LA bench, while at the same time lifting Boston spirits considerably. With the clock winding down several minutes later and the game finally knotted, Wilt at last signalled his coach that he was ready to re-enter the fray. Van Breda Kolff—obviously irritated by his giant star's apparent lack of grit and dedication—ignored Wilt's signals and stuck with replacement Mel Counts down to the final buzzer. The game as well as the Lakers' title chances evaporated when Boston's Don Nelson rattled home a short jumper just ahead of the final gun.

Unmolested by the absent Chamberlain down the stretch, Russell closed out his career with a relentless 48-minute performance that included 21 crucial rebounds. Thus while LA players and fans suffered yet another humiliating title defeat at the hands of the hated Celtics (the sixth of the decade), Boston's remarkable player coach suffered the lesser disappointment of not having his arch rival on the floor to heighten the waning moments of their final shootout. And Van Breda Kolff would experience considerable regrets of his own in the face of the embarrassing incident when he soon learned that this final rift with his disgruntled franchise player had not only lost him a championship ring but had also cost him his plush NBA coaching job.

Kareem's Most Unforgettable Sky-Hook (May 10, 1974)

Milwaukee Bucks 102, Celtics 101 (2OT) (NBA Finals Game 6)

It wasn't always a player adorned in Boston green and white making the improbable and season-saving last-ditch clutch shot, though in retrospect it often seems as though it

Lew Alcindor established huge credentials at UCLA as the greatest collegiate big man ever, then turned the NBA on its head when he arrived in Milwaukee as Kareem Abdul-Jabbar.

was. But there were sometimes balls that bounced astray and shots that uncharacteristically caromed in the other direction, and none was more memorable that Kareem's dagger-like skyhook that extended a drama-filled championship series and in the process delayed still another apparently destined Boston championship party.

The season that had ended the Celtics' long reign in early summer of 1969 and the one that opened with the heralded debut of 7 foot-2 inch Lew Alcindor in the autumn of the same year were bookends to perhaps the greatest overnight transition in the history of professional basketball. The first glorious campaign of Alcindor's unprecedented 20-year career (played in its bulk with his new-found identity as Kareem Abdul-Jabbar) would, for one thing, witness the first season since 1950 that the Boston Celtics did not field a playoff-round entrant. The demoralized Beantowners of new coach Tom Heinsohn in fact finished a lowly sixth in the seven-team Eastern Division they had for so long so thoroughly dominated. Russell's retirement had indeed signalled the end of basketball's greatest dynasty ever, and Boston would continue to slide and to lose far more games than it won over the next two dreadful seasons.

With the arrival of Alcindor in Milwaukee in 1969, the age of the truly dominant big man (Russell and Chamberlain aside) had now finally arrived in the NBA. While Wilt

had been a unstoppable offensive force and Russell an unmoveable defensive pillar, the young Alcindor now promised to combine the very best talents of both in a single incomparable basket-making and basket-defending machine. Alcindor overnight also transformed the expansion Milwaukee Bucks (who had won out for his services over their expansion partners in Phoenix and also over the rival upstart pro league which played with a red-white-and-blue striped ball) into a supremely efficient championship unit. Aided by the pickup of veteran backcourt ace Oscar Robertson to compliment their giant center, the Bucks were celebrating a league title in only Alcindor's second season. They were also lodged at the top of the postseason heap across the next several campaigns. And when Boston's fortunes were quickly resurrected a couple of seasons down the road under the coaching guidance of Heinsohn and on-floor leadership of Dave Cowens, it was again Milwaukee and Alcindor (now known as Jabbar, after a name change in his third season) who provided the biggest roadblock to renewed Celtics prominence.

The showdown came in Jabbar's fifth NBA season, which was also Cowens's fourth campaign. Boston had appeared bound for a title a season earlier when Heinsohn's unit set an NBA record for victories with 68; but then an overconfident Boston crew had stumbled against the defense-minded New York Knicks, who had the where-withal to stop Boston's polished fast-breaking attack. A severe injury to franchise anchor John Havlicek in the showdown series with New York also scuttled the Boston cause. Now a year later Boston was back on another championship course when they collided with Milwaukee (owner of the year's best record) in the final playoff round.

It would be a series in which neither team could ever string together repeat victories, and thus Boston's eventual

Dave Cowens guards Kareem during the 1974 title game which followed on the heels of Abdul-Jabbar's most memorable sky-hook. Boston won easily to post a twelfth world championship.

victory margin came with their destruction of Milwaukee's home court advantage in the opening contest. But it was the game-six Boston Garden shootout in which Boston championship celebrations were unexpectedly delayed that remains the year's most noteworthy contest. Cowens fell into early foul trouble and watched from the bench while the visitors opened a first-half dozen-point spread. The Celtics still trailed by half that amount late in the contest but battled back gamely to force an overtime. A basket off a lucky-bounce rebound enabled Havlicek to be the momentary hero and force a second extra session. Havlicek also scored nine of Boston's eleven in the second overtime, including a rainbow hook over Kareem with seven seconds still showing that appeared to signal a victory party.

But on this particular night Lady Luck was not sitting comfortably in the Boston corner. Kareem was handed the ball on the final inbounds play and although the Bucks had planned a Jabbar screen and a final shot by Jon McGlockin the play was fortunately busted up by the tight Boston defense. With no options left, the smooth Jabbar dribbled to the baseline and launched easily the most famous of all his many skyhook tosses. The ball found only net and swished cleanly home for a stunning 102-101 Milwaukee victory that temporarily postponed the expected Boston victory dance and also etched the famed Jabbar offense move forever into the catalog of the NBA's most deadly offensive weapons.

Glenn McDonald is captured here during his career moment, as he sinks two free throws to give him six crucial points during a dramatic third overtime session versus the upstart Phoenix Suns.

Three Controversial Overtimes
(June 4, 1976)

Celtics 128, Phoenix Suns 126 (3OT)
(NBA Finals Game 5)

There is hardly ever any serious debate when it comes to selecting either the greatest postseason game or the greatest-ever game in NBA annals. The place of honor is always given—almost automatically—to the triple-overtime affair in Boston which was filled with more unpredictable nail-biting action than any other single basketball game in recorded memory. Ironically, however, the most memorable and even the most heroic roles in what yet remains the most unforgettable of all Boston Celtics games were filled not by Russell, Havlicek, Cousy, Bird or any other luminary from Boston's distinguished roll call of storied hall-of-famers. The pivotal roles were instead reserved for a pair of normally unsung ballplayers who suited up for the opponents' side, and also for a harried if noble game official, plus an unruly Boston grandstand throng that almost stole all the thunder and even the final victory from their beloved green-clad heroes.

It is an time-worn sports axiom that the best game officials are those who are never noticed while they ply their professional trade. Richie Powers was indeed one of the best ever to blow the whistle in the NBA, though at times he unfortunately grabbed far more than his share of the limelight usually reserved exclusively for the players. The most infamous moment for Powers came during the climactic seconds of perhaps the most famous game in NBA history—certainly the most memorable moment in the sparkling postseason annals of the storied Boston Celtics. On the night of June 4, 1976, the Celtics and Phoenix Suns locked horns in a three-overtime heart-wrencher during which Boston outlasted the spunky underdogs 128-126 and thus captured a crucial Game 5 of the championship series—a series which provided a springboard to the club's thirteenth league championship banner. It was a game that would witness easily the most bizarre chain of events ever to unfold in an NBA title round (or anywhere else in NBA history for that matter), and Richie Powers stood smack in the middle of all that rapidly transpired.

A couple of dramatic shots by ex-Celtic Paul Westphal first knotted the game during regulation play. True fireworks, however, were saved for the closing moments of the second overtime stanza, when an off-balance 15-footer by John Havlicek gave Boston a 111-110 margin as time seemed to expire. As joyous mayhem covered the Boston Garden parquet floor the unflappable Powers signalled that

Phoenix had successfully called a timeout with but two ticks of the clock still remaining. The further complication—if one were somehow needed—was the fact that the desperate Suns did not actually have a legal timeout remaining when Westphal signaled for stoppage.

In the wild melee that followed Powers was struck in the face by an irate fan who had rushed onto the floor to protest, and a full-blown riot next broke out before police and players from both teams could restore some semblance of order. When both order and play resumed the clever ploy by Westphal suddenly paid rich dividends: Boston's Jo Jo White sank a penalty free throw, but Phoenix now had the ball at midcourt for a desperation shot which Gar Heard somehow sank to trigger a third nailbiting overtime period. Eventually Boston prevailed and Powers escaped with his life and his reputation still largely intact. Richie Powers had also been squarely on the firing lines for the famed deciding game of the 1970 New York and Los Angeles NBA title confrontation—an equally famous game in which Willis Reed made his dramatic and inspiring last-second appearance (returning from a serious game-five injury) and launched an emotional New York championship party. But what happened in Madison Square Garden in May 1970 was altogether mild compared to the wild night in Boston six postseasons later.

Gar Heard is surrounded by Havlicek (#17), Westphal (center) and Paul Silas (right) during the marathon playoff game in Boston Garden in which his own dramatic last-second shot (along with Westphal's gutsy time-out call) would play a vital role.

If Powers' role in postponing the Boston victory party had been highly significant, it was the former Celtic—Westphal—who almost completely ruined the evening and also the season for the hometown forces. At one point in his career Paul Westphal was considered the best athlete at his playmaking position to be found anywhere in the NBA. An electrifying guard out of the University of Southern California, Westphal had dulled campus memories of Trojan great Bill Sharman and had also become a career 1,000-point scorer, although he never earned All-American honors or broke any important school offensive records. Entering the pros as a 1972 first-round pick of the Boston Celtics, Westphal quickly launched a red-letter pro career that easily outstripped his moderate collegiate credentials. Sharman's USC protégé was not destined to remain in Boston long, however, even if a solid rookie campaign off the bench in 1973 contributed heavily to the league's best regular-season record and a still-standing franchise mark of 68 league victories.

Contract squabbles arose on the heals of the team's 1974 NBA title and Westphal was sent packing to Phoenix in exchange for Charlie Scott (who himself had earlier been dealt to the Suns for Paul Silas, in one of Auerbach's most astute front office moves). The stage was set by the Westphal-Scott trade for a single great irony coloring the remainder of Paul Westphal's NBA career. Despite his early unhappy departure from Boston Garden, Westphal would nonetheless now be fated to become a feature player in what may well be the most storied moment of Boston Celtics postseason history.

That moment came in 1976, during the three-overtime Boston Garden NBA Finals thriller which saw the Celtics turn the tide toward a second league title in three years. The pivotal game still hung in the balance when Westphal came back to haunt his former team by scoring 9 of his current team's final 11 points to fashion a 95-all tie at the end of regulation play. Curtis Perry's jumper off a Westphal steal also gave the Suns a one-point lead in the final minute of the second overtime session. John Havlicek's desperation shot next put the hometown forces once again in the driver's seat with only seconds left on the game clock. Amidst the pandemonium that followed Havlicek's heave, Westphal managed to call the timeout which Phoenix no longer had, a brilliant ploy since—although it permitted Jo Jo White to sink a technical free throw for a 112-110 Boston lead—it also allowed Phoenix one last half-court possession which would result in the memorable game-extending desperation bucket by Garfield Heard. Westphal's heroics were not enough in the end to salvage the series or even to rescue the see-saw game. His brilliant time-out call would nonetheless be sufficient to secure his own lasting spot among the most memorable architects of indelible NBA postseason heroics.

Bird's Famous Steal
(May 26, 1987)

BOSTON

Celtics 108, Detroit Pistons 107
(Eastern Conference Finals Game 5)

It was the second most famous pilfering in storied ballclub annals and likely the second most memorable in all of basketball history. And if it hadn't been for Havlicek's earlier slight-of-hand trick and Johnny Most's immortal call of that rare parallel moment back in 1965, what Bird did to Isiah Thomas in the postseason of 1987 might have held a bigger place still in our collective NBA memories. Among so many indelible Larry Bird highlight moments this one was hardly the defining sequence of a hall-of-fame career. And while it did salvage a postseason series—had Detroit won that game, their follow-up Game 6 triumph would have put them in the NBA Finals with Los Angeles—it did not lead (like Havlicek's similar act of larceny) to preserving a championship season. Nonetheless, few postseason games have ever ended with quite such a startling turn of events for the favored home team.

Bird's heroics came in the waning seconds of the pivotal game of a hard-fought Eastern Conference Finals series which had witnessed the upstart Pistons extending the defending league champions to the very limit of their endurance. With Detroit owning the ball and the game's lead in the final seconds of play, the usually adept Isiah Thomas released a careless inbounds toss which the alert Bird intercepted with only five seconds still showing. With miraculous body control the sometimes awkward-appearing Boston star instantaneously fed the ball blindly over his shoulder to a cutting Dennis Johnson for the winning bucket that capped a stunning 108-107 Boston comeback. Riding the momentum of that play Boston (after a rebound Pistons' victory in Detroit) was then able to close out the stubborn series back on their home floor four nights later.

Bird's steal in the end represented only a final gasp for a beleaguered Boston team that had started the season with hefty hopes of being the first league champion to repeat a title since the collapse of the Russell era two decades earlier. But little by little that dream had quickly unravelled as Boston suffered through one of its most ill-fated seasons ever. In reality this was the very year that marked a final hurrah for the now fading Bird epoch, and thus also the season that launched a Celtics slide that has never stopped worsening since. It had started with the tragic death of Len Bias in the shadows of the 1986 college draft. The second major blow of that year—far more gradual in nature—had been the disintegration of a Boston bench that had only a year earlier been the strongest anywhere. Walton was struck down first with his recurring foot injuries, Scott Wedman was forced out with a bad heel, and Jerry Sichting was kayoed by a rare virus. Bird's heroic effort against Detroit was thus barely enough to stave off what appeared to be inevitable defeat for a rapidly fading team. And that defeat came soon enough—in the form of a six-game blitzing during the final round at the hands of a crack Lakers outfit and its star, Magic Johnson, who was playing at the very top of his own incomparable game.

The game today remembered for Bird's remarkable split-second anticipation which spelled disaster for Detroit was also noteworthy for another far less artistic moment involving Robert Parish and Detroit's arch bad guy, Bill Laimbeer. A skirmish between the two centers results in a huge fine and suspension for Parish, who was docked $7,500 and forced to the sidelines for the vital following game at Detroit. The penalty—which was administered because Parish had unleashed a volley of punches at his antagonistic rival—was noteworthy as the second largest in league history, trailing only the $10,000 fee once levied against Kermit Washington for his savage attack on Rudy Tomjanovich a decade earlier.

AP/Wide World Photos

Bird celebrates a most unlikely playoff victory over Detroit moments after his own incredible steal saved the day for Boston. Bird's steal ranks second only to Havlicek's in Boston basketball lore.

Bird versus Wilkins
(May 22, 1988)

Celtics

Celtics 118, Atlanta Hawks 116
(Eastern Conference Semifinals Game 7)

Boston basketball history is littered with a litany of great one-on-one individual battles: Cousy against Slater Martin (with both Minneapolis and St. Louis), Havlicek and Jerry West, Dave Cowens head-to-head with Kareem Abdul-Jabbar, Paul Silas against Dave DeBusschere, Bird versus Julius Erving, Bird and Magic, Heinsohn alongside Pettit, and of course Bill Russell versus Wilt Chamberlain. Most were played out over numerous contests spread across season after season. But perhaps the most memorable individual shootout was confined to a single postseason game.

Pro basketball is known for its classic one-on-one matchups and its spectacular shootouts between individual stars. Today's fans frequently thrill to confrontations between the league's towering young centers, or contests of long-distance marksmanship between hot-handed outside bombers, but never has there been a more spectacular single night of head-to-head fireworks than the one staged in the Boston Garden on the evening of May 22, 1988. Veteran reporter Jack McCallum of *Sports Illustrated*, a writer who has covered the NBA scene for three decades, called it "one of the most dramatic shootouts in NBA history." Kevin McHale had an even more colorful description (and also a better close-range view) when he later described the scene as being "like two western gunfighters waiting to blink."

The dramatic setting was the seventh and final game of the NBA's 1988 Eastern Conference semifinal playoff series. The Boston Celtics and Atlanta Hawks were battling each other for the right to advance to a final series against Detroit for the conference title, and also for a chance to play against the Western Conference winner (destined to be the Los Angeles Lakers) for the NBA world championship. Each team was led by its own superstar high-scoring forward and both of these stars were now at the very peak of their illustrious careers. For Boston it was Larry Bird, who many now consider the best passer and long-range shooting forward to ever play the game. For Atlanta it was Dominique Wilkins, the league's most spectacular dunker and also perhaps its best one-on-one player. Just a couple of months earlier, Bird and Wilkins (who logged 29 points) had been the two starters at forward for the victorious Eastern Conference team in the league's annual mid-season All-Star Game shootout against the Western Conference elite. Now they were squaring off face-to-face as bitter postseason opponents.

Rarely do such publicized matchups between oppos-

ing superstar players during playoff action ever quite live up to the overreaching expectations of fans and the sports media. Usually one or both of the stars involved have only mediocre nights under the pressures of the moment. Sometimes it is another less famous player from one of the two teams who rises to the occasion and proves the true star of the evening. This time, however, the main actors would remain on center stage and together would certainly meet everyone's loftiest anticipations. Before the action was finished on this memorable night at the storied Boston Garden—scene of so many earlier legendary showdowns— Bird and Wilkins would stage one of the most dramatic and hard-fought struggles ever savored by courtside wittnesses in the long and colorful history of professional basketball.

The Celtics were again one of basketball's showcase teams in 1988 and the legendary Bird was the brighter of the two stars in the eyes of most NBA fans. Bird had of course already earned an almost-certain spot in basketball's Naismith Hall of Fame: he already wore three NBA championship rings. Wilkins, though, was also coming off the best season of his brief career. He had averaged over 30 points a game for the entire campaign and had trailed only Chicago's Michael Jordan as the league's best individual scorer for the 1987-88 season (his fifth in the league).

Wilkins had also led the Hawks (runners-up in the Central Division) to an unexpected showing against the favored Celtics (the runaway Atlantic Division winners) in the first six games of the best-of-seven second-round postseason series. The underdog Atlanta team had fought Boston to a tie, with each club winning once on the road. Now everything was on the line in the single vital game that would finally end the season for one of these two proud teams.

Wilkins, guarded by Kevin McHale, was sensationally hot from the very start of the game. Bird started more slowly. While McHale tried to defend Wilkins at one end of the floor, Wilkins would shift off McHale and guard Bird at the other end of the court. Bird was clearly harassed by tough defense thrown up by Wilkins and had only 14 points after the first 36 minutes of play.

The fourth quarter saw Wilkins and Bird put on an absolutely amazing shooting display. McHale again offered the best description of that final twelve minutes of scintillating action: "The final quarter was like two warriors standing at arm's length and relentlessly punching each other." A whole nation of spectators was watching on television which only made the rare performance more special still. Wilkins burned the nets all night from everywhere on the floor. Entering the final quarter, the Atlanta star had already scored 31 points. Now he upped his shooting a notch and poured in 16 more in the final stanza for a game-high 47 total. Bird was equal to the Wilkins fourth period onslaught and then some: Boston's ace seemed on fire and he too threw down long-range jumpers and driving layups at a phenomenal pace. Bird would drop in nine of his ten shots down the stretch for 34 points of his own.

The final ten minutes of this special playoff game was one of the most priceless sequences in pro basketball history. Simply put, it showcased the very best that two of the sport's greatest players could muster under almost excruciating pressure. For those final ten minutes the wild shootout continued without any seeming break in the action or the tension. Down through the final minutes there was a seemingly endless string of dramatic baskets by Bird and Wilkins at both ends of the floor. Wilkins hit a 20-foot jumper with 5:57 remaining on the clock to tie the score at 99; Bird immediately answered with a leaning left-handed hook from ten feet out. Wilkins's following jumper from the top of the key only 17 seconds later again knotted the score. Bird immediately swished a 17-footer to make it 103-101, Boston. Atlanta next rushed the ball to the opposite end of the floor and Wilkins banked home another 10-footer to create still another deadlock. Each clutch play by Bird was answered by another equally clutch shot by Wilkins.

The final minute saw five vital baskets as the game wore down to its dramatic conclusion. With 45 seconds remaining, Wilkins's two clutch free throws cut the Boston lead to 112-109. Nineteen second later Bird swept past Wilkins for a running scoop shot, making the lead 114-109. With 20 seconds left Wilkins missed a slam dunk but then put back his own rebound. It was now 114-111. Bird immediately inbounded the ball with a crisp pass to Danny Ainge, who collected two points on a goal-tending violation. The Hawks answered, however, with four more points in the final 16 seconds, while the Celtics collected only two. Then Wilkins was fouled with only a single second left on the scoreboard clock and Boston still in the lead by a three-point spread.

Dominique Wilkins made his first free throw but had only one option with his second foul shot. The Hawks still trailed by two and a one-point shot was therefore worthless. Wilkins would have to attempt a miss, grab his own rebound, then try a desperation heave that might cause a tie if it found the net. But the plan quickly backfired as Wilkins's intentional miss bounced harmlessly off the rim and into the hands of Boston center Robert Parish just as the final buzzer sounded.

The Celtics somehow held on to win by the narrow margin of 118-116. Bird made 15 of his 24 shots during the contest, as well as all three free throws he attempted. Wilkins also excelled, making 19 out of 33 from the floor, and 8 of nine from the charity stripe. But Bird missed only one shot and had racked up 20 points in the important fourth quarter, four more than Wilkins, and Wilkins failed

in his desperate attempt to pull out the game from the foul line in the closing seconds. The 14,890 fans in attendance (the customary Boston Garden sellout) slumped in their seats exhausted after the final whistle. The Hawks players were crushed after so valiant an effort.

It would take some time for Wilkins and his Atlanta teammates to grasp the full meaning of that single loss in Boston Garden. For in the end this one unforgettable defeat would have a far greater effect on the Atlanta Hawks, and especially on Dominique Wilkins, than the mere ending of another season's playoff dream. It was a game, instead, that from this point on would shape the career of Atlanta's biggest-ever star. A win and a trip to the conference finals might well have been the highlight of Wilkins's career, but in the end the Hawks had not won. A clutch performance by Larry Bird had overshadowed Wilkins's own brilliance that night. Bird's showdown victory had even seemed to slam the door on future superstardom for Atlanta's Dominique Wilkins.

Wilkins would later talk about how Bird's clutch performance and his own team's loss that night had influenced the way fans and writers saw his own career in future years. "I think that single game is why I have never been given a lot of attention," observed Wilkins in an interview with a reporter from *Sport* magazine. Wilkins would go on to suggest that it was probably also this single game, more than any other, which would cause league officials to bypass him in 1991 when selecting NBA stars for the United States Olympic Dream Team roster. It was an all-star team that Wilkins very badly wanted to make. Like other elite NBA players, he too wanted a chance to pocket an almost certain Olympic gold medal in Barcelona; but it was an aging veteran Larry Bird, at the very end of his career, who was selected instead. "Had we won the game in Boston," muses Wilkins, "I think that all might have played out very different."

Two Dozen Less Memorable Boston Celtics Moments

January 3, 1946—Boston defeats Toronto's Huskies in Maple Leafs Gardens wearing makeshift uniforms consisting of black sweaters with white adhesive tape attached to mark the jersey letters and numbers. It was the only time in their half-century-plus history that the Boston ballclub was not adorned in their familiar green and white colors.

March 28, 1948—Boston makes its first postseason playoff appearance ever with a 79-72 Boston Garden loss to the Western Division Chicago Stags. The crowd of 2,842 was the smallest Garden gathering of the entire season, establishing the indisputable fact that Hub fans were not yet turned on to pro basketball's "second season" back in the earliest BAA days.

February 17, 1952—Auerbach and Milwaukee Hawks head coach Doxie Moore wrestle each other to the floor during an explosion of tempers which mars an already sloppy 97-95 Milwaukee victory in Moline, Illinois. The ugly brawl rapidly expanded to involve the entire benchs from both squads. (Milwaukee had that very season joined the league via transfer of the Tri-Cities Blackhawks team, owned by Ben Kerner, earlier coached by Auerbach himself, and soon to be relocated once again to St. Louis.)

February 21, 1952—In one of the early NBA's most bizarre game-night promotions, Boston takes the home floor at the stroke of midnight for a "Milkman's Special" game against the Detroit Pistons. The late-starting NBA fare followed a performance of the popular Ice Follies and the uninspired and anticlimactic roundball contest dragged out to a 88-67 Boston win witnessed by 2,368 sleepy Boston Garden patrons.

February 28, 1952—Bob Cousy joined Chuck Cooper on a train ride home to Boston after the pioneering black ballplayer (the first of his race drafted by an NBA team) was denied a hotel room on the eve of a scheduled Celtics game in North Carolina. Auerbach would also, almost a decade later, send some of his black players home from Louisville after they were denied restaurant service on the eve of a scholarship fund exhibition contest at the University of Kentucky arena. Together these were disagreeable enough incidents, but they also foreshadowed the Boston Celtics' commendable role in fostering race relations and in eventual fullscale NBA integration. Beyond Cooper's pioneering debut, Russell was both the league's first black superstar and also North American pro sport's first black head coach. And in 1965 the Celtics would also be the first NBA club to feature an all-black starting lineup.

March 17, 1954—In another of the frequent brutal pre-shot-clock-era games between Boston and Syracuse, the Celtics drop a 96-95 decision in a rugged overtime game in Boston Garden. The flavor of the unsightly affair was adequately captured by the fact that there were 46 fouls called against the Nats and 35 whistled against the home club.

March 27, 1954—Boston is eliminated from the postseason by the Syracuse Nats in a melee-marred ball game which remains to this day the wildest of NBA playoff history. The brutal contest was delayed 25 minutes by brawling and police and security forces had to take the floor to end the fistacuffs and restore both order and ball-playing activities. Two top Nats stars—Dolph Schayes and Paul Seymour—left the floor with fight-related injuries but Syracuse prevailed anyway by a 83-76 count.

February 27, 1955—Boston nipped the Hawks 62-57 in Milwaukee in a sleep-inducing game which long held the record for the lowest point totals for two teams during the post-shot-clock NBA era. The normally high-scoring Celtics are a surprising team to set this dubious mark, since they more than any other NBA club had taken advantage of the new shot-clock regulations and had been the first league outfit to average triple figures in both points scored and points allowed.

April 6, 1957—In one of his most colorful if most outrageous unsportsmanlike acts, Red Auerbach punches St. Louis Hawks owner Ben Kerner in the mouth prior to the Celtics game-three loss in the NBA Finals. The immediate cause of hostilities was a dispute over the height of one of the baskets, but the two hotheaded rivals had been feuding ever since Auerbach quit in midseason 1950 as Kerner's coach with the then Tri-Cities Blackhawks.

April 2, 1958—Bill Russell is forced to leave the third game of the championship series with St. Louis due to a severely swollen left ankle. Russell would not return until the sixth and final contest, and without their lanky center at full speed the Celtics are unable to defend a league title they had won a season earlier, during Russell's rookie campaign.

April 1, 1962—The usually inspired Philadelphia-Boston postseason rivalry turned ugly during Game 5 of the Eastern Conference Finals as Boston won 119-104 in a game that looked more like a World Wrestling Federation event than an NBA contest. Fisticuffs began when Warriors guard Guy Rodgers apparently sucker-punched Carl Braun, and a lengthy string of similar altercations would quickly follow. The most famous of the distasteful scenes which ensued was the one in which Sam Jones grabbed a photographer's stool in the effort of defending himself against a much larger and usually mild-mannered Wilt Chamberlain.

January 10, 1967—Already "officially" retired Red Auerbach was ejected from the sidelines during the NBA All-Star Game (won by the West 135-120) in San Francisco. This was Red's eleventh and final time coaching the Eastern Division all-star squad (an honor earned as coach of the previous year's postseason division champions) and he ungraciously picked a most characteristic way to make his final curtain call.

April 11, 1967—Boston is eliminated in an Eastern Division Finals series by Philadelphia and thus loses the NBA title for the only time during the entire decade of the '60s. The powerful 76ers capped the lopsided five-game series on their home floor with a 140-116 rout during which they thoroughly embarrassed the defending champions 75-46 in the second half.

March 12, 1972—The Celtics retire Bill Russell's famed "Number 6" but do so behind closed doors in a private pregame ceremony. Russell had refused to attend the event if it was going to be staged with the arena full of spectators. Bill Russell—the most private and unorthodox of superstars—would also later fail to show up for his own induction into the Naismith Memorial Basketball Hall of Fame in Springfield, thus maintaining his consistent protest against traditional honors and recognitions.

January 3, 1978—After eight-plus seasons on the job, Tom Heinsohn is relieved of his position as head coach, making him the first of only two Boston head coaches to be dismissed in midseason. The second to suffer a similar fate would be Heinsohn's own replacement, Tom "Satch" Sanders, who would himself last only a dozen games into the following campaign.

January 31, 1978—The 488-game ironman streak of Jo Jo White comes to an end during a 104-94 Boston victory against Indiana's Pacers in the unlikely venue of Springfield, Massachusetts, home of the sport's hall of fame. The game had been originally scheduled into the Hartford Civic Center, but was moved when that building's roof collapsed after an excreptionally heavy snowfall.

February 12, 1979—High-scoring but selfish gunner Bob McAdoo is acquired from New York by owner John Y. Brown (at his wife's urging) for three highly valued future draft picks. Auerbach doesn't approve of the deal and is in fact so upset by it that he seriously considers leaving his longtime Boston post for a front office job with the rival New York Knicks. McAdoo, for his part, would later prove to be excellent trade bait for one of Red Auerbach's subsequent franchise-building deals.

February 18, 1985—Larry Bird enjoys perhaps the most impressive night of his glory-filled career while only barely missing a quadruple-double with 30 points, 12 rebounds, 10 assists and 9 steals. In typical Larry Bird fashion, the Boston star refuses to pursue individual headlines and achieve the almost certain rare statistical feat when he elects not to re-enter the meaningless one-sided game in Utah during any of the fourth quarter.

June 17, 1986—With the most ill-fated draft day move in league history Boston selects Maryland superstar Len Bias with its second overall first-round pick. Bias would die two days later of a concaine overdose suffered in his University of Maryland dormitory room. It was a blow to Boston's long-term post-Bird rebuilding plans from which the ballclub has still never fully recovered.

March 25, 1988—In very un-Celtic-like fashion Boston blows a huge 75-45 lead over the final 19 minutes of an exciting Boston Garden contest with the Philadelphia Sixers. The unaccountable loss would also mark the first-ever win at Boston Garden for a young hall-of-fame-bound Philadelphia star named Charles Barkley.

February 4, 1993—Larry Bird's number "33" is retired and raised to the rafters in Boston Garden. Bird's departure was especially painful for Boston fans since his unmatched career had been shortened considerablly by injuries which may have robbed several additional seasons of stardom for Bird and several additional NBA championship banners for the tradition-rich franchise.

April 29, 1993—Budding franchise star Reggie Lewis collapses during the first quarter of Boston's 112-101 opening game playoff win in Charlotte. On June 2nd Lewis would be diagnosed as having heart abnormalities and then released from round-the-clock medical care. Then on July 27th the young star would die suddenly of a full-fledged heart attack suffered while shooting baskets in a pickup game.

June 14, 1994—Former popular role player M.L. Carr is appointed vice president and director of basketball operations in what soon turns out to be perhaps the most ill-advised front office move in Boston club history. The short reign of Carr as both de facto general manager and head coach will see the ballclub stumble to its worst performances ever.

January 20, 1995—The Celtics and Lakers square off for the final time in Boston Garden and Los Angeles comes away with a hard-fought 120-118 victory. With this game ended easily the most historic rivalry in NBA history in the most cherished and celebrated building the sport has ever known. This was indeed a sad night for Boston-based and LA-based basketball traditionalists.

April 5, 1995—The once-glorious Celtics drop the final game ever played in the once-proud Boston Garden, falling to Orlando 95-92 and dropping the opening-round playoff series in only four games. Only a week earlier, in the first game of this series, Boston had also suffered through its worst drubbing in ballclub history, being blitzed 124-77 by the traditionless expansion Orlando Magic.

Nick Anderson (left) and Donald Royal put the squeeze on Celtics guard Sherman Douglas during the opening game of a most disappointing 1995 postseason series with the Orlando Magic.

BOSTON *Celtics*

BOSTON *Celtics*

CHAPTER VIII ──────────
The Celtics Coaches

No franchise in pro basketball circles is more closely associated with a single coach than are the Boston Celtics with Red Auerbach. This reality might appear strange enough on the surface, given the 33 seasons that separate Auerbach's retirement from the present, and also the fact that his 16 seasons on the bench represent only a fraction over thirty percent of franchise history. Yet so great was Auerbach's impact on the NBA record books and on the definition of a franchise identity that for most long-time fans to this day he remains the sum and substance of the Boston Celtics. And the fact that he was a major player in all office decisions down to the current decade has not hurt the perception either.

But there have been other memorable Boston coaches as well, and the dozen men who have filled the slot in pre-Auerbach and post-Auerbach seasons have all brought their own colorful and oftentimes controversial images to the scene. Seven have been former Boston players who grew into their bench roles through long service on the playing floor in Boston Garden. Five were Auerbach's players and his own handpicked choices to direct ballclub fortunes. Four besides Auerbach have claimed world championships and three have done it twice. In fact, no other franchise in NBA history can claim has many championship coaches, even if Auerbach is left entirely out of the mix. In brief, Red's interns have themselves built a most impressive

Transcendental Graphics

Having long-since abandoned the bench for the front office, Red Auerbach nevertheless remained a coach at heart. The number one redhead here gives pointers to one of his prized draft recruits and fellow carrot-top, center Dave Cowens.

Honey Russell celebrates with his Seton Hall team (which includes All-American Walter Dukes, hugged by Russell) after winning the 1953 NIT postseason college tournament. A half-decade earlier, Russell was nowhere near as successful in his role as first coach of the Boston Celtics.

championship legacy.

Of the dozen coaches beyond Auerbach who have directed Celtics fortunes down through the club's fifty-plus seasons, only two—Tom Heinsohn in 1978 and his replacement Tom Sanders the following winter—have ever suffered the indignity of mid-season replacement. Transitions have been for the most part been very smooth in Boston. But no matter how the picture is painted, most of the glorious Boston winning has come with but five men—Auerbach, Russell, Heinsohn, Bill Fitch and K. C. Jones. And the most impressive career records—in terms of winning percentage if not championship banners—have fallen to the latter pair. But even the relentless losers like Honey Russell and Doggie Julian in early franchise history and M. L. Carr and Rick Pitino in the most recent campaigns have been mentors of special distinction whose careers have been filled up with both relentless success and unique distinction. Together they build one of the richest chapters in Boston Celtics franchise history.

John "Honey" Russell
(1946-48)

The Boston Celtics didn't actually begin their franchise history with Arnold "Red" Auerbach at the reins, although sometimes in seems that way. In reality the doors swung open on the first several seasons of BAA action with Auerbach running the show for the short-lived Washington Capitols franchise and another future Hall-of-Famer entrenched on the bench for Walter Brown's club in the Boston Garden. John "Honey" Russell suffered two painfully long losing seasons with the fledgling Celtics, a tenure which was hardly a fitting middle chapter to what had already been a somewhat brief but altogether spectacular college coaching career during the late thirties and early forties at Seton Hall University.

Russell took over the Pirates' cage program in 1936 and

quickly built it into one of the strongest in the nation. His teams won a then-record 43 straight games between 1934 and 1941, a stretch when he had as his centerpiece player one of the great college backcourt men of all-time in future pro star Bobby Davies. But when Seton Hall dropped its basketball operations during World War II Russell's college coaching career ended suddenly and quite unexpectedly.

Russell would next return to the ABL, where he had already been a star player during the league's heyday between 1925 and 1931 and had paced the Cleveland Rosenblums to the ABL title during the league's inaugural season. On returning to a now watered-down ABL in the mid-forties, the forty-plus-year-old mentor again saw service as an active player in addition to his coaching duties. And he pulled a rarest of doubles for one stress-filled season, coaching both an ABL club in Trenton (New Jersey) and the Manhattan collegians simultaneously.

Russell might never have coached anywhere other than Seton Hall after his start there in 1936 had the university not dropped its basketball program for a spell in the years surrounding World War II. For Russell those war years were instead filled with duties as a player-coach in the ABL pro circuit and also his stint at Manhattan College. The opening of the BAA immediately after the war provided a new opportunity and Honey Russell received a summons from Boston Garden president Walter Brown to handle bench duties for the new pro club in New England. It was a rather dismal two-year stint for Russell in Boston that featured only two bright spots. They both came the second and final season when the Boston club boasted one of the league's best offensive threats in Ed Sadowski (the first bright spot) and rode Sadowski's talents to a postseason playoff spot (the second) despite an overall losing record.

Russell had not actually been Walter Brown's original choice for the job of kicking off the Boston Celtics franchise. The savvy promoter may not have known much about basketball in the early going but he did know marketing and thus his first priority had been a local drawing card to give his neophyte franchise a bit of credibility. The job had thus been offered to Frank Keaney a longtime fixture at Rhode Island University whose two most recent teams with All-American Ernie Calverley had made headlines with strong postseason performances in the then-prestigious Madison Square Garden NIT. Keaney had initially agreed to come on board but then at the eleventh hour in August withdrew when serious health problems got in the way. It was a bad break for Brown and the new BAA club. And it was probably also a bad break, as it turned out, for Brown's second choice, John Russell.

Russell would return to Seton Hall in 1950 and would prove in the process that he was still a master of the college game, producing another series of fine teams and another string of All-American stars. Especially potent were the clubs featuring Walter Dukes at center and Rich Regan in the backcourt, both future successful NBA warriors. A 1953 Russell-coached team featuring Dukes and Regan captured an NIT crown by blitzing St. John's and sat second in that year's final AP and UPI national polls. By career's end his seventeen years at Seton Hall had produced an impressive 294-129 winning record. But most important about Russell's split college tenure was the manner in which it offered a microcosm of basketball's evolution. In the professional game he had begun as a barnstorming player and would close by serving as first coach for what would turn out to be the modern sport's most legendary team. And in the college ranks he stood squarely at the fountainhead of the sport's mid-century explosion into a major-arena big-time entertainment spectacle.

Celtics Alvin "Doggie" Julian (1948-50)

If there is a single forgotten figure in Boston Celtics coaching history it is the man who preceded Red Auerbach on the job. Only M. L. Carr has posted a more dismal record during a brief tenure on the Boston bench than did Alvin "Doggie" Julian in the two pioneering seasons that marked the transition from the BAA to the NBA. But Julian's overall coaching career was anything but a dismal failure. And even his years in Boston had their memorable moments and pioneering influence.

A three-sports star at Bucknell University in the early '20s, Alvin Julian briefly tried his hand at professional baseball (as a catcher with the Reading International League club) and also at high school football and basketball coaching before taking on his first major college coaching assignment in 1936 at Muhlenberg (Pennsylvania) College. But big-time success came only when he took over the basketball program at Holy Cross in the immediate post-Word War II years and enjoyed both an NCAA championship (1946-47) with the Crusaders and the chance to mentor such outstanding ballplayers as George Kaftan, Frank Oftring, Joe Mullaney and Bob Cousy. Julian nearly had back-to-back NCAA champions in Cousy's first two seasons as a college player; the 1947-48 Crusaders made it back to the national semifinals before falling to Adolph Rupp's eventual winners from Kentucky. A 67-10 winning mark in three campaigns at Holy Cross (53-7 over the final two seasons) became the springboard to an offer from Walter Brown to take over the pro ballclub in Boston in time for its third season of operation.

Julian's successes with the Celtics were less noticeable than his predecessor's. The first campaign matched the winning percentage of the previous season over the course of an expanded BAA schedule which featured sixty instead

Alvin "Doggy" Julian earned New England fame as head coach of the 1947 NCAA champion Holy Cross team before taking over the reins of the Boston Celtics in 1948. Julian was known affectionalately as "The Weeper" for his sideline antics, which often involved an ever-present towel.

notable NCAA tournament upset of a national powerhouse West Virginia team featuring Jerry West. Another highlight was the appearance on his mid-fifties teams of future NBA standout Rudy LaRusso who would rank with Cousy and Kaftan as the best players Julian ever coached.

A final highlight of Doggie Julian's collegiate coaching career would be his service as president of the national coaches fraternity (NABC) and his role in that capacity in expanding the NCAA postseason tournament to its larger format beginning with the decade of the sixties. It was perhaps this administrative role more than his 388-358 coaching ledger (over 32 years) that would justify an election in 1967 to the Naismith Memorial Basketball Hall of Fame. The college coaching record was solid enough, however, to suggest one obvious interpreation of Doggie Julian's rather lame 47-81 record in the NBA with the Boston Celtics. It was not so much the coaching as the lack of ballplayers that explains the also-ran status of those early pre-Cousy and pre-Auerbach Boston teams.

BOSTON

Bill Russell
(1966-69)

When Red Auerbach began pondering retirement sometime shortly before his eighth straight world title he was faced with a daunting puzzle. In his own absence from the bench, who could possibly manage Bill Russell and thus assure future Boston successes? If the answer was inscrutible to many, it was quite obvious to the genius Auerbach. The only possible solution to the paradox was Bill Russell himself. But it was an idea that was first pushed openly by recently retired star Tom Heinsohn, even if it may have already also occurred to Auerbach himself. Heinsohn reputedly suggested the idea to his former coach at a luncheon meeting originally arranged to sound out Heinsohn's own interest in the soon-to-be-vacant job.

Bill Russell the bench coach would of course never match Bill Russell the terrorizing player. Russell the coach remained Russell the player as well, and he won another pair of world titles only because his coaching persona could always in the end count on his playing persona to save the day. There has in fact never been a playing coach in major sports history whose successes relied quite so heavily on his own athletic performances. If Russell had made Auerbach a coaching genius with his own presence in the Boston lineup, he could undoubtedly do the same for himself.

Yet at times the two roles also got in each other's way. There was, for one example, the game that Russell almost lost in the final championship series of his career by taking himself off the floor. In the championship series with LA during Russell's final season at the helm the team was facing a desperate situation in Game 4 that might have left them

of 48 games. A year later the club fell from the fifth to the sixth and bottom rung of the Eastern Division in an expanded league which had changed its name from BAA to NBA. At least Honey Russell had Big Ed Sadowski in the year before Julian arrived to add some scoring punch. Julian's first pro team didn't own a double figure scorer among its regular starters; his two biggest point makers both saw restricted duty, with Mel Reibe logging 11.0 per game before finishing the season in Providence and his former Holy Cross ace Ed Kaftan averaging a team-best 14.5 but dressing for only 21 games. A season later Sonny Hertzberg and Bob Kinney contributed double-figure scoring as starters but Kaftan proved far less productive once he logged more game time.

Released from his Boston contract by Walter Brown after his mediocre two seasons which spanned the switch from the BAA to NBA league format, Julian returned to the New England college ranks for a 17-year stint which started (3-23 in 1951) and ended (3-21 in 1966) slowly but peaked in the late fifties with a pair of 20-win teams that returned to NCAA postseason action. There were three Ivy League championships at Dartmouth during his best stretch and a

Four new NBA head coaches enjoy a laugh at the 1966 NBA draft meetings in New York. Included are (l to r): Bill Russell of Boston, John Kerr of Chicago, Alex Hannum of Philadelphia, and ex-Celtic Bill Sharman of San Francisco. Russell was blazing new trails as the league's first African-American head coach.

in a deep hole, down three games to one. The Lakers led by a single point with only seven seconds remaining in what would have been a devastating loss. Sam Jones unleashed a final desperate shot of the type that had so often rescued the Celtics in the past. This time Jones slipped while firing up the ball but nonetheless let the desperate missile fly. In any such situation the Celtics always had a trump card to play; even if such a wild shot was off the mark there was always the chance that Russell would be able to guide it home. This time, however, Russell as coach had taken himself off the floor (a fact Jones overlooked in the heat of the tense closing seconds); but this time Celtic mystique was also still alive and the shot by Jones fell in on its own.

The three years that found Russell on the bench as the first black mentor in American sports history are also three of the most exciting and drama-drenched in Boston Celtics annals. First came a landmark rare Boston loss that resulted largely because Wilt Chamberlain for once that season became a team player who had a sufficient supporting cast placed around him in Philadelphia to assure invincibility for the long-suffering 76ers. Philadelphia routed Boston in the playoffs in only five games. And then came two of the

most surprising championship eleventh-hour victories in ballclub history. Despite trailing Philadelphia in the divisional race again in 1968, the Celtics finally jelled in postseason and earned another title only after becoming the first team in league history to come back from a postseason 3-1 deficit (against Chamberlain and the 76ers in the Division Finals). A year later it was an even more miraculous year-end finish, highlighted by Sam Jones's above-mentioned miraculous shot in game four against an LA ballclub that had been strengthened by acquiring old-rival Wilt Chamberlain.

Russell's first season at the helm suggested that the Boston club might now be over the hill, and also that a large part of the Boston winning formula might have in truth been the now departed Cousy and the just-retired Auerbach. In retrospect, of course, the temporary slide of the first post-Auerbach season seemed to have more to do with Chamberlain's own sudden transformation into a clone of Russell than it did with anything else. K. C. Jones had been talked into postponing retirement for a year in order to help his old USF college roommate adjust to the dual roles of coaching while still carrying much of the load as a player. If the team Auerbach had left in Russell's hands on the court was now aging there was little sign they were slowing much and the team's 60 victories outstripped every past season but two. Bailey Howell had been added as another 20-point scorer and Sam Jones (22.1) and Havlicek (21.4) also continued to carry the offensive load. The truth by season's end was simply that the Philadelphia team which went 68-13 was so good that none of the other great Celtics clubs of the decade coached by Auerbach could have derailed them either.

If there were doubts that the Celtics had any more in them or that Russell could spark a revival as the teams "official" coaching leader these were quickly answered in the second post-Auerbach season, then reconfirmed in Russell's final year at the helm. There was no question that the team was aging: Russell and Sam Jones were both 34 (Jones slightly over and Russell slightly under). Howell was 31 and Sanders was also nearing thirty. The key to continued success was that Russell the coach adopted a new formula for continued championship runs. The team would largely forget about regular season action and concentrate its energies and resources on a final year-end burst when victories meant the most. Divisional championships were hollow victories after all. Thus the Russell-coached teams were the first to introduce a modern attitude that marked the new reality of the NBA: only the "second season" counted for much. If Russell had a small legacy as coach that supplemented his huge legacy as player it was precisely this insight about the way to approach the new "second" season that awaited teams each April and May. It was one more bit of oddball Russell philosophy that worked to enhance the ultimate reputation of Bill Russell as basketball's master psychologist.

Tom Heinsohn
(1969-78)

Tom Heinsohn was Boston's most reluctant coach. It took a good deal of Red Auerbach persuasion to get Tommy into the position in the first place. Heinsohn was approached on two different occasions before finally agreeing to accept the post: he hastily turned down the task of trying to manage Bill Russell at the time of Auerbach's 1966 retirement, then took on the burden of rebuilding the Celtics in the wake of Russell's 1969 departure because he agreed with Auerbach that he had thick enough skin to survive the unfamiliar spate of losing the team was almost certain to face. Heinsohn—despite recent successes in the insurance business—was also still attached enough to the Celtics clan to also agree with Auerbach that the job of coaching the team still belonged within the immediate family. Once Heinsohn had the post he also seemed at

times to be a reluctant winner and he was certainly never a very happy one. His courtside behavior was often outrageous and even embarrassing, and he would spend most of the coming decade chafing under the lack of respect connected with coaching a team that most believed was still Auerbach's.

But as in playing days, Heinsohn was a winner nonetheless. His resurrection of Celtics winning ways in the early and mid-seventies has to rank as one of the most successful coaching reclamation processes of pro basketball history. There was only one losing season to be discounted as a rebuilding year; there were only two seasons without playoff appearances; by his fourth and fifth seasons on the job he was already directing first a division champion and then another world champion. No one had ever stepped into a coaching situation where there were bigger shoes to fill—both Russell's and Auerbach's! No coach ever had more sudden and gapping holes to fill: Sam Jones had departed along with Russell; K. C. Jones left a mere season earlier; Bailey Howell and Larry Siegfried bowed out during Heinsohn's first season on the job. None ever faced larger shadows or more inflated expectations. Celtics fans—even if they were scarcer than might be expected in Boston had been conditioned to expecting championships annually as though they were an officially scheduled league event.

Auerbach had been caught completely off guard by Russell's retirement which he didn't think would happen for several more seasons. Heinsohn's hiring was so last-minute that he had less than a week to prepare before his first group of rookies reported for pre-season camp. The challenge for Heinsohn's first season on the bench, of course, was simply that he didn't have much of a team. The biggest problem was obviously that of replacing Bill Russell the ballplayer. The job was handed to a new acquisition named Henry Finkel who had been picked up from the Houston Rockets for spare change, and the experiment quickly proved an even bigger disaster than perhaps anyone had anticipated. The plodding Finkel was rotated with a muscular but small Jim "Bad News" Barnes and a slender 6-9 second-year recruit out of Grambling named Rich Johnson. The three together didn't come close to the rebound totals posted by Russell even in his final campaign. Opponents were no longer intimidated driving the lane against Boston and when Sanders went down with a season-ending injury in February the team was lucky to limp home three games ahead of last-place Detroit. A page was also turned when Heinsohn made a gutsy rebuilding move halfway through the winter and replaced veteran guards Larry Siegfried and Emmette Bryant with Jo Jo White and Don Chaney, two recent first-round draft picks. The move would be paying big dividends before another season was out.

Another unanticipated reward of that first dismal season for Heinsohn and the rest of the Boston braintrust

John Havlicek and Tom Heinsohn celebrate Heinsohn's first NBA championship as a head coach, the 1974 crown earned in a seven-game series with Milwaukee and Kareem Abdul-Jabbar.

second coming of Bill Russell—for all the difference in his appearance, personality and playing style. He also evolved into the most unusual post-position player in NBA history. At first Heinsohn and Auerbach were not at all certain whether the new arrival in camp was a potential replacement for Russell, or instead a surprise second coming of John Havlicek, an oversized forward who would undoubtedly have major impact but not necessarily answer their desperate need at the center position. Heinsohn resolved the issue with a bold piece of strategy: he designed an offensive that would exploit all of Cowens's inherent strengths (speed, mobility, and a Havlicek-like frenetic energy) and minimize all of his rather obvious weaknesses (height and bulk to compete with behemoths like Chamberlain, Nate Thurmond and Abdul-Jabbar). Cowens would be Heinsohn's low-post player, but he would roam farther outside than traditional NBA centers, outrun taller defenders, and overpower smaller forwards that might be assigned to guard him. If a large part of the story was Cowens' innate abilities, certainly another portion of the saga was Heinsohn's brilliant strategies for utilizing Cowens and his special talents.

was a top draft pick, and it was with that draft pick that Red Auerbach engineered a brilliant draft-day plan that more than anything saved Heinsohn's coaching career. On the eve of Heinsohn's second season the Boston Celtics inherited Dave Cowens, an unknown quantity out of Florida State whose team (and thus his own skills) had received little national exposure due to an NCAA television ban of the school. And what Auerbach and Heinsohn and the Boston fans and media got was far, far more than they had ever anticipated. Cowens' fierce rebounding and intensity all over the floor revitalized the ballclub almost overnight, put fans back in the stands, and launched an immediate on-court ressurection of Celtics fortunes that wildly outstripped even the most ambitious hopes among Boston Garden regulars.

Cowens quickly evolved into the needed replacement for Bill Russell, and at moments even appeared to be the

With the combination of Cowens and Havlicek and the reconstruction of the Boston backcourt (White the shooter and Chaney the defender replacing Siegfried and Bryant) Heinsohn soon had the makings of the third best team in Boston history. It didn't hurt that he also had the veterans John Havlicek and Don Nelson on the floor filling vital leadership roles. And Heinsohn's own genius was again demonstrtated when he moved veteran Don Nelson back into the starting lineup and converted newly acquired Paul Silas into the latest phenomenal Boston sixth man. It was certainly not a team that could equal the revolving squads led by first Cousy and Sharman and then Russell and Sam Jones during the dynasty period a decade earlier. Nor was it one that could match up with the Bird-Parish-McHale outfit to come a decade later. But it was a good enough unit for several seasons to allow Tom Heinsohn to build his own legacy as a winning NBA coach.

Much has been written about Heinsohn's career-long role as a scapegoat in Boston. As a player he had been Auerbach's designated whipping boy, the one player implaccable enough for Red to berate in the locker room whenever he wanted to stir up his team. (Cousy, Russell and Sharman were all exceptionally sensative to public criticism and had to be handled with kid gloves, but Heinsohn never flinched even if he knew that he was an inappropriate victim of Auerbach's rage.) This scapegoat's role also unfortunately shadowed Heinsohn as a coach, however, and his mentoring genius was always nearly as underrated as were his playing-days contributions. The team was considered to be Auerbach's creation and the Boston public never took Coach Heinsohn very seriously; his reputation for fuming, sulking, and throwing temper tantrums on the sideline didn't help improve the unfavorable image.

An illustration of both Heinsohn's brilliance as a coach and his inescapable fate as an underappreciated lacky is found in the circumstances surrounding the exciting 1974 championship finals versus Milwaukee and Kareem Abdul-Jabbar. The entire series had been a brilliant chess match between Heinsohn and his assistant John Killilea and Milwaukee head man Larry Costello and his assistant Hubie Brown. The visiting team won each of the final four games and Jabbar's clutch overtime skyhook in Boston Garden sent the evenly matched teams into Milwaukee for the game-seven winner-take-all match. Boston's strategy throughout the series had been the one employed against Milwaukee all year, with scrappy Cowens going head-to-head against the bigger Jabbar. Before the final shootout the Boston brass met behind closed doors with Bob Cousy sitting in as unofficial consultant. Heinsohn opted for a change in strategy and convinced both Auerbach and Cousy of the wisdom of his plan. Jabbar would now be double and tripled teamed with Cowens now fronting the big man and Paul Silas stationing himself behind. It was a gamble since the redesigned defense would leave Bucks forward Cornell Warner largely unguarded; Heinsohn reportedly quipped that he was willing to give Warner his chance to achieve greatness. The ploy worked brilliantly: Warner scored exactly one point in 29 minutes, Jabbar was held without a point for a full quarter, Cowens ran wild with 28 points and 14 rebounds, and Boston ran off with the easy 102-87 victory that restored Boston at the top of the league's elite. The moment for Heinsohn was only partially dulled by the next morning's Boston sportspage headlines which unfairly but quite typically read: COUSY STRATEGY SAVES CELTICS.

In the end Heinsohn matched Fitch and K. C. Jones in championships won; he won more games at the Boston helm than anyone but Auerbach. Fitch and Jones never suffered with weak rosters even for a single season—they both had Bird, McHale, and Parish for starters. Auerbach owned Russell, Cousy, Sharman, The Jones Boys, Heinsohn himself. But Heinsohn as coach was dealt far less cards, and the one ace he did draw—Dave Cowens—was in large part a creature of his own molding.

In brief, Tom Heinsohn may have done more with the hand dealt him than any NBA coach before or since. He got shamefully little credit for his original brilliant scheme for utilizing Cowens, or for his radical coaching gamble in the memorable 1974 Game 7 which brought him his first coaching title and also punctuated Boston's overnight return to prominence. But one fact was nonetheless unavoidable. Five short years after his first depleted team—the one later referred to by wags and historians as "The Finkel Era"—had been the laughingstock of the entire league he had brought the hated Celtics back into the winner's circle. Heinsohn had worked his magic during the early seventies even faster than Auerbach back in the early fifties. Even if he had one invaluable redhead in the lineup and another in the front office to aid the process, Heinsohn himself had drawn the x's and o's and had also inspired his revamped lineup to respond. He alone benched Siegfried and Bryant in favor of White and Chaney, matched Cowens against all-star centers six inches taller, and convinced Silas that the sixth man assignment was a worthwhile one. If he was a whipping boy much of the time and a raving lunatic some of the time, Heinsohn was nonetheless a born winner all of the time. That was the reason, of course, that the wily Auerbach had handed him the job in the first place.

B O S T O N

Tom "Satch" Sanders
(1978-79)

Tom Sanders was always only a stop-gap measure on the Boston bench. The long-time assistant and former playing star took over the ballclub in what was perhaps the darkest hour of its proud history. And he remained on the job for the shortest tenure in club history—62 games spread over parts of two forgettable seasons. It was a time when nothing but chaos and turmoil seemed to surround what had long been one of the proudest outfits in all of professional sports. The club owned by Walter Brown and his family for more than two decades had now experienced seven ownership changes in a dozen seasons and was about the undergo an eighth. These recent ownerships had been corporate entities and bottom dollar businessmen with little knowledge of the NBA and zero feeling for Celtics traditon. It had gotten so frustrating for Auerbach that he had come within inches of taking a job running the hated New York Knicks. And the players above all had stopped caring, their feelings for the most part summed up in the Curtis Rowe observation that there were no Ws and Ls on the weekly

Tom Sanders discusses strategy with assistant (and future head coach) K.C. Jones, during Sanders' first Boston Garden appearance as the Boston Celtics' head man.

chapters in ballclub annals. Short-term owner Irv Levin had attempted to force Heinsohn into resignation by embarrassing him by having GM Auerbach run a number of practices but the ploy would not coerce the failing coach into abandoning his guaranteed contract. By mid-season 1977-78 with the team standing 11-23 overall and having only two road wins, Heinsohn was axed. It was the first time a Boston coach had ever been relieved with a campaign in progress. And it would be Heinsohn's old teammate, Sanders, who would be handed the temporary task of cleaning up the resulting oncourt and locker room mess.

Sanders had been brought back to the Celtics family as Heinsohn's assistant that very season, five years after retiring as a player, and after a handful of years coaching locally in the college ranks at low-profile Harvard University. As an NBA head coach Sanders would not thrive for long. In fact he didn't thrive at all. He did salvage something from the remaining months of the season with a miniscule improvement (21-27), but there was no evidence that much spirit had returned to the Boston locker room. After only fourteen games of a new season (with the record at 2 and 12) Satch Sanders was also gone and Dave Cowens took over as part of the club's second (and far less successful) experiment with a star player serving simultaneously as bench coach. The first Boston coach to replace a fired forerunner in midstream now himself became the club's second in-season coaching firing. But Sanders did leave behind one personnel transaction under his brief tenure that was about to pay huge dividends just around the corner. As his own assistant Sanders had brought back another ex-teammate, K. C. Jones, the very man who was destined to led a new glory era in Boston only a handful of seasons down the road.

paychecks.

Sanders was a Celtics anomaly, a behind-the-scenes guy who even more than Heinsohn never got his full due for his numerous, valuable and versatile contributions. On a seemingly invincible team laced with stars and known for its stockpile of offensive weapons, plus a defense built around Russell inside and K. C. Jones outside, Sanders was a crucial if not always appreciated cog in the dynasty machinery. He was the second defensive enforcer, a player with an exceptionally narrow and precisely defined on-floor role which he always filled to a tee. He was the final element in Auerbach's master plan to have a defensive intimidator at each of the key positions: Russell the shotblocker under the hoop in the low pivot, Jones the ballhawk harassing the league's best playmakers, and Sanders squeezing the corner shooter who was usually an opponent's biggest gunner. Whether it was Elgin Baylor, or Bob Pettit, or Dolph Schayes, or later Rick Barry—they all had their hands full and their game slowed versus the tenacious Sanders. No one on the Celtics, or elsewhere in the NBA for that matter, was a better one-on-one straight-up defender. Sanders would nightly delight in shutting down the opponent's high-scoring forward, thus continually forcing the ball and the hesitant opposition shooter straight toward the waiting shotblocker in the middle of the lane.

The circumstances leading up the Tom Heinsohn's demise as Celtics coach thus provided one of the bleakest

Dave Cowens
(1979)

Even true diehard Celtics boosters often have trouble remembering that Dave Cowens ever coached in Boston. For one thing, his short tenure came during one of the least memorable epochs in club annals. For a second, he logged the second fewest bench games of any Boston mentor and did so for only part of a single dreadful season. But most importantly, Cowens the player has always dwarfed Cowens the coach in a way that was even more extreme than the cases of three predecessors who also occupied both roles— Bill Russell, Tom Heinsohn and Satch Sanders. When Russell was player-coach he won a pair of titles which added a bit of luster and a punctuation mark to his tenure filling both roles. Cowen's time on the job was, by contrast, utterly forgettable.

As a player Cowens was indisputably the boldest and most surprisingly successful experiment in team history. Like Russell, he too had revolutionized the way the position of NBA center was played. And whereas Russell's innovations were all on the defensive end, Cowens correspondingly revamped the notion of mobile pivot-position offensive play. Now he would again follow Russell's model as a team floor leader turned into a playing coaching. Unfortunately this time around the experiment wasn't such an obvious success. Even Auerbach apparently didn't work miracles every time with his innovative manipulations. But if just one experiment worked with Cowens (the one that had him running the league's bigger centers away from the basket to guard his arsenal of longer-range jump shots and hooks) that was enough in the annals of a single ballclub.

Cowens' one partial season in filling both coaching and playing roles likely contributed heavily to his own career burnout. With so many holes to fill on the roster and so many teammates that no longer played hard or seemed cut in his own mold, Cowens griped at year's end that the thankless coaching job was painfully like running a day care center. And a 29-53 ledger (27-41 after Cowens took over)—the worst since Auerbach stepped aboard back in 1950—didn't help renew any tired spirits. Cowens was perhaps most frustrated by highly touted ex-UCLA Bruin, Curtis Rowe, who played out his last Boston season with little show of real enthusiasm, as well as by Billy Knight (booed mercilessly by Garden fans for his "soft" play) and Bob McAdoo (an un-Celtic-like gunner brought to town in an unpopular trade). The beleaguered coach had to supply much of the offensive action himself (16.8 ppg.), trailing only Cornbread Maxwell (19.0) among team scorers. (He was also number two rebounder after Maxwell.) There would be only one more season in the cards (Bird's rookie outing) before Dave Cowens would admit that his own enthusiasm for the game was now almost entirely gone.

On the heels of the final game of 1979 Cowens brusquely resigned as head coach; at the outset of Bird's second season a year and a half later a frustrated Cowens announced his retirement from active play (he returned for a 40-game cameo in Milwaukee two years later) when he realized that waning skills were diminishing both his game and his pride. But the one partial season that Cowens did

coach was in the end a lot like Heinsohn's first year on the job. It was a year devoted entirely to surviving a holding pattern until a new franchise saviour would come along. Cowens had himself been that savior for Heinsohn. This time it would be Larry Bird waiting in the wings.

BOSTON
Bill Fitch
(1979-83)

Fitch sits alongside Dick Motta and Gene Shue in the triumverate of three-decade also-ran NBA coaches who have steadily padded their resumes with mountainous victory totals simply by clinging to miraculous runs of longevity. Thus while Fitch has steadily climbed the ladder among the all-time winningest NBA mentors he has at the same time proven to be the game's unrivaled relentless loser. The "up" side of the Bill Fitch story is the fact that only Lenny Wilkens has won more games (1120 to 944 at the end of 1998); the more eye-catching "down" side is that no one has come close to losing as many (1106). Admittedly coaching with the Cleveland Cavaliers throughout the 1970s, and then the sadsack New Jersey Nets and Los Angeles Clippers throughout the '90s, has not lent itself to stashing large numbers in the win column. During the intervening decade the former Coe College (Iowa) player and coach enjoyed what must at the time have seemed like paradise assignments in both Boston and Houston and took enough advantage to post three Atlantic Division championships and an NBA crown (during Larry Bird's third season) at the first post, and then a runaway Midwest Division banner and second trip to the NBA Finals (versus his old Boston team) when blessed with the Twin Towers (Olajuwon and Sampson) in Houston. Ironically neither of his two NBA coach-of-the-year trophies came in those two heady seasons, however. The first was garnered with a surprising Cleveland outfit that captured the 1976 Central Division race and featured stellar guards Jim Chones and Campy Russell. The second came in his debut Boston season (1980) where a miracle 32-game turnaround in ballclub fortunes had seemingly far more to do with a rookie sensation named Larry Bird than it did with the arrival of a replacement veteran head coach.

But if Bill Fitch was one of the sport's biggest losers in backwater outposts like Los Angeles, Cleveland and New Jersey, he was nonetheless one of the league's most effective winners when he was finally handed a full deck in Boston. Like baseball's Casey Stengel with the New York Yankees, Bill Fitch became the prime exemplar of a coaching truism—give a talented veteran mentor a bunch of worthless losers on his roster and he will be as ineffective as the next chump; load his roster with future hall of famers and he will miraculously transform into a hall of famer himself.

himself not to grow up with the Celtics system as a former Boston player, Fitch also seemed to be just that right kind of coach for Larry Bird's debut. The biggest factor in the perfect marriage of veteran coach and novice player was that Bird had been raised with an immense respect for authority and a willing hunger to take instruction from his mentors. Under a laissez faire boss who gave his players free rein, the prized rookie might well have flounder despite his immense unchallenged talents. Bird even as a raw rookie respected hard work, and Fitch was the hardest working coach the young Larry Bird had ever seen.

Perhaps the largest contribution of Fitch's coaching stay in Boston, however, is the one he has never been given adequate credit for. It was his role in the maneuvers that brought both Robert Parish and Kevin McHale to Boston in time for Bird's second

Rookie Larry Bird listens intently as another Boston newcomer, head coach Bill Fitch, reacts to the oncourt action at Boston Garden.

Fitch proved again what Stengel had earlier proved on the baseball diamond. The players make the coach and not vice versa. Even the genius that was Auerbach never won much of anything before he had an overgrown human shot-swatting defender named Bill Russell in the fold.

Fitch's tenure was therefore successful in hindsight largely because of the coinciding arrival on the Boston scene of Auerbach's latest draft day coup, Larry Bird. But Fitch himself was at least partially responsible for the Celtics turnaround at the start of a new decade. He was hand-picked by Auerbach for the job because of the near miracles he had just accomplished with an expansion ballclub in Cleveland. Over a half-dozen seasons he had painstakingly constructed a club that by 1976 had captured a Central Division crown and challenged the title-bound Celtics in the Conference Finals. It was the notion of the new coach that the "soft" Celtics teams of the past few seasons had fallen on such hard times because they had forgotten (or refused) to play hard-nosed NBA-style defense. Fitch boasted an ambitious work ethic (for himself and his players) and a well-drawn plan for driving his new team toward immediate improvement. And some of the new reinforcments which included veteran guard Nate Archibald and rugged reserve center Rick Robey would help immensely in the renewed driven for success.

The ex-Marine who was the first coach since Auerbach

season in the league. When Auerbach consummated the deal that corralled Parish for the number one pick Boston was still sitting on (from an earlier trade with Detroit that had unloaded Bob McAdoo) as well as the number three overall selection (which was Golden State's), Auerbach himself was not convinced that Purdue's Joe Barry Carroll was not the player Boston really needed. Fitch prevailed in forcing the trade (and thus letting Carroll go to Golden State, but reeling in McHale); then Auerbach himself took credit for the entire transaction in subsequent years. In his insightful book *Ever Green: The Boston Celtics* (1990), respected Boston sportswriter Dan Shaunghnessy would later contend that Fitch's lingering jealousy over Auerbach's ruthless commandering of credit for the Parish and McHale acquisitions would play a very significant role in Fitch's eventual souring on the job and then his departure from the organization.

The dealing for Parish and McHale paid immediate dividends in Boston no matter who the chief architect might have been. The pieces were now all in place and Bill Fitch himself reaped the rewards with three more sensational seasons. But it was a joyride that could not be sustained for very long under the militaristic coach's intense approach to training and team management. The Celtics of course would survive as an elite outfit for much of the decade and enjoy an even brighter renaissance halfway into

Bird's career. But Bill Fitch himself would not make the grade for long and would not stay on board long enough to reap the full rewards of a legendary team which he as much as Auerbach or anyone else had constructed and then molded into the league's latest scourge.

Celtics
K.C. Jones
(1983-88)

K. C. Jones may well be another exemplar of the Bill Fitch principle: the one that argues for players underpinning coaches' reputations and not vice versa. Jones enjoyed five years on the Boston bench with a nightly lineup that consisted of Bird, Parish and McHale on the front wall and Dennis Johnson at the backcourt controls. An immediate result was the most relentless winning of games in franchise history. But then Jones—just like Fitch—also did his own considerable amount of molding, though the taciturn manner of the hall-of-fame guard was an even further

assurance that the bulk of his impact on players and team performance would—again like Fitch's—go largely unappreciated. Jones may have always lived in the shadows of Bill Russell as a collegiate and professional ballplayer. And as a coach he may never have entirely climbed out from under Red Auerbach's still all-enveloping image. But no coach anywhere ever did a better job for five seasons running when it came to relentless winning with impeccable class. But then again none ever had a more potent lineup to work with.

When Jones took the Boston coaching job in 1983 on the heels of four Bill Fitch seasons that produced three 60-win campaigns it might have appeared to the outsider that Fitch would have been a particularly tough act to follow. This might have been the case even if one took into consideration the previous coaching successes that Jones had already enjoyed with the Washington Bullets. But by the time Fitch was run off, Jones was a most popular and welcomed replacement in the eyes of most of the Boston ballplayers. More importantly he was also a most welcomed shift—from Auerbach's perspective—even if it had been Red himself who was once so high on Fitch only a handful of seasons earlier.

Jones was a quiet font of coaching experience and knowledge who inspired supreme confidence in his players and always held their complete respect almost to the last man at the end of the bench (the one who receives little playing time and is thus most prone to dissatisfaction). He allowed players a degree of freedom to freelance and be themselves within his disciplined on-court system. He was open to input and made team members feel a part of the close-bound unit. And he enhanced his respect in all quarters when he matched Fitch's heady debut with his own three inaugural 60-win seasons, then nearly maintained the pace for his final two seasons despite increased challenges, especially from Pat Riley's perfectly jelled "Showtime" Lakers.

Bird peaked under Jones and took home two of his NBA team trophies during the Jones coaching era. The five-year span was also enhanced by the full emergence of the all-time front wall of Bird, Parish and McHale. And Jones missed by the narrowest of margins of taking his club the the NBA Finals in all five of his seasons on the job. That would have been a perfect record of success that ranked right up there alongside the feats that marked Auerbach's glowing tenure back in the sixties. Few coaches before or since ever boasted regular-season and postseason victory percentages to compare with those Jones recorded.

K.C. Jones reacts to the flow of the game from the Boston bench in late-season 1988, shortly after it was announced that Jones would retire at season's end and be replaced by his assistant Jimmy Rodgers (seated at right).

AP/Wide World Photos

B O S T O N

Jimmy Rodgers
(1988-90)

Five of Auerbach's followers were former players well ingrained in the Celtics system of selfless team play. A sixth, Jimmy Rodgers, was a longtime assistant who carried on the legacy of family tradition in the Boston coaching ranks. Unfortunately for Rodgers, by the time he inherited the job from K. C. Jones things were already winding down on the Bird-Parish-McHale era. Without a fresh infusion of immense talent—something that was never forthcoming—it was predictable that Rodgers would sail rough waters after taking over the Celtics ship. And the first season under the new mentor got off to the worst of all possible starts when the franchise player—Larry Bird—immediately fell victim to a season-ending injury.

Rodgers had joined the Celtics family as one of Bill Fitch's assistants and he later continued to fill that role under K. C. Jones. Given the glut of winning successes during those first nine Larry Bird seasons (eight divisional titles and three NBA crowns) it was an excellent school for learning the trade and also a perfect opportunity for having some winning tradition rub off. Auerbach, for one, thought that Rodgers was a most excellent pupil and even thought so highly of the assistant as head coaching material that he once denied the New York Knicks permission to speak with Rodgers about one of their own coaching openings.

Auerbach displayed that supreme faith by bumping K. C. Jones to the front office in 1989 and handing the job to the seasoned Jimmy Rodgers. It was not Red's worst move ever, but it certainly didn't pan out as one of his most memorable gambles either.

Even with Bird in decline, Rodgers managed to post some solid successes. The unanticipated loss of Bird in his maiden outing can at least partially excuse a thoroughly average beginning for Rodgers; with Bird revived a second campaign proved almost lucrative with 52 wins and a climb back near the top of the division. But Rodgers suffered by comparisons to his predecessor and tension was in the air between him in his players almost from the start. It only took a disastrous collapse in the opening 1990 playoff round with New York (in which the Celtics lost three straight and blew a 2-0 series lead) to ring the sudden death knell on Rodgers' short tenure in Boston.

Chris Ford
(1990-95)

There were many plusses to the five year tenure of Chris Ford, which began with two division titles in Larry Bird's final seasons. But there was also plenty of trying misfortune and rare bad luck, especially during two final campaigns of backsliding and backbiting which began the current Boston swoon of the mid and late '90s. There was the inevitable departure of "The Big Three" unit which had anchored Boston clubs for a full decade, and there was also the tragic 1993 death of team captain Reggie Lewis. Chris Ford may not have been the best Boston coach (that was obviously Auerbach by any measure, with K. C. Jones a close second and nobody else but maybe Bill Fitch even in the running), and he certainly wasn't close to being the worst (a distinction that M. L. Carr now holds without any serious challengers). But there is little dispute that he was by far the unluckiest.

The biggest blows were the injuries that robbed Bird and McHale of their final few potentially productive years, and the heart disease suffered by Reggie Lewis that robbed the team of its emotional leader and also its top performer for perhaps many

Still a Celtics assistant, Jim Rodgers gestures while explaining a point in practice to center Robert Parish, number 00 in the foreground.

AP/Wide World Photos

Chris Ford experienced both the fortune and misfortune of coaching Boston during the final Larry Bird seasons of the early 1990s.

seasons to come. But what seemed to exasperate Ford the most as head coach was the total ineptitude of his final couple of teams and his inability to get those disinterested and disloyal groups to perform even the most basic of the game's fundamentals. It was perhaps fading superstar Dominique Wilkins with his one-year mercenary layover during the final season at Boston Garden who cursed the beleaguered Ford with his largest dose of understandable frustration. Gone were the days where team came first, Celtics Pride enveloped the entire franchise, and any newly arriving touted rookie or veteran castoff from another team was nothing special until he proved himself worthy of wearing the famed green and white uniform. In his final distasteful go-around Ford—who himself had played alongside a young Bird and an aging Cowens—was saddled with a group that played defense without enthusiasm and offense without much style or skill, and he spent much of the final winter chewing out his tuned-out and turned-off lackluster forces.

Ford's career does boast one special highlight though— the rare distinction of being one of only four rookie NBA mentors (the others are Ed Macauley, Billy Cunningham and Pat Riley) to serve as a head coach in the NBA All-Star Game. And while he never garnered a championship ring as a head bench man, he did earlier pick up an earlier pair as an assistant to K. C. Jones, making him one of four Celtics alumni (with Russell, Heinsohn and Jones) to earn coveted championship rings in Boston as both player and coach.

BOSTON

M.L. Carr
(1995-97)

Carr was always a relentless winner when he wore a playing uniform, and he was also the fortunate beneficiary of a slew of talented teammates to make his own role all the easier. When it came to coaching the good fortune of an excellent surrounding cast was never there, however. And the results were predictable—the two worst seasons in the storied history of the Boston Celtics franchise. But Carr's negative coaching legacy had an added twist that seemed to even further sour the mix. For the same two seasons when he rode the bench as head coach, the likeable Carr also sported the lofty titles of director of basketball operations and executive vice-president. There were few to blame above since the head coach was also in charge of a large piece of the operation. And in short order a once-popular role player from the glorious Celtics past became a much-maligned bench boss who felt the sting of criticism from hordes of frustrated Boston patrons.

Carr didn't assume the head coaching role in Boston under the best of circumstances. Chris Ford had finally stepped aside after the successes of his first three seasons had evaporated into a pair of losing backsliding campaigns, the first of which had left the team out of the playoffs for the first time in fifteen years and the second of which had ended in the embarrassing first-round postseason blitzing by the expansion Orlando Magic which had rung down the curtain on the historic Boston Garden. The new coach was now one with no frontline bench experience, and the team he inherited from Ford was one in need of a complete overhaul. The frontcourt of Pervis Ellison, Rick Fox and Xavier McDaniel had little skill or interest when it came to playing tough defense; the backcourt of Dee Brown (6-1) and Sherman Douglas (6-1) was one of the smallest in the league; and a bench comprised of Dino Radja, Greg Minor, and Eric Williams among others was painfully thin by NBA standards.

But the biggest problems of all seemed to be the misplaced self-confidence that motivated basketball operations director Carr to select himself as Ford's replacement, as well as blind support of board chairman Paul Gaston, who was seemingly overly impressed with Carr's skills as a motivational speaker and thus willing to discount altogether is complete lack of coaching preparation in the pros or at any other level. Critics from every quarter were predicting dire results from Boston's uncharacteristically bizarre front office move and it didn't take long for all the naysayers to be proven right on the mark. Carr for his own part was enthused about the prospects, noting that his dual role would be unique in NBA circles and seeing it all as an opportunity to evaluate talent from a coaching and managerial position simultaneously and thus fully comprehend his team's needs. The problem for the most part was that the personal needs were so stark that they might easily have been assessed adequately by any season ticket holder. It was addressing the needs and turning the ballclub in a different direction that required a coaching genius that M. L. Carr apparently didn't have.

What started off as a merely bad season in Carr's first winter on the circuit (33-49, only two games worse that Ford's team of the previous year) turned into full blown disaster by year two. The 1997 edition was not only the worst team in franchise history by every measure but also easily the worst in the watered-down NBA of the current moment. Boston trailed the pack in virtually every team statistical category and seemed to invent new ways to lose almost every night they took the floor. Opponents shot a league-high .503 percentage from the floor against them and the ballclub was a woeful 6 and 35 in one-sided games decided by double-figure margins. Hot rookie Antoine Walker was the only Boston bright spot and only seemed to emphasize the derth of talent around him. Once promising European important Dino Radja missed 57 games due to injury and even a year-end deal to unload Radja and clear over $5 million from the salary cap (picking up veterans Michael Cage and Clarence Weatherspoon from Philadelphia in the process) turned sour when the unwanted forward failed to pass his Philadelphia physical.

The disaster of Carr's two-year tenure as bench coach had perhaps only a single silver lining. It did ultimately present the opportunity for landing supersuccessful Rick Pitino to tackle the considerable challenge of restoring some amount of respect to the Boston Celtics basketball family. It will be certainly the biggest rebuilding task of franchise history. Carr had seemingly overnight put the team in its deepest hole in a half century of operations. And since he was his own front office boss he had no one else to blame for the unprecedented catastrophe, or even anyone else to share part of the burden with him. In a five-decade-plus run of unparalleled coaching successes the Boston Celtics had at long last discovered that even the most storied franchise is not entirely immune to a complete coaching collapse now and again.

Rick Pitino
(1997-99)

Rick Pitino is Boston's hope for the new millennium. Certainly he is the biggest franchise investment ever when it comes down to measurement in pure dollar amounts. No star player—not even Larry Bird in the modern era—has ever come on board in Boston with anything like the 10-year $70 million package that was thrown at Pitino in the wake of the wreckage left behind my M. L. Carr's brief coaching tenure. And so far—after a pair of mediocre rebuilding campaigns—the jury is still out on the man who has already produced one of the largest modern-day legends in college basketball circles.

When Pitino took over as Boston's thirteen head coach he immediately pushed all the right buttons for devoted Celtics watchers by vowing to work harder than perhaps even Red Auerbach could possibly imagine to rebuild sagging Celtics on-court fortunes. It was a bold promise but certainly not an unreasonable or inappropriate one given how much the ballclub was about to pay for his valued services. And not an unreasonable gesture either considering how much franchise front office control was about to be handed over to a wildly successful collegiate mentor flush with recent NCAA championship successes at the University of Kentucky.

The most thankless assignment in basketball coaching history has long been that of living up to the legend of Adolph Rupp in Kentucky, and Rick Pitino a few years back nearly pulled it off. Had he stayed around in the Blue Grass State a few more seasons he might even have done so eventually. As it was he twice took the Wildcats to the NCAA title game in his final two seasons on the job, he won five SEC crowns in eight campaigns, he put Kentucky back in the NCAA winners circle for the first time in nearly two decades with a 1996 national title, won 28 games four seasons in a row, and had UK consistently ranked near the top of the national polls throughout most of his tenure. After a single losing campaign in 1990 his next half-dozen Wildcat juggernaut teams averaged a seasonal record of 27-8 and finished as low as second in the Southeastern Conference only once. His final Kentucky team which posted an eye-popping 35-5 year-long mark clawed its way into an NCAA title match with Cinderella Arizona and nearly put together one of the strongest postseason runs in storied Kentucky cage history. Pitino was *The Sporting News* selection as college coach of the year in both 1987 at Providence and also 1991 in Lexington, and managed to fulfill his grossly inflated mission by adding to the impressive collection of UK national championship trophies. Maddening consistency was thus the final measure of Kentucky's biggest coaching idol outside of Rupp—just as

Rick Pitino has so far enjoyed few highlight moments in Boston, but there were many occasions for celebration during the glory years with Kentucky. Here Coach Pitino and his team celebrate with the traditional on-floor coach's shower after the Wildcats captured the 1995 Southeastern Conference year-end tournament.

it had been with the Baron himself—and for six final seasons between 1992 and 1997 the Pitino-led Wildcats posted Rupp-like records, never winning fewer that 27 nor losing more than seven games.

If Pitino almost succeeded in replacing one living legend in Kentucky, his chances of repeating the trick in the NBA ranks with Boston seem far less likely of accomplishment. He has, admittedly, already tasted pro success in an earlier short stint at the reins of the New York Knicks (1988 and 1989), posting an overall 90-74 ledger and one sterling 52-30 campaign which was the best in New York since Red Holzman's championship run in the early seventies. But tackling the ghost of Red Holzman and Willis Reed or even that of Adolph Rupp was one thing. Taking on the shadows cast by Red Auerbach is yet quite another. Boston fans—with a third of the NBA's title banners already hanging from the ceiling of the new Fleet Center—will hardly settle for anything short of another minidynasty. And it is likely that Pitino, or any successor, will only turn that trick if and when the next Bill Russell or Larry Bird happens to come along.

The Boston Coaching Record

A third of a century after his retirement from the bench Red Auerbach is still the most legendary name in NBA coaching circles—the composite Miller Huggins, Joe McCarthy and Casey Stengel of the pro basketball coaching fraternity, with Connie Mack and John McGraw thrown in for good measure. Yet only once (in his penultimate season of 1965) was Auerbach formally tabbed as an NBA Coach of the Year—partially due admittedly to the fact that such an honor was not instituted (1963) until he already owned five of his nine championship rings. Two other Celtics head coaches (Heinsohn and Fitch) have captured the same

formal honor, leaving only three top coaching trophies in the Boston display case despite 16 world championships—a third of the entire total the league has presented—and five different championship coaches. Perhaps the explanation is a widespread assumption through the years that with players like Russell, Cousy, Heinsohn, Havlicek, Cowens and Bird in the fold coaching the Celtics was likely the cushiest assignment in the NBA.

But there are other surprises as well to be gleaned from scanning the year-by-year Boston coaching record. The nonpareil Auerbach holds only the third best lifetime winning percentage among franchise coaches—trailing both K. C. Jones and Bill Fitch and barely outstripping Russell and Heinsohn—and his postseason winning ratio (individual games won and lost) is also third best (after Jones and Russell) in Boston club annals. Great coaching in Boston certainly began with Auerbach, but it obviously didn't always end there.

Boston has also turned out more players who eventually became coaches in either the pro or college ranks that any other franchise. The total number now approaches close to fifty and the list that begins with Heinsohn, Russell, Sharman, Cousy, K. C. Jones, Chris Ford, Don Nelson, Danny Ainge, Don Chaney, Paul Silas, Dave Cowens and Larry Bird features only the celebrated names whose successes have graced the NBA. Since the day that Auerbach retired back in 1966 there have been ten men who have held the clipboard at the end of the Boston bench and a full seven have been former playing members of the Boston Celtics family, trained and nurtured by the top dog redhead himself. And of those who weren't—Fitch, Rodgers and now Pitino—only the first has had more than passing success at the job. If there is indeed something tangible in the concept of Celtic Pride its fullest and most obvious measure is found in the sideline performances of the handful of men who have been Red Auerbach's successors and also his chief disciples.

Boston Celtics Head Coaching Legacy

Coach	Years (Seasons)	Regular Season Record	Post-Season Record	Titles
John "Honey" Russell	1946-48 (2)	42-66 (.389)	1-2 (.333)	-
Alvin "Doggie" Julian	1948-50 (2)	47-81 (.367)	Did Not Qualify	-
Arnold "Red" Auerbach	1950-66 (16)	795-397 (.667)	90-58 (.608)	9
Bill Russell	1966-69 (3)	162-83 (.661)	28-18 (.609)	2
Tom Heinsohn	1969-78 (9)	427-263 (.619)	47-33 (.588)	2
Tom "Satch" Sanders	1978 (2)	23-39 (.371)	Did Not Qualify	-
Dave Cowens	1978-79 (1)	27-41 (.397)	Did Not Qualify	-
Bill Fitch	1979-83 (4)	242-86 (.738)	26-19 (.578)	1
K. C. Jones	1983-88 (5)	**308-102 (.751)**	**65-37 (.737)**	2
Jim Rodgers	1988-90 (2)	94-70 (.573)	2-6 (.250)	0
Chris Ford	1990-95 (5)	222-188 (.541)	13-16 (.448)	0
M. L. Carr	1995-97 (2)	48-116 (.296)	Did Not Qualify	-
Rick Pitino	1997-99 (2)	55-77 (.417)	Has Not Qualified	-
Totals	**1946-99 (53)**	**2492-1609 (.608)**	**272-189 (.590)**	**16**

BOSTON Celtics
Celtics

CHAPTER IX ————————————————

A Quintet of Legendary Sidecourt Personalities

Few pro franchises in any sport have boasted such rock solid consistency in their off-court management as has the NBA basketball club operated out of Boston. Of the league's original eleven teams only the Boston Celtics and New York Knicks continue to operate in the same city under the same nickname. And only baseball's Brooklyn-Los Angeles Dodgers with two ownerships and three field managers over the recent half-century, or the long moribund Philadelphia A's owned, operated and managed by one Connie Mack for the century's entire first half, provide comparable examples of front office stablity.

For nearly fifty years two men alone have guided Boston's front-office NBA fortunes as well as managed its oncourt performances. Original owner Walter Brown (who controlled club operations for the first 18 seasons) was far more than a pioneering franchise mogul; it is Brown as much as anyone else who deserves the full credit for launching the shaky enterprise originally known as the Basketball Association of America (BAA) and thus building the foundation on which America's current-day top professional sport now securely sits. If James Naismith is the true father of basketball and legendary Kansas University coach Phog Allen is (in Naismith's own pronouncement) the father of basketball coaching, then Walter Brown indeed may be the father of professional basketball as we today know it. But it was not until Brown was inspired to hire an obscure coach named Auerbach in the century's middle year that his franchise ever amounted to much. The enterprise to which Walter Brown gave birth has been for most of its life run by a brazen basketball folk hero who is rivalled only by John Wooden in the collegiate ranks for miraculous year-in and year-out winning and who knows absolutely no peer at any level when it came to building the sport in its modern image.

After Red Auerbach and Walter Brown there is pre-

ciously little left to occupy our attention when it comes to the history of Boston Celtics front office operations. Yet there have been a small handful of other notable figures who have also graced the ballclub's off-court operations. Jan Volk has operated behind the Auerbach shadows for much of the past decade in a noble effort to rebuild sagging franchise fortunes. Bill Mokray remains a little-known figure of immense historical significance. And one other memorable character survived for almost as long as Auerbach while serving as the Hub fan's airwaves link to the hometown heroes and their ongoing championship sagas. The byword in Boston has always been consistency. But local color has played its own dominant role in the fortunes of basketball's most successful franchise. How could it be otherwise for a team with Walter Brown lurking in the shadows, Auerbach flamboyantly pacing on the sidelines, and Johnny Most reaching out over the airwaves to four decades of listeners among basketball's most proud and knowledgable fans.

Celtics
Red Auerbach
Author of Celtic Mystique

Arnold "Red" Auerbach's NBA coaching career, in hindsight at least, will forever be bound up with two legendary athletes who contributed mightily to his Boston Celtics dynasty and its almost unimaginable successes, yet who also serve today to diminish somewhat unfairly his own immense two-decade coaching achievements. There is little doubt that the often irascible Auerbach would not have won quite so relentlessly in Boston without the sleight-handed Bob Cousy to run his offense or without towering Bill Russell to anchor his unique model for a fast-breaking offensive machine. Naysayers have long contended that Auerbach's victories can never be separated out from

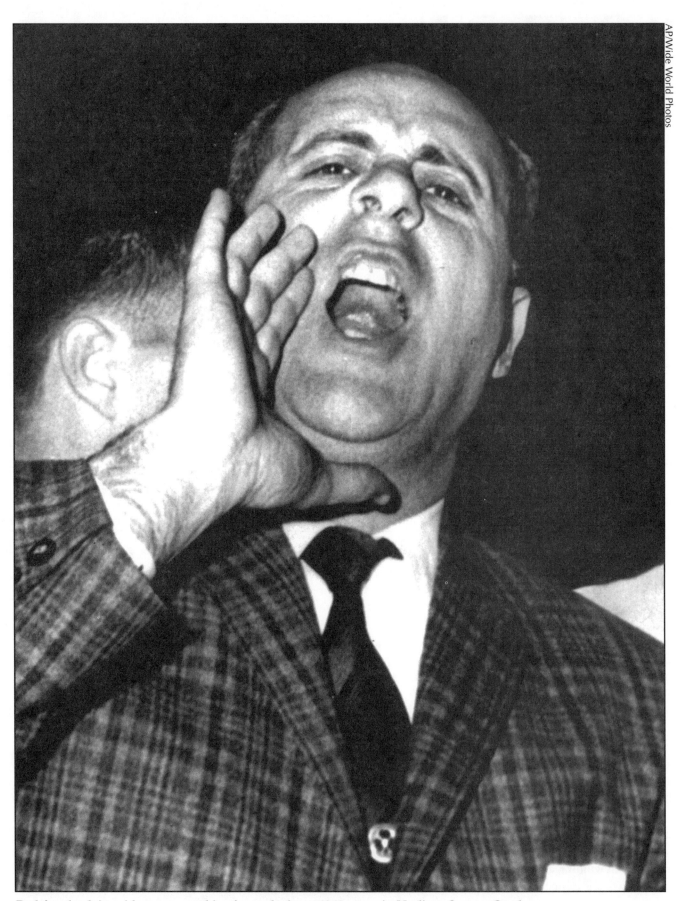

Red Auerbach in mid-career coaching form, during a 1960 game in Madison Square Garden.

Russell's. And those same nigglers are quick to point out that Auerbach only ended up with Cousy quite against his wishes and despite his own best efforts to block the local hero's presence in a Boston uniform.

The story of Auerbach's unplanned acquisition of Cousy and his painstakingly orchestrated acquisition of Russell together reveal much about the combined role of rare luck and unmatched acumen in shaping his own coaching and administrative career. Cousy was one player Auerbach had seemingly little use for in the beginning. The newly arrived Boston mentor tried to avoid the popular favorite on draft day of 1950 and was clearly annoyed by the hounding he at first received from the Boston area press to draft the local hero and Holy Cross All-American. Auerbach even squared off with the hometown media in his earliest press conference when he uttered words that were among his most famous. "Am I here to win games," chided Auerbach, "or to please the local yokels?"

Auerbach opted for 6-11 Charlie Share from Bowling Green while Cousy was a draft choice of the Tri-Cities Blackhawks. But the Hawks immediately dealt Cousy to Chicago which almost as immediately folded its own franchise operations. Cousy was then thrown into a dispersal draft with popular veterans Max Zaslofsky and Andy Phillip and went by default to Boston which owned the last of the three available "special" picks. In the end, Bob Cousy wound up in the Boston camp despite Auerbach's best efforts, but then again the stubborn coach was quick to demonstrate that he was quite wise enough to exploit the new talent once he owned him.

With Russell it was a different matter altogether. Here the ingenious Auerbach had done his homework thoroughly, knew precisely what he wanted and how to manipulate other owners and GMs to get it, and saw in the rough-cut gem that was Bill Russell what other club directors failed entirely to see. That fortuitous insight was soon to give victory-minded Auerbach all the edge he ever needed. Auerbach was alerted early (tipped off by his former George Washington University coach Bill Reinhart) to the raw potential in the San Francisco University defensive star and from the beginning seemed to see in Russell's latent talents the key to reshaping his own imbalanced team and thus altering the entire NBA's future course as well. Auerbach envi-

sioned the fast-break (learned from Reinhart at George Washington) as the key to turning around his middling ballclub, but he also knew precisely the kind of player he needed to make his scheme work. That player was built precisely in the image that corresponded to Bill Russell. With Ed Macauley in the center slot and Cousy and Sharman in the backcourt Boston already boasted plenty of shooting power (they were the NBA's highest-scoring team) but little defense (they gave up the most points) and less rebounding. The fast-break would work as a strategy only if it was anchored by a stellar rebounder and shot-blocker who could sweep the defensive boards and deliver lightning-fast outlet passes to a streaking Cousy. Russell fit the job description to a tee.

Once he had deemed Russell the answer to his plan the clever Boston mentor still had to do some fancy manipulating to bring the future star to Boston. Rochester owned the top 1956 draft pick but was almost certain not to pursue Russell for purely financial reasons. Sihugo Green thus became the answer to a classic trivia question (who was drafted ahead of Russell in 1956?). St. Louis in second slot likely would not grab Russell either, but the risk here was far greater. Auerbach knew that Russell would not be a saleable item in racially tense St. Louis. But Hawks owner

Pro Basketball's Ten Winningest Coaches

Coach	Teams (Years)	Record (Pct.)
Lenny Wilkens	Seattle, Portland, Seattle, Cleveland, Atlanta	1,170-876 (.573)
Red Auerbach	Boston Celtics	938-479 (.662)
Bill Fitch	LA Clippers, New Jersey, Houston, Boston, Cleveland	927-1,041 (.471)
Dick Motta	Chicago, Washington, Dallas, Sacramento	918-965 (.487)
Jack Ramsay	Philadelphia, Buffalo, Portland, Indiana	864-783 (.525)
Pat Riley	LA Lakers, New York Knicks, Miami Heat	859-360 (.705)
Larry Brown	Carolina (ABA), Denver (ABA) New Jersey, San Antonio, LA Clippers, Indiana	853-587 (.592)
Don Nelson,	Milwaukee, Golden State, New York Knicks	851-629 (.575)
Cotton Fitzsimmons	Phoenix, Atlanta, Buffalo, Sacramento, San Antonio	832-775 (.518)
Gene Shue	Baltimore, Philadelphia, San Diego, Washington, LA Clippers	784-861- (.477)

The two master architects of Celtic hardcourt magic—Walter Brown in top hat and dripping Red Auerbach with his ever-present cigar—celebrate the clinching of the team's first-ever Eastern Division crown (and first trip to the NBA Finals) during the franchise's eleventh season. Also present are Russell (top left), Heinsohn (#15), Cousy (to Auerbach's right), Loscutoff (#18), Andy Phillip (#17), Jack Nichols (#16), Ramsey (#23) and Sharman (#21).

Ben Kerner was not about to let him go to Boston without plenty of "appropriate" compensation. The deal that was finally struck (sending the Hawks all-star Ed Macauley and hot prospect Cliff Hagan) not only cemented Boston's future, but it also strengthened a prime rival—Kerner's Hawks—and in the process created a blockbuster postseason confrontation with St. Louis over the next half-decade that would remain one of the league's showcase events of its first quarter-century.

It is not surprising to find such carping about Auerbach's achievements in Boston—claims that he gained his first true star, Cousy, against his own will and best judgement, and also that he won only because Russell and Cousy were regularly in the lineup—since in his own day he was one of the least-popular coaches on the scene with fans, media, and even rival players, and especially with his rivals in the coaching fraternity. Auerbach from the start had as much of a knack for alienating the general populace (especially his bench rivals) as he did for winning championships. Especially despised was his on-court behavior during Boston's many triumphs across the decade known for "Celtic Mystique." Red's flaunted victory cigar—which

he would light on the bench in closing moments of games when victory was in the bag—remained throughout the late '50s and '60sthe most universally hated sight to be found anywhere around the league.

But despite this veneer of broad-based unpopularity, Auerbach's record for sixteen seasons as a Boston head coach speaks eloquently for itself. No NBA coach has won so much, so consistently, and for so long a string. (Lenny Wilkens' victories now exceed Auerbach's by 200 and counting, but Wilkens' winning percentage is one hundred points lower and his championships (one) are miniscule.) Red's teams dominated an era which may well have been the league's most balanced and most competitive, despite all the Boston winning. If it can be claimed that Boston won only because it had Russell and to a lesser extent Cousy or Heinsohn or Sharman, then the credit must again nonetheless fall in large part to Auerbach and not merely the star players themselves. It was the coach's genius after all that had envisioned the new directions the game would inevitably take with a player like Russell. It had also been Boston's bossman who arranged the coup that brought Russell to Boston in the first place, and then molded the elements of a winning team around the game's greatest defensive player. And if Auerbach was at first sceptical about Cousy, nonetheless he knew precisely how to exploit the great ballhandler and stellar playmaker once he had the other pieces of his powerhouse team set into place.

Even when his coaching time ran out Auerbach continued to display a unique flair for organizational genius. First he would select Russell to replace himself on the bench, thus choosing rather fortuitously the only man who could possibly have done the job properly at the time. Auerbach of course again immediately saw what others may well not have seen, and this time it was the fact that no one else could have stepped in to manage the equally cantakerous Russell but Bill Russell himself. Then in the 1970s, having retained control of the club as GM, the still-fiery Auerbach would once more rebuild Boston's fortunes around the latent coaching skills of one of his former players. This time it would be Tom Heinsohn who would be the exceptional beneficiary. Having built two powerhouse teams in two different decades, Auerbach was not quite done as he entered his fourth decade at the helm of franchise fortunes. As Boston's performance again seemed about to sag in the wake of Heinsohn's era (as coach) and then the Dave Cowens era (as star player), Auerbach would pull off yet one final coup which would bring Boston its most popular and talented player ever—Larry Bird—and establish in the process yet another remarkable chapter of Boston NBA invincibility.

The ingenious move that brought Bird to Boston and reopened the Celtic Mystique was in reality a series of transactions that not only landed Bird but brought on board at the same time both Robert Parish and Kevin McHale. The key this time was a deal with San Francisco, not unlike the earlier deal with St. Louis involving Russell. Auerbach had first plucked Bird from the 1978 draft, even though the Indiana State star was only a junior and would not join the club until another full season had passed. Now with the 1980 draft he shipped veteran Bob McAdoo to Detroit for the number one pick, then swapped the pick to San Francisco (which coveted Purdue center Joe Barry Carroll) in exchange for established center Parish and a lower draft selection that was pencilled in to be McHale.

The Warriors would get what they wanted, even if it was not by any stretch what they needed. The trio brought to Boston by Auerbach's latest maneuvers—Bird, McHale, Parish—would eventually comprise what many still believe to be the greatest front line in the history of the sport. The immediate victims this time around were thus the San Francisco Warriors, who had gambled in a big way on seven-foot prospect Carroll and ultimately lost in an even bigger way for their boldness. Acquiring McHale and Parish was a big enough coup in itself, but the capturing of Bird had been without question the league's biggest deal of the

first half of the new decade. Much of the credit again would fall to Auerbach's rare insight into players whose potential was even greater than commonly perceived. McHale and Parish would provide championship backbone. Bird would shine for a decade and more and even turn out to be Red Auerbach's final on-court legacy.

Auerbach might well have extended his own reputation and the Boston dynasty record still a bit farther if another draft-day gamble—that involving Maryland star Len Bias—had not taken a bizarre eleventh-hour tragic turn that even basketball's most astute front office genius could never have anticipated. (Auerbach plucked Bias with the number two 1986 pick, but the All-American died two days later of a cocaine overdose.) With the Len Bias fiasco the great Boston mastermind would finally be beaten by Fate's cruel hand. But one such loss in five still left Auerbach miles ahead of the pack when it came down to an unmatched lifetime track record for building charismatic championship teams around true franchise superstars, stars for whom others were not quite so willing to mortagage their own front-office futures.

It is not an insignificant fact that while Auerbach owned some of the sport's best team-oriented and championship-driven players, he never had a league scoring champion, something that Boston to this day has never enjoyed. In the end this rare insight into team-concept individual talent was Auerbach's greatest genius. It was getting Cousy, Heinsohn, Russell, K.C. Jones, Sam Jones, Cowens and finally Bird into Boston uniforms in the first place that was Red Auerbach's special calling and also his indelible claim to future fame.

BOSTON
Walter Brown
Godfather of the NBA

In the beginning there was Walter Brown—both in the history of the Boston Celtics and the history of the entire National Basketball Association itself. The man who was co-owner and president of the Boston Celtics during their remarkable dynasty seasons was also one of the original founders (along with a half-dozen or so other National and American Hockey League arena owners) of the Basketball Association of America which would soon transform itself into the NBA. But up until his moment of inspiration about the potential of a new sporting operation built on basketball, Brown had almost no contact with Naismith's popular indoor game. As the son of George Brown, a highly successful Boston sports promoter and general manager of the Boston Arena, he was educated in the finest New England schools (Boston Latin and Exeter Academy) and apprenticed in his father's sports promotion business. But that business was mostly oriented toward the sport of ice

Walter Brown is flanked by Cousy and Easy Ed Macauley (#22) in a mid-fifties ceremony honoring the Boston team's two top players. Macauley was always a personal favorite of the generous and fatherly team owner.

hockey, and young Walter's earliest distinction in sports management was that he coached the first American team (in 1933) to win a world amateur hockey title (by defeating a Toronto team in Prague, Czechoslovakia).

Walter Brown's basketball interest was strictly a pragmatic affair. Having replaced his father as general manager of the Garden-Arena Corporation (which now operated the newer Boston Garden as well as Boston Arena), his main duties by the end of World War II were the operation of the Boston NHL franchise, operation of the Ice Capades (for which he was vice-president and treasurer), and filling up both Boston arenas with as many sporting and entertainment dates as possible. Chafing under the fact that his Boston Garden sat idle half the nights of the year, and noting the increased national (if not local) interest in college basketball during wartime years, Brown was soon approaching other East Coast hockey-oriented arena owners (like Arthur Wirtz who ran Chicago Stadium, Al Sutphin who operated Cleveland's AHL franchise and arena, Mike Uline who ran an arena but not a hockey club in Washington, and Ned Irish whose venue was Madison Square Garden) to consider the risky but potentially lucrative gamble of a pro basketball circuit. It would be a risky venture indeed, since all previous attempts at drawing large

audiences for basketball at the professional level had eventually collapsed, and also since most of the promoters involved (with the exception of Irish who had made his mark with promoting college basketball doubleheaders in New York) knew little if anything about the plodding sport of basketball.

The motives behind founding a new pro circuit known as the BAA reveal much about the lamentable if perhaps promising status of pro basketball in the mid-forties. Hockey club owners and arena managers—like Brown—simply wanted to fill their venues on off-nights (when hockey games, circuses, or ice capades and ice follies were not on their docket) and thus reduce overhead costs on under-used buildings. The model had already been provided by one of their number—Ned Irish, the basketball director for Madison Square Garden—who during pre-war years had amassed a personal fortune by promoting college contests, at the same time also demonstrating beyond question the money-making potential of basketball. With his Garden-based college twinbills Irish had also stimulated a growing nationwide interest in the sport.

Brown and his partners in the BAA venture thus knew preciously little about basketball, beyond the fact that it hopefully meant ticket-buying customers. After all, the college teams drew legions of paying fans with bouncing balls and arching set shots. The commissioner they would trust to run their hastily pasted together operation—American Hockey League czar Maurice Podoloff—had himself never even seen a basketball contest before taking over his new administrative assignment. (Podoloff had become connected with the venture when Chicago's Art Wirtz had agreed to lend his support only if Russian-born Podoloff, whom he respected for his business acumen in running the AHL, were brought on as chief operating officer.) In reality, Podoloff knew almost as little about hockey as he did about basketball, but a league president is not hired to coach or to make and interrupt playing rules, only to orchestrate business deals, market a product, and adjudicate club owners' petty disputes. Podoloff would soon enough prove a genius at the trade.

The two most important pioneering figures of the fledgling cage circuit would of course be Boston's Walter Brown (who as Boston Garden president would operate the newly founded Boston Celtics) and New York's Ned Irish (now adding ownership of the BAA Knickerbockers to his other Madison Square Garden basketball duties). Brown—along with Max Kase, sports editor of New York's *Journal-American*—had

Walter Brown greets new Celtics player Don Barksdale, acquired via a trade with the Baltimore Bullets in November 1953. Having broken new ground by drafting Chuck Cooper in 1950, Brown now was the first owner to boast two African-American players in his NBA lineup.

been more responsible than anyone for coming up with the original BAA idea. Kase had been lobbying for the concept ever since he promoted a 1944 game in Manhattan for war relief and had hoped himself to own the New York entry, but he was forced to the sidelines when Ned Irish decided he didn't want any interlopers on his own city-wide basketball monopoly. Irish, of course, had already made his lasting mark on the history of the college game in basketball's reigning capital. His tireless promotion of college double and tripleheaders in the thirties and throughout the war years had put the college sport on firm footing in Gotham. Now Irish hoped to exercise similar impact in the same

building with the newly formed professional league. And Brown up in Boston would quickly prove to be pro basketball's biggest and most successful gambler. Over the next half-decade his novel experiments with a league all-star contest (first held in Boston Garden in 1951), black ballplayers (launched with the 1950 drafting of Chuck Cooper out of Duquesne), and a coach named Auerbach (hired that same season) were destined to cement the league's bright future.

Brown remained one of the major individual influences on the direction of pro basketball's boom-industry development during the two rapid-growth decades which immediately followed World War II. For a handful of the game's innovators one single moment of pure inspiration—let's say a significant rule change or fortuitous player signing or unprecedented promotional gimmick—would constitute a lifetime's work. One example of this narrowness of inventive genius would be Syracuse club owner Danny Biasone with his shot clock concept in 1954, and another would be James Naismith himself, with his peach baskets and his novel indoor non-contact game back in 1891. Walter Brown, on the other hand, had at least four such moments of pure inspiration and each one radically altered the present and future pro basketball scene.

It was Brown, first off, who as much as anyone had conceived (and enthusiastically pushed) the original idea for a true national professional league which could pack arenas in larger cities and exploit the national hunger for high-quality pro sports entertainment. The fledgling league into which he dragged such fellow sports moguls as Irish, Sutphin, Lou Pieri in Providence, and Uline in Washington, would over only a handful of winters evolve as the infant NBA. But the early going was not easy for the league, and it was particularly rough for Walter Brown in Boston where hockey was the game of choice and basketball had such small popularity or priority that it wasn't even taught

AP/Wide World Photos

Owner Walter Brown accepts a trophy for the 1963 NBA Championship from commissioner Walter Kennedy. The ceremony occurred during the January 1964 NBA All-Star Game staged in Boston Garden.

already quit two coaching jobs in the league—one at Washington after three successful seasons when Uline wouldn't issue a long-term contract, and the other with the Tri-Cities Blackhawks in the middle of his first year when owner Ben Kerner traded a valued ballplayer without consulting him.

If Auerbach wasn't entirely Brown's own idea, he would quickly make his fortuitous new boss look like a genius when he turned a team that had been 89 and 151 in four years under its first two coaches (Honey Russell and Doggie Julian) into a consistent regular-season winner (even if also a regular postseason loser) that only finished as low as break-even once during his first decade on the job. And the Auerbach deal was still news when owner Brown pulled off his third bold ploy and the one that from a broad historical perspective would have the grandest impact of all. Brown with Auerbach's blessing and connivance shocked the establishment of the infant pro basketball circuit when he boldly selected the first black player drafted by the NBA with his second-round June 1950 pick of Duquesne's star forward Chuck Cooper. The move came after Brown and Auerbach had upset many of the locals in bypassing home-town favorite Bob Cousy (the popular Holy Cross All-American) in the first round to grab towering Bowling Green center Charlie Share. Share seemed to Auerbach a better choice for crafting a well-balanced team that could rebound and defend, but then was immediately rendered useless to the club when Boston also obtained Ed Macauley in a special dispersal draft to distribute players from the defunct St. Louis Bombers.

NBA owners had regularly avoided black ballplayers before Brown's bold move mainly for economic reasons; The Harlem Globetrotters' own Abe Saperstein demanded exclusive claim on the top college black talent and annual exhibitions with NBA clubs were too lucrative to risk offending the volatile Saperstein. When Saperstein responded to Brown's move by suggesting he might not be interested in visiting Boston Garden any longer, the Boston owner responded that this was just fine, since he was no longer welcome.

Finally, as if all his earlier strokes of pure genius were not already quite enough, Walter Brown also inaugurated the institution soon to be known as the NBA All-Star Game and soon to provide the young league with one of its most popular showcase events. But again the idea was not entirely Brown's, though certainly the actions to make it a reality were. Attracted to the concept dreamed up by NBA publicist Haskell Cohen, the risk-loving Boston owner gambled his reputation and much of his team's thin coffers by agreeing to host and cover all expenses for the first All-

in physical education classes in the local public schools and had been dropped as an interscholastic sport in the decades between the two world wars. To make matters worse, the local sports pages refused to cover the team's games or even allot space for reporting boxscores.

Without an educated fan base or a native basketball culture at hand, Brown's team hardly drew flies in early seasons and the committed owner was pressured by his own Boston Garden Corporation (which rapidly lost $460,000) to give up the venture after only two winters. But Brown was stubborn and unwilling to abandon the ballclub which was a charter team in a league he had founded. With an assist from Lou Pieri, whose Providence team folded after three seasons but who was willing to join as a Boston partner, Brown bought controlling interest in the team in 1950. In subsequent winters he would mortgage his own home and personal property to keep the operation going.

For his second inspirational act Brown brought Arnold "Red" Auerbach to Boston as his third coach for the floundering Celtics team he now owned and operated in the first season under the league's new NBA label. In fairness to the historical record, it was a management decision that was thrust upon Walter Brown by his new partner Lou Pieri, who agreed to invest in the club only if a new coach was brought in, and if that coach was the already successful but quirky Arnold "Red" Auerbach, who had

Star event to be staged at Boston Garden in March of 1951. The game was a surprising and resounding success, drawing better than 10,000 customers to a thrill-packed game that featured Celtics center Ed Macauley as the most valuable player. The event served its announced function, to draw some national media attention at mid-season to a struggling and often-ignored league in only its fifth season. It encored in Boston Garden the following winter and has been a league staple ever since.

Walter Brown also soon put into place basketball's greatest-ever dynasty team consisting mainly of Cousy (eventually acquired in a special dispersal draft from the defunct Chicago Stags), Russell, Sharman, Heinsohn, Frank Ramsey, K.C. Jones and Sam Jones, although this last blockbuster achievement was perhaps more than anything else the doing of his hand-picked coach and general manager, Red Auerbach. Brown's biggest role in the later franchise building of the late fifties and early sixties may have been the behind-the-scenes assist he lent to the deal which brought Bill Russell to Boston. The trade with St. Louis which obtained the number two draft pick the Celtics planned to spend on Russell could only bear fruit if Boston held some guarantee from Rochester owner Les Harrison that the Royals would not pluck the USF defensive star with their own top choice. Brown provided Harrison with the needed plum, quietly offering a much-coveted annual visit from the Brown-controlled Ice Capades that spelled valued revenue for Harrison's Rochester arena.

Many professional basketball players have had uniform numbers retired in their honor and the Celtics far outdistance all other pro sports franchises with 19 such honorees. But only one NBA owner has been accorded this ultimate distinction. Among the banners hosted to the rafters in Boston Garden (and later moved to the new Fleet Center) was one bearing the number "1"—a number never won by any Boston Celtics player and now permanently ineligible for active wearing. In October 1964—a month after his premature death at age 59—that number was permanently retired in Walter Brown's honor. It was a fitting symbol of the fact that—despite all the Auerbach coaching genius and all the Russell and Cousy athletic talent and oncourt magic—there would never have been even a single Boston Celtics championship without the initial efforts and long-term sacrifices of club founder Walter Brown.

William G. "Bill" Mokray, the famed author and statistician who was first editor of the official NBA Guide *and also a one-time director of basketball operations at the Boston Garden. Mokray was elected to the Naismith Memorial Basketball Hall of Fame in 1965.*

Bill Mokray
The Numbers Man

Twenty-two members of the Naismith Memorial Basketball Hall of Fame have spent all or part of their careers with the proud Boston Celtics franchise, and of these nearly two dozen legends only two have earned their place in some capacity other than that of player or coach. These two immortal special "contributors" to basketball's legacy are original Boston franchise owner Walter Brown and long-time NBA statistics guru Bill Mokray.

Mokray was first smitten with a love for basketball numerology while attending Passaic (NJ) High School during the era of Ernest Blood's "Wonder Teams" of the early '20s, a series of legendary squads which won 159 games without defeat. The young Mokray compiled statistics and detailed records for these teams, thus fueling his early passion for the numerical side of the sport. A student at Rhode Island State College during the early years of coach Frank Keaney's racehorse fast-break basketball tradition, Mokray would sign on after graduation as the school's first sports publicity director and work arduously for more than a decade publicizing the Rams colorful style of play.

But the true calling of Bill Mokray would be finally found after 1944 when he took over the post of basketball director for the Boston Garden, a position which lead directly to a final assignment as public relations director for the Boston Celtics once that BAA franchise was established by Walter Brown in the shadows of World War II. While laboring in a variety of promotion-oriented positions for the Celtics over the next quarter-century Mokray also voraciously collected NBA statistics and published numerous analytical articles for the Converse Rubber Company's ground-breaking publication known as the *Basketball Yearbook*. But his greatest efforts in pioneering the field of basketball record keeping came with his founding and editing of the *Official NBA Guide*, his authoring of a history of basketball for *Encyclopedia Britannica* (1957), and his writing of the 900-page landmark *Ronald Basketball Encyclopedia* (1963). Years before baseball would discover Bill James and sabermetrics, basketball had already found Bill Mokray.

Jan Volk
Behind-the-Scenes Genius

There was a time when Arnold "Red" Auerbach was the entire show when it came to on-court and off-the-court operations of the Boston Celtics. Or at least it always seemed that way, at least from the time of Walter Brown's death in 1964 (when he added the title of general manager to those of vice president and coach) until 1984 (when he handed the GM title to Jan Volk, the third man in club history—after Brown and Auerbach—to hold the lofty post). And most of the time it indeed was the top redhead alone at the controls, despite the counterclaims of those who have from time-to-time downplayed the role of

Jan Volk had huge shoes to fill indeed when he took over in 1984 from Red Auerbach as the Boston Celtics general manager and chief basketball architect.

Auerbach's true genius.

But for most of the past dozen or more years there has been another "genius" operating behind the scenes in Boston. It has been general manager Jan Volk throughout most of the 1990s who has pulled most of the strings in the Boston Celtics front office. Volk's tenure as architect of Celtics oncourt fortunes began with the fifth season of the Larry Bird era and stretched until the recent appearance of Rick Pitino, when Chris Wallace also arrived from the Miami Heat as part of the Pitino package to become only the fourth GM in franchise history. It was a stretch that culminated in some of the bleakest seasons of ballclub history yet also peaked early on with some of the most success-strewn campaigns of the third great Boston Celtics championship epoch.

Volk has been a major part of five world championship teams in Boston (one as general manager and another as assistant GM) and was an instrumental figure after 1979 in molding ballclubs which won ten Atlantic Division titles, five Eastern Conference crowns, and three NBA titles. If the first two great Celtics eras—those of first Russell and later Cowens—were Auerbach creations, the third (the Larry Bird Era) has been at least partly a Jan Volk extravaganza. But unlike front office architects of Auerbach's earlier generation, Volk is a part of the new breed of NBA front office operatives whose training and orientation has been in the business and legal worlds and not in the locker rooms and on the basketball courts. Trained in law at Columbia University, Volk's 26-year tenure with the Celtics began in the strictly business operations end of the franchise and included positions along the way as ticket sales director, manager of equipment purchases, traveling secretary, and eventually business manager, legal counsel and vice president. By the mid-seventies he had convinced Auerbach that the changing NBA landscape made his legal expertise vital in the negotiating and drafting of player contracts. As an assistant GM and general manager (after July 11, 1984) Volk quickly established himself in Boston as one of the league's leading experts on NBA salary cap matters, one of the vital areas of modern-day ballclub management.

The largest feather in Volk's managerial cap is certainly the world championship team of 1986 (last of the Bird era) which is widely acknowledged as one of the great ballclubs of franchise and also league history. In addition to his role as principal architect of Boston's 16th NBA title banner, the tenure of the club's second-longest-reigning general manager has included such memorable deals as the 1984 trade of Gerald Henderson to Seattle for the draft pick used to land ill-starred Len Bias; the acquisition of Bill Walton from the LA Clippers in exchange for Cedric Maxwell (the key deal in constructing the 1986 team); trade-route acquisitions of Jerry Sichting and Fred Roberts; a 1992 Brian Shaw for Sherman Douglas deal with the Miami Heat; free agent signings of Xavier McDaniel and Dominique Wilkins; and the top draft day selections of Reggie Lewis, Brian Shaw and Dee Brown.

Jan Volk has now departed the Boston scene and in his wake the Boston Celtics have turned a new corner at the dawn of the Rick Pitino era. Pitino (along with his hand-picked GM Chris Wallace) will now have to be nothing short of spectacular if he hopes to extend in timely fashion the several decades of an Auerbach-Volk winning tradition.

BOSTON
Johnny Most
Basketball's Most Famous Voice

Baseball's radio voices were once as much a part of the game's nostalgia as were the sport's colorful star athletes themselves. Mel Allen, Red Barber, Connie Desmond, Ernie Harwell, Bob Elston, Harry Caray and Bob Prince were for legions of fans in dozens of cities the very soul of the game they described daily. Basketball has never been such a radio-oriented game and few long-time broadcasters have enjoyed such an intimate connection with a team's evolving history. Johnny Most—four-decade voice of the Boston Celtics—is almost the singular exception, though LA Lakers fans may have an argument that Chick Hearn has equal stature as a rare broadcasting prototype.

Outside of Boston, Most's immortality—like Russ Hodges in baseball, whose radio call immortalized Bobby

A frail but still enthusiastic Johnny Most returns to the booth as color commentator only a few months after a 1983 stroke had temporarily sent him to the sidelines.

The gravel-throated voice of the Boston Celtics here seen in action from his favorite perch during the 1974 season.

Thomson's "shot heard 'round the world"—rests with a single momentary call of ephemeral hardcourt action. When John Havlicek stepped in front of Chet Walker to pick off Hal Greer's wayward inbounds pass and preserve Boston's championship string during the 1965 Eastern Division Finals he created a moment that would implant into the national consciousness not only his own legendary career but also that of the man who called the action for Boston radio listeners. Most's franatic description of the scene still lives in the collective memory of a generation of New England basketball fans: *"Greer is putting the ball in play. He gets it out deep . . . (pause) . . . And Havlicek steals it! Over to Sam Jones! Havlicek stole the ball! It's all over! It's all over! Johnny Havlicek is being mobbed by the fans! It's all over! Johnny Havlicek stole the ball!"*

The memorable moment came less than a third of the way into Johnny Most's long tenure (1953-1989) in the Celtics radio booth and was only a small part of the legend for those who could tune in his broadcasts regularly during the Cousy-Russell dynasty years and the two up-and-down decades that followed. Most was perhaps best celebrated over the years (and best beloved among Boston fans) for his colorful creations of a large cast of villains among rival players and teams. By casting Chamberlain and Guy Rodgers in Philadelphia or Oscar Robertson in Cincinnati or Rudy LaRusso in Los Angeles as arch enemies of the

Boston cause—players to be despised—Most spiced and legitimized the team's biggest rivalries for thousands of local fans. The Goliath Wilt who battled Russell and complained (endlessly, according to Most) of his rough treatment by the energized Celtics was a natural target for derision. Most waxed profound about the showboating of Guy Rodgers (which in the announcer's view could never match the class act that was Cousy), and about Luke Jackson's roughhouse tactics on the 76ers' front line, and also about Oscar's favored status with league officials (Oscar seemingly never committed a foul). And he also immortalized two rugged role players in Washington when he dubbed Ricky Mahorn and Jeff Ruland as the hated and villainous "McFilthy and McNasty" whose mission was to disrupt the noble Celtics' cause.

Like most sports broadcasting giants Most seemed to have nothing in his on-air manner that fit him for the job. His voice was pure gravel, his style was annoyingly machine-gun-like ("rat-a-tat-tat") in anything but small doses, his personality was always acerbic (he had long-running feuds with arena security forces that tried to limit his on-air smoking and coffee guzzling at courtside), and he wore his onesided love for the home team squarely on his sleeve, for which Boston fans loved him all the more. But Most was genuine and passionate and brought basketball to full life on the airwaves for 36 long seasons. Most's era, stretching from the arrival of Auerbach to the peak seasons of Larry Bird, covered nearly the entire span of NBA history. But the large bulk of that career came before the high-ratings television popularity which has been the league's boasting point for the last decade. In an age when fans did not yet flood into NBA arenas in droves, televised basketball was far more occasional than unbiquitous and pro basketball—even in the dynasty city of Boston—was therefore still only the third or fourth most popular game in town. Throughout those building-block periods of NBA history Johnny Most remained a vital link to nightly action for New England airwaves rooters who followed the ebb and flow of one the America's most cherished dynasty ballclubs.

BOSTON Celtics
Boston Celtics
Statistical Appendices

CHAPTER X

All-Time Franchise Record: 2496-1605, .609 Pct. (1946-1999)
NBA Championships (16): 1956-57, 1958-59, 1959-60, 1960-61, 1961-62, 1962-63, 1963-64, 1964-65, 1965-66, 1967-68, 1968-69, 1973-74, 1975-76, 1980-81, 1983-84, 1985-86
Greatest Franchise Players: Bill Russell (1956-1969) and Larry Bird (1979-1992)
All-Time Leading Scorer: John Havlicek (26,395 Points, 1962-1978)
Most Successful Coach: Red Auerbach (795-397, .667 Pct., 1950-1968)
All-Time Franchise Team: Bill Russell (C), Larry Bird (F), John Havlicek (F), Bob Cousy (G), Sam Jones (G)

YEAR-BY-YEAR IN BOSTON CELTICS HISTORY

Season	Record	Finish	Coach(es)	Scoring Leader(s)	Playoffs (W-L Record)
Key: * = Tied for Position					
Basketball Association of America					
1946-47	22-38	5th*	John Russell	Connie Simmons (10.3)	Did Not Qualify
1947-48	20-28	3rd	John Russell	Ed Sadowski (19.4)	Lost in 1st Round (1-2)
1948-49	25-35	5th	Alvin Julian	George Kaftan (14.5)	Did Not Qualify
National Basketball Association					
1949-50	22-46	6th	Alvin Julian	Bob Kinney (11.1)	Did Not Qualify
1950-51	39-30	2nd	Red Auerbach	Ed Macauley (20.4)	Lost in 1st Round (0-2)
1951-52	39-27	2nd	Red Auerbach	Bob Cousy (21.7)	Lost in 1st Round (1-2)
1952-53	46-25	3rd	Red Auerbach	Ed Macauley (20.3)	Lost in 2nd Round (3-3)
1953-54	42-30	2nd	Red Auerbach	Bob Cousy (19.2)	Lost in 2nd Round (2-4)
1954-55	36-36	3rd	Red Auerbach	Bob Cousy (21.1)	Lost in 2nd Round (3-4)
1955-56	39-33	2nd	Red Auerbach	Bill Sharman (19.9)	Lost in 1st Round (1-2)
1956-57	44-28	1st	Red Auerbach	Bill Sharman (21.1)	**NBA Champions** (7-3)
1957-58	49-23	1st	Red Auerbach	Bill Sharman (22.3)	Lost in NBA Finals (6-5)
1958-59	52-20	1st	Red Auerbach	Bill Sharman (20.4)	**NBA Champions** (8-3)
1959-60	59-16	1st	Red Auerbach	Tom Heinsohn (21.7)	**NBA Champions** (8-5)
1960-61	57-22	1st	Red Auerbach	Tom Heinsohn (21.3)	**NBA Champions** (8-2)
1961-62	60-20	1st	Red Auerbach	Tom Heinsohn (22.1)	**NBA Champions** (8-6)
1962-63	58-22	1st	Red Auerbach	Sam Jones (19.7)	**NBA Champions** (8-5)
1963-64	59-21	1st	Red Auerbach	John Havlicek (19.9)	**NBA Champions** (8-2)
1964-65	62-18	1st	Red Auerbach	Sam Jones (25.9)	**NBA Champions** (8-4)
1965-66	54-26	2nd	Red Auerbach	Sam Jones (23.5)	**NBA Champions** (11-6)
1966-67	60-21	2nd	Bill Russell	John Havlicek (21.4)	Lost in 2nd Round (4-5)
1967-68	54-28	2nd	Bill Russell	Sam Jones (21.3)	**NBA Champions** (12-7)

Bill Russell with Red Auerbach.

1968-69	48-34	4th	Bill Russell	John Havlicek (21.6)	**NBA Champions** (12-6)
1969-70	34-48	6th	Tom Heinsohn	John Havlicek (24.2)	Did Not Qualify
1970-71	44-38	3rd	Tom Heinsohn	John Havlicek (28.9)	Did Not Qualify
1971-72	56-26	1st	Tom Heinsohn	John Havlicek (27.5)	Lost in 2nd Round (5-6)
1972-73	68-14	1st	Tom Heinsohn	John Havlicek (23.8)	Lost in 2nd Round (7-6)
1973-74	56-26	1st	Tom Heinsohn	John Havlicek (22.6)	**NBA Champions** (12-6)
1974-75	60-22	1st	Tom Heinsohn	Dave Cowens (20.4)	Lost in 3rd Round (6-5)
1975-76	54-28	1st	Tom Heinsohn	Dave Cowens (19.0)	**NBA Champions** (12-6)
1976-77	44-38	2nd	Tom Heinsohn	Jo Jo White (19.6)	Lost in 2nd Round (5-4)
1977-78	32-50	3rd	Tom Heinsohn	Dave Cowens (18.6)	Did Not Qualify
			Tom Sanders		
1978-79	29-53	5th	Tom Sanders	Bob McAdoo (24.8)	Did Not Qualify
			Dave Cowens		
1979-80	61-21	1st	Bill Fitch	Larry Bird (21.3)	Lost in 3rd Round (5-4)
1980-81	62-20	1st	Bill Fitch	Larry Bird (21.2)	**NBA Champions** (12-5)
1981-82	63-19	1st	Bill Fitch	Larry Bird (22.9)	Lost in 3rd Round (7-5)
1982-83	56-26	2nd	Bill Fitch	Larry Bird (23.6)	Lost in 2nd Round (2-5)
1983-84	62-20	1st	K. C. Jones	Larry Bird (24.2)	**NBA Champions** (15-8)
1984-85	63-19	1st	K. C. Jones	Larry Bird (28.7)	Lost in NBA Finals (13-8)
1985-86	67-15	1st	K. C. Jones	Larry Bird (25.8)	**NBA Champions** (15-3)
1986-87	59-23	1st	K. C. Jones	Larry Bird (28.1)	Lost in NBA Finals (13-10)
1987-88	57-25	1st	K. C. Jones	Larry Bird (29.9)	Lost in 3rd Round (9-8)
1988-89	42-40	3rd	Jimmy Rodgers	Kevin McHale (22.5)	Lost in 1st Round (0-3)
1989-90	52-30	2nd	Jimmy Rodgers	Larry Bird (24.3)	Lost in 1st Round (2-3)
1990-91	56-26	1st	Chris Ford	Larry Bird (19.4)	Lost in 2nd Round (5-6)

1991-92	51-31	1st	Chris Ford	Reggie Lewis (20.8)	Lost in 2nd Round (6-4)
1992-93	48-34	2nd	Chris Ford	Reggie Lewis (20.8)	Lost in 1st Round (1-3)
1993-94	32-50	5th	Chris Ford	Dee Brown (15.5)	Did Not Qualify
1994-95	35-47	3rd	Chris Ford	Dominique Wilkins (17.8)	Lost in 1st Round (1-3)
1995-96	33-49	5th	M.L. Carr	Dino Radja (19.7)	Did Not Qualify
1996-97	15-67	7th	M.L. Carr	Antoine Walker (17.5)	Did Not Qualify
1997-98	36-46	6th	Rick Pitino	Antoine Walker (22.4)	Did Not Qualify
1999*	19-31	5th	Rick Pitino	Antoine Walker (18.7)	Did Not Qualify

*Strike-shortened season (February 5-May 5)

ALL-TIME BOSTON CELTICS INDIVIDUAL PLAYER RECORDS

Celtics Individual Career Leaders and Record Holders (1946-1998)

Scoring Average	Larry Bird (24.3 ppg., 1979-1992)
Points Scored	John Havlicek (26,395)
Games Played	John Havlicek (1,270)
Minutes Played	John Havlicek (46,471)
Field Goal Pct.	Cedric Maxwell (.559)
Free Throws Made	John Havlicek (5,369)
Free-Throw Pct.	Larry Bird (.886)
Rebounds	Bill Russell (21,620)
Rebound Average	Bill Russell (22.5 rpg.)
Assists	Bob Cousy (6,945)
Personal Fouls	John Havlicek (3,281)
Consecutive Games Played	Jo Jo White (488, 1-21-1972 to 1-29-1978)

Celtics Individual Single-Season Records (1946-1998)

Scoring Average	Larry Bird (29.9 ppg., 1987-88)
Points Scored	John Havlicek (2,338, 1970-71)
Field Goals Made	Larry Bird (918, 1984-85)
Field Goal Percentage	Cedric Maxwell (.609, 1979-80)
Free Throws Made	Cedric Maxwell (574, 1978-79)
Free Throw Percentage	Bill Sharman (.932, 1958-59)
Rebounds	Bill Russell (1,930, 1963-64)
Rebound Average	Bill Russell (24.7 rpg., 1963-64)
Assists	Bob Cousy (715, 1959-60)
Steals	Larry Bird (167, 1996-97)
	Larry Bird (166, 1985-86)
Blocked Shots	Robert Parish (214, 1980-81)
3-Pt. Field Goals	Danny Ainge (148, 1987-88)
Personal Fouls	Charlie Scott (356, 1975-76)
Disqualifications	Tom Sanders (19, 1964-65)
Minutes Played	John Havlicek (3,689, 1971-72)

Celtics Individual Single-Game Records (1946-1998)

Points Scored	Larry Bird (60, 3-12-85 vs. Atlanta, at New Orleans)
Field Goals Made	Larry Bird (22, 3-12-85 vs. Atlanta at New Orleans)
	Larry Bird (22, 4-12-87 vs. New York)
	Kevin McHale (22, 3-3-85 vs. Detroit)
Free Throws Made	Nate Archibald (20, 1-16-80 vs. Chicago)
Rebounds	Bill Russell (51, 2-5-60 vs. Syracuse Nats)
3-Point Field Goals Made	Dee Brown (8, 2-4-98 vs. Dallas)
Assists	Bob Cousy (28, 2-27-59 vs. Minneapolis Lakers)
Blocked Shots	Kevin McHale (9, 4-16-82 vs. New Jersey)
	Robert Parish (9, 3-17-82 vs. Atlanta)
	Kevin McHale (9, 1-21-83 vs. Chicago)
Steals	Larry Bird (9, 2-18-85 vs. Utah)

Larry Bird

BOSTON CELTICS CAREER LEADERS

Career Games Played
1. **John Havlicek** — **1,270**
2. Robert Parish — 1,106
3. Kevin McHale — 971
4. Bill Russell — 963
5. Bob Cousy — 917
6. Tom Sanders — 916
7. Larry Bird — 897
8. Don Nelson — 872
9. Sam Jones — 871
10. Dave Cowens — 726

Career Minutes Played
1. **John Havlicek** — **46,471**
2. Bill Russell — 40,726
3. Robert Parish — 34,977
4. Larry Bird — 34,443
5. Bob Cousy — 30,131
6. Kevin McHale — 30,118
7. Dave Cowens — 28,551
8. Jo Jo White — 26,770
9. Sam Jones — 24,285
10. Tom Sanders — 22,164

Career Points Scored
1. **John Havlicek** — **26,395**
2. Larry Bird — 21,791
3. Robert Parish — 18,245
4. Kevin McHale — 17,335
5. Bob Cousy — 16,955
6. Sam Jones — 15,411
7. Bill Russell — 14,522
8. Dave Cowens — 13,192
9. Jo Jo White — 13,181
10. Bill Sharman — 12,287

John Havlicek

Career Scoring Average (Minimum of 2 Seasons)
1. **Larry Bird** — **24.3 ppg.**
2. John Havlicek — 20.8
3. Antoine Walker — 20.0
4. Ed Macauley — 18.9
5. Tom Heinsohn — 18.6
6. Bob Cousy — 18.5
7. Jo Jo White — 18.3
8. Dave Cowens — 18.2
9. Bill Sharman — 18.1
10. Bailey Howell — 18.0
11. Kevin McHale — 17.9

Points in a Single Game
1. **Larry Bird** — **60 (March 12, 1985 vs. Atlanta Hawks at New Orleans)**
2. Kevin McHale — 56 (March 3, 1985 vs. Detroit Pistons at Boston Garden)
3. Larry Bird — 53 (March 30, 1983 vs. Indiana Pacers at Boston Garden)
4. Sam Jones — 51 (October 29, 1965 vs. Detroit Pistons at Detroit)
5. Larry Bird — 50 (November 10, 1989 vs. Atlanta Hawks at Boston Garden)
6. Larry Bird — 50 (March 10, 1986 vs. Dallas Mavericks at Dallas)
7. Antoine Walker — 49 (January 7, 1998 vs. Washington Wizards at Washington)

8	Larry Bird	49 (March 15, 1992 vs. Portland Trailblazers at Boston Garden)
9	Larry Bird	49 (February 15, 1988 vs. Phoenix Suns at Phoenix)
10	Larry Bird	49 (January 27, 1988 vs. Washington Bullets at Boston Garden)

Career Field Goal Attempts

1	**John Havlicek**	**23,930**
2	Larry Bird	17,334
3	Bob Cousy	16,465
4	Sam Jones	13,745
5	Robert Parish	13,558
6	Bill Russell	12,930
7	Jo Jo White	12,782
8	Kevin McHale	12,334
9	Dave Cowens	12,193
10	Tom Heinsohn	11,787

Career Field Goals Made

1	**John Havlicek**	**10,513**
2	Larry Bird	8,591
3	Robert Parish	7,483
4	Kevin McHale	6,830
5	Sam Jones	6,271
6	Bob Cousy	6,167
7	Bill Russell	5,687
8	Jo Jo White	5,648
9	Dave Cowens	5,608
10	Tom Heinsohn	4,773

Field Goal Percentage (2,000 Attempts)

1	**Cedric Maxwell**	**.559 (2,786-4,984)**
2	Kevin McHale	.554 (6,830-12,334)
3	Robert Parish	.552 (7,483-13,558)
4	Kevin Gamble	.518 (2,067-3,988)
5	Rick Robey	.510 (1,144-2,241)
6	Dino Radja	.497 (1,516-3,052)
7	Larry Bird	.496 (8,591-17,334)
8	Gerald Henderson	.489 (1,467-3,002)
9	Reggie Lewis	.488 (3,198-6,550)
10	Danny Ainge	.487 (2,537-5,210)

Career Free Throws Attempted

1	**John Havlicek**	**6,589**
2	Bob Cousy	5,753
3	Bill Russell	5,614
4	Kevin McHale	4,554
5	Robert Parish	4,491
6	Larry Bird	4,471
7	Sam Jones	3,572
8	Ed Macauley	3,518
9	Cedric Maxwell	3,496
10	Bill Sharman	3,451

Career Free Throws Made

1	**John Havlicek**	**5,369**
2	Bob Cousy	4,621
3	Larry Bird	3,960
4	Kevin McHale	3,634
5	Robert Parish	3,279
6	Bill Russell	3,148

Bill Russell holds the Celtics' all-time individual career rebounding record with 21,620 rebounds.

7	Bill Sharman	3,047
8	Sam Jones	2,869
9	Cedric Maxwell	2,738
10	Ed Macauley	2,724

Career Free Throw Percentage (Minimum of 1,500 Attempts)

1	**Larry Bird**	**.886 (3,960-4,471)**
2	Bill Sharman	.883 (3,047-3,451)
3	Larry Siegfried	.855 (1,500-1,755)
4	Dennis Johnson	.840 (1,527-1,817)
5	Jo Jo White	.833 (1,892-2,270)
6	Reggie Lewis	.824 (1,479-1,794)
7	John Havlicek	.815 (5,369-6,589)
8	Frank Ramsey	.804 (2,480-3,083)
9	Bob Cousy	.803 (4,621-5,753)
10	Sam Jones	.803 (2,869-3,572)

Career Assists

1	**Bob Cousy**	**6,945**
2	John Havlicek	6,114
3	Larry Bird	5,695
4	Bill Russell	4,100
5	Jo Jo White	3,686
6	Dennis Johnson	3,486
7	K.C. Jones	2,904
8	Dave Cowens	2,828
9	Tiny Archibald	2,563
10	Danny Ainge	2,422

Rebounds

1	**Bill Russell**	**21,620**
2	Robert Parish	11,051
3	Dave Cowens	10,170
4	Larry Bird	8,974
5	John Havlicek	8,007
6	Kevin McHale	7,122
7	Tom Sanders	5,798
8	Tom Heinsohn	5,749
9	Bob Cousy	4,781
10	Don Nelson	4,517

Personal Fouls

1	**John Havlicek**	**3,281**
2	Robert Parish	3,125
3	Tom Sanders	3,044
4	Dave Cowens	2,783
5	Kevin McHale	2,758
6	Bill Russell	2,592
7	Tom Heinsohn	2,454
8	Larry Bird	2,279
9	Bob Cousy	2,231
10	Frank Ramsey	2,158

Disqualifications

1	Tom Sanders	94
2	Frank Ramsey	87
3	Dave Cowens	86

4 Tom Heinsohn	58
5 Robert Parish	53
6 Bob Brannum	42
7 Don Chaney	40
8 Jim Loscutoff	40
9 Cedric Maxwell	32
10 Bob Donham	31

BOSTON CELTICS RETIRED UNIFORM NUMBERS (21)

Personality (Number)	Retirement Ceremony Date
Robert Parish (00)	January 18, 1998
Walter Brown (1, Owner)	October 17, 1964
Red Auerbach (2, Coach)	January 4, 1985
Dennis Johnson (3)	December 13, 1991
Bill Russell (6)	March 12, 1972
Jo Jo White (10)	April 9, 1982
Bob Cousy (14)	October 16, 1963 (Bob Cousy Day on March 17, 1963)
Tom Heinsohn (15)	October 15, 1966
Tom "Satch" Sanders (16)	January 1973
John Havlicek (17)	October 13, 1978
Dave Cowens (18)	February 8, 1981
Jim Loscutoff (18)	No Ceremony ("Loscy" retired but number worn by Cowens)
Don Nelson (19)	No Ceremony
Bill Sharman (21)	October 15, 1966
Ed Macauley (22)	October 16, 1963
Frank Ramsey (23)	No Ceremony
Sam Jones (24)	March 9, 1969
K. C. Jones (25)	February 12, 1967
Kevin McHale (32)	January 30, 1994
Larry Bird (33)	February 4, 1993
Reggie Lewis (35)	March 22, 1995

CELTICS IN NAISMITH MEMORIAL BASKETBALL HALL OF FAME (25)

Personality	Status	Year of Induction
Ed Macauley	Player	1960
Andy Phillip	College Player	1961
John (Honey)Russell	Player	1964
Walter Brown	Contributor	1965
Bill Mokray	Contributor	1965
Alvin (Doggie) Julian	Coach	1967
Arnold (Red) Auerbach	Coach	1968
Bob Cousy	Player	1970
Bill Russell	Player	1974
Bill Sharman	Player	1975
Frank Ramsey	Player	1981
John Havlicek	Player	1983
Sam Jones	Player	1983
Tom Heinsohn	Player	1986
Bob Houbregs	Player	1987
Pete Maravich	Player	1987
Clyde Lovellette	Player	1988
K.C. Jones	Player	1989
Dave Bing	Player	1990
Nate (Tiny) Archibald	Player	1991
Dave Cowns	Player	1991
Bill Walton	Player	1993

Bailey Howell	Player	1997
Larry Bird	Player	1998
Arnie Risen	Player	1998

BOSTON CELTICS TOP DRAFT PICKS

Key: * = never played with Boston Celtics

1947	Eddie Ehlers (Purdue)
1948	George Hauptfuehrer (Harvard)*
1949	Tony Lavelli (Yale)
1950	Charlie Share (Bowling Green)*
1951	Ernie Barrett (Kansas State)
1952	Bill Staufer (Missouri)*
1953	Frank Ramsey (Kentucky)
1954	Togo Palazzi (Holy Cross)
1955	Jim Loscutoff (Oregon)
1956	Bill Russell (San Francisco)
1957	Sam Jones (North Carolina Central)
1958	Ben Swain (Texas Southern)
1959	John Richter (North Carolina State)

Red Auerbach presenting the Celtics' 1978 top draft pick, Larry Bird, with his #33 jersey.

1960	Tom Sanders (NYU)
1961	Gary Phillips (Houston)
1962	John Havlicek (Ohio State)
1963	Bill Green (Colorado State)*
1964	Mel Counts (Oregon State)
1965	Ollie Johnson (San Francisco)*
1966	Jim Barnett (Oregon)
1967	Mal Graham (NYU)
1968	Don Chaney (Houston)
1969	Jo Jo White (Kansas)
1970	Dave Cowens (Florida State)
1971	Clarence Glover (Western Kentucky)
1972	Paul Westphal (South California)
1973	Steve Downing (Indiana)
1974	Glenn McDonald (Long Beach State)
1975	Tom Boswell (South Carolina)
1976	Norm Cook (Kansas)
1977	Cedric Maxwell (UNC-Charlotte)
1978	Larry Bird (Indiana State)
1979	NONE
1980	Kevin McHale (Minnesota)
1981	Charles Bradley (Wyoming)
1982	Darren Tillis (Cleveland State)
1983	Greg Kite (BYU)
1984	Michael Young (Houston)*
1985	Sam Vincent (Michigan State)
1986	Len Bias (Maryland)*
1987	Reggie Lewis (Northeastern)
1988	Brian Shaw (UC-Santa Barbara)
1989	Michael Smith (BYU)
1990	Dee Brown (Jacksonville)
1991	Rick Fox (North Carolina)
1992	Jon Barry (Georgia Tech)*
1993	Acie Earl (Iowa)
1994	Eric Montross (North Carolina)
1995	Eric Williams (Providence)
1996	Antoine Walker (Kentucky)
1997	Chauncey Billips (Colorado)
1998	Paul Pierce (Kansas)

BOSTON CELTICS CAPTAINS

Bob Cousy (1950-63)
Bill Russell (1963-69)
John Havlicek (1969-78)
Dave Cowens (1978-80)
Larry Bird (1980-92)
Reggie Lewis (1992-93)
Robert Parish (1993-94)
Dee Brown and Dominique Wilkins (1994-95)
Dee Brown (1995-96)
Rick Fox (1996-97)
Dee Brown, Pervis Ellison, and Antoine Walker (1997-98)

Boston Celtics Front Office and Bench Personnel

Celtics Presidents
Walter Brown (1946-63)
Lou Pieri (1963-65)

Former Celtics captains Bob Cousy and Bill Russell.

Jack Waldron (1965-67)
Clarence Adams (1967-68)
Jack Waldron (1968-70)
Red Auerbach (1970-97)
Rick Pitino (1997-99)

Celtics General Managers
Walter Brown (1946-50)
Red Auerbach (1950-64) (Basketball Operations)
Walter Brown (1950-64) (Business Operations)
Red Auerbach (1964-84)
Jan Volk (1984-97)
Dave Gavitt (1990-94) (Senior Executive Vice President)
M.L. Carr (1994-97) (Director of Basketball Operations)
Chris Wallace (1997-99)

Celtics Head Coaches
John (Honey) Russell (1946-48)
Alvin (Doggie) Julian (1948-50)
Red Auerbach (1950-1966)
Bill Russell (1968-69) as player-coach
Tom Heinsohn (1969-78) (fired January 3, 1978)
Tom Sanders (1978)
Dave Cowens (1978-79)
Bill Fitch (1979-83)
K.C. Jones (1983-88)
Jimmy Rodgers (1988-90)
Chris Ford (1990-95)
M.L. Carr (1995-97)
Rick Pitino (1997-99)

Red Auerbach—head coach from 1950-1966.

Bill Fitch—head coach from 1979-1983.

Celtics Assistant Coaches
Danny Silva (1946-48)
Henry McCarthy (1948-50)
Art Spector (1949-50)
John Killilea (1972-77)
Tom Sanders (1977-78)
K.C. Jones (1977-83) (1996-97)
Bob MacKinnon (1978-79)
Jimmy Rodgers (1980-88)
Chris Ford (1983-90)
Ed Badger (1984-88)
Lanny Van Eman (1988-90)
Don Casey (1990-96)
Jon P. Jennings (1990-94)
Dennis Johnson (1993-97)
John Kuester (1995-97)
Winston Bennett (1997-98)
Jim O'Brien (1997-99)
John Carroll (1997-99)
Lester Conner (1998-99)
Andy Enfield (1998-99)

Celtics Physicians
Dr. Robert Steinsieck (1958-59)
Dr. John Doherty (1959-69)
Dr. Thomas Silva (1969-87)
Dr. Arnold Scheller (1987-99)

Celtics Trainers
Harry Cohen (1946-58)
Edward (Buddy) LeRoux (1958-67)
John DeLauri (1967-71)
Frank Challant (1971-79)
Ray Melchiorre (1979-87)
Ed Lacerte (1987-99)

ALL-TIME BOSTON CELTICS ROSTER AND PLAYER STATISTICS (complete through 1998 season)

Sources: Boston Celtics 1998-99 Media Guide and The Official NBA Basketball Encyclopedia, 2nd Edition (Alex Sachare, Editor)

Alaa Abdelnaby (6-10, Duke 1990) (wore Celtics #4)

Statistics	G	MIN	FGM-FGA-PCT	FTM-FTA-PCT	REBS	STL	AST	PTS-PPG
Celtics (1992-94)	76	1311	243-472-.515	92-125-.736	346	21	20	578-**7.6**
NBA	202	2694	502-1005-.500	205-286-.717	732	56	72	1209-**6.0**

Zaid Abdul-Aziz (aka Don Smith) (6-9, Iowa State 1968) (wore Celtics #54)

Statistics	G	MIN	FGM-FGA-PCT	FTM-FTA-PCT	REBS	STL	AST	PTS-PPG
Celtics (1977-78)	2	24	3-13-.231	2-3-.667	15	1	3	8-**4.0**
NBA	505	11023	1769-4138-.428	1019-1400-.728	4065	131	601	4557-**9.0**

Mark Acres (6-11, Oral Roberts 1985) (wore Celtics #42)

Statistics	G	MIN	FGM-FGA-PCT	FTM-FTA-PCT	REBS	STL	AST	PTS-PPG
Celtics (1987-89)	141	1783	163-317-.514	97-159-.610	416	48	61	424-**3.0**
NBA	375	5982	514-1016-.506	308-463-.665	1525	137	180	1343-**3.6**

Danny Ainge (6-5, BYU 1981) (wore Celtics #44)

Statistics	G	MIN	FGM-FGA-PCT	FTM-FTA-PCT	REBS	STL	AST	PTS-PPG
Celtics (1981-89)	556	15603	2537-5210-.487	835-963-.867	1534	671	2422	6257-**11.3**
NBA	1042	27755	4643-9905-.469	1676-1980-.846	2768	1133	4199	11964-**11.5**

Jerome Anderson (6-5, West Virginia 1975) (wore Celtics #42)

Statistics	G	MIN	FGM-FGA-PCT	FTM-FTA-PCT	REBS	STL	AST	PTS-PPG
Celtics (1975-76)	22	126	25-45-.556	11-16-.688	13	3	6	61-**2.8**
NBA	49	290	51-104-.490	25-36-.694	25	9	16	127-**2.6**

Kenny Anderson (6-1, Georgia Tech 1993) (wore Celtics #7)

Statistics	G	MIN	FGM-FGA-PCT	FTM-FTA-PCT	REBS	STL	AST	PTS-PPG
Celtics (1997-99)	95*	2868	429-1031-.416	237-295-.803	276	120	538	1158-**12.2**

*Total includes games also played with Portland Trail Blazers and Toronto Raptors in 1997-98

NBA	519	17213	2807-6744-.416	1778-2235-.796	1767	817	3813	7826-**15.1**

Nate (Tiny) Archibald (6-1, Texas-El Paso 1970) (wore Celtics #7)

Statistics	G	MIN	FGM-FGA-PCT	FTM-FTA-PCT	REBS	STL	AST	PTS-PPG
Celtics (1978-83)	363	11324	1567-3338-.469	1401-1773-.790	683	326	2563	4550-**12.5**
NBA	876	31159	5899-12682-.467	4664-5760-.810	2046	719	6476	16481-**18.8**

Nate Archibald

Dennis Awtry

Jim Ard (6-9, Cincinnati 1970) (wore Celtics #34)

Statistics	G	MIN	FGM-FGA-PCT	FTM-FTA-PCT	REBS	STL	AST	PTS-PPG
Celtics (1974-78)	204	2550	292-815-.358	169-243-.695	788	43	142	753-**3.7**
NBA	218	2666	300-831-.361	171-246-.695	820	00	149	771-**3.5**

Dennis Awtrey (6-10, Santa Clara 1970) (wore Celtics #34)

Statistics	G	MIN	FGM-FGA-PCT	FTM-FTA-PCT	REBS	STL	AST	PTS-PPG
Celtics (1978-79)	23	247	17-44-.386	16-20-.800	47	3	20	50-**2.2**
NBA	733	14159	1382-3009-.459	752-1154-.652	3342	186	1467	3516-**4.8**

John Bach (6-2, Fordham 1948) (wore Celtics #17)

Statistics	G	MIN	FGM-FGA-PCT	FTM-FTA-PCT	REBS	STL	AST	PTS-PPG
Celtics (1948-49)	34	NA	34-119-.286	51-75-.680	NA	NA	25	119-**3.5**
NBA (BAA) same								

John Bagley (6-0, Boston College 1983) (wore Celtics #5)

Statistics	G	MIN	FGM-FGA-PCT	FTM-FTA-PCT	REBS	STL	AST	PTS-PPG
Celtics (1989-93)	137	2934	332-749-.443	102-140-.729	257	99	796	777-**5.7**
NBA	665	17120	2359-5398-.437	970-1245-.779	1729	755	3980	5802-**8.7**

Tom Barker (6-11, Hawaii 1976) (wore Celtics #35)

Statistics	G	MIN	FGM-FGA-PCT	FTM-FTA-PCT	REBS	STL	AST	PTS-PPG
Celtics (1978-79)	12	131	21-48-.438	11-15-.733	30	4	6	53-**4.4**
NBA	98	1830	250-592-.422	139-201-.692	520	43	75	639-**6.5**

Don Barksdale (6-6, UCLA 1947) (wore Celtics #7 and #17)

Statistics	G	MIN	FGM-FGA-PCT	FTM-FTA-PCT	REBS	STL	AST	PTS-PPG
Celtics (1953-55)	135	3148	423-1114-.380	369-563-.655	890	NA	246	1215-**9.0**
NBA	262	7460	1016-2747-.370	863-1307-.660	2088	NA	549	2895-**11.0**

Jim (Bad News) Barnes (6-8, Texas Western 1964) (wore Celtics #28)

Statistics	G	MIN	FGM-FGA-PCT	FTM-FTA-PCT	REBS	STL	AST	PTS-PPG
Celtics (1968-70)	126	1644	270-636-.425	160-220-.727	544	NA	79	700-**5.6**
NBA	454	9455	1548-3607-.429	901-1317-.684	2939	NA	377	3997-**8.8**

Marvin Barnes (6-9, Providence 1974) (wore Celtics #27)

Statistics	G	MIN	FGM-FGA-PCT	FTM-FTA-PCT	REBS	STL	AST	PTS-PPG
Celtics (1978-79)	38	796	133-271-.491	43-66-.652	177	38	53	309-**8.1**
NBA	171*	3718	638-1444-.442	293-436-.672	946	145	252	1569-**9.2**

*Also played in ABA with St. Louis Spirit

Jim Barnett (6-4, Oregon 1966) (wore Celtics #11)

Statistics	G	MIN	FGM-FGA-PCT	FTM-FTA-PCT	REBS	STL	AST	PTS-PPG
Celtics (1966-67)	48	383	78-211-.370	42-62-.677	53	NA	41	198-**4.1**
NBA	732	17410	3326-7642-.435	1884-2363-.797	2259	131	2232	8536-**11.7**

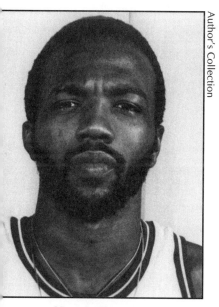

Marvin Barnes

Dave Bing

Tom Boswell

Ernie Barrett (6-3, Kansas State 1951) (wore Celtics #23)

Statistics	G	MIN	FGM-FGA-PCT	FTM-FTA-PCT	REBS	STL	AST	PTS-PPG
Celtics (1953-56)	131	2092	267-724-.369	107-143-.748	343	NA	229	641-**4.9**
NBA	same							

Dana Barros (5-11, Boston College 1989) (wore Celtics #11)

Statistics	G	MIN	FGM-FGA-PCT	FTM-FTA-PCT	REBS	STL	AST	PTS-PPG
Celtics (1995-99)	234	5878	938-2039-.460	353-407-.867	482	219	881	2586-**11.1**
NBA	688	16669	2826-6098-.463	1092-1271-.859	1343	665	2516	7707-**11.2**

Tony Battie (6-11, Texas Tech 1998) (wore Celtics #40)

Statistics	G	MIN	FGM-FGA-PCT	FTM-FTA-PCT	REBS	STL	AST	PTS-PPG
Celtics (1999)	50	1121	147-283-.519	41-61-.672	204	29	53	335-**6.7**
NBA	115	2627	381-808-.472	114-165-.691	555	83	113	879-**7.6**

Kenny Battle (6-6, Illinois 1989) (wore Celtics #8)

Statistics	G	MIN	FGM-FGA-PCT	FTM-FTA-PCT	REBS	STL	AST	PTS-PPG
Celtics (1991-93)	11	75	9-17-.529	10-10-1.000	20	2	2	28-**2.5**
NBA	134	1795	243-842-.504	137-189-.725	327	98	106	627-**4.7**

Moe (Morris) Becker (6-1, Duquesne 1941) (wore Celtics #5)

Statistics	G	MIN	FGM-FGA-PCT	FTM-FTA-PCT	REBS	STL	AST	PTS-PPG
Celtics (1946-47)	6	NA	5-22-.227	3-4-.750	NA	NA	1	13-**2.2**
NBA (BAA)	43	NA	70-358-.196	22-44-.500	NA	NA	30	162-**3.8**

Hank Beenders (6-6, LIU) (wore Celtics #6)

Statistics	G	MIN	FGM-FGA-PCT	FTM-FTA-PCT	REBS	STL	AST	PTS-PPG
Celtics (1948-49)	8	NA	6-28-.214	7-9-.778	NA	NA	3	19-**2.4**
NBA (BAA)	111	NA	348-1313-.265	239-348-.687	NA	NA	53	935-**8.4**

Bob Bigelow (6-7, Pennsylvania 1975) (wore Celtics #34)

Statistics	G	MIN	FGM-FGA-PCT	FTM-FTA-PCT	REBS	STL	AST	PTS-PPG
Celtics (1977-78)	4	17	3-12-.250	0-0-.000	4	0	0	6-**1.5**
NBA	94	762	91-220-.414	52-71-.732	111	19	42	234-**2.5**

Chauncey Billips (6-3, Colorado 1999) (wore Celtics #4)

Statistics	G	MIN	FGM-FGA-PCT	FTM-FTA-PCT	REBS	STL	AST	PTS-PPG
Celtics (1997-98)	51	1296	177-454-.390	147-180-.817	113	77	217	565-**11.1**
NBA	12	3704	471-1244-.379	383-438-.874	286	165	487	1517-**12.1**

Dave Bing (6-3, Syracuse 1966) (wore Celtics #44)

Statistics	G	MIN	FGM-FGA-PCT	FTM-FTA-PCT	REBS	STL	AST	PTS-PPG
Celtics (1977-78)	80	2256	422-940-.449	244-296-.824	212	79	300	1088-**13.6**
NBA	901	32769	6962-15769-.441	4403-5683-.775	3420	483	5397	18327-**20.3**

Larry Bird (6-9, Indiana State 1979) (wore Celtics #33, retired in his honor)

Statistics	G	MIN	FGM-FGA-PCT	FTM-FTA-PCT	REBS	STL	AST	PTS-PPG
Celtics (1979-92)	897	34443	8591-17334-.496	3960-4471-.886	8974	1556	5695	21791-**24.3**
NBA	same							

Otis Birdsong (6-3, Houston 1977) (wore Celtics #12)

Statistics	G	MIN	FGM-FGA-PCT	FTM-FTA-PCT	REBS	STL	AST	PTS-PPG
Celtics (1988-89)	13	108	18-36-.500	0-2-.000	13	3	9	37-**2.8**
NBA	696	21627	5347-10562-.506	1801-2748-.655	2072	858	2260	12544-**18.0**

James Blackwell (6-0, Dartmouth 1991) (wore Celtics #8)

Statistics	G	MIN	FGM-FGA-PCT	FTM-FTA-PCT	REBS	STL	AST	PTS-PPG
Celtics (1994-95)	9	61	6-10-.600	2-3-.667	8	3	6	14-**1.6**
NBA	same							

Meyer (Mike) Bloom (6-6, Temple) (wore Celtics #10)

Statistics	G	MIN	FGM-FGA-PCT	FTM-FTA-PCT	REBS	STL	AST	PTS-PPG
Celtics (1947-48)	14	NA	46-169-.272	37-57-.649	NA	NA	14	129-**9.2**
NBA (BAA)	93	NA	209-821-.255	216-303-.713	NA	NA	70	634-**6.8**

Ron Bonham (6-5, Cincinnati 1964) (wore Celtics #21)

Statistics	G	MIN	FGM-FGA-PCT	FTM-FTA-PCT	REBS	STL	AST	PTS-PPG
Celtics (1964-66)	76	681	167-427-.390	144-173-.836	113	NA	30	478-**6.3**
NBA	same (also played in ABA with Indiana Pacers)							

Tom Boswell (6-9, South Carolina State, South Carolina 1975) (wore Celtics #31)

Statistics	G	MIN	FGM-FGA-PCT	FTM-FTA-PCT	REBS	STL	AST	PTS-PPG
Celtics (1975-78)	170	2507	401-790-.508	203-282-.720	665	54	172	1005-**5.9**
NBA	366	7046	1096-2058-.533	623-860-.724	1709	142	591	2821-**7.7**

Bruce Bowen (6-7, Cal State-Fullerton 1993) (wore Celtics #12)

Statistics	G	MIN	FGM-FGA-PCT	FTM-FTA-PCT	REBS	STL	AST	PTS-PPG
Celtics (1997-99)	91	1799	148-391-.379	87-146-.596	226	108	109	410-**4.5**
NBA	92	1800	148-391-.379	87-146-.596	226	108	109	410-**4.5**

Harry (Big Hesh) Boykoff (6-10, St. John's 1947) (wore Celtics #24)

Statistics	G	MIN	FGM-FGA-PCT	FTM-FTA-PCT	REBS	STL	AST	PTS-PPG
Celtics (1950-51)	48*	NA	126-336-.375	74-100-.740	220	NA	60	326-**6.8**

*also played with Tri-Cities Blackhawks

NBA	109	NA	414-1034-.400	277-362-.765	220	NA	209	1105-**10.1**

Charles Bradley (6-5, Wyoming 1981) (wore Celtics #35)

Statistics	G	MIN	FGM-FGA-PCT	FTM-FTA-PCT	REBS	STL	AST	PTS-PPG
Celtics (1981-83)	102	871	124-298-.416	88-152-.579	116	46	50	336-**3.3**
NBA	110	910	127-305-.416	93-159-.585	119	46	55	347-**3.2**

Bob Brannum (6-5, Kentucky, Michigan State) (wore Celtics #18)

Statistics	G	MIN	FGM-FGA-PCT	FTM-FTA-PCT	REBS	STL	AST	PTS-PPG
Celtics (1951-55)	279	6576	653-1863-.351	436-689-.633	1944	NA	494	1742-**6.2**
NBA	338	6576*	887-2581-.344	681-1044-.652	1944*	NA	699	2455-**7.3**

*Minutes and rebounds NA from first two seasons with Sheboygan Redskins

Carl Braun (6-5, Colgate 1949) (wore Celtics #4)

Statistics	G	MIN	FGM-FGA-PCT	FTM-FTA-PCT	REBS	STL	AST	PTS-PPG
Celtics (1961-62)	48	414	78-207-.377	20-27-.741	50	NA	71	176-**3.7**
NBA	788	18409	3912-10211-.383	2801-3484-.804	2122	NA	2892	10625-**13.5**

Frank Brickowski (6-9, Penn State 1981) (wore Celtics #34)

Statistics	G	MIN	FGM-FGA-PCT	FTM-FTA-PCT	REBS	STL	AST	PTS-PPG
Celtics (1996-97)	17	255	32-73-.438	10-14-.714	34	5	15	81-**4.8**
NBA	731	16278	2873-5538-.519	1501-2028-.740	3410	644	1384	7302-**10.0**

Al Brightman (6-2, Morris Harvey, Long Beach State 1959) (wore Celtics #8)

Statistics	G	MIN	FGM-FGA-PCT	FTM-FTA-PCT	REBS	STL	AST	PTS-PPG
Celtics (1946-47)	58	NA	223-870-.256	121-193-.627	NA	NA	60	567-**9.8**
NBA (BAA)	same							

Dee Brown (6-2, Jacksonville 1990) (wore Celtics #7)

Statistics	G	MIN	FGM-FGA-PCT	FTM-FTA-PCT	REBS	STL	AST	PTS-PPG
Celtics (1990-98)	476	13665	2104-4698-.448	979-1181-.829	1302	174	1883	5512-**11.6**
NBA	556	15590	2428-5500-.441	1058-1279-.827	1495	769	2127	6439-**11.6**

Emmette Bryant (6-1, DePaul 1964) (wore Celtics #7)

Statistics	G	MIN	FGM-FGA-PCT	FTM-FTA-PCT	REBS	STL	AST	PTS-PPG
Celtics (1968-70)	151	3005	407-1008-.404	200-281-.712	461	NA	407	1014-**6.7**
NBA	566	11451	1501-3665-.410	720-1043-.690	1593	NA	1700	3722-**6.6**

Quinn Buckner (6-3, Indiana 1976) (wore Celtics #28)

Statistics	G	MIN	FGM-FGA-PCT	FTM-FTA-PCT	REBS	STL	AST	PTS-PPG
Celtics (1982-85)	226	3672	460-1077-.427	154-241-.639	411	255	637	1074-**4.8**
NBA	719	16245	2546-5527-.461	830-1264-.657	1969	1337	3114	5929-**8.2**

Junior Burrough (6-8, Virginia 1995) (wore Celtics #5)

Statistics	G	MIN	FGM-FGA-PCT	FTM-FTA-PCT	REBS	STL	AST	PTS-PPG
Celtics (1995-96)	61	496	64-170-.376	61-93-.656	109	15	15	189-**3.1**
NBA	same							

Elbert (Al) Butler (6-2, Niagara 1961) (wore Celtics #9)

Statistics	G	MIN	FGM-FGA-PCT	FTM-FTA-PCT	REBS	STL	AST	PTS-PPG
Celtics (61-62)	5	47	13-29-.448	5-NA-NA	13	NA	4	31-**6.2**
NBA	234	5055	930-2119-.439	422-571-.739	696	NA	530	2282-**9.8**

Rick Carlisle (6-5, Maine, Virginia 1984) (wore Celtics #34)

Statistics	G	MIN	FGM-FGA-PCT	FTM-FTA-PCT	REBS	STL	AST	PTS-PPG
Celtics (1984-87)	157	1236	148-348-.425	45-60-.750	128	30	164	346-**2.2**
NBA	188	1461	178-422-.422	55-71-.775	141	42	201	422-**2.2**

M.L. (Michael Leon) Carr (6-6, Guilford 1973) (wore Celtics #30)

Statistics	G	MIN	FGM-FGA-PCT	FTM-FTA-PCT	REBS	STL	AST	PTS-PPG
Celtics (1979-85)	363	5810	910-2023-.450	432-570-.758	818	303	484	2285-**6.3**
NBA	604*	14216	2330-4954-.470	1160-1555-.746	2595	867	1112	5853-**9.7**

*Also played in ABA with St. Louis Spirit

M.L Carr

Chuck Connors

Don Chaney (6-5, Houston 1968) (wore Celtics #42 and #12)

Statistics	G	MIN	FGM-FGA-PCT	FTM-FTA-PCT	REBS	STL	AST	PTS-PPG
Celtics (1968-80)	652	14865	2287-5180-.442	1114-1432-.778	2572	344	1268	5689-**8.7**
NBA	742	17406	2513-5738-.438	1189-1532-.776	2913	492	1593	6216-**8.4**

Carlos Clark (6-4, Mississippi 1983) (wore Celtics #40)

Statistics	G	MIN	FGM-FGA-PCT	FTM-FTA-PCT	REBS	STL	AST	PTS-PPG
Celtics (1983-85)	93	689	83-204-.407	57-71-.803	86	43	65	223-**2.4**
NBA	same							

Charles Claxton (7-0, Georgia 1995) (wore Celtics #51)

Statistics	G	MIN	FGM-FGA-PCT	FTM-FTA-PCT	REBS	STL	AST	PTS-PPG
Celtics (1995-96)	3	7	1-2-.500	0-2-.000	2	0	0	2-**0.7**
NBA	same							

Ben Clyde (6-7, Florida State 1974) (wore Celtics #33)

Statistics	G	MIN	FGM-FGA-PCT	FTM-FTA-PCT	REBS	STL	AST	PTS-PPG
Celtics (1974-75)	25	157	31-72-.431	7-9-.778	41	5	5	69-**2.8**
NBA	same							

Gene Conley (6-9, Washington State 1952) (wore Celtics #17)

Statistics	G	MIN	FGM-FGA-PCT	FTM-FTA-PCT	REBS	STL	AST	PTS-PPG
Celtics (1952-61)	235	3696	505-1404-.360	237-362-.655	1587	NA	110	1247-**5.3**
NBA	351	5791	833-2244-.371	403-613-.657	2212	NA	201	2069-**5.9**

Marty Conlon (6-11, Providence 1990) (wore Celtics #0 and #30)

Statistics	G	MIN	FGM-FGA-PCT	FTM-FTA-PCT	REBS	STL	AST	PTS-PPG
Celtics (1996-97)	74	1614	214-454-.471	144-171-.842	195	46	104	574-**7.8**
NBA	351	6063	935-1865-.501	471-641-.735	1257	139	365	2356-**6.7**

Kevin (Chuck) Connors (6-7, Seton Hall) (wore Celtics #11)

Statistics	G	MIN	FGM-FGA-PCT	FTM-FTA-PCT	REBS	STL	AST	PTS-PPG
Celtics (1946-48)	53	NA	99-393-.252	41-87-.471	NA	NA	41	239-**4.5**
NBA (BAA)	same (also played in NBL with Rochester Royals)							

Norm Cook (6-9, Kansas 1977) (wore Celtics #52)

Statistics	G	MIN	FGM-FGA-PCT	FTM-FTA-PCT	REBS	STL	AST	PTS-PPG
Celtics (1976-77)	25	138	27-72-.375	9-17-.529	27	10	5	63-**2.5**
NBA	27	148	28-75-.373	9-17-.529	30	10	6	65-**2.4**

Chuck Cooper (6-5, Duquesne 1950) (wore Celtics #11, #9, #5)

Statistics	G	MIN	FGM-FGA-PCT	FTM-FTA-PCT	REBS	STL	AST	PTS-PPG
Celtics (1950-54)	272	5071*	639-1873-.341	572-774-.739	1807	NA	494	1850-**6.8**

*Minutes not available from 1950-51 season

NBA	409	7964	933-2750-.339	859-1156-.743	2431	NA	734	2725-**6.7**

Chris Corchiani (6-1, North Carolina State 1991) (wore Celtics #12)

Statistics	G	MIN	FGM-FGA-PCT	FTM-FTA-PCT	REBS	STL	AST	PTS-PPG
Celtics (1993-94)	51	467	40-94-.426	26-38-.684	44	22	86	117-**2.3**
NBA	112	1313	131-311-.421	133-163-.816	129	73	243	416-**3.7**

Mel Counts (7-0, Oregon State 1964) (wore Celtics #11)

Statistics	G	MIN	FGM-FGA-PCT	FTM-FTA-PCT	REBS	STL	AST	PTS-PPG
Celtics (1964-66)	121	1593	321-821-..391	178-219-.613	697	NA	69	820-**6.8**
NBA	789	13723	2665-6122-.435	1186-1552-.764	4756	85	1100	6516-**8.3**

Bob Cousy lays up a shot against the St. Louis Hawks.

Bob Cousy (6-1, Holy Cross 1950) (wore Celtics #14, retired number in his honor)

Statistics	G	MIN	FGM-FGA-PCT	FTM-FTA-PCT	REBS	STL	AST	PTS-PPG
Celtics (1950-63)	917	30131	6167-16465-.375	4621-5753-.803	4781	NA	6945	16955-**18.5**
NBA	924	30165	6168-16468-.375	4624-5756-.803	4786	NA	6955	16960-**18.4**

Dave Cowens (6-8 1/2, Florida State 1970) (wore Celtics #18, retired in his honor)

Statistics	G	MIN	FGM-FGA-PCT	FTM-FTA-PCT	REBS	STL	AST	PTS-PPG
Celtics (1970-80)	726	28551	5608-12193-.460	1975-2527-.782	10170	569	2828	13192-**18.2**
NBA	766	29565	5744-12499-.460	2027-2590-.783	10444	599	2910	13516-**17.6**

Hal Crisler (6-3, San Jose State) (wore Celtics #15)

Statistics	G	MIN	FGM-FGA-PCT	FTM-FTA-PCT	REBS	STL	AST	PTS-PPG
Celtics (1946-47)	4	NA	2-6-.333	2-2-1.000	NA	NA	0	6-**1.5**
NBA (BAA) same								

Tony Dawson (6-7, Florida State 1989) (wore Celtics #45)

Statistics	G	MIN	FGM-FGA-PCT	FTM-FTA-PCT	REBS	STL	AST	PTS-PPG
Celtics (1994-95)	2	13	3-8-.375	1-1-1.0001	3	0	1	8-**4.0**
NBA	same							

Todd Day (6-6, Arkansas 1992) (wore Celtics #13)

Statistics	G	MIN	FGM-FGA-PCT	FTM-FTA-PCT	REBS	STL	AST	PTS-PPG
Celtics (1995-97)	152	3913	675-1745-.384	456-592-.769	532	185	219	2027-**13.4**
NBA	394	10928	1862-4569-.408	1187-1596-.744	1483	478	620	5389-**13.7**

Darren Daye (6-8, UCLA 1983) (wore Celtics #20)

Statistics	G	MIN	FGM-FGA-PCT	FTM-FTA-PCT	REBS	STL	AST	PTS-PPG
Celtics (1986-88)	108	1379	213-419-.508	93-152-.612	200	54	146	519-**4.8**
NBA	328	5208	849-1730-.491	525-771-.681	844	191	672	2225-**6.8**

Andrew DeClercq (6-10, Florida 1995) (wore Celtics #45)

Statistics	G	MIN	FGM-FGA-PCT	FTM-FTA-PCT	REBS	STL	AST	PTS-PPG
Celtics (1997-99)	95	1781	197-397-.496	120-197-.609	455	98	69	514-**5.4**
NBA	221	3893	473-939-.504	298-479-.622	984	175	131	1244-**5.6**

Dick Dickey (6-1, North Carolina State 1950) (wore Celtics #23)

Statistics	G	MIN	FGM-FGA-PCT	FTM-FTA-PCT	REBS	STL	AST	PTS-PPG
Celtics (1951-52)	45	440	40-136-.294	47-69-.681	81	NA	50	127-**2.8**
NBA	same							

Ernie DiGregorio (6-0, Providence 1973) (wore Celtics #7)

Statistics	G	MIN	FGM-FGA-PCT	FTM-FTA-PCT	REBS	STL	AST	PTS-PPG
Celtics (1977-78)	27	274	47-109-.431	12-13-.923	27	12	66	106-**3.9**
NBA	312	7859	1268-3052-.415	461-511-.902	610	190	1594	2997-**9.6**

Bill Dinwiddie (6-7, New Mexico Highlands 1966) (wore Celtics #27)

Statistics	G	MIN	FGM-FGA-PCT	FTM-FTA-PCT	REBS	STL	AST	PTS-PPG
Celtics (1969-71)	61	717	123-328-.375	54-74-.730	209	NA	34	300-**4.9**
NBA	220	2760	404-1095-.369	166-272-.610	720	NA	129	974-**4.4**

Bob Doll (6-5, Colorado 1942) (wore Celtics #19)

Statistics	G	MIN	FGM-FGA-PCT	FTM-FTA-PCT	REBS	STL	AST	PTS-PPG
Celtics (1948-50)	94	NA	265-785-.338	155-231-.671	NA	NA	225	685-**7.3**
NBA (BAA/NBL)	196	NA	633-2211-.286	387-585-.662	NA	NA	273	1653-**8.4**

Bob Donham (6-2, Ohio State 1950) (wore Celtics #12)

Statistics	G	MIN	FGM-FGA-PCT	FTM-FTA-PCT	REBS	STL	AST	PTS-PPG
Celtics (1950-54)	273	NA	662-1379-.480	494-975-.570	1071	NA	706	1818-**6.7**
NBA	same							

Sherman Douglas (6-1, Syracuse 1989) (wore Celtics #4 and #20)

Statistics	G	MIN	FGM-FGA-PCT	FTM-FTA-PCT	REBS	STL	AST	PTS-PPG
Celtics (1991-96)	269	7657	1191-2524-.472	558-862-.647	605	241	2129	2981-**11.1**
NBA	576	17204	2817-5759-.489	1320-1959-.674	1376	650	3915	7081-**12.3**

Steve Downing (6-8, Indiana 1973) (wore Celtics #32)

Statistics	G	MIN	FGM-FGA-PCT	FTM-FTA-PCT	REBS	STL	AST	PTS-PPG
Celtics (1973-75)	27	146	21-66-.318	22-40-.550	41	5	11	64-**2.4**
NBA	same							

Nate Driggers (6-4, Montevallo 1995) (wore Celtics #27)

Statistics	G	MIN	FGM-FGA-PCT	FTM-FTA-PCT	REBS	STL	AST	PTS-PPG
Celtics (1996-97)	15	132	13-43-.302	10-14-.714	22	3	6	36-**2.4**
NBA	same							

Terry Duerod (6-2, Detroit 1979) (wore Celtics #40)

Statistics	G	MIN	FGM-FGA-PCT	FTM-FTA-PCT	REBS	STL	AST	PTS-PPG
Celtics (1980-82)	53	260	64-150-.427	17-26-.654	20	8	18	151-**2.8**
NBA	143	1977	429-928-.462	80-119-.672	160	63	170	961-**6.7**

Bob Duffy (6-4, Tulane) (wore Celtics #17)

Statistics	G	MIN	FGM-FGA-PCT	FTM-FTA-PCT	REBS	STL	AST	PTS-PPG
Celtics (1946-47)	6	NA	2-7-.286	4-4-1.000	NA	NA	0	8-**1.3**
NBA (BAA)	17	NA	7-32-.219	5-7-.714	NA	NA	0	19-**1.1**

Andy Duncan (6-6, Kentucky, William & Mary) (wore Celtics #21)

Statistics	G	MIN	FGM-FGA-PCT	FTM-FTA-PCT	REBS	STL	AST	PTS-PPG
Celtics (1950-51)	14	NA	7-40-.175	15-22-.682	30	NA	8	29-**2.1**
NBA (BAA/NBL)	136	NA	294-720-.408	158-265-.596	30*	NA	101	746-**5.5**

*Rebound totals not available for 1948-1950 seasons

Acie Earl (6-10, Iowa 1993) (wore Celtics #55)

Statistics	G	MIN	FGM-FGA-PCT	FTM-FTA-PCT	REBS	STL	AST	PTS-PPG
Celtics (1993-95)	104	1357	177-440-.402	122-189-.646	292	30	14	476-**4.6**
NBA	193	2512	361-896-.403	258-387-.667	517	63	61	980-**5.1**

Tyus Edney (5-10, UCLA 1995) (wore Celtics #20)

Statistics	G	MIN	FGM-FGA-PCT	FTM-FTA-PCT	REBS	STL	AST	PTS-PPG
Celtics (1997-98)	52	623	93-216-.431	88-111-.793	55	51	139	277-**5.3**
NBA	202	4480	548-1347-.407	462-578-.799	369	200	856	1622-**8.0**

Blue (Theodore) Edwards (6-4, East Carolina 1989) (wore Celtics #30)

Statistics	G	MIN	FGM-FGA-PCT	FTM-FTA-PCT	REBS	STL	AST	PTS-PPG
Celtics (1994-95)	31	507	83-195-.426	43-48-.896	65	19	47	220-**7.1**
NBA	599	16158	2663-5548-.480	1050-1362-.771	2126	625	1178	6636-**11.1**

Ed Ehlers (6-3, Purdue 1947) (wore Celtics #4)

Statistics	G	MIN	FGM-FGA-PCT	FTM-FTA-PCT	REBS	STL	AST	PTS-PPG
Celtics (1947-49)	99	NA	286-1000-.286	228-369-.618	NA	NA	177	800-**8.1**
NBA (BAA)	same							

Don Eliason (6-2, Hamline 1942) (wore Celtics #14)

Statistics	G	MIN	FGM-FGA-PCT	FTM-FTA-PCT	REBS	STL	AST	PTS-PPG
Celtics (1946-47)	1	NA	0-1-.000	0-0-.000	NA	NA	0	0-**0.0**
NBA (BAA)	same							

Pervis Ellison (6-10, Louisville 1989) (wore Celtics #29)

Statistics	G	MIN	FGM-FGA-PCT	FTM-FTA-PCT	REBS	STL	AST	PTS-PPG
Celtics (1994-98)	163	3086	343-681-.504	169-255-.663	895	86	131	855-**5.2**
NBA	435	11284	1805-3529-.511	824-1198-.688	3091	283	675	4435-**10.2**

Wayne Embry (6-8, Miami-Ohio 1958) (wore Celtics #28)

Statistics	G	MIN	FGM-FGA-PCT	FTM-FTA-PCT	REBS	STL	AST	PTS-PPG
Celtics (1966-68)	150	1817	340-842-.404	191-329-.581	615	NA	94	871-**5.8**
NBA	831	21763	3993-9067-.440	2394-3741-.640	7544	NA	1194	10380-**12.5**

Gene Englund (6-5, Wisconsin 1941) (wore Celtics #10)

Statistics	G	MIN	FGM-FGA-PCT	FTM-FTA-PCT	REBS	STL	AST	PTS-PPG
Celtics (1949-50)	24	NA	55-148-.372	86-106-.811	NA	NA	17	196-**8.2**
NBA (NBL/BAA)	46	NA	104-274-.380	152-192-.792	NA	NA	41	360-**7.8**

John Ezersky (6-3, St. John's) (wore Celtics #10 and #16)

Statistics	G	MIN	FGM-FGA-PCT	FTM-FTA-PCT	REBS	STL	AST	PTS-PPG
Celtics (1948-50)	34	NA	104-321-.324	84-131-.641	NA	NA	51	292-**8.6**
NBA (NBL/BAA)	135	NA	366-1270-.288	299-447-.669	NA	NA	169	1031-**7.6**

Phil Farbman (6-2, CCNY 1948) (wore Celtics #8)

Statistics	G	MIN	FGM-FGA-PCT	FTM-FTA-PCT	REBS	STL	AST	PTS-PPG
Celtics (1948-49)	21	NA	21-78-.269	30-38-.789	NA	NA	18	72-**3.4**
NBA (BAA)	48	NA	50-163-.307	55-81-.679	NA	NA	36	155-**3.2**

Warren (Bill) Fenley (6-3, Manhattan) (wore Celtics #7)

Statistics	G	MIN	FGM-FGA-PCT	FTM-FTA-PCT	REBS	STL	AST	PTS-PPG
Celtics (1946-47)	33	NA	31-138-.225	23-45-.511	NA	NA	16	85-**2.6**
NBA (BAA)	same							

Eric Fernsten (6-10, San Francisco 1975) (wore Celtics #45)

Statistics	G	MIN	FGM-FGA-PCT	FTM-FTA-PCT	REBS	STL	AST	PTS-PPG
Celtics (1979-82)	144	912	128-281-.456	72-112-.643	200	28	46	328-**2.3**
NBA	218	1643	193-434-.445	131-194-.675	372	52	82	517-**2.4**

Henry Finkel (7-0, Dayton 1966) (wore Celtics #29)

Statistics	G	MIN	FGM-FGA-PCT	FTM-FTA-PCT	REBS	STL	AST	PTS-PPG
Celtics (1969-75)	436	5277	817-1858-.440	371-572-.649	1605	10*	2005	2005-**4.6**

*Steals totals not available before 1973-74 season

NBA	551	6866	1125-2508-.449	540-816-.662	2151	10*	426	2790-**5.1**

Jack ("The Shot") Foley (6-3, Holy Cross 1962) (wore Celtics #21)

Statistics	G	MIN	FGM-FGA-PCT	FTM-FTA-PCT	REBS	STL	AST	PTS-PPG
Celtics (1962-63)	5	46	13-26-.500	6-8-.750	7	NA	0	32-**6.4**
NBA	11	83	20-51-.392	13-15-.867	16	NA	5	53-**4.8**

Chris Ford (6-5, Villanova 1972) (wore Celtics #42)

Statistics	G	MIN	FGM-FGA-PCT	FTM-FTA-PCT	REBS	STL	AST	PTS-PPG
Celtics (1978-82)	309	9058	1357-2973-.456	354-476-.744	708	367	1021	3194-**10.3**
NBA	794	22043	3160-6874-.460	868-1188-.731	2394	1152	2719	7314-**9.2**

Rick Fox (6-7, North Carolina 1991) (wore Celtics #44)

Statistics	G	MIN	FGM-FGA-PCT	FTM-FTA-PCT	REBS	STL	AST	PTS-PPG
Celtics (1991-97)	444	10990	1788-3862-.463	892-1155-.772	1733	552	1250	4759-**10.7**
NBA	614	15587	2447-5293-.462	1195-1563-.765	2269	708	1704	6530-**10.6**

Chris Ford

John Havlicek

Kevin Gamble (6-5, Iowa 1987) (wore Celtics #34)

Statistics	G	MIN	FGM-FGA-PCT	FTM-FTA-PCT	REBS	STL	AST	PTS-PPG
Celtics (1988-94)	436	10988	2067-3988-.518	670-821-.816	1112	360	1003	4895-**11.2**
NBA	649	14508	2562-5106-.502	802-990-.810	1457	470	1300	6154-**9.5**

Jack Garfinkel (6-0, St. John's 1941) (wore Celtics #15)

Statistics	G	MIN	FGM-FGA-PCT	FTM-FTA-PCT	REBS	STL	AST	PTS-PPG
Celtics (1946-49)	92	NA	207-754-.275	62-88-.705	NA	NA	134	476-**5.2**
NBA (BAA)	same							

Ward Gibson (6-5, Creighton 1947) (wore Celtics #4)

Statistics	G	MIN	FGM-FGA-PCT	FTM-FTA-PCT	REBS	STL	AST	PTS-PPG
Celtics (1949-50)	2	NA	3-4-.750	1-4-.250	NA	NA	1	7-**3.5**
NBA	32	NA	67-195-.344	42-64-.656	NA	NA	37	176-**5.5**

Artis Gilmore (7-2, Jacksonville 1971) (wore Celtics #53)

Statistics	G	MIN	FGM-FGA-PCT	FTM-FTA-PCT	REBS	STL	AST	PTS-PPG
Celtics (1987-88)	47	521	58-101-.574	48-91-.527	148	10	12	164-**3.5**
NBA	909	29685	5732-9572-.599*	4114-5768-.713	9161	470	1777	15579-**17.1**

*NBA record

Clarence Glover (6-8, Western Kentucky 1971) (wore Celtics #28)

Statistics	G	MIN	FGM-FGA-PCT	FTM-FTA-PCT	REBS	STL	AST	PTS-PPG
Celtics (1971-72)	25	119	25-55-.455	15-32-.469	46	NA	4	65-**2.6**
NBA	same							

Mal Graham (6-1, NYU 1967) (wore Celtics #11)

Statistics	G	MIN	FGM-FGA-PCT	FTM-FTA-PCT	REBS	STL	AST	PTS-PPG
Celtics (1967-69)	100	889	130-327-.398	67-102-.657	118	NA	75	327-**3.3**
NBA	same							

Ron Grandison (6-8, New Orleans 1987) (wore Celtics #31)

Statistics	G	MIN	FGM-FGA-PCT	FTM-FTA-PCT	REBS	STL	AST	PTS-PPG
Celtics (1988-89)	72	528	59-142-.415	59-80-.738	92	18	42	177-**2.5**
NBA	75	553	61-146-.418	65-90-.722	103	19	43	187-**2.5**

Wyndol Gray (6-1, Harvard, Bowling Green) (wore Celtics #4)

Statistics	G	MIN	FGM-FGA-PCT	FTM-FTA-PCT	REBS	STL	AST	PTS-PPG
Celtics (1946-47)	55	NA	139-476-.292	72-124-.581	NA	NA	47	350-**6.4**
NBA (BAA/NBL)	67	NA	145-513-.283	73-128-.570	NA	NA	50	363-**5.4**

Rickey Green (6-0, Michigan 1977) (wore Celtics #13)

Statistics	G	MIN	FGM-FGA-PCT	FTM-FTA-PCT	REBS	STL	AST	PTS-PPG
Celtics (1991-92)	26	367	45-101-.446	13-18-.722	24	17	68	106-**4.1**
NBA	946	23271	3594-7669-.469	1643-2035-.807	1819	1348	5221	8870-**9.4**

Sihugo Green (6-2, Duquesne 1956) (wore Celtics #28)

Statistics	G	MIN	FGM-FGA-PCT	FTM-FTA-PCT	REBS	STL	AST	PTS-PPG
Celtics (1965-66)	10	92	12-31-.387	8-16-.500	11	NA	9	32-**3.2**
NBA	504	13132	1732-4481-.387	1172-1735-.676	2152	NA	1655	4636-**9.2**

Gene Guarilia (6-5, George Washington 1959) (wore Celtics #20)

Statistics	G	MIN	FGM-FGA-PCT	FTM-FTA-PCT	REBS	STL	AST	PTS-PPG
Celtics (1959-63)	129	1082	168-447-.376	77-126-.611	294	NA	36	413-**3.2**
NBA	same							

Charles (Chick) Halbert (6-9, West Texas State 1942) (wore Celtics #11)

Statistics	G	MIN	FGM-FGA-PCT	FTM-FTA-PCT	REBS	STL	AST	PTS-PPG
Celtics (1948-49)	33	NA	99-338-.293	112-188-.596	NA	NA	61	310-**9.4**
NBA (BAA)	303	NA	910-2900-.314	851-1344-.633	539*	NA	438	2671-**8.8**

*Rebounds not availble before 1950-51 season

Steve Hamer (7-0, Tennessee 1996) (wore Celtics #42)

Statistics	G	MIN	FGM-FGA-PCT	FTM-FTA-PCT	REBS	STL	AST	PTS-PPG
Celtics (1996-97)	35	268	30-57-.526	16-29-.552	60	2	7	76-**2.2**
NBA	same							

Thomas Hamilton (7-2, Pittsburgh 1997) (wore Celtics #30)

Statistics	G	MIN	FGM-FGA-PCT	FTM-FTA-PCT	REBS	STL	AST	PTS-PPG
Celtics (1995-96)	11	70	9-31-.290	7-18-.389	22	0	1	25-**2.3**
NBA	same							

Cecil Hankins (6-1, Oklahoma A&M 1946) (wore Celtics #5)

Statistics	G	MIN	FGM-FGA-PCT	FTM-FTA-PCT	REBS	STL	AST	PTS-PPG
Celtics (1947-48)	25	NA	23-116-.198	24-35-.686	NA	NA	8	70-**2.8**
NBA (BAA/NBL)	80	NA	140-507-.276	114-185-.616	NA	NA	22	394-**4.9**

Phil Hankinson (6-8, Pennsylvania 1973) (wore Celtics #20)

Statistics	G	MIN	FGM-FGA-PCT	FTM-FTA-PCT	REBS	STL	AST	PTS-PPG
Celtics (1973-75)	31	187	56-114-.491	10-13-.769	57	4	6	122-**3.9**
NBA	same							

Reggie Hanson (6-8, Kentucky 1991) (wore Celtics #34)

Statistics	G	MIN	FGM-FGA-PCT	FTM-FTA-PCT	REBS	STL	AST	PTS-PPG
Celtics (1997-98)	8	26	3-6-.500	0-0-.000	6	2	1	6-**0.8**
NBA	same							

Bob (Gabby) Harris (6-7, Oklahoma A&M 1949) (wore Celtics #13 and #18)

Statistics	G	MIN	FGM-FGA-PCT	FTM-FTA-PCT	REBS	STL	AST	PTS-PPG
Celtics (1950-54)	263	5768*	636-1626-.391	461-734-.628	1824	NA	373	1733-**6.6**

*Minutes not available for 1950-1951 seasons

Statistics	G	MIN	FGM-FGA-PCT	FTM-FTA-PCT	REBS	STL	AST	PTS-PPG
NBA	325	5768*	804-2091-.385	601-957-.628	1824	NA	502	2209-**6.8**

Tony Harris (6-3, New Orleans 1990) (wore Celtics #43)

Statistics	G	MIN	FGM-FGA-PCT	FTM-FTA-PCT	REBS	STL	AST	PTS-PPG
Celtics (1993-95)	8	106	12-39-.308	31-34-.912	10	4	8	56-**7.0**
NBA	14	147	16-55-.290	33-38-.868	11	5	8	66-**4.7**

John Havlicek (6-5, Ohio State 1962) (wore Celtics #17, retired number in his honor)

Statistics	G	MIN	FGM-FGA-PCT	FTM-FTA-PCT	REBS	STL	AST	PTS-PPG
Celtics (1962-78)	1270	46471	10513-23930-.439	5369-6589-.815	8007	476*	6114	26395-**20.8**

*Steals not available before 1973-74 season

NBA   same

Michael Hawkins (6-0, Xavier-Ohio 1995) (wore Celtics #5)

Statistics	G	MIN	FGM-FGA-PCT	FTM-FTA-PCT	REBS	STL	AST	PTS-PPG
Celtics (1996-97)	29	326	29-68-.426	12-15-.800	31	16	64	80-**2.8**
NBA	53	529	43-108-.398	15-18-.833	56	19	91	116-2.2

John Hazen (6-2, Indiana State) (wore Celtics #3 and #10)

Statistics	G	MIN	FGM-FGA-PCT	FTM-FTA-PCT	REBS	STL	AST	PTS-PPG
Celtics (1948-49)	6	NA	6-17-.353	6-7-.857	NA	NA	3	18-**3.0**

NBA (BAA)   same

Tom Heinsohn (6-7, Holy Cross 1956) (wore Celtics #15, retired number in his honor)

Statistics	G	MIN	FGM-FGA-PCT	FTM-FTA-PCT	REBS	STL	AST	PTS-PPG
Celtics (1956-65)	654	19254	4773-11787-.405	2648-3353-.790	5749	NA	1318	12194-**18.6**

NBA   same

Tom Heinsohn (#15) goes up against the St. Louis Hawks' Bob Pettit (#9).

Dickie (Dixon) Hemric (6-6, Wake Forest 1955) (wore Celtics #20)

Statistics	G	MIN	FGM-FGA-PCT	FTM-FTA-PCT	REBS	STL	AST	PTS-PPG
Celtics (1955-57)	138	2384	270-717-.377	323-483-.669	703	NA	102	863-**6.3**
NBA	same							

Gerald Henderson (6-2, Virginia Commonwealth 1978) (wore Celtics #43)

Statistics	G	MIN	FGM-FGA-PCT	FTM-FTA-PCT	REBS	STL	AST	PTS-PPG
Celtics (1979-84)	400	8152	1467-3002-.489	559-768-.728	638	418	1107	3521-**8.8**
NBA	871	18856	3079-6526-.472	1412-1820-.776	1453	939	3141	7773-**8.9**

Conner Henry (6-7, California- Santa Barbara 1986) (wore Celtics #43)

Statistics	G	MIN	FGM-FGA-PCT	FTM-FTA-PCT	REBS	STL	AST	PTS-PPG
Celtics (1986-88)	46	312	49-131-.374	19-27-.704	37	7	39	132-**2.9**
NBA	93	756	108-286-.378	56-74-.757	83	21	102	305-**3.3**

Clarence (Kleggie) Hermsen (6-9, Minnesota 1948) (wore Celtics #10)

Statistics	G	MIN	FGM-FGA-PCT	FTM-FTA-PCT	REBS	STL	AST	PTS-PPG
Celtics (1950-53)	81*	62**	193-675-.283	158-242-.653	467	NA	96	544-**6.7**

*Also played for Tri-Cities Blackhawks in 1950-51 and Indianapolis Olympians in 1952-53
**Minutes not available before 1952-53 season

	G	MIN	FGM-FGA-PCT	FTM-FTA-PCT	REBS	STL	AST	PTS-PPG
NBA (NBL/BAA)	288	62**	962-3243-.297	745-1139-.654	467***	NA	366	2669-**9.3**

***Rebounds not available before 1950-51 season

Sidney Hertzberg (6-0, CCNY) (wore Celtics #4)

Statistics	G	MIN	FGM-FGA-PCT	FTM-FTA-PCT	REBS	STL	AST	PTS-PPG
Celtics (1949-51)	133	NA	481-1516-.317	366-461-.794	260*	NA	444	1328-**10.0**
NBA	293	NA	946-3166-.299	671-847-.792	260*	NA	618	2563-**8.7**

*Rebounds not available before 1950-51 season

Jack Hewson (6-6, Temple 1948) (wore Celtics #17)

Statistics	G	MIN	FGM-FGA-PCT	FTM-FTA-PCT	REBS	STL	AST	PTS-PPG
Celtics (1947-48)	24	NA	22-89-.247	21-30-.700	NA	NA	1	65-**2.7**
NBA (BAA)	same							

Mel Hirsch (5-6, Brooklyn 1943) (wore Celtics #3)

Statistics	G	MIN	FGM-FGA-PCT	FTM-FTA-PCT	REBS	STL	AST	PTS-PPG
Celtics (1946-47)	13	NA	9-45-.200	1-2-.500	NA	NA	10	19-**1.5**
NBA (BAA) same								

Charlie Hoefer (5-9, Hofstra) (wore Celtics #3)

Statistics	G	MIN	FGM-FGA-PCT	FTM-FTA-PCT	REBS	STL	AST	PTS-PPG
Celtics (1946-48)	42	NA	79-335-.236	63-101-.624	NA	NA	27	221-**5.3**
NBA (BAA)	65	NA	133-533-.250	95-147-.646	NA	NA	36	361-**5.6**

Bob Houbregs (6-8, Washington 1953) (wore Celtics #4)

Statistics	G	MIN	FGM-FGA-PCT	FTM-FTA-PCT	REBS	STL	AST	PTS-PPG
Celtics (1954-55)	64	1326*	148-386-.383	129-182-.709	297	NA	86	425-**6.6**

*Also played for Baltimore Bullets and Fort Wayne Pistons

	G	MIN	FGM-FGA-PCT	FTM-FTA-PCT	REBS	STL	AST	PTS-PPG
NBA	281	6725	906-2245-.404	799-1108-.721	1552	NA	500	2611-**9.3**

Bailey Howell (6-7, Mississippi State 1959) (wore Celtics #18)

Statistics	G	MIN	FGM-FGA-PCT	FTM-FTA-PCT	REBS	STL	AST	PTS-PPG
Celtics (1966-70)	323	9909	2290-4766-.480	1232-1666-.739	2717	NA	493	5812-**18.0**
NBA	950	30627	6515-13585-.480	4740-6224-.762	9383	NA	1853	17770-**18.7**

Jay Humphries (6-3, Colorado 1984) (wore Celtics #5)

Statistics	G	MIN	FGM-FGA-PCT	FTM-FTA-PCT	REBS	STL	AST	PTS-PPG
Celtics (1994-95)	6	52	4-9-.444	2-4-.500	3	2	10	10-**1.7**
NBA	776	22913	3498-7337-.477	1549-1981-.782	1993	1146	4330	8762-**11.3**

Tracy Jackson (6-6, Notre Dame 1981) (wore Celtics #11)

Statistics	G	MIN	FGM-FGA-PCT	FTM-FTA-PCT	REBS	STL	AST	PTS-PPG
Celtics (1981-82)	11	66	10-26-.385	6-10-.600	12	3	5	26-**2.4**
NBA	129	1797	279-602-.463	134-179-.749	243	78	132	694-**5.4**

John Janisch (6-3, Valparaiso 1946) (wore Celtics #17)

Statistics	G	MIN	FGM-FGA-PCT	FTM-FTA-PCT	REBS	STL	AST	PTS-PPG
Celtics (1947-48)	3	NA	1-7-.143	1-2-.500	NA	NA	0	3-**1.0**
NBA (BAA/NBL)	70	NA	297-1033-.288	140-214-.654	NA	NA	51	734-**10.5**

Dennis Johnson (6-4, Pepperdine 1976) (wore Celtics #3, retired number in his honor)

Statistics	G	MIN	FGM-FGA-PCT	FTM-FTA-PCT	REBS	STL	AST	PTS-PPG
Celtics (1983-90)	541	18321	2617-5873-.446	1527-1817-.840	1757	654	3486	6805-**12.6**
NBA	1100	35954	5832-13100-.445	3791-4754-.797	4249	1477	5499	15535-**14.1**

Rich Johnson (6-9, Grambling 1968) (wore Celtics #26)

Statistics	G	MIN	FGM-FGA-PCT	FTM-FTA-PCT	REBS	STL	AST	PTS-PPG
Celtics (1968-71)	97	1074	200-442-.452	57-93-.613	265	NA	39	457-**4.7**
NBA	same (also played in ABA with Florida Floridians, Carolina Cougars and Pittsburgh Pipers)							

Damon Jones (6-3, Houston 1998) (wore Celtics #13)

Statistics	G	MIN	FGM-FGA-PCT	FTM-FTA-PCT	REBS	STL	AST	PTS-PPG
Celtics (1997-98)	24	344	43-119-.361	14-17-.824	44	13	42	125-**5.2**
NBA	same							

Dontaé Jones (6-8, Mississippi State 1997) (wore Celtics #13)

Statistics	G	MIN	FGM-FGA-PCT	FTM-FTA-PCT	REBS	STL	AST	PTS-PPG
Celtics (1998-99)	15	91	19-57-.33	0-0-.000	9	2	5	44-**2.9**
NBA	same							

Johnny Jones (6-7, Los Angeles State 1967) (wore Celtics #27)

Statistics	G	MIN	FGM-FGA-PCT	FTM-FTA-PCT	REBS	STL	AST	PTS-PPG
Celtics (1967-68)	51	475	86-253-.340	42-68-.618	114	NA	26	214-**4.2**
NBA	same (also played in ABA with Kentucky Colonels)							

Dennis Johnson

Billy Knight

K.C. Jones (6-1, San Francisco 1956) (wore Celtics #27 and #25, retired in his honor)

Statistics	G	MIN	FGM-FGA-PCT	FTM-FTA-PCT	REBS	STL	AST	PTS-PPG
Celtics (1958-67)	676	17501	1919-4961-.387	1173-1814-.647	2399	NA	2908	5011-**7.4**
NBA	same							

Popeye Jones (6-8, Murray State 1992) (wore Celtics #4)

Statistics	G	MIN	FGM-FGA-PCT	FTM-FTA-PCT	REBS	STL	AST	PTS-PPG
Celtics (1997-99)	32*	558	72-178-.404	28-36-.777	154	8	33	174-**5.4**

*Total includes games also played with Toronto Raptors in 1997-98

NBA	340	9459	1224-2694-.454	387-521-.743	3020	132	511	2853-**8.4**

Sam Jones (6-4, North Carolina Central 1957) (wore Celtics #24, retired in his honor)

Statistics	G	MIN	FGM-FGA-PCT	FTM-FTA-PCT	REBS	STL	AST	PTS-PPG
Celtics (1993-94)	871	24285	6271-13745-.456	2869-3572-.803	4305	NA	2209	15411-**17.7**
NBA	same							

Jeff Judkins (6-6, Utah 1978) (wore Celtics #32)

Statistics	G	MIN	FGM-FGA-PCT	FTM-FTA-PCT	REBS	STL	AST	PTS-PPG
Celtics (1978-80)	146	2195	434-863-.503	181-222-.816	257	110	192	1060-**7.3**
NBA	272	3421	596-1248-.478	267-329-.812	427	147	282	1482-**5.4**

George Kaftan (6-3, Holy Cross 1948) (wore Celtics #9)

Statistics	G	MIN	FGM-FGA-PCT	FTM-FTA-PCT	REBS	STL	AST	PTS-PPG
Celtics (1948-50)	76	NA	315-850-.371	208-323-.644	NA	NA	206	838-**11.0**
NBA (BAA)	212	1335*	586-1585-.370	422-649-.650	424**	NA	399	1594-**7.5**

*Minutes not available before 1951-52 season
**Rebounds not available before 1950-51 season

Tony Kappen (5-10, No College) (wore Celtics #5)

Statistics	G	MIN	FGM-FGA-PCT	FTM-FTA-PCT	REBS	STL	AST	PTS-PPG
Celtics (1946-47)	18	NA	25-91-.275	24-38-.632	NA	NA	6	74-**4.1**
NBA (BAA)	59	NA	128-537-.238	128-161-.795	NA	NA	28	384-**6.5**

Gerard Kelly (6-2, Marshall) (wore Celtics #14 and #24)

Statistics	G	MIN	FGM-FGA-PCT	FTM-FTA-PCT	REBS	STL	AST	PTS-PPG
Celtics (1946-47)	43	NA	91-313-.291	74-111-.667	NA	NA	21	256-**6.0**
NBA (BAA)	46	NA	94-323-.291	74-112-.661	NA	NA	21	262-**5.7**

Tom Kelly (6-2, NYU 1948) (wore Celtics #6)

Statistics	G	MIN	FGM-FGA-PCT	FTM-FTA-PCT	REBS	STL	AST	PTS-PPG
Celtics (1948-49)	27	NA	73-218-.335	45-73-.616	NA	NA	38	191-**7.1**
NBA (BAA) same								

Toby Kimball (6-8, Connecticut 1965) (wore Celtics #26)

Statistics	G	MIN	FGM-FGA-PCT	FTM-FTA-PCT	REBS	STL	AST	PTS-PPG
Celtics (1966-67)	38	222	35-97-.361	27-40-.675	146	NA	13	97-**2.6**
NBA	571	10439	1383-3251-.425	704-1229-.573	3870	NA	571	3470-**6.1**

Maurice (Maury) King (6-3, Kansas 1957) (wore Celtics #19)

Statistics	G	MIN	FGM-FGA-PCT	FTM-FTA-PCT	REBS	STL	AST	PTS-PPG
Celtics (1959-60)	1	19	5-8-.625	0-1-.000	4	NA	2	10-**10.0**
NBA	38	973	99-249-.398	28-35-.800	106	NA	144	226-**5.9**

Stacey King (6-11, Oklahoma 1989) (wore Celtics #41)

Statistics	G	MIN	FGM-FGA-PCT	FTM-FTA-PCT	REBS	STL	AST	PTS-PPG
Celtics (1996-97)	5	33	5-7-.714	2-3-.667	9	0	1	12-**2.4**
NBA	438	7406	1071-2240-.478	673-952-.707	1460	173	387	2819-**6.4**

Greg Kite (#50) tries to score over the head of the Sixers' Charles Barkley.

Bob Kinney (6-6, Rice 1942) (wore Celtics #22)

Statistics	G	MIN	FGM-FGA-PCT	FTM-FTA-PCT	REBS	STL	AST	PTS-PPG
Celtics (1948-50)	81	NA	308-845-.364	255-411-.620	NA	NA	126	871-**10.8**
NBA (BAA/NBL)	118	NA	394-1116-.353	337-554-.608	NA	NA	177	1125-**9.5**

Greg Kite (6-11, Brigham Young 1983) (wore Celtics #50)

Statistics	G	MIN	FGM-FGA-PCT	FTM-FTA-PCT	REBS	STL	AST	PTS-PPG
Celtics (1983-88)	241	1916	153-378-.405	72-169-.426	472	27	70	378-**1.6**
NBA	669	10003	713-1617-.441	282-574-.491	2585	171	344	1709-**2.6**

Joe Kleine (7-0, Arkansas 1985) (wore Celtics #53)

Statistics	G	MIN	FGM-FGA-PCT	FTM-FTA-PCT	REBS	STL	AST	PTS-PPG
Celtics (1988-93)	329	4833	589-1274-.461	265-339-.782	1378	85	170	1447-**4.4**
NBA	989	15055	1928-4264-.452	854-1078-.792	4052	268	632	4723-**4.8**

Billy Knight (6-6, Pittsburgh 1974) (wore Celtics #35)

Statistics	G	MIN	FGM-FGA-PCT	FTM-FTA-PCT	REBS	STL	AST	PTS-PPG
Celtics (1978-79)	40	1119	219-436-.502	118-146-.808	173	31	66	556-**13.9**
NBA	671	18412	4064-8026-.506	2399-2892-.830	3037	627	1435	10561-**15.7**

Travis Knight (7-0, Connecticut 1996) (wore Celtics #40)

Statistics	G	MIN	FGM-FGA-PCT	FTM-FTA-PCT	REBS	STL	AST	PTS-PPG
Celtics (1997-98)	74	1503	193-438-.441	81-103-.786	365	54	104	482-**6.5**
NBA	182	3184	400-843-.474	165-232-.711	812	106	174	980-**5.4**

Bart Kofoed (6-4, Kearney State 1987) (wore Celtics #12)

Statistics	G	MIN	FGM-FGA-PCT	FTM-FTA-PCT	REBS	STL	AST	PTS-PPG
Celtics (1992-93)	7	41	3-13-.231	11-14-.786	1	2	10	17-**2.4**
NBA	111	702	58-150-.387	43-70-.614	56	19	108	162-**1.5**

Harold Kottman (6-8, Culver-Stockton 1946) (wore Celtics #9)

Statistics	G	MIN	FGM-FGA-PCT	FTM-FTA-PCT	REBS	STL	AST	PTS-PPG
Celtics (1946-47)	53	NA	59-188-.314	47-101-.465	NA	NA	17	165-**3.1**
NBA (BAA)	same							

Wayne Kreklow (6-4, Drake 1979) (wore Celtics #20)

Statistics	G	MIN	FGM-FGA-PCT	FTM-FTA-PCT	REBS	STL	AST	PTS-PPG
Celtics (1980-81)	25	100	11-47-.234	7-10-.700	12	2	9	30-**1.2**
NBA	same							

Steve Kuberski (6-8, Bradley 1969) (wore Celtics #11 and #33)

Statistics	G	MIN	FGM-FGA-PCT	FTM-FTA-PCT	REBS	STL	AST	PTS-PPG
Celtics (1969-78)	499	7285	1185-2829-.419	559-731-.765	1998	26*	300	2929-**5.9**

*Steals not available before 1973-74 season

NBA	568	7897	1254-3005-.417	606-790-.767	2146	38*	338	3114-**5.5**

Frank Kudelka (6-2, St. Mary's-California) (wore Celtics #21)

Statistics	G	MIN	FGM-FGA-PCT	FTM-FTA-PCT	REBS	STL	AST	PTS-PPG
Celtics (1950-51)	62*	NA	179-518-.346	83-119-.697	158	NA	105	441-**7.1**

*Also played with Washington Capitols

NBA	228	2150**	614-1853-.331	414-585-.708	521***	NA	490	1642-**7.2**

**Minutes not available before 1951-52 season
***Rebounds anot available before 1950-51 season

Tony Lavelli (6-3, Yale 1949) (wore Celtics #4 and #11)

Statistics	G	MIN	FGM-FGA-PCT	FTM-FTA-PCT	REBS	STL	AST	PTS-PPG
Celtics (1949-50)	56	NA	162-436-.372	168-197-.853	NA	NA	40	492-**8.8**
NBA	86	NA	194-529-.367	203-238-.853	59*	NA	63	591-**6.9**

*Rebounds not available before 1950-51 season

Ed Leede (6-3, Dartmouth 1948) (wore Celtics #5)

Statistics	G	MIN	FGM-FGA-PCT	FTM-FTA-PCT	REBS	STL	AST	PTS-PPG
Celtics (1949-51)	121	NA	293-877-.335	363-505-.719	118*	NA	225	949-**7.8**

*Rebounds not available before 1950-51 season
NBA same

Reggie Lewis (6-7, Northeastern 1987) (wore Celtics #35, retired in his honor)

Statistics	G	MIN	FGM-FGA-PCT	FTM-FTA-PCT	REBS	STL	AST	PTS-PPG
Celtics (1987-93)	450	14674	3198-6550-.488	1479-1794-.824	1938	569	1153	7902-**17.6**
NBA	same							

Todd Lichti (6-4, Stanford 1989) (wore Celtics #30)

Statistics	G	MIN	FGM-FGA-PCT	FTM-FTA-PCT	REBS	STL	AST	PTS-PPG
Celtics (1993-94)	4	48	6-14-.429	7-14-.500	8	5	6	19-**4.8**
NBA	237	4240	733-1595-.460	385-488-.789	505	179	325	1870-**7.9**

Alton Lister (7-0, Arizona State 1981) (wore Celtics #53)

Statistics	G	MIN	FGM-FGA-PCT	FTM-FTA-PCT	REBS	STL	AST	PTS-PPG
Celtics (1995-97)	110	1163	79-173-.453	62-93-.686	419	14	28	220-**2.0**
NBA	946	18921	2511-4899-.513	1269-2126-.597	5985	350	913	6292-**6.7**

Brad Lohaus (7-0, Iowa 1987) (wore Celtics #54)

Statistics	G	MIN	FGM-FGA-PCT	FTM-FTA-PCT	REBS	STL	AST	PTS-PPG
Celtics (1987-89)	118	1456	239-516-.463	85-108-.787	280	41	98	566-**4.8**
NBA	647	10276	1535-3486-.440	377-513-.735	1377	306	709	3835-**5.9**

Jim Loscutoff (6-5, Oregon 1955) (wore Celtics #18, retired in his honor)

Statistics	G	MIN	FGM-FGA-PCT	FTM-FTA-PCT	REBS	STL	AST	PTS-PPG
Celtics (1955-64)	511	9431	1333-3868-.345	490-750-.653	2808	NA	353	3156-**6.2**
NBA	same							

Clyde Lovellette (6-9, Kansas 1952) (wore Celtics #4 and #34)

Statistics	G	MIN	FGM-FGA-PCT	FTM-FTA-PCT	REBS	STL	AST	PTS-PPG
Celtics (1962-64)	106	1005	289-681-.424	118-155-.761	303	NA	51	696-**6.6**
NBA	704	19075	4784-10795-.443	2379-3141-.757	6663	NA	1097	11947-**17.0**

Albert (Al) Lucas (6-3, Fordham) (wore Celtics #20)

Statistics	G	MIN	FGM-FGA-PCT	FTM-FTA-PCT	REBS	STL	AST	PTS-PPG
Celtics (1948-49)	2	NA	1-3-.333	0-0-.000	NA	NA	0	2-**1.0**

NBA (BAA) same (also played in NBL with Sheybogan Redskins)

Ed Macauley (6-8, St. Louis 1949) (wore Celtics #22, retired in his honor)

Statistics	G	MIN	FGM-FGA-PCT	FTM-FTA-PCT	REBS	STL	AST	PTS-PPG
Celtics (1950-56)	416	13385*	2579-5796-.447	2724-3518-.774	3367	NA	1521	7882-**18.9**

*Minutes not available before 1951-52 season

NBA	641	18071*	3742-8589-.436	3750-4929-.761	4325	NA	2079	11234-**17.5**

John Mahnken (6-8, Georgetown 1945) (wore Celtics #16)

Statistics	G	MIN	FGM-FGA-PCT	FTM-FTA-PCT	REBS	STL	AST	PTS-PPG
Celtics (1949-53)	153	1352*	198-647-.306	88-135-.652	314*	NA	180	484-**3.2**

*Minutes and rebounds not available before 1951-52 season

NBA	414	1352*	966-3557-.272	456-702-.650	533*	NA	539	2388-**5.8**

Francis (Mo) Mahoney (6-4, Brown 1950) (wore Celtics #19)

Statistics	G	MIN	FGM-FGA-PCT	FTM-FTA-PCT	REBS	STL	AST	PTS-PPG
Celtics (1952-53)	6	34	4-10-.400	4-5-.800	7	NA	1	12-**2.0**
NBA	8	45	4-12-.333	4-5-.800	9	NA	2	12-**1.5**

Reggie Lewis

Pete Maravich

Pete (Pistol Pete) Maravich (6-5, LSU 1970) (wore Celtics #44)

Statistics	G	MIN	FGM-FGA-PCT	FTM-FTA-PCT	REBS	STL	AST	PTS-PPG
Celtics (1979-80)	26	442	123-249-.494	50-55-.909	38	9	29	299-**11.5**
NBA	658	24316	6187-14025-.441	3564-4344-.820	2747	587*	3563	15948-**24.2**

*Steals not available before 1973-74 season

Saul Mariaschin (5-11, Harvard 1947) (wore Celtics #4)

Statistics	G	MIN	FGM-FGA-PCT	FTM-FTA-PCT	REBS	STL	AST	PTS-PPG
Celtics (1947-48)	43	NA	125-463-.270	83-117-.709	NA	NA	60	333-**7.7**
NBA (BAA)	same							

Tony Massenburg (6-9, Maryland 1990) (wore Celtics #41)

Statistics	G	MIN	FGM-FGA-PCT	FTM-FTA-PCT	REBS	STL	AST	PTS-PPG
Celtics (1991-92)	7	46	4-9-.444	2-4-.500	9	0	0	10-**1.4**
NBA	266	5795	752-1570-.479	455-658-.691	1407	119	124	1959-**7.4**

Cedric (Cornbread) Maxwell (6-8, UNC-Charlotte 1977) (wore Celtics #30 and #31)

Statistics	G	MIN	FGM-FGA-PCT	FTM-FTA-PCT	REBS	STL	AST	PTS-PPG
Celtics (1977-85)	607	18495	2786-4984-.559	2738-3496-.783	4023	549	1390	8311-**13.7**
NBA	835	23769	3433-6293-.546	3598-4592-.784	5261	671	1862	10465-**12.5**

Bob McAdoo (6-9, North Carolina 1973) (wore Celtics #11)

Statistics	G	MIN	FGM-FGA-PCT	FTM-FTA-PCT	REBS	STL	AST	PTS-PPG
Celtics (1978-79)	20	637	167-334-.500	77-115-.670	141	12	40	411-**20.6**
NBA	852	28327	7420-14751-.503	3944-5229-.754	8048	751	1951	18787-**22.1**

John McCarthy (6-1, Canisius 1956) (wore Celtics #21)

Statistics	G	MIN	FGM-FGA-PCT	FTM-FTA-PCT	REBS	STL	AST	PTS-PPG
Celtics (1963-64)	28	206	16-48-.333	5-13-.385	35	NA	24	37-**1.3**
NBA	316	8828	958-2714-.353	534-859-.622	1145	NA	1184	2450-**7.8**

Walter McCarty (6-10, Kentucky 1996) (wore Celtics #0)

Statistics	G	MIN	FGM-FGA-PCT	FTM-FTA-PCT	REBS	STL	AST	PTS-PPG
Celtics (1997-99)	114	2999	359-907-.396	184-251-.733	479	134	217	969-**8.5**
NBA	149	3191	385-975-.395	192-265-.725	502	141	230	1033-**6.9**

Xavier McDaniel (6-7, Wichita State 1985) (wore Celtics #31)

Statistics	G	MIN	FGM-FGA-PCT	FTM-FTA-PCT	REBS	STL	AST	PTS-PPG
Celtics (1992-95)	232	5616	1090-2309-.472	424-579-.732	1189	150	397	2626-**11.3**
NBA	788	23851	5525-11300-.489	2116-2949-.718	4964	752	1701	13235-**16.8**

Glenn McDonald (6-6, Long Beach State 1974) (wore Celtics #30)

Statistics	G	MIN	FGM-FGA-PCT	FTM-FTA-PCT	REBS	STL	AST	PTS-PPG
Celtics (1974-76)	137	1414	261-638-.409	68-93-.731	203	47	92	590-**4.3**
NBA	146	1493	269-672-.400	71-97-.732	219	51	99	609-**4.2**

Kevin McHale (6-10, Minnesota 1980) (wore Celtics #32, retired in his honor)

Statistics	G	MIN	FGM-FGA-PCT	FTM-FTA-PCT	REBS	STL	AST	PTS-PPG
Celtics (1980-93)	971	30118	6830-12334-.554	3634-4554-.798	7122	344	1670	17335-**17.9**
NBA	same							

Horace (Bones) McKinney (6-6, North Carolina 1946) (wore Celtics #17)

Statistics	G	MIN	FGM-FGA-PCT	FTM-FTA-PCT	REBS	STL	AST	PTS-PPG
Celtics (1950-52)	107*	1083**	238-745-.319	123-161-.764	373***	NA	196	599-**5.6**

*Also played with Washington Capitols in 1950-51

NBA	318	1083**	1145-3844-.298	704-990-.711	373***	NA	503	2994-**9.4**

**Minutes not available before 1951-52 season
***Rebounds not available before 1950-51 season

Dick Mehen (6-6, Tennessee 1947) (wore Celtics #13)

Statistics	G	MIN	FGM-FGA-PCT	FTM-FTA-PCT	REBS	STL	AST	PTS-PPG
Celtics (1950-51)	66*	NA	192-532-.361	90-123-.732	223	NA	188	474-**7.2**

*Also played with Baltimore Bullets and Fort Wayne Pistons in 1950-51

NBA	193	2294**	832-2182-.381	405-571-.709	505***	NA	550	2069-**10.7**

**Minutes not available before 1951-52 season   ***Rebounds not available before 1950-51 season

Ron Mercer (6-7, Kentucky 1999) (wore Celtics #5)

Statistics	G	MIN	FGM-FGA-PCT	FTM-FTA-PCT	REBS	STL	AST	PTS-PPG
Celtics (1997-99)	121	4213	820-1852-.443	271-329-.824	435	192	280	1919-**15.9**
NBA	same							

Ed Mikan (6-8, DePaul 1948) (wore Celtics #16)

Statistics	G	MIN	FGM-FGA-PCT	FTM-FTA-PCT	REBS	STL	AST	PTS-PPG
Celtics (1953-54)	9	71	8-24-.333	5-9-.556	20	NA	3	21-**2.3**
NBA	323	2779*	799-2493-.320	565-747-.756	1093**	NA	296	2163-**6.7**

*Minutes not available before 1951-52 season
**Rebounds not available before 1950-51 season

Dirk Minniefield (6-3, Kentucky 1983) (wore Celtics #11)

Statistics	G	MIN	FGM-FGA-PCT	FTM-FTA-PCT	REBS	STL	AST	PTS-PPG
Celtics (1987-88)	61	868	83-173-.480	27-32-.844	75	44	190	196-**3.2**
NBA	222	3801	493-1050-.470	176-238-.739	367	196	845	1187-**5.3**

Greg Minor (6-6, Louisville 1994) (wore Celtics #9)

Statistics	G	MIN	FGM-FGA-PCT	FTM-FTA-PCT	REBS	STL	AST	PTS-PPG
Celtics (1994-99)	277	5144	794-1662-.478	290-378-.767	741	156	384	1902-**6.9**
NBA	same							

Mark Minor (6-5, Ohio State 1972) (wore Celtics #27)

Statistics	G	MIN	FGM-FGA-PCT	FTM-FTA-PCT	REBS	STL	AST	PTS-PPG
Celtics (1972-73)	4	20	1-4-.250	3-4-.750	4	NA	2	5-**1.3**
NBA	same							

Xavier McDaniel

Eric Montross (7-0, North Carolina 1994) (wore Celtics #0)

Statistics	G	MIN	FGM-FGA-PCT	FTM-FTA-PCT	REBS	STL	AST	PTS-PPG
Celtics (1994-96)	139	3747	503-921-.546	217-396-.548	918	48	79	1223-**8.8**
NBA	311	6843	765-1494-.512	265-530-.500	1774	93	165	1795-**5.8**

Rex Morgan (6-5, Jacksonville 1970) (wore Celtics #20)

Statistics	G	MIN	FGM-FGA-PCT	FTM-FTA-PCT	REBS	STL	AST	PTS-PPG
Celtics (1970-72)	62	416	57-152-.375	58-85-.682	91	NA	39	172-**2.8**
NBA	same							

Dwight Morrison (6-8, Idaho 1954) (wore Celtics #15)

Statistics	G	MIN	FGM-FGA-PCT	FTM-FTA-PCT	REBS	STL	AST	PTS-PPG
Celtics (1954-56)	142	2137	209-524-.399	116-204-.569	796	NA	135	534-**3.8**
NBA	155	2216	218-550-.396	119-208-.572	822	NA	135	555-**3.6**

Joe Mullaney (6-0, Holy Cross 1959) (wore Celtics #17)

Statistics	G	MIN	FGM-FGA-PCT	FTM-FTA-PCT	REBS	STL	AST	PTS-PPG
Celtics (1949-50)	37	NA	9-70-.129	12-15-.800	NA	NA	52	30-**0.8**
NBA	same							

Todd Mundt (7-0, Delta State 1993) (wore Celtics #51)

Statistics	G	MIN	FGM-FGA-PCT	FTM-FTA-PCT	REBS	STL	AST	PTS-PPG
Celtics (1995-96)	33	151	16-41-.390	5-8-.625	28	2	3	37-**1.1**
NBA	same							

George Munroe (5-11, Dartmouth 1943) (wore Celtics #6)

Statistics	G	MIN	FGM-FGA-PCT	FTM-FTA-PCT	REBS	STL	AST	PTS-PPG
Celtics (1947-48)	21	NA	27-91-.297	17-26-.654	NA	NA	3	71-**3.4**
NBA (BAA)	80	NA	191-714-.268	103-159-.648	NA	NA	20	485-**6.1**

Dick Murphy (6-1, Manhattan) (wore Celtics #5)

Statistics	G	MIN	FGM-FGA-PCT	FTM-FTA-PCT	REBS	STL	AST	PTS-PPG
Celtics (1946-47)	7	NA	1-17-.059	0-4-.000	NA	NA	3	2-**0.3**
NBA (BAA)	31	NA	15-75-.200	4-9-.444	NA	NA	8	34-**1.1**

Willie Naulls (6-6, UCLA 1956) (wore Celtics #12)

Statistics	G	MIN	FGM-FGA-PCT	FTM-FTA-PCT	REBS	STL	AST	PTS-PPG
Celtics (1963-66)	220	4307	951-2370-.401	372-464-.802	1011	NA	208	2274-**10.3**
NBA	716	20620	4526-11145-.406	2253-2774-.812	6508	NA	1114	11305-**15.8**

Don Nelson (6-6, Iowa 1962) (wore Celtics #19, retired in his honor)

Statistics	G	MIN	FGM-FGA-PCT	FTM-FTA-PCT	REBS	STL	AST	PTS-PPG
Celtics (1965-76)	872	18970	3717-7672-.484	2534-3296-.769	4517	43*	1354	9968-**11.4**

*Steals not available before 1973-74

NBA	1053	21685	4017-8373-.480	2864-3744-.765	5192	65	1526	10898-**10.3**

Jack Nichols (6-7, Washington 1948) (wore Celtics #16)

Statistics	G	MIN	FGM-FGA-PCT	FTM-FTA-PCT	REBS	STL	AST	PTS-PPG
Celtics (1953-58)	329	8077	1107-3004-.369	618-798-.774	2197	NA	556	2932-**8.6**
NBA	504	10703*	2013-5462-.369	1219-1620-.752	2782**	NA	964	5245-**10.4**

*Minutes not available before 1952-53 season
**Rebounds not available before 1950-51 season

Rich Niemann (7-0, St. Louis 1968) (wore Celtics #27)

Statistics	G	MIN	FGM-FGA-PCT	FTM-FTA-PCT	REBS	STL	AST	PTS-PPG
Celtics (1969-70)	6	18	2-5-.400	2-2-1.000	6	NA	2	6-**1.0**
NBA	40	290	46-111-.414	21-27-.778	106	NA	18	113-**2.8**

Bob (Bevo) Nordmann (6-10, St. Louis 1961) (wore Celtics #34)

Statistics	G	MIN	FGM-FGA-PCT	FTM-FTA-PCT	REBS	STL	AST	PTS-PPG
Celtics (1964-65)	3	25	3-5-.600	0-0-.000	8	NA	3	6-**2.0**
NBA	133	1628	237-516-.459	97-198-.490	517	NA	73	571-**4.3**

George Nostrand (6-8, Wyoming 1946) (wore Celtics #3)

Statistics	G	MIN	FGM-FGA-PCT	FTM-FTA-PCT	REBS	STL	AST	PTS-PPG
Celtics (1948-50)	45	NA	127-403-.315	118-186-.634	NA	NA	60	372-**8.3**
NBA (BAA)	221	NA	678-2222-.305	448-832-.538	NA	NA	184	1804-**8.2**

Stan Noszka (6-1, Duquesne 1943) (wore Celtics #10 and #11)

Statistics	G	MIN	FGM-FGA-PCT	FTM-FTA-PCT	REBS	STL	AST	PTS-PPG
Celtics (1947-49)	52	NA	57-220-.259	39-65-.600	NA	NA	29	153-**2.9**
NBA (BAA)	110	NA	256-913-.280	148-222-.667	NA	NA	68	660-**6.0**

Julius Nwosu (6-10, Liberty 1993) (wore Celtics #0)

Statistics	G	MIN	FGM-FGA-PCT	FTM-FTA-PCT	REBS	STL	AST	PTS-PPG
Celtics (1996-97)	Injured and did not play							
NBA	23	84	9-28-.321	13-17-.765	24	0	3	31-**1.3**

Dermott (Dermie) O'Connell (6-0, Holy Cross 1949) (wore Celtics #7)

Statistics	G	MIN	FGM-FGA-PCT	FTM-FTA-PCT	REBS	STL	AST	PTS-PPG
Celtics (1948-50)	58	NA	159-590-.269	63-114-.553	NA	NA	129	381-**6.6**
NBA (BAA)	82	NA	198-740-.268	77-145-.531	NA	NA	156	473-**5.8**

Jimmy Oliver (6-6, Purdue 1991) (wore Celtics #27)

Statistics	G	MIN	FGM-FGA-PCT	FTM-FTA-PCT	REBS	STL	AST	PTS-PPG
Celtics (1993-94)	44	540	89-214-.426	25-33-.758	46	16	33	216-**4.9**
NBA	75	835	132-325-.406	44-57-.772	78	27	54	323-**4.3**

Enoch (Bud) Olsen (6-8, Louisville 1962) (wore Celtics #25)

Statistics	G	MIN	FGM-FGA-PCT	FTM-FTA-PCT	REBS	STL	AST	PTS-PPG
Celtics (1968-69)	7	43	7-19-.368	0-6-.000	14	NA	4	14-**2.0**
NBA	369	4218	653-1542-.423	286-517-.553	1111	NA	293	1592-**4.3**

Togo Palazzi (6-4, Holy Cross 1964) (wore Celtics #12)

Statistics	G	MIN	FGM-FGA-PCT	FTM-FTA-PCT	REBS	STL	AST	PTS-PPG
Celtics (1954-57)	169*	2220	456-1197-.381	266-359-.741	590	NA	121	1178-**7.0**
*Also played with Syracuse Nationals in 1956-57								
NBA	324	4344	937-2429-.386	508-696-.730	1113	NA	233	2382-**7.4**

Robert Parish (7-1, Centenary 1976) (wore Celtics #00, retired number in his honor)

Statistics	G	MIN	FGM-FGA-PCT	FTM-FTA-PCT	REBS	STL	AST	PTS-PPG
Celtics (1980-94)	1106	34977	7483-13558-.552	3279-4491-.730	7601	873	1679	18245-**16.5**
NBA	1611*	45704	9614-17914-.537	4106-5694-.721	14715	1219	2180	23334-**14.5**
*NBA Record								

Jim Paxson (6-6, Dayton 1979) (wore Celtics #4)

Statistics	G	MIN	FGM-FGA-PCT	FTM-FTA-PCT	REBS	STL	AST	PTS-PPG
Celtics (1987-90)	157	2959	487-1058-.460	211-254-.831	178	94	293	1196-**7.6**
NBA	784	21357	4545-9134-.498	2011-2493-.807	1593	951	2300	11199-**14.3**

Andy Phillip (6-2, Illinois 1947) (wore Celtics #17)

Statistics	G	MIN	FGM-FGA-PCT	FTM-FTA-PCT	REBS	STL	AST	PTS-PPG
Celtics (1956-58)	137	2640	202-550-.367	130-208-.625	339	NA	289	534-**3.9**
NBA	701	15378*	2323-6318-.368	1738-2499-.695	2395**	NA	3759	6384-**9.1**

*Minutes not available before 1951-52 season

**Rebounds not available before 1949-50 season

Robert Parish

Ed Pinckney

Gary Phillips (6-3, Houston 1961) (wore Celtics #21)

Statistics	G	MIN	FGM-FGA-PCT	FTM-FTA-PCT	REBS	STL	AST	PTS-PPG
Celtics (1961-62)	67	713	110-310-.355	50-86-.581	107	NA	64	270-**4.0**
NBA	348	6932	926-2500-.370	467-742-.629	903	NA	665	2319-**6.7**

Paul Pierce (6-7, Kansas 1999) (wore Celtics #34)

Statistics	G	MIN	FGM-FGA-PCT	FTM-FTA-PCT	REBS	STL	AST	PTS-PPG
Celtics (1999)	48	1632	284-647-.439	139-195-.713	309	82	115	791-**16.5**
NBA	same							

Ed Pinckney (6-9, Villanova 1985) (wore Celtics #54)

Statistics	G	MIN	FGM-FGA-PCT	FTM-FTA-PCT	REBS	STL	AST	PTS-PPG
Celtics (1988-94)	340	6517	725-1359-.533	610-757-.806	1799	256	282	2060-**6.1**
NBA	793	15698	1915-3577-.535	1548-2024-.765	3952	612	727	5378-**6.8**

Dave Popson (6-10, North Carolina 1987) (wore Celtics #42)

Statistics	G	MIN	FGM-FGA-PCT	FTM-FTA-PCT	REBS	STL	AST	PTS-PPG
Celtics (1990-91)	19	64	13-32-.406	9-10-.900	14	1	2	35-**1.8**
NBA	41	196	32-79-.405	12-16-.750	46	4	13	76-**1.9**

Vitaly Potapenko (6-10, Wright State 1997) (wore Celtics #52)

Statistics	G	MIN	FGM-FGA-PCT	FTM-FTA-PCT	REBS	STL	AST	PTS-PPG
Celtics (1999)	50*	1394	204-412-.495	91-155-.587	332	35	75	499-**10.0**
*Total includes games also played with Cleveland Cavaliers in 1999								
NBA	210	4044	624-1323-.472	285-424-.672	862	88	172	1534-**7.3**

Kevin Pritchard (6-3, Kansas 1990) (wore Celtics #12)

Statistics	G	MIN	FGM-FGA-PCT	FTM-FTA-PCT	REBS	STL	AST	PTS-PPG
Celtics (1991-92)	11	136	16-34-.471	14-18-.778	11	3	30	46-**4.2**
NBA	73	909	104-263-.395	76-95-.800	76	33	111	289-**4.0**

Dino Radja (6-11, Croatia) (wore Celtics #40)

Statistics	G	MIN	FGM-FGA-PCT	FTM-FTA-PCT	REBS	STL	AST	PTS-PPG
Celtics (1993-97)	224	7308	1516-3052-.497	701-954-.735	1883	201	356	3733-**16.7**
NBA	same							

Frank Ramsey (6-3, Kentucky 1953) (wore Celtics #23, retired in his honor)

Statistics	G	MIN	FGM-FGA-PCT	FTM-FTA-PCT	REBS	STL	AST	PTS-PPG
Celtics (1954-64)	623	15330	2949-7382-.399	2480-3083-.804	3410	NA	1134	8378-**13.**
NBA	same							

John Richter (6-9, North Carolina State 1959) (wore Celtics #16)

Statistics	G	MIN	FGM-FGA-PCT	FTM-FTA-PCT	REBS	STL	AST	PTS-PPG
Celtics (1959-60)	66	808	113-332-.340	59-117-.504	312	NA	27	285-**4.3**
NBA	same							

Mel Riebe (5-11, Ohio University) (wore Celtics #7 and #9)

Statistics	G	MIN	FGM-FGA-PCT	FTM-FTA-PCT	REBS	STL	AST	PTS-PPG
Celtics (1947-49)	81	NA	374-1242-.301	164-270-.607	NA	NA	145	912-**10.0**
NBA (BAA)	146	NA	650-2140-.304	275-443-.621	NA	NA	212	1575-**10.8**

Eric Riley (7-0, Michigan 1993) (wore Celtics #44)

Statistics	G	MIN	FGM-FGA-PCT	FTM-FTA-PCT	REBS	STL	AST	PTS-PPG
Celtics (1999)	35	337	28-54-.519	22-31-.710	99	9	13	78-**2.2**
NBA	186	1968	218-478-.456	138-196-.704	479	54	60	574-**3.1**

Arnie Risen (6-9, Ohio State) (wore Celtics #19)

Statistics	G	MIN	FGM-FGA-PCT	FTM-FTA-PCT	REBS	STL	AST	PTS-PPG
Celtics (1955-58)	174	3651	442-1197-.369	390-563-.693	1199	NA	191	1274-**7.3**
NBA	637	12690*	2610-6850-.381	2413-3451-.699	5011**	NA	1058	7633-**12.0**

*Minutes not available before 1951-52 season

**Rebounds not available before 1950-51 season

Ramon Rivas (6-10, Temple 1988) (wore Celtics #45)

Statistics	G	MIN	FGM-FGA-PCT	FTM-FTA-PCT	REBS	STL	AST	PTS-PPG
Celtics (1988-89)	28	91	12-31-.387	16-25-.640	24	4	3	40-**1.4**
NBA	same							

Bill Roberts (6-9, Wyoming) (wore Celtics #5)

Statistics	G	MIN	FGM-FGA-PCT	FTM-FTA-PCT	REBS	STL	AST	PTS-PPG
Celtics (1948-49)	26	NA	36-109-.330	9-19-.474	NA	NA	13	81-**3.1**
NBA (BAA)	117	NA	166-489-.339	72-102-.706	NA	NA	65	404-**3.5**

Fred Roberts (6-10, Brigham Young 1982) (wore Celtics #31)

Statistics	G	MIN	FGM-FGA-PCT	FTM-FTA-PCT	REBS	STL	AST	PTS-PPG
Celtics (1986-88)	147	2111	300-600-.500	252-318-.792	352	38	143	852-**5.8**
NBA	752	14123	2175-4312-.504	1345-1686-.798	2217	390	943	5738-**7.6**

Rick Robey (6-10, Kentucky 1978) (wore Celtics #53)

Statistics	G	MIN	FGM-FGA-PCT	FTM-FTA-PCT	REBS	STL	AST	PTS-PPG
Celtics (1978-83)	339	6442	1122-2241-.510	541-858-.631	1693	154	433	2829-**8.3**
NBA	493	8824	1498-2993-.501	726-1117-.650	2301	220	611	3723-**7.6**

Larry Robinson (6-5, Centenary 1990) (wore Celtics #4)

Statistics	G	MIN	FGM-FGA-PCT	FTM-FTA-PCT	REBS	STL	AST	PTS-PPG
Celtics (1991-92)	1	6	1-5-.200	0-0-.000	2	0	1	2-**2.0**
NBA	47	519	79-191-.414	21-40-.525	66	24	45	181-**3.9**

Curtis Rowe

Charlie Scott

Roy Rogers (6-10, Alabama 1996) (wore Celtics #99)

Statistics	G	MIN	FGM-FGA-PCT	FTM-FTA-PCT	REBS	STL	AST	PTS-PPG
Celtics (1997-98)	9	37	3-8-.375	1-2-.500	5	2	1	7-**0.8**
NBA	91	1885	247-491-.503	55-96-.573	391	23	47	550-**6.0**

Ken Rollins (6-0, Kentucky 1948) (wore Celtics #4)

Statistics	G	MIN	FGM-FGA-PCT	FTM-FTA-PCT	REBS	STL	AST	PTS-PPG
Celtics (1952-53)	43	426	38-115-.330	22-27-.815	45	NA	46	98-**2.3**
NBA	168	426*	326-1056-.309	165-220-.750	45*	NA	344	817-**4.9**

*Minutes and rebounds not available before 1952-53 season

Curtis Rowe (6-7, UCLA 1971) (wore Celtics #41)

Statistics	G	MIN	FGM-FGA-PCT	FTM-FTA-PCT	REBS	STL	AST	PTS-PPG
Celtics (1976-79)	183	4323	589-1251-.471	288-404-.714	1308	53	221	1466-**8.0**
NBA	590	18277	2821-5847-.482	1231-1756-.701	4264	199	932	6873-**11.6**

Bill Russell (6-10, San Francisco 1956) (wore Celtics #6, retired number in his honor)

Statistics	G	MIN	FGM-FGA-PCT	FTM-FTA-PCT	REBS	STL	AST	PTS-PPG
Celtics (1956-69)	963	40726	5687-12930-.440	3148-5614-.561	21620	NA	4100	14522-**15.1**
NBA	same							

Ed Sadowski (6-5, Seton Hall 1940) (wore Celtics #22)

Statistics	G	MIN	FGM-FGA-PCT	FTM-FTA-PCT	REBS	STL	AST	PTS-PPG
Celtics (1947-48)	47	NA	308-953-.323	294-422-.697	NA	NA	74	910-**19.4**
NBA (BAA)	229	NA	1276-3605-.354	1027-1473-.697	NA	NA	416	3579-**15.6**

Kenny Sailors (5-10, Wyoming 1946) (wore Celtics #13)

Statistics	G	MIN	FGM-FGA-PCT	FTM-FTA-PCT	REBS	STL	AST	PTS-PPG
Celtics (1950-51)	60	NA	181-533-.340	131-180-.728	120	NA	150	493-**8.2**
NBA	276	NA	1255-3813-.329	970-1362-.712	120*	NA	781	3480-**12.6**

*Rebounds not available before 1950-51 season

Bill Russell

Frankie Sanders (6-6, Southern University 1978) (wore Celtics #45)

Statistics	G	MIN	FGM-FGA-PCT	FTM-FTA-PCT	REBS	STL	AST	PTS-PPG
Celtics (1978-79)	24	216	55-119-.462	22-27-.815	51	7	17	132-**5.5**
NBA	69	665	139-323-.430	74-90-.822	131	37	69	352-**5.1**

Tom Sanders (6-6, NYU 1960) (wore Celtics #16, retired in his honor)

Statistics	G	MIN	FGM-FGA-PCT	FTM-FTA-PCT	REBS	STL	AST	PTS-PPG
Celtics (1960-73)	916	22164	3416-7988-.428	1934-2520-.767	5798	NA	1026	8766-**9.6**
NBA	same							

Woodrow (Woodie) Sauldsberry (6-7, Texas Southern 1957) (wore Celtics #18)

Statistics	G	MIN	FGM-FGA-PCT	FTM-FTA-PCT	REBS	STL	AST	PTS-PPG
Celtics (1965-66)	39	530	80-249-.321	11-22-.500	142	NA	15	171-**4.4**
NBA	462	12788	2189-6288-.348	552-905-.610	3618	NA	498	4930-**10.7**

Fred (James) Saunders (6-7, Syracuse 1974) (wore Celtics #20)

Statistics	G	MIN	FGM-FGA-PCT	FTM-FTA-PCT	REBS	STL	AST	PTS-PPG
Celtics (1976-78)	94	1294	214-486-.440	49-70-.700	260	33	96	477-**5.1**
NBA	210	2899	487-1099-.443	133-195-.682	624	93	224	1107-**5.3**

Dwayne Schintzius (7-2, Florida 1990) (wore Celtics #55)

Statistics	G	MIN	FGM-FGA-PCT	FTM-FTA-PCT	REBS	STL	AST	PTS-PPG
Celtics (1999)	16	67	4-16-.250	3-4-.750	19	0	8	11-**0.7**
NBA	217	1950	256-633-.404	74-116-.638	536	30	93	587-**2.7**

Fred Scolari (5-10, San Francisco 1943) (wore Celtics #24)

Statistics	G	MIN	FGM-FGA-PCT	FTM-FTA-PCT	REBS	STL	AST	PTS-PPG
Celtics (1954-55)	59	619	76-249-.305	39-49-.796	77	NA	93	191-**3.2**
NBA	534	6573*	2132-6651-.321	1750-2139-.818	857**	NA	1406	6014-**11.3**

*Minutes not available before 1951-52 season

**Rebounds not available before 1950-51 season

Charlie Scott (6-6, North Carolina 1970) (wore Celtics #11)

Statistics	G	MIN	FGM-FGA-PCT	FTM-FTA-PCT	REBS	STL	AST	PTS-PPG
Celtics (1975-78)	156	5574	1124-2528-.445	480-626-.767	650	214	680	2728-**17.5**
NBA	560	19278	4113-9266-.444	1809-2344-.772	2034	608*	2696	10037-**17.9**

*Steals not available before 1973-74 season

Ed Searcy (6-6, St. John's 1974) (wore Celtics #32)

Statistics	G	MIN	FGM-FGA-PCT	FTM-FTA-PCT	REBS	STL	AST	PTS-PPG
Celtics (1975-76)	4	12	2-6-.333	2-2-1.000	0	0	1	6-**1.5**
NBA	same							

Jim Seminoff (6-2, Southern California) (wore Celtics #15)

Statistics	G	MIN	FGM-FGA-PCT	FTM-FTA-PCT	REBS	STL	AST	PTS-PPG
Celtics (1948-50)	123	NA	238-770-.309	293-407-.720	NA	NA	478	769-**6.3**
NBA (BAA)	231	NA	535-1737-.308	437-642-.681	NA	NA	630	1507-**6.5**

Earl Shannon (5-11, Rhode Island) (wore Celtics #20)

Statistics	G	MIN	FGM-FGA-PCT	FTM-FTA-PCT	REBS	STL	AST	PTS-PPG
Celtics (1948-49)	5	NA	2-11-.182	1-4-.250	NA	NA	4	5-**1.0**
NBA (BAA)	134	NA	402-1318-.305	352-589-.598	NA	NA	177	1156-**8.6**

Howard (Howie) Shannon (6-3, Kansas State 1948) (wore Celtics #8)

Statistics	G	MIN	FGM-FGA-PCT	FTM-FTA-PCT	REBS	STL	AST	PTS-PPG
Celtics (1949-50)	67	NA	222-646-.344	143-182-.786	NA	NA	174	587-**8.8**
NBA	122	NA	514-1448-.355	295-371-.795	NA	NA	299	1323-**10.8**

Bill Sharman (6-1, Southern California 1950) (wore Celtics #21, retired in his honor)

Statistics	G	MIN	FGM-FGA-PCT	FTM-FTA-PCT	REBS	STL	AST	PTS-PPG
Celtics (1951-61)	680	21793	4620-10807-.428	3047-3451-.883	2683	NA	2062	12287-**18.1**
NBA	711	21793*	4761-11168-.426	3143-3559-.883	2779	NA	2101	12665-**17.8**

*Minutes not available before 1951-52 season

Brian Shaw (6-6, California-Santa Barbara 1988) (wore Celtics #20)

Statistics	G	MIN	FGM-FGA-PCT	FTM-FTA-PCT	REBS	STL	AST	PTS-PPG
Celtics (1988-92)	178	5509	809-1792-.451	348-421-.827	815	195	1163	1969-**11.1**
NBA	639	16551	2089-5113-.409	806-1021-.789	2368	592	3179	5279-**8.3**

Jerry Sichting (6-1, Purdue 1979) (wore Celtics #12)

Statistics	G	MIN	FGM-FGA-PCT	FTM-FTA-PCT	REBS	STL	AST	PTS-PPG
Celtics (1985-88)	184	3532	481-892-.539	106-120-.883	216	104	435	1083-**5.9**
NBA	598	12732	1789-3531-.507	515-601-.857	817	439	1962	4141-**6.9**

Larry Siegfried (6-3, Ohio State 1961) (wore Celtics #20)

Statistics	G	MIN	FGM-FGA-PCT	FTM-FTA-PCT	REBS	STL	AST	PTS-PPG
Celtics (1963-70)	466	11401	1960-4747-.413	1500-1755-.855	1318	NA	1532	5420-**11.6**
NBA	550	13632	2149-5248-.409	1662-1945-.854	1567	NA	1950	5960-**10.8**

Paul Silas (6-7, Creighton 1964) (wore Celtics #35)

Statistics	G	MIN	FGM-FGA-PCT	FTM-FTA-PCT	REBS	STL	AST	PTS-PPG
Celtics (1972-76)	325	10540	1367-3112-.439	1010-1394-.725	4004	179*	864	3744-**11.5**

*Steals not available before 1973-74 season

	G	MIN	FGM-FGA-PCT	FTM-FTA-PCT	REBS	STL	AST	PTS-PPG
NBA	1254	34989	4293-9949-.432	3196-4748-.673	12357	358*	2572	11782-**9.4**

Connie Simmons (6-8, No College) (wore Celtics #10)

Statistics	G	MIN	FGM-FGA-PCT	FTM-FTA-PCT	REBS	STL	AST	PTS-PPG
Celtics (1946-48)	92	NA	354-1134-.312	160-243-.658	NA	NA	79	868-**9.4**
NBA (BAA)	598	7036*	2180-6211-.351	1499-2211-.678	2294**	NA	940	5859-**9.8**

*Minutes not available before 1951-52 season

**Rebounds not available before 1950-51 season

Paul Silas

Kevin Stacom

John Simmons (6-1, NYU) (wore Celtics #6)

Statistics	G	MIN	FGM-FGA-PCT	FTM-FTA-PCT	REBS	STL	AST	PTS-PPG
Celtics (1946-47)	60	NA	120-429-.280	78-127-.614	NA	NA	29	318-**5.3**
NBA (BAA)	same							

Charles Smith (6-1, Georgetown 1989) (wore Celtics #13)

Statistics	G	MIN	FGM-FGA-PCT	FTM-FTA-PCT	REBS	STL	AST	PTS-PPG
Celtics (1989-91)	65	549	62-140-.443	56-81-.691	71	36	109	180-**2.8**
NBA	same							

Derek Smith (6-6, Louisville 1982) (wore Celtics #43)

Statistics	G	MIN	FGM-FGA-PCT	FTM-FTA-PCT	REBS	STL	AST	PTS-PPG
Celtics (1990-91)	2	16	1-4-.250	3-4-.750	0	1	5	5-**2.5**
NBA	408	9825	2031-4074-.499	1125-1495-.753	1300	265	866	5232-**12.8**

Doug Smith (6-10, Missouri 1991) (wore Celtics #34)

Statistics	G	MIN	FGM-FGA-PCT	FTM-FTA-PCT	REBS	STL	AST	PTS-PPG
Celtics (1995-96)	17	92	14-39-.359	5-8-.625	22	3	4	33-**1.9**
NBA	296	5833	1020-2399-.425	313-405-.773	1234	224	400	2356-**8.0**

Garfield Smith (6-9, Kentucky 1968) (wore Celtics #33)

Statistics	G	MIN	FGM-FGA-PCT	FTM-FTA-PCT	REBS	STL	AST	PTS-PPG
Celtics (1970-72)	63	415	70-182-.390	28-87-.322	132	NA	17	168-**2.7**
NBA	same (also played in ABA with San Diego Conquistadors)							

Michael Smith (6-10, Brigham Young 1989) (wore Celtics #11)

Statistics	G	MIN	FGM-FGA-PCT	FTM-FTA-PCT	REBS	STL	AST	PTS-PPG
Celtics (1989-91)	112	1009	231-486-.475	75-91-.824	156	15	122	545-**4.9**
NBA	same							

Art Spector (6-4, Villanova) (wore Celtics #12)

Statistics	G	MIN	FGM-FGA-PCT	FTM-FTA-PCT	REBS	STL	AST	PTS-PPG
Celtics (1946-50)	169	NA	322-1149-.280	208-362-.575	NA	NA	143	852-**5.0**
NBA (BAA)	same							

Kevin Stacom (6-4, Providence 1974) (wore Celtics #27)

Statistics	G	MIN	FGM-FGA-PCT	FTM-FTA-PCT	REBS	STL	AST	PTS-PPG
Celtics (1974-79)	296	3878	679-1601-.424	210-272-.772	443	96	440	1568-**5.3**
NBA	347	4539	769-1844-.417	242-315-.768	511	111	524	1781-**5.1**

Ed Stanczak (6-1, No College) (wore Celtics #19 and #21)

Statistics	G	MIN	FGM-FGA-PCT	FTM-FTA-PCT	REBS	STL	AST	PTS-PPG
Celtics (1950-51)	17	NA	11-48-.229	35-43-.814	34	NA	6	57-**3.4**
NBA	74	NA	170-504-.337	238-313-.760	34*	NA	73	578-**7.8**

*Rebounds not available before 1950-51 season

Derek Strong (6-8, Xavier-Ohio 1990) (wore Celtics #31)

Statistics	G	MIN	FGM-FGA-PCT	FTM-FTA-PCT	REBS	STL	AST	PTS-PPG
Celtics (1994-95)	70	1344	149-329-.453	141-172-.820	375	24	44	441-**6.3**
NBA	408	7909	1001-2318-.432	904-1148-.787	2061	184	280	2916-**7.1**

Gene (Eugene) Stump (6-2, DePaul 1947) (wore Celtics #13)

Statistics	G	MIN	FGM-FGA-PCT	FTM-FTA-PCT	REBS	STL	AST	PTS-PPG
Celtics (1947-49)	99	NA	252-827-.305	116-167-.695	NA	NA	74	620-**6.3**
NBA (BAA)	148	NA	315-1040-.303	153-221-.692	NA	NA	118	783-**5.3**

Ben (Bennie) Swain (6-8, Texas Southern 1958) (wore Celtics #16)

Statistics	G	MIN	FGM-FGA-PCT	FTM-FTA-PCT	REBS	STL	AST	PTS-PPG
Celtics (1958-59)	58	708	99-244-.406	67-110-.609	262	NA	29	265-**4.6**
NBA	same							

Dan Swartz (6-4, Kentucky 1956) (wore Celtics #12)

Statistics	G	MIN	FGM-FGA-PCT	FTM-FTA-PCT	REBS	STL	AST	PTS-PPG
Celtics (1962-63)	39	335	57-150-.380	61-72-.847	88	NA	21	175-**4.5**
NBA	same							

Larry Sykes (6-9, Xavier-Ohio 1995) (wore Celtics #54)

Statistics	G	MIN	FGM-FGA-PCT	FTM-FTA-PCT	REBS	STL	AST	PTS-PPG
Celtics (1995-96)	1	2	0-0-.000	0-0-.000	2	0	0	0-**0.0**
NBA	same							

Brett Szabo (6-11, Augustana 1991) (wore Celtics #43)

Statistics	G	MIN	FGM-FGA-PCT	FTM-FTA-PCT	REBS	STL	AST	PTS-PPG
Celtics (1996-97)	70	662	54-121-.446	45-61-.738	165	16	17	76-**2.2**
NBA	same							

Zan Tabak (7-0, Croatia) (wore Celtics #55)

Statistics	G	MIN	FGM-FGA-PCT	FTM-FTA-PCT	REBS	STL	AST	PTS-PPG
Celtics (1997-98)	18	232	26-55-.473	7-13-.538	58	5	12	59-**3.3**
NBA	135	1964	307-593-.518	118-200-.590	484	37	92	732-**5.4**

Earl Tatum (6-6, Marquette 1976) (wore Celtics #43)

Statistics	G	MIN	FGM-FGA-PCT	FTM-FTA-PCT	REBS	STL	AST	PTS-PPG
Celtics (1978-79)	3	38	8-20-.400	4-5-.800	4	0	1	20-**6.7**
NBA	262	5229	1109-2415-.459	288-386-.746	682	319	507	2508-**9.6**

Tom Thacker (6-2, Cincinnati 1963) (wore Celtics #12)

Statistics	G	MIN	FGM-FGA-PCT	FTM-FTA-PCT	REBS	STL	AST	PTS-PPG
Celtics (1967-68)	65	782	114-272-.419	43-84-.512	161	NA	69	271-**4.2**
NBA	218	2187	307-828-.371	107-222-.482	522	NA	222	721-**3.3**

David Thirdkill (6-8, Bradley 1982) (wore Celtics #45)

Statistics	G	MIN	FGM-FGA-PCT	FTM-FTA-PCT	REBS	STL	AST	PTS-PPG
Celtics (1985-87)	62	463	64-129-.496	60-100-.600	84	12	17	188-**3.0**
NBA	179	1469	189-414-.457	131-232-.565	209	47	84	510-**2.8**

John Thomas (6-9, Minnesota 1997) (wore Celtics #55)

Statistics	G	MIN	FGM-FGA-PCT	FTM-FTA-PCT	REBS	STL	AST	PTS-PPG
Celtics (1997-98)	33	368	41-80-.513	26-33-.788	70	19	13	108-**3.3**
NBA	93	1128	126-236-.534	68-102-.667	240	39	32	320-**3.4**

John Thompson (6-10, Providence 1964) (wore Celtics #5 and #18)

Statistics	G	MIN	FGM-FGA-PCT	FTM-FTA-PCT	REBS	STL	AST	PTS-PPG
Celtics (1964-66)	74	771	98-239-.410	66-111-.595	260	NA	19	262-**3.5**
NBA	same							

Darren Tillis (6-11, Cleveland State 1982) (wore Celtics #52)

Statistics	G	MIN	FGM-FGA-PCT	FTM-FTA-PCT	REBS	STL	AST	PTS-PPG
Celtics (1982-83)	15	44	7-23-.304	2-6-.333	9	0	2	16-**1.1**
NBA	124	1256	184-435-.423	57-91-.626	314	20	42	425-**3.4**

Lou Tsioropoulos (6-5, Kentucky 1953) (wore Celtics #20 and #29)

Statistics	G	MIN	FGM-FGA-PCT	FTM-FTA-PCT	REBS	STL	AST	PTS-PPG
Celtics (1956-59)	157	2977	337-1070-.315	236-329-.717	751	NA	165	910-**5.8**
NBA	same							

Andre Turner (5-11, Memphis State 1986) (wore Celtics #7)

Statistics	G	MIN	FGM-FGA-PCT	FTM-FTA-PCT	REBS	STL	AST	PTS-PPG
Celtics (1986-87)	3	18	2-5-.400	0-0-.000	2	0	1	4-**1.3**
NBA	170	2523	307-727-.422	139-182-.764	263	137	535	767-**4.5**

Bill Walton   **Jo Jo White**

Kelvin Upshaw (6-2, Utah 1986) (wore Celtics #7)

Statistics	G	MIN	FGM-FGA-PCT	FTM-FTA-PCT	REBS	STL	AST	PTS-PPG
Celtics (1988-90)	37	604	85-188-.452	18-26-.692	49	21	125	192-**5.2**
NBA	120	1518	267-589-.453	101-127-.795	145	81	257	649-**5.4**

Virgil Vaughn (6-4, Kentucky Wesleyan) (wore Celtics #17)

Statistics	G	MIN	FGM-FGA-PCT	FTM-FTA-PCT	REBS	STL	AST	PTS-PPG
Celtics (1946-47)	17	NA	15-78-.192	15-28-.536	NA	NA	10	45-**2.6**
NBA (BAA)	same (also played in NBL with Syracuse Nationals)							

Sam Vincent (6-2, Michigan State 1985) (wore Celtics #11)

Statistics	G	MIN	FGM-FGA-PCT	FTM-FTA-PCT	REBS	STL	AST	PTS-PPG
Celtics (1985-87)	103	806	119-298-.399	116-125-.928	75	30	128	355-**3.4**
NBA	396	7527	1163-2591-.449	764-885-.863	819	268	1543	3106-**7.8**

Stojko Vrankovic (7-2, Croatia) (wore Celtics #52 and #11)

Statistics	G	MIN	FGM-FGA-PCT	FTM-FTA-PCT	REBS	STL	AST	PTS-PPG
Celtics (1990-92)	50	276	39-84-.464	17-30-.567	79	1	9	95-**1.9**
NBA	same							

Antoine Walker (6-9, Kentucky 1998) (wore Celtics #8)

Statistics	G	MIN	FGM-FGA-PCT	FTM-FTA-PCT	REBS	STL	AST	PTS-PPG
Celtics (1996-99)	206	7787	1601-3794-.422	649-1041-.623	1936	310	598	4059-**19.7**
NBA	same							

Brady Walker (6-6, Brigham Young 1948) (wore Celtics #13)

Statistics	G	MIN	FGM-FGA-PCT	FTM-FTA-PCT	REBS	STL	AST	PTS-PPG
Celtics (1949-50)	68	NA	218-583-.374	72-114-.632	NA	NA	109	508-**7.5**
NBA (BAA)	228	699*	673-1772-.380	257-406-.633	549**	NA	328	1603-**7.0**

*Minutes not available before 1951-52 season

**Rebounds not available before 1950-51 season

Mike (Red) Wallace (6-1, Scranton) (wore Celtics #13)

Statistics	G	MIN	FGM-FGA-PCT	FTM-FTA-PCT	REBS	STL	AST	PTS-PPG
Celtics (1946-47)	24	NA	55-224-.246	21-48-.438	NA	NA	20	131-**5.5**
NBA (BAA)	61	NA	225-809-.278	106-196-.541	NA	NA	58	556-**9.1**

Bill Walton (6-11, UCLA 1974) (wore Celtics #5)

Statistics	G	MIN	FGM-FGA-PCT	FTM-FTA-PCT	REBS	STL	AST	PTS-PPG
Celtics (1985-88)	90	1658	241-437-.551	152-217-.700	575	39	174	634-**7.0**
NBA	468	13250	2552-4900-.521	1111-1683-.660	4923	380	1590	6215-**13.3**

Gerry Ward (6-4, Boston College 1963) (wore Celtics #4)

Statistics	G	MIN	FGM-FGA-PCT	FTM-FTA-PCT	REBS	STL	AST	PTS-PPG
Celtics (1964-65)	3	30	2-18-.111	1-1-1.000	5	NA	6	5-**1.7**
NBA	169	2049	202-567-.356	138-216-.639	294	NA	237	542-**3.2**

Kermit Washington (6-8, American University 1973) (wore Celtics #26)

Statistics	G	MIN	FGM-FGA-PCT	FTM-FTA-PCT	REBS	STL	AST	PTS-PPG
Celtics (1977-78)	32	866	137-263-.521	102-136-.750	335	28	42	376-**11.8**
NBA	507	12815	1778-3382-.526	1110-1691-.656	4232	403	695	4666-**9.2**

Ron Watts (6-6, Wake Forest 1965) (wore Celtics #12)

Statistics	G	MIN	FGM-FGA-PCT	FTM-FTA-PCT	REBS	STL	AST	PTS-PPG
Celtics (1965-67)	28	92	12-46-.261	16-23-.696	39	NA	2	40-**1.4**
NBA	same							

Marcus Webb (6-9, Alabama 1991) (wore Celtics #41)

Statistics	G	MIN	FGM-FGA-PCT	FTM-FTA-PCT	REBS	STL	AST	PTS-PPG
Celtics (1992-93)	9	51	13-25-.520	13-21-.619	10	1	2	39-**4.3**
NBA	same							

Scott Wedman (6-7, Colorado 1974) (wore Celtics #8 and #20)

Statistics	G	MIN	FGM-FGA-PCT	FTM-FTA-PCT	REBS	STL	AST	PTS-PPG
Celtics (1982-87)	271	4026	757-1630-.464	137-190-.721	573	110	281	1689-**6.2**
NBA	906	25927	5153-10713-.481	1526-1923-.794	4355	846	1771	11916-**13.2**

Rick Weitzman (6-2, Northeastern 1967) (wore Celtics #26)

Statistics	G	MIN	FGM-FGA-PCT	FTM-FTA-PCT	REBS	STL	AST	PTS-PPG
Celtics (1967-68)	25	75	12-46-.261	9-13-.692	10	NA	8	33-**1.3**
NBA	same							

Matt Wenstrom (7-1, North Carolina 1993) (wore Celtics #50)

Statistics	G	MIN	FGM-FGA-PCT	FTM-FTA-PCT	REBS	STL	AST	PTS-PPG
Celtics (1993-94)	11	37	6-10-.600	6-10-.600	12	0	0	18-**1.6**
NBA	same							

David Wesley (6-0, Baylor 1992) (wore Celtics #4)

Statistics	G	MIN	FGM-FGA-PCT	FTM-FTA-PCT	REBS	STL	AST	PTS-PPG
Celtics (1994-97)	207	6475	922-2133-.432	513-670-.766	645	344	1193	2627-**12.7**
NBA	398	11710	1612-3606-.447	945-1202-.786	1063	622	2167	4570-**11.5**

Paul Westphal (6-4, Southern California 1972) (wore Celtics #44)

Statistics	G	MIN	FGM-FGA-PCT	FTM-FTA-PCT	REBS	STL	AST	PTS-PPG
Celtics (1972-75)	224	3228	669-1357-.493	298-395-.754	373	117*	475	1636-**7.3**

*Steals not available before 1973-74 season

NBA	823	20947	5079-10084-.504	2596-3166-.820	1580	1022*	3591	12809-**15.6**

Jo Jo White (6-3, Kansas 1969) (wore Celtics #10, retired number in his honor)

Statistics	G	MIN	FGM-FGA-PCT	FTM-FTA-PCT	REBS	STL	AST	PTS-PPG
Celtics (1969-79)	717	26770	5648-12782-.442	1892-2270-.833	3071	561*	3686	13188-**18.3**

*Steals not available before 1973-74 season

NBA	837	29941	6169-13884-.444	2060-2471-.834	3345	686*	4095	14399-**17.2**

Lucian (Skip) Whittaker (6-1, Kentucky 1952) (wore Celtics #5)

Statistics	G	MIN	FGM-FGA-PCT	FTM-FTA-PCT	REBS	STL	AST	PTS-PPG
Celtics (1954-55)	3	15	1-6-.167	0-0-.000	1	NA	1	2-**0.7**
NBA	same							

Sidney Wicks (6-9, UCLA 1971) (wore Celtics #12)

Statistics	G	MIN	FGM-FGA-PCT	FTM-FTA-PCT	REBS	STL	AST	PTS-PPG
Celtics (1976-78)	163	5055	897-1939-.463	527-793-.665	1497	131	340	2321-**14.2**
NBA	760	25762	5046-11002-.459	2711-3955-.685	6620	592*	2437	12803-**16.8**

*Steals not available before 1973-74 season

Dominique Wilkins (6-8, Georgia 1982) (wore Celtics #12)

Statistics	G	MIN	FGM-FGA-PCT	FTM-FTA-PCT	REBS	STL	AST	PTS-PPG
Celtics (1994-95)	77	2423	496-1169-.424	266-340-.782	401	61	166	1370-**17.8**
NBA	1047	37861	9913-21457-.462	6002-7396-.812	7098	1374	2661	26534-**25.3**

Art (Hambone) Williams (6-1, California Poly 1963) (wore Celtics #7)

Statistics	G	MIN	FGM-FGA-PCT	FTM-FTA-PCT	REBS	STL	AST	PTS-PPG
Celtics (1970-74)	303	4057	494-1098-.450	220-290-.759	758	44*	959	1208-**4.0**

*Steals not available before 1973-74 season

NBA	541	9329	1175-2872-.409	526-722-.729	1700	44*	2377	2876-**5.3**

Earl Williams (6-7, Winston-Salem 1974) (wore Celtics #52)

Statistics	G	MIN	FGM-FGA-PCT	FTM-FTA-PCT	REBS	STL	AST	PTS-PPG
Celtics (1978-79)	20	273	54-123-.439	14-24-.583	105	12	12	122-**6.1**
NBA	146	1882	290-671-.432	84-177-.475	814	62	126	664-**4.5**

Eric Williams (6-8, Providence 1995) (wore Celtics #55)

Statistics	G	MIN	FGM-FGA-PCT	FTM-FTA-PCT	REBS	STL	AST	PTS-PPG
Celtics (1995-97)	136	3905	615-1366-.450	528-734-.719	546	128	199	1763-**12.7**
NBA	178	4830	719-1646-.437	670-918-.730	648	159	248	2119-**11.9**

Lorenzo Williams (6-9, Stetson 1991) (wore Celtics #43)

Statistics	G	MIN	FGM-FGA-PCT	FTM-FTA-PCT	REBS	STL	AST	PTS-PPG
Celtics (1992-93)	22	151	16-31-.516	2-7-.286	44	4	5	34-**1.5**
NBA	231	5348	318-695-.458	81-213-.380	1552	129	243	717-**3.1**

Ray Williams (6-3, Minnesota 1977) (wore Celtics #20)

Statistics	G	MIN	FGM-FGA-PCT	FTM-FTA-PCT	REBS	STL	AST	PTS-PPG
Celtics (1984-85)	23	459	55-143-.385	31-46-.674	57	30	90	147-**6.4**
NBA	655	18462	3962-8794-.451	2143-2673-.802	2370	1198	3779	10158-**15.5**

Sly Williams (6-7, Rhode Island 1980) (wore Celtics #35)

Statistics	G	MIN	FGM-FGA-PCT	FTM-FTA-PCT	REBS	STL	AST	PTS-PPG
Celtics (1985-86)	6	54	5-21-.238	7-12-.583	15	1	2	17-**2.8**
NBA	305	6617	1322-2765-.478	672-971-.692	1287	328	603	3327-**10.9**

Willie Williams (6-7, Florida State 1970) (wore Celtics #28)

Statistics	G	MIN	FGM-FGA-PCT	FTM-FTA-PCT	REBS	STL	AST	PTS-PPG
Celtics (1970-71)	16	56	6-32-.188	3-5-.600	10	NA	2	15-**0.9**
NBA	25	105	10-42-.238	3-5-.600	23	NA	8	23-**0.9**

Bobby Wilson (6-1, Wichita State 1974) (wore Celtics #42)

Statistics	G	MIN	FGM-FGA-PCT	FTM-FTA-PCT	REBS	STL	AST	PTS-PPG
Celtics (1976-77)	25	131	19-59-.322	11-13-.846	9	3	14	49-**2.0**
NBA	143	1498	345-809-.426	102-132-.773	167	52	110	792-**5.5**

Joe Wolf (6-11, North Carolina 1987) (wore Celtics #42)

Statistics	G	MIN	FGM-FGA-PCT	FTM-FTA-PCT	REBS	STL	AST	PTS-PPG
Celtics (1992-93)	2	9	0-1-.000	1-2-.500	3	0	0	1-**0.5**
NBA	532	9003	1028-2401-.428	326-418-.780	1806	237	566	2398-**4.5**

A. J. Wynder (6-2, Fairfield 1987) (wore Celtics #12)

Statistics	G	MIN	FGM-FGA-PCT	FTM-FTA-PCT	REBS	STL	AST	PTS-PPG
Celtics (1990-91)	6	39	3-12-.250	6-8-.750	3	1	8	12-**2.0**
NBA	same							

SEASON-BY-SEASON HISTORICAL SUMMARIES

1946-47 (BAA)
Regular Season: 22-38, Tied for 5th Place (last place) in Eastern Division
Post-Season: Did Not Compete
Coach: John (Honey) Russell
Leading Scorer: Connie Simmons (10.3 ppg.)
Boston's League Leaders: None

1947-48 (BAA)
Regular Season: 20-28, 3rd Place in Eastern Division
Post-Season (1-2): Lost in Quarterfinals to Chicago Stags (1-2)
Coach: John (Honey) Russell
Leading Scorer: Ed Sadowski (19.4 ppg., 3rd in league)
Boston's League Leaders: None

1948-49 (BAA)
Regular Season: 25-35, 5th Place in Eastern Division
Post-Season: Did Not Compete
Coach: Alvin (Doggie) Julian
Leading Scorer: George Kaftan (14.5 ppg.)
Boston's League Leaders: None

1949-50
Regular Season: 22-46, 6th Place (last place) in Eastern Division
Post-Season: Did Not Compete
Coach: Alvin (Doggie) Julian
Leading Scorer: Bob Kinney (11.1 ppg.)
Boston's League Leaders: None
NBA Awards: None

1950-51
Regular Season: 39-30, 2nd Place in Eastern Division
Post-Season (0-2): Lost in Division Semifinals to New York Knicks (0-2)
Coach: Red Auerbach
Leading Scorer: Ed Macauley (20.4 ppg., 3rd in league)
All-Star Game Players: Bob Cousy; Ed Macauley (MVP)
Boston's League Leaders: None
NBA Awards: NBA All-Star Game MVP (Ed Macauley)

1951-52
Regular Season: 39-27, 2nd Place in Eastern Division
Post-Season (1-2): Lost in Division Semifinals to New York Knicks (1-2)
Coach: Red Auerbach
Leading Scorer: Bob Cousy (21.7 ppg., 3rd in league)

All-Star Game Players: Bob Cousy; Ed Macauley
Boston's League Leaders: None
NBA Awards: None

1952-53
Regular Season: 46-25, 3rd Place in Eastern Division
Post-Season (3-3): Won in Division Semifinals over Syracuse Nats (2-0); lost in Division Finals to New York Knicks (1-3)
Coach: Red Auerbach
Leading Scorer: Ed Macauley (20.3 ppg., 3rd in league) and Bob Cousy (19.8 ppg., 4th in league)
All-Star Game Players: Bob Cousy; Ed Macauley; Bill Sharman
Boston's League Leaders: Bill Sharman (Free Throw Percentage); Bob Cousy (Assists)
NBA Awards: None

1953-54
Regular Season: 42-30, 2nd Place (tie) in Eastern Division
Post-Season (2-4): Survived in Division Round Robin (2-2 versus Syracuse Nats and New York Knicks); lost in Division Finals to Syracuse Nats (0-2)
Coach: Red Auerbach
Leading Scorer: Bob Cousy (19.2 ppg., 2nd in league) and Ed Macauley (18.9 ppg., 3rd in league)
All-Star Game Players: Bob Cousy (MVP); Ed Macauley; Bill Sharman
Boston's League Leaders: Ed Macauley (Field Goal Percentage); Bill Sharman (Free Throw Percentage); Bob Cousy (Assists)
NBA Awards: NBA All-Star Game MVP (Bob Cousy)

1954-55
Regular Season: 36-36, 3rd Place in Eastern Division
Post-Season (3-4): Won in Division Semifinals over New York Knicks (2-1); lost in Division Finals to Syracuse Nats (1-3)
Coach: Red Auerbach
Leading Scorer: Bob Cousy (21.1 ppg., 3rd in league)
All-Star Game Players: Bob Cousy; Ed Macauley; Bill Sharman (MVP)
Boston's League Leaders: Bill Sharman (Free Throw Percentage); Bob Cousy (Assists)
NBA Awards: NBA All-Star Game MVP (Bill Sharman)

1955-56
Regular Season: 39-33, 2nd Place in Eastern Division
Post-Season (1-2): Lost in Division Semifinals to Syracuse Nats (1-2)
Coach: Red Auerbach
Leading Scorer: Bill Sharman (19.9 ppg., 6th in league) and Bob Cousy (18.8 ppg., 7th in league)
All-Star Game Players: Bob Cousy; Ed Macauley; Bill Sharman
Boston's League Leaders: Bill Sharman (Free Throw Percentage); Bob Cousy (Assists); Arnie Risen (Disqualifications)
NBA Awards: None

1956-57 (NBA Champions)
Regular Season: 44-28, 1st Place in Eastern Division
Post-Season (7-3): Won in Division Finals over Syracuse Nats (3-0); won in NBA Championship Finals over St. Louis Hawks (4-3)
Coach: Red Auerbach
Leading Scorer: Bill Sharman (21.1 ppg., 7th in league) and Bob Cousy (20.6 ppg., 8th in league)
All-Star Game Players: Bob Cousy (MVP); Tom Heinsohn; Bill Sharman; Red Auerbach (Coach)
Boston's League Leaders: Bill Sharman (Free Throw Percentage); Bob Cousy (Assists)
NBA Awards: NBA MVP (Bob Cousy); NBA Rookie of the Year (Tom Heinsohn); NBA All-Star Game MVP (Bob Cousy)

1957-58
Regular Season: 49-23, 1st Place in Eastern Division
Post-Season (6-5): Won in Division Finals over Philadelphia Warriors (4-1); lost in NBA Championship Finals to St. Louis Hawks (2-4)
Coach: Red Auerbach
Leading Scorer: Bill Sharman (22.3 ppg., 6th in league)
All-Star Game Players: Bill Russell; Bob Cousy; Bill Sharman; Red Auerbach (Coach)
Boston's League Leaders: Bob Cousy (Assists); Bill Russell (Rebounds)
NBA Awards: NBA MVP (Bill Russell)

1958-59 (NBA Champions)
Regular Season: 52-20, 1st Place in Eastern Division
Post-Season (8-3): Won in Division Finals over Syracuse Nats (4-3); won in NBA Championship Finals over Minneapolis Lakers (4-0)
Coach: Red Auerbach
Leading Scorer: Bill Sharman (20.4 ppg., 8th in league) and Bob Cousy (20.0 ppg., 9th in league)
All-Star Game Players: Bill Russell; Bob Cousy; Bill Sharman; Red Auerbach (Coach)
Boston's League Leaders: Bill Sharman (Free Throw Percentage); Bob Cousy (Assists); Bill Russell (Rebounds and Minutes Played)
NBA Awards: None

1959-60 (NBA Champions)
Regular Season: 59-16, 1st Place in Eastern Division
Post-Season (8-5): Won in Division Finals over Philadelphia Warriors (4-2); won in NBA Championship Finals over St. Louis Hawks (4-3)
Coach: Red Auerbach
Leading Scorer: Tom Heinsohn (21.7 ppg., 8th in league)
All-Star Game Players: Bill Russell; Bob Cousy; Bill Sharman; Red Auerbach (Coach)
Boston's League Leaders: Bob Cousy (Assists); Bill Russell (Minutes Played)
NBA Awards: None

1960-61 (NBA Champions)
Regular Season: 57-22, 1st Place in Eastern Division
Post-Season (8-2): Won in Division Finals over Syracuse Nats (4-1); won in NBA Championship Finals over St. Louis Hawks (4-1)
Coach: Red Auerbach
Leading Scorer: Tom Heinsohn (21.3 ppg.)
All-Star Game Players: Bill Russell; Bob Cousy; Tom Heinsohn; Red Auerbach (Coach)
Boston's League Leaders: Bill Sharman (Free Throw Percentage)
NBA Awards: NBA MVP (Bill Russell)

1961-62 (NBA Champions)
Regular Season: 60-20, 1st Place in Eastern Division
Post-Season (8-6): Won in Division Finals over Philadelphia Warriors (4-3); won in NBA Championship Finals over Los Angeles Lakers (4-3)
Coach: Red Auerbach
Leading Scorer: Tom Heinsohn (22.1 ppg.)
All-Star Game Players: Bill Russell; Bob Cousy; Tom Heinsohn; Sam Jones; Red Auerbach (Coach)
Boston's League Leaders: None
NBA Awards: NBA MVP (Bill Russell)

1962-63 (NBA Champions)
Regular Season: 58-22, 1st Place in Eastern Division
Post-Season (8-5): Won in Division Finals over Cincinnati Royals (4-3); won in NBA Championship Finals over Los Angeles Lakers (4-2)
Coach: Red Auerbach
Leading Scorer: Sam Jones (19.7 ppg.)
All-Star Game Players: Bob Cousy; Bill Russell (MVP); Tom Heinsohn; Red Auerbach (Coach)
Boston's League Leaders: Frank Ramsey (Disqualifications)
NBA Awards: NBA MVP (Bill Russell); NBA All-Star Game MVP (Bill Russell)); NBA All-Rookie Team (John Havlicek)

1963-64 (NBA Champions)
Regular Season: 59-21, 1st Place in Eastern Division
Post-Season (8-2): Won in Division Finals over Cincinnati Royals (4-1); won in NBA Championship Finals over San Francisco Warriors (4-1)
Coach: Red Auerbach
Leading Scorer: John Havlicek (19.9 ppg., 10th in league)
All-Star Game Players: Bill Russell; Tom Heinsohn; Sam Jones; Red Auerbach (Coach)
Boston's League Leaders: Bill Russell (Rebounds)
NBA Awards: None

1964-65 (NBA Champions)
Regular Season: 62-18, 1st Place in Eastern Division
Post-Season (8-4): Won in Division Finals over Philadelphia Sixers (4-3); won in NBA Championship Finals over Los Angeles Lakers (4-1)
Coach: Red Auerbach
Leading Scorer: Sam Jones (25.9 ppg., 4th in league)
All-Star Game Players: Bill Russell; Red Auerbach (Coach); Tom Heinsohn (injured)
Boston's League Leaders: Bill Russell (Rebounds); Tom Sanders (Disqualifications)
NBA Awards: NBA MVP (Bill Russell); NBA Coach of the Year (Red Auerbach)

1965-66 (NBA Champions)
Regular Season: 54-26, 2nd Place in Eastern Division
Post-Season (11-6): Won in Division Semifinals over Cincinnati Royals (3-2); won in Division Finals over Philadelphia Sixers (4-1); won in NBA Championship Finals over Los Angeles Lakers (4-3)
Coach: Red Auerbach
Leading Scorer: Sam Jones (23.5 ppg., 10th in league)
All-Star Game Players: Bill Russell; John Havlicek; Sam Jones; Red Auerbach (Coach)
Boston's League Leaders: Larry Siegfried (Free Throw Percentage); Tom Sanders (Disqualifications)
NBA Awards: None

1966-67
Regular Season: 60-21, 2nd Place in Eastern Division
Post-Season (4-5): Won in Division Semifinals over New York Knicks (3-1); lost in Division Finals to Philadelphia Sixers (1-4)
Coach: Bill Russell (player coach)
Leading Scorer: John Havlicek (21.4 ppg., 7th in league)
All-Star Game Players: Bill Russell; John Havlicek; Bailey Howell; Red Auerbach (Coach)
Boston's League Leaders: None
NBA Awards: None

1967-68 (NBA Champions)
Regular Season: 54-28, 2nd Place in Eastern Division
Post-Season (12-7): Won in Division Semifinals over Detroit Pistons (4-2); won in Division Finals over Philadelphia Sixers (4-3); won in NBA Championship Finals over Los Angeles Lakers (4-2)
Coach: Bill Russell (player coach)
Leading Scorer: Sam Jones (21.3 ppg.)
All-Star Game Players: Bill Russell; John Havlicek; Sam Jones
Boston's League Leaders: None
NBA Awards: None

1968-69 (NBA Champions)
Regular Season: 48-34, 4th Place in Eastern Division
Post-Season (12-6): Won in Division Semifinals over Philadelphia Sixers (4-1); won in Division Finals over New York Knicks (4-2); won in NBA Championship Finals over Los Angeles Lakers (4-3)
Coach: Bill Russell (player coach)
Leading Scorer: John Havlicek (21.6 ppg.)
All-Star Game Players: Bill Russell; John Havlicek
Boston's League Leaders: Larry Siegfried (Free Throw Percentage)
NBA Awards: None

1969-70
Regular Season: 34-48, 6th Place in Eastern Division
Post-Season: Did Not Compete
Coach: Tom Heinsohn
Leading Scorer: John Havlicke (24.2 ppg., 8th in league)
All-Star Game Players: John Havlicek
Boston's League Leaders: None
NBA Awards: NBA All-Rookie Team (Jo Jo White)

1970-71

Regular Season: 44-38, 3rd Place in Atlantic Division

Post-Season: Did Not Compete

Coach: Tom Heinsohn

Leading Scorer: John Havlicek (28.9 ppg., 2nd in league)

All-Star Game Players: John Havlicek; Jo Jo White

Boston's League Leaders: John Havlicek (Minutes Played); Dave Cowens (Personal Fouls)

NBA Awards: NBA Rookie of the Year (Dave Cowens); NBA All-Rookie Team (Dave Cowens)

1971-72

Regular Season: 56-26, 1st Place in Atlantic Division

Post-Season (5-6): Won in Conference Semifinals over Atlanta Hawks (4-2); lost in Conference Finals to New York Knicks (1-4)

Coach: Tom Heinsohn

Leading Scorer: John Havlicek (27.5 ppg., 3rd in league)

All-Star Game Players: John Havlicek; Dave Cowens; Jo Jo White; Tom Heinsohn (Coach)

Boston's League Leaders: John Havlicek (Minutes Played); Dave Cowens (Personal Fouls)

NBA Awards: None

1972-73

Regular Season: 68-14, 1st Place in Atlantic Division

Post-Season (7-6): Won in Conference Semifinals over Atlanta Hawks (4-2); lost in Conference Finals to New York Knicks (3-4)

Coach: Tom Heinsohn

Leading Scorer: John Havlicek (23.8 ppg., tied for 9th in league)

All-Star Game Players: John Havlicek; Dave Cowens (MVP); Jo Jo White; Tom Heinsohn (Coach)

Boston's League Leaders: None

NBA Awards: NBA MVP (Dave Cowens); NBA Coach of the Year (Tom Heinsohn); NBA All-Star Game MVP (Dave Cowens)

1973-74 (NBA Champions)

Regular Season: 56-26, 1st Place in Atlantic Division

Post-Season (12-6): Won in Conference Semifinals over Buffalo (4-2); won in Conference Finals over New York Knicks (4-1); won in NBA Championship Finals over Milwaukee Bucks (4-3)

Coach: Tom Heinsohn

Leading Scorer: John Havlicek (22.6 ppg., 9th in league)

All-Star Game Players: John Havlicek; Jo Jo White; Dave Cowens; Tom Heinsohn (Coach)

Boston's League Leaders: None

NBA Awards: NBA Finals MVP (John Havlicek)

1974-75

Regular Season: 60-22, 1st Place in Atlantic Division

Post-Season (6-5): Won in Conference Semifinals over Houston Rockets (4-1); lost in Conference Finals to Washington Bullets (2-4)

Coach: Tom Heinsohn

Leading Scorer: Dave Cowens (20.4 ppg.)

All-Star Game Players: John Havlicek; Paul Silas; Jo Jo White; Dave Cowens

Boston's League Leaders: Don Nelson (Field Goal Percentage)

NBA Awards: None

1975-76 (NBA Champions)

Regular Season: 54-28, 1st Place in Atlantic Division

Post-Season (12-6): Won in Conference Semifinals over Buffalo (4-2); won in Conference Finals over Cleveland Cavaliers (4-2); won in NBA Championship Finals over Phoenix Suns (4-2)

Coach: Tom Heinsohn

Leading Scorer: Dave Cowens (19.0 ppg.)

All-Star Game Players: John Havlicek; Jo Jo White; Dave Cowens; Tom Heinsohn (Coach)

Boston's League Leaders: Charlie Scott (Personal Fouls)

NBA Awards: NBA Finals MVP (Jo Jo White)

1976-77
Regular Season: 44-38, 2nd Place in Atlantic Division
Post-Season (5-4): Won in Conference First Round over San Antonio Spurs (2-0); lost in Conference Semifinals to Philadelphia Sixers (3-4)
Coach: Tom Heinsohn
Leading Scorer: Jo Jo White (19.6 ppg.)
All-Star Game Players: John Havlicek; Jo Jo White; Dave Cowens (injured)
Boston's League Leaders: None
NBA Awards: None

1977-78
Regular Season: 32-50, 3rd Place in Atlantic Division
Post-Season: Did Not Compete
Coach: Tom Heinsohn (11-23) and Tom Sanders (21-27)
Leading Scorer: Dave Cowens (18.6 ppg.)
All-Star Game Players: John Havlicek; Dave Cowens
Boston's League Leaders: None
NBA Awards: None

1978-79
Regular Season: 29-53, 5th Place (last place) in Atlantic Division
Post-Season: Did Not Compete
Coach: Tom Sanders (2-12) and Dave Cowens (27-41)
Leading Scorer: Bob McAdoo (24.8 ppg., 4th in league)
All-Star Game Players: None
Boston's League Leaders: Cedric Maxwell (Field Goal Percentage)
NBA Awards: None

1979-80
Regular Season: 61-21, 1st Place in Atlantic Division
Post-Season (5-4): Won in Conference Semifinals over Houston Rockets (4-0); lost in Conference Finals to Philadelphia Sixers (1-4)
Coach: Bill Fitch
Leading Scorer: Larry Bird (21.3 ppg.)
All-Star Game Players: Larry Bird; Nate Archibald
Boston's League Leaders: Cedric Maxwell (Field Goal Percentage)
NBA Awards: NBA Executive of the Year (Red Auerbach); NBA Coach of the Year (Bill Fitch); NBA Rookie of the Year (Larry Bird); NBA All-Rookie Team (Larry Bird)

1980-81 (NBA Champions)
Regular Season: 62-20, Tied for 1st Place in Atlantic Division
Post-Season (12-5): Won in Conference Semifinals over Chicago Bulls (4-0); won in Conference Finals over Philadelphia Sixers (4-3); won in NBA Championship Finals over Houston Rockets (4-2)
Coach: Bill Fitch
Leading Scorer: Larry Bird (21.2 ppg.)
All-Star Game Players: Larry Bird; Nate Archibald (MVP); Robert Parish
Boston's League Leaders: None
NBA Awards: NBA Finals MVP (Cedric Maxwell); NBA All-Star Game MVP (Nate Archibald); NBA All-Rookie Team (Kevin McHale)

1981-82
Regular Season: 63-19, 1st Place in Atlantic Division
Post-Season (7-5): Won in Conference Semifinals over Washington Bullets (4-1); lost in Conference Finals to Philadelphia Sixers (3-4)
Coach: Bill Fitch
Leading Scorer: Larry Bird (22.9 ppg., tied for 9th in league)
All-Star Game Players: Larry Bird (MVP); Nate Archibald; Robert Parish; Bill Fitch (Coach)
Boston's League Leaders: None
NBA Awards: NBA All-Star Game MVP (Larry Bird)

1982-83
Regular Season: 56-26, 2nd Place in Atlantic Division
Post-Season (2-5): Won in Eastern Conference First Round over Atlanta Hawks (2-1); lost in Eastern Conference Semifinals to Milwaukee Bucks (0-4)
Coach: Bill Fitch
Leading Scorer: Larry Bird (23.6 ppg.)
All-Star Game Players: Larry Bird; Robert Parish
Boston's League Leaders: None
NBA Awards: None

1983-84 (NBA Champions)
Regular Season: 62-20, 1st Place in Atlantic Division
Post-Season (15-8): Won in Conference First Round over Washington Bullets (3-1); won in Conference Semifinals over New York Knicks (4-3); won in Conference Finals over Milwaukee Bucks (4-1); won in NBA Championship Finals over Los Angeles Lakers (4-3)
Coach: K.C. Jones
Leading Scorer: Larry Bird (24.2 ppg., 7th in league)
All-Star Game Players: Larry Bird; Kevin McHale; Robert Parish; K.C. Jones (Coach)
Boston's League Leaders: Larry Bird (Free Throw Percentage)
NBA Awards: NBA MVP (Larry Bird); NBA Finals MVP (Larry Bird); NBA Sixth Man of the Year (Kevin McHale)

1984-85
Regular Season: 63-19, 1st Place in Atlantic Division
Post-Season (13-8): Won in Conference First Round over Cleveland Cavaliers (3-1); won in Conference Semifinals over Detroit Pistons (4-2); won in Conference Finals over Philadelphia Sixers (4-1); lost in NBA Championship Finals to Los Angeles Lakers (2-4)
Coach: K.C. Jones
Leading Scorer: Larry Bird (28.7 ppg., 2nd in league)
All-Star Game Players: Larry Bird; Dennis Johnson; Robert Parish; K.C. Jones (Coach)
Boston's League Leaders: None
NBA Awards: NBA MVP (Larry Bird); NBA Sixth Man of the Year (Kevin McHale)

1985-86 (NBA Champions)
Regular Season: 67-15, 1st Place in Atlantic Division
Post-Season (15-3): Won in Conference First Round over Chicago Bulls (3-0); won in Conference Semifinals over Atlanta Hawks (4-1); won in Conference Finals over Milwaukee Bucks (4-0); won in NBA Championship Finals over Houston Rockets (4-2)
Coach: K.C. Jones
Leading Scorer: Larry Bird (25.8 ppg., 4th in league)
All-Star Game Players: Larry Bird; Kevin McHale; Robert Parish; K.C. Jones (Coach)
Boston's League Leaders: Larry Bird (Free Throw Percentage)
NBA Awards: NBA MVP (Larry Bird); NBA Finals MVP (Larry Bird); NBA Sixth Man of the Year (Bill Walton)

1986-87
Regular Season: 59-23, 1st Place in Atlantic Division
Post-Season (13-10): Won in Conference First Round over Chicago Bulls (3-0); won in Conference Semifinals over Milwaukee Bucks (4-3); won in Conference Finals over Detroit Pistons (4-3); lost in NBA Championship Finals to Los Angeles Lakers (2-4)
Coach: K.C. Jones
Leading Scorer: Larry Bird (28.1 ppg., 4th in league)
All-Star Game Players: Larry Bird; Kevin McHale; Robert Parish; K.C. Jones (Coach)
Boston's League Leaders: Kevin McHale (Field Goal Percentage); Larry Bird (Free Throw Percentage)
NBA Awards: None

1987-88
Regular Season: 57-25, 1st Place in Atlantic Division
Post-Season (9-8): Won in Conference First Round over New York Knicks (3-1); won in Conference Semifinals over Atlanta Hawks (4-3); lost in Conference Finals to Detroit Pistons (2-4)
Coach: K.C. Jones
Leading Scorer: Larry Bird (29.9 ppg., 3rd in league)
All-Star Game Players: Larry Bird; Danny Ainge; Kevin McHale

Boston's League Leaders: Kevin McHale (Field Goal Percentage)
NBA Awards: None

1988-89
Regular Season: 46-36, 3rd Place in Atlantic Division
Post-Season (0-3): Lost in Conference First Round to Detroit Pistons (0-3)
Coach: Jimmy Rodgers
Leading Scorer: Kevin McHale (22.5 ppg.)
All-Star Game Players: Kevin McHale
Boston's League Leaders: None
NBA Awards: None

1989-90
Regular Season: 52-30, 2nd Place in Atlantic Division
Post-Season (2-3): Lost in Conference First Round to New York Knicks (2-3)
Coach: Jimmy Rodgers
Leading Scorer: Larry Bird (24.3 ppg.)
All-Star Game Players: Larry Bird; Kevin McHale; Robert Parish
Boston's League Leaders: Larry Bird (Free Throw Percentage)
NBA Awards: None

1990-91
Regular Season: 56-26, 1st Place in Atlantic Division
Post-Season (5-6): Won in Conference First Round over Indiana Pacers (3-2); lost in Conference Semifinals to Detroit Pistons (2-4)
Coach: Chris Ford
Leading Scorer: Larry Bird (19.4 ppg.)
All-Star Game Players: Kevin McHale; Robert Parish; Chris Ford (Coach); Larry Bird (injured)
Boston's League Leaders: None
NBA Awards: NBA All-Rookie Team (Dee Brown)

1991-92
Regular Season: 51-31, 1st Place in Atlantic Division
Post-Season (6-4): Won in Conference First Round over Indiana Pacers (3-0); lost in Conference Semifinals to Cleveland Cavaliers (3-4)
Coach: Chris Ford
Leading Scorer: Reggie Lewis (20.8 ppg.)
All-Star Game Players: Reggie Lewis; Larry Bird (injured)
Boston's League Leaders: None
NBA Awards: None

1992-93
Regular Season: 48-34, 2nd Place in Atlantic Division
Post-Season (1-3): Lost in Conference First Round to Charlotte Hornets (1-3)
Coach: Chris Ford
Leading Scorer: Reggie Lewis (20.8 ppg.)
All-Star Game Players: None
Boston's League Leaders: None
NBA Awards: None

1993-94
Regular Season: 32-50, 5th Place in Atlantic Division
Post-Season: Did Not Compete
Coach: Chris Ford
Leading Scorer: Dee Brown (15.5 ppg.)
All-Star Game Players: None
Boston's League Leaders: None
NBA Awards: NBA Rookie of the Month, November (Dino Radja)

1994-95
Regular Season: 35-47, 3rd Place in Atlantic Division
Post-Season (1-3): Lost in Conference First Round to Orlando Magic (1-3)
Coach: Chris Ford
Leading Scorer: Dominique Wilkins (17.8 ppg.)
All-Star Game Players: None
Boston's League Leaders: None
NBA Awards: None

1995-96
Regular Season: 33-49, 5th Place in Atlantic Division
Post-Season: Did Not Compete
Coach: M.L. Carr
Leading Scorer: Dino Radja (19.7 ppg.)
All-Star Game Players: None
Boston's League Leaders: None
NBA Awards: None

1996-97
Regular Season: 15-67, 7th Place (last place) in Atlantic Division
Post-Season: Did Not Compete
Coach: M.L. Carr
Leading Scorer: Antoine Walker (17.5 ppg.)
All-Star Game Players: None
Boston's League Leaders: None
NBA Awards: NBA All-Rookie Team (Antoine Walker)

1997-98
Regular Season: 36-46, 6th Place in Atlantic Division
Post-Season: Did Not Compete
Coach: Rick Pitino
Leading Scorer: Antoine Walker (22.4 ppg.)
All-Star Game Players: Antoine Walker
Boston's League Leaders: None
NBA Awards: NBA All-Rookie Team (Ron Mercer)

1999 (Strike-Shortened Season)
Regular Season: 19-31, 5th Place in Atlantic Division
Post-Season: Did Not Compete
Coach: Rick Pitino
Leading Scorer: Antoine Walker (18.7 ppg.)
All-Star Game Players: All-Star Game Cancelled
Boston's League Leaders: None
NBA Awards: None

Appendix

Boston Celtics Annotated Bibliography

Like the moribund Brooklyn Dodgers of baseball's past, Red Auerbach's Boston Celtics are basketball's most literary team, and dozens of books have chronicled the history of the glory-bound ballclub and also the basketball lives of its many legendary ballplayers. The below twenty-five selections stand among the most essential volumes for any diehard Boston Celtics fan's personal basketball library.

Annotated List of Twenty-Five Boston Celtics Classics

Araton, Harvey and Filip Bondy. *The Selling of the Green: The Financial Rise and Moral Decline of the Boston Celtics*. New York: HarperCollins, 1992.

An irreverent history which boldly (and correctly) claims to be the first cold and critical analysis of the seldom-talked-about underside of American sports' most powerful and successful dynasty franchise. The intention (largely successful if sometimes prejudiced and less than objective in its viewpoint) is to expose the dynamics of marketing, finance and race that drive the $30-million-a-year Boston sports machine. Most brutal is the treatment of Auerbach who is belittled for distaining Cousy in the 1950 college draft, chastized for taking undue credit for what is seen here as Bill Fitch's acquisitions of Parish and McHale, exposed for rejecting Bird as a collegian until persuaded otherwise by an unheralded Celtics scout, and condemned as racist for insensitivities to Russell's treatment at the hands of Boston fans. This book is a boon to Celtics haters the world over, but is also informative reading for any student of NBA marketing and NBA politics.

Auerbach, Red (with Joe Fitzgerald). *Red Auerbach: An Autobiography*. New York: G. P. Putnam's Sons, 1977.

Auerbach, Red (with Joe Fitzgerald). *On and Off the Court*. New York and London: Collier-Macmillan Publishers, 1985.

A pair of unvarnished memoirs provide vintage Auerbach, polished and focussed by the veteran *Boston Herald* columnist who has become the famed redhead's professional literary mouthpiece. The architect of Boston's 1960s-era basketball dynasty expounds fully on his philosophies of coaching, his frustrations with coaches who micromanage, his intimate memories of his two biggest stars (Russell and Cousy) and also of some of his less touted role-players who got the most out of their abilities, and also such off-court matters as methods of dealing with drugs in sports and the important distinctions between athletic heroes and athletic celebrities. Few if any other volumes provide quite as much insight into both Auerbach and the legendary team he almost singlehandedly constructed.

Bjarkman, Peter C. *The Biographical History of Basketball*. Chicago: Masters Press (NTC/Contemporary Books), 1999.

While not about the Celtics per se, this unique encyclopedic volume offers profiles of the basketball lives and contributions of 500-plus figures ranking among the cage sport's most influential on-court and off-court celebrities. An early overview chapter (100 pages) detailing the capsule history of professional basketball (there is also a similar chapter on the college game) provides an important backdrop for understanding the evolution of the Boston Celtics franchise.

Bjarkman, Peter C. *The History of the NBA*. New York and Avenel, New Jersey: Crescent Books (Random House Outlet Books), 1992.

Though a near-decade out of date and increasingly hard to find, this remains perhaps the most lavishly illustrated coffeetable format history of the NBA and its larger-than-life high-flying individual stars. Hundreds of archive photos are supplemented with fast-paced historical text and full statistical appendices. Chapter 3 ("Celtic Mystique, 1957-69") details the Auerbach-Cousy-Russell years with considerable and careful detail.

Clary, Jack. *Basketball's Great Dynasties: The Celtics*. New York: Smithmark (W.H. Smith), 1992.

A succinct capsule coffetable franchise history most notable for its colorful collection of approximately 100 archive photographs. Each Celtics era is recounted in synopsis form and all the important heroes and highlights are present here, even if sometimes rather mundanely treated. This is neither the most gripping nor the most insightful team history, but it is nevertheless a good starting point for the uninitiated.

Cousy, Bob (and Bob Ryan). *Cousy on the Celtic Mystique*. New York: McGraw-Hill Publishers, 1988.

The best "insider's view" of the nuts and bolts of basketball's greatest team during their most memorable epoch. Boston's most articulate former player and most talented hoops beat writer combine forces to provide a history and personal memoir full of passion and surprising candor. Cousy tackles and in most cases resolves most of the intriguing issues surrounding "Celtics mystique" and the Auerbach-led ballclubs which proudly wore the label. Was Auerbach himself a coaching genius or a fortunate beneficiary of an endless stream of talented players (especially Russell and Cousy himself)? Has the "mystique" bogged down recent and less-talented Boston teams? And is the so-called "mystique" a real factor in franchise successes, or only a carefully cultivated and arduously marketed illusion? Cousy at every turn offers some most insightful and surprising assessments.

Cousy, Bob (as told to Al Hirshberg). *Basketball is My Life*. Englewood Cliffs, New Jersey: Prentice-Hall Publishers, 1957.

Cousy's first among a handful of personal memoirs, this one was released at the apex of his career and at the outset of the Auerbach-Cousy-Russell dynasty era. This is easily the best source for memories of Cousy's early non-basketball life, his college glories at Holy Cross, and his first half-dozen pre-Russell seasons with coach Auerbach. The volume is also a treasure trove for its rendering of the flavor of life on the road in the earliest decade of the barnstorming NBA.

Cousy, Bob (with Ed Linn). *The Last Load Roar*. Englewood Cliffs, New Jersey: Prentice-Hall, 1964.

The events leading up to the culminating sixth game of the 1963 NBA Finals, followed by a near moment-by-moment recounting of events of Bob Cousy's dramatic final contest in a Boston Celtics uniform. This is Cousy's own blow-by-blow reworking of that gripping farewell performance - the one in which the beloved "Houdini of the Hardwood" dribbled out the game's concluding seconds and then tossed the ball toward the rafters as the season's final buzzer sounded. It was not only one of the most memorable moments of Cousy's career and of Boston franchise history, but in this delightful rendering it also becomes one of the most cherished and savored moments of Boston Celtics literature.

Devaney, John. *Bob Cousy*. New York: G.P. Putnam's Sons (Toronto: Longmans Canada Limited), 1965. (Juvenile)

Still the most readible and entertaining Cousy biography, despite the fact that it was written for a juvenile audience and contains little treatment of the behind-the-scenes tribulations and tensions which were always a part of the Auerbach dynasty years. While the treatment is often the saccharine fare typical of most '50s-vintage kids biographies, nonetheless the essence of the magnetism of Cousy's hold on a generation of early NBA fans emerges in fine detail. There are no better word-portraits available anywhere of the deft behind-the-back passing and dribbling and the exciting run-and-gun floor generalship which was the essence of Cousy's unparalleled backcourt game.

Greenfield, Jeff. *The World's Greatest Team - A Portrait of the Boston Celtics, 1957-69*. New York: Random House, 1976.

The ultimate capsule portrait of the most glorious dozen-year epoch in both NBA and Boston Celtics history. A brilliant journalist and longtime contributing editor to *Sport* magazine, Greenfield offers the most informative chapter ever written on Bill Russell's uneven relationship with Boston fans, as well as unmatched explanations for the oncourt successes and off-court problems (including mediocre hometown fan support) of pro basketball's greatest dynasty ballclub. Greenfield is also unmatched in his brief portraits of the other Celtics standbys of the 1960s-era: Cousy, Sharman, Frank Ramsey, Jim Loscutoff, Heinsohn, Sam and K.C. Jones, Havlicek, Satch Sanders, and Don Nelson. And the included chapter on arch-rival Wilt Chamberlain is also one of the most useful essays ever penned on the enigmatic Big Dipper who was both Boston's much-valued foil and Russell's much-needed antagonist.

Havlicek, John (and Bob Ryan). *Hondo: Celtic Man in Motion*. Englewood Cliffs, New Jersey: Prentice-Hall Publishers, 1977.

Personal reflections of the nearly retired (during his final season) Boston star on his own career and on the Boston Celtics franchise that was its cornerstone. Havlicek spans the Celtics dynasty from Cousy and Russell (versus Chamberlain) to Cowens and Jo Jo White (versus Abdul-Jabbar). An inspirational and passionate treatment from one of the most inspirational and passionate performers in both Boston Celtics and NBA annals.

Lazenby, Roland (Introduction by Bob Ryan*). The NBA Finals: The Official Illustrated History*. Dallas, Texas: Taylor Publishing Company, 1990.

A lavishly illustrated and historically detailed account of each NBA season's final championship showdowns becomes in large part a paean to Boston postseason glories. This is not surprising, given the fact that 19 of the 44 championship series (43%) have involved the Celtics in either a winning (16 times) or losing (3 times) role. No single book is better for background scenarios, headline on-court matchups, thrilling individual performances and shot-by-shot game details of NBA basketball's finest showcase event.

Levine, Lee Daniel. *Bird: The Making of an American Sports Legend*. New York: McGraw-Hill Publishers, 1988.

The only thorough and objective Bird biography which focus largely on his playing years in Boston. In an unauthorized and unsanctioned profile, Levine chronicles the remarkable rags-to-riches success saga which underlies Bird's college and NBA careers, yet at the same time artfully explores with equal precision the personal meanings which Bird derived from the sport during his private and public odyssey from small-town backwater Indiana to big-city NBA limelight.

May, Peter. *The Big Three: The Best Frontcourt in the History of Basketball*. New York and London: Simon and Schuster, 1994.

Delightful thesis-driven account which argues for Bird, Parish and McHale as the best frontcourt in the history of basketball. Oldtimers and hardliners may still reasonably hold out for the Minneapolis Lakers trio of George Mikan, Jim Pollard and Vern Mikkelsen during the early fifties. But May's case is persuasively presented, and in the process he also captures the full flavor and records the most impressive achievements of the third great epoch (following those of Russell-Cousy in the sixties and Cowens-Havlicek in the seventies) in Boston Celtics team history.

McCallum, Jack. *Unfinished Business - On and Off the Court with the 1990-91 Boston Celtics*. New York: Summit Books (Simon and Schuster), 1992.

A veteran *Sports Illustrated* columnist tackles the story behind one of the most crucial and exciting seasons in the history of one of the most successful sports franchises ever. McCallum's tale is one of dramatic transition, both on and off the court, in a season which witnessed Red Auerbach's fading from the front office scene, Larry Bird's final postseason hurrahs which mark a sad ending to a glorious era, and Dee Brown's roller coaster ride from off-court legal scrapes to All-Star Weekend slam dunk glories and a dawning love affair with the Boston fans. The book's highlight is perhaps the author's candid exploration of an awkward relationship forged between Bird and Kevin McHale as the two fading stars make a final desperate effort to capture one final NBA championship in the twilight of their remarkable careers.

Powers, John. *The Short Season - A Boston Celtics Diary, 1977-1978*. New York: Harper and Row, 1979.

Day-by-day dairy entries of the Celtics *Boston Globe* beat writer evolve into an engaging book-length treatment of one of the most tumultuous seasons for the legendary franchise. As the final turbulent season of Tom Heinsohn's coaching tenure unfolds with episodes of increasing devisiveness and on-court disaster (with the team winning its fewest games and losing the most since the 1950 arrival of Red Auerbach), readers are treated to an intimate inside view of the locker room, airport, restaurant and road trip tensions that once severely tested the very foundations of the always-proud Celtics winning tradition.

Russell, Bill (as told to William McSweeny). *Go Up for Glory*. New York: Coward-McCann Publishers, 1966.

Basketball's biggest superstar before Magic, Bird and MJ offers an unvarnished personal account of his considerable and often heroic struggles as a lonely warrior, a black pioneer in race relations, and an unparalleled champion athlete. In what is also appropriately billed as a "no-punches-pulled" story of professional basketball, Russell paints the game's top stars and coaches as "Machiavellis of the ball court, crack psychologists who learn to 'psyche' their opponents, to outguess them and put them off their stride, to understand and exploit the referees in every game." No single book is any better at fully revealing this "inner game" which remains the essence of yesterday's and today's pro basketball.

Russell, Bill and Taylor Branch. *Second Wind: The Memoirs of an Opinionated Man*. New York: Random House, 1979.

Jacket notes warn that "this is not just one more autobiography filled with anecdotes about past athletic glories" and that "basketball occupies less than half of this book" and is thus hardly a dominating theme. Always-outspoken Bill Russell provides a true classic of sports literature with his probing self-examination and exploration of what it meant to be a personal and racial misfit at the center (literally) of one of the sportsworld's most legendary and celebrated teams. If the reader is interested in modern-era athletic heroes as real people, then this is the one book he or she should read to the exclusion of all others.

Ryan, Bob and Dick Raphael. *The Boston Celtics - The History, Legends, and Images of America's Most Celebrated Team*. Reading, Massachusetts: Addison-Wesley Publishers, 1989.

Much-valued joint-effort from the team's longest-reigning beat writer and its revered official team photographer. Raphael's intimate portraits and skillful game-action scenes are adequately paralleled by Ryan's episodic prose history. An era-by-era structure contains inside analysis of Auerbach's role in building the Boston dynasty, plus season-by-season and championship-by-championship highlights of the crucial games and the memorable heroic individual performances. Statistical appendices offer an all-time roster and career leaders in all major offensive categories. Highlight chapters capsulize all-time opponents ("The Villains"), unforgettable one-on-one "over-the-years" matchups, crucial trades and draft choices ("Great Pickups"), vital role players ("Sixth Men"), and of course the pantheon of immortals ("Retired Numbers"). No single team history yet published offers as much variety as this special coffee-table format edition.

Schron, Bob and Kevin Stevens. *The Bird Era: A History of the Boston Celtics, 1978-1988*. Boston: Quinlan Press, 1988.

An always delightful and often insightful journey through both highs and lows of the latest chapter of the Boston Celtics dynasty reign. Bird is the touchstone here, but not the only focus of a thorough-going history which provides player profiles, examinations and recountings of key games and crucial series, and a candid review of usual successes and occasional mistakes in front office and bench management. The fast-paced and engaging narrative text is supplemented with dozens of black and white action photos and a center insert of full-color portraits of top stars (Maxwell, McHale, Bird and Dennis Johnson, Parish, Ainge, Walton, DJ, and Bird). Here is this author's personal favorite title for its effective portrayal of a special magic which long was Boston Garden basketball tradition.

Shaughnessy, Dan. *Ever Green, The Boston Celtics - A History in the Words of Their Players, Coaches, Fans and Foes, from 1946 to the Present*. New York: St. Martin's Press, 1990.

A useful chronological review of team history which provides both historical context and a valued oral history approach in the form of extensive observations and quotations from players, opponents, coaches and hometown fans. There is equal treatment here of the lean seasons which both preceded (in the late forties and early fifties) and followed (with the late '70s and late '80s) the apex of the Russell-Cousy dynasty seasons. And equal voice is also given to some of the notable "hangers-on" of Celtics history - the Henry Finkels, Chris Fords, Paul Silases, Gene Conleys and M. L. Carrs, among others, who often provide the most off-beat and telling bench-eye views of unfolding franchise history.

Shaughnessy, Dan. *Seeing Red - The Red Auerbach Story*. ("Forward" by Larry Bird). New York: Crown Publishers, 1994.

The most recent hagiography on Auerbach, penned by one of the Boston's most talented and prolific sportswriters. What is billed on the jacket as the first-ever fullscale biography of Auerbach is in reality a rehashing (if often more lively telling) of personal tales earlier unfolded in several of Red's own ghost-written memoirs. While Shaughnessy's treatment adds little truly new to the Auerbach profile, his vivid portrait nonetheless successfully brings to full life one of the sportsworld's most engaging personalities and also one of basketball's most historically important personages.

Shaw, Mark. *Larry Legend*. Chicago: Masters Press (NTC/Contemporary Books), 1998.

This most recent Bird biography focusses more on Indiana connections than past Boston glories - especially the heady college years at Indiana State and current successes as two-year head coach of the front-running Indiana Pacers. Perhaps the most insightful look at what makes Bird tick - as a man, a ballplayer, and especially a coach. And there is plenty here on Boston years as well, though little that has not also been fully covered elsewhere.

Shouler. Ken. *The Experts Pick Basketball's Best 50 Players in the Last 50 Years*. Lenexa, Kansas: Addax Publishing Group, 1998.

Larry Bird tops the best-ever forwards list and Bill Russell heads up the all-time centers, with Bob Cousy (guards, number 8), Nate "Tiny" Archibald (guards, number 13), Pete Maravich (guards, number 12), John Havlicek (forwards, number 6), Kevin McHale (forwards, number 10), Dominique Wilkins (forwards, number 17), Dave Cowens (centers, number 8), Robert Parish (centers, number 14), Bob McAdoo (centers, number 14), and Artis Gilmore (centers, number 16) also among Boston alumni singled out here for immortality. Arguments for Bird and Russell are especially articulate and persuasive.

Ten Additional Boston Celtics Titles of Interest

Auerbach, Arnold (Red). *Basketball for the Player, the Fan, and the Coach*. New York: Simon and Schuster, 1952.

Auerbach, Red and Paul Sann. *Red Auerbach: Winning the Hard Way*. Boston: Little, Brown and Company, 1966.

Bird, Larry (with Bob Ryan). *Drive: The Story of My Life*. ("Forward" by Earvin "Magic" Johnson). New York: Doubleday, 1989.

Corn, Frederick Lynn. *Basketball's Magnificent Bird: The Larry Bird Story*. New York: Random House (Zander Hollander Sports Book), 1982. (Juvenile Biography)

Cousy, Bob (with John Devaney). *The Killer Instinct*. New York and Toronto: Random House, 1975.

Heinsohn, Tommy and Joe Fitzgerald. *Give 'Em the Hook*. New York and London: Prentice-Hall Press, 1988.

Hirshberg, Al. *Bill Russell of the Boston Celtics*. New York: Julian Messner Publishers, 1963. (Juvenile Biography)

Jones, K. C. (with Jack Warner). *Rebound: The Autobiography of K. C. Jones and An Inside Look at the Champion Boston Celtics*. Boston: Quinlan Press, 1986.

Kavanagh, Jack. *Sports Great Larry Bird*. Enslow Sports Great Series. Hillsdale, New Jersey: Enslow Publishers, 1992. (Juvenile Biography)

Sullivan, George. *The Picture History of the Boston Celtics*. Indianapolis and New York: The Bobbs-Merrill Company, 1981.

BOSTON *Celtics* 1999-2002

Celtics Pride Turns New Page for New Century

Born in the long shadows of World War II, the Boston professional basketball franchise spent more than a decade climbing out of mediocrity and building foundations for a winning tradition. Once the league's upper echelons were reached in the late fifties, the Boston Celtics would spend most of the next half-century entrenched as the sport's most dominant force and the league's most storied Cinderella franchise.

Between Red Auerbach's first league championship in April 1957 and a final Boston appearance in the league finals under Auerbach protégé K. C. Jones in June 1987, the history of the National Basketball Association is largely synonymous with the history of the fabled Boston Celtics. In the late fifties with Cousy and Sharman leading the charge, Boston drastically changed the appearance of pro basketball with Red Auerbach's high-powered fast-break-style offense. Throughout the sixties the Boston Celtics of Bill Russell and John Havlicek owned the greatest dynasty in the history of American professional sports—eight straight years as the reigning world champions. In the

seventies there was one glorious franchise revival with overachieving Dave Cowens and in the eighties yet another with the overachieving Larry Bird. It was only in the mid-nineties, when aging Red Auerbach had finally given up front-office control of the franchise he had painstakingly built and nurtured and Larry Bird had been forced into premature retirement by nagging injuries, that Boston's proud Celtics once more fell on lean times. By the time the NBA was celebrating its 50-year Silver Anniversary, the Celtics franchise had finally and surprisingly come full cycle.

The late nineties were arguably the most frustrating span in franchise history. Storied Boston Garden finally met the wrecking ball five years into the decade. A luxurious new home in the spacious Fleet Center—complete with replica parquet floor—inherited only mediocre teams, and the only visible signs of a continuing proud Celtics tradition were the rows of 16 championship banners and 21 retired uniform numbers now hanging from the rafters of the replacement arena. These were hardly "genuine" Boston Celtics that now

Rick Pitino's coaching style, developed successfully at the college level, wasn't received well by the pros. AP/Wide World Photos

took the floor, with lineup names like Dana Barros, Popeye Jones, Ron Mercer and Walter McCarty. An untimely experiment with one of college basketball's most relentlessly successful coaches quickly proved an unprecedented disaster when Rick Pitino brought his micromanagement style into the world of the laid-back professionals. The final few years of the twentieth century were indeed a barren wasteland for once-proud if not altogether spoiled Boston Celtics fans.

With a new millennium and a new era of NBA basketball there have already been substantial signs that Boston's remarkable swoon might indeed be only temporary. Two bright stars—a tandem of the best forwards found anywhere in the league—saw the ball club through the leanest of times under the experiment with Pitino. With Paul Pierce and Antoine Walker still anchoring the lineup, the necessary building blocks for franchise revival seemed firmly in place. That a coaching change might spark a new direction in team fortunes appeared to be very much the case after Pitino's inevitable departure. Jim O'Brien's welcomed arrival in midseason 2001 lit an immediate fire under the long-dormant Celtics. After a pair of seasons demonstrating only painfully slow progress, the 2002 NBA campaign has suddenly reawakened genuine hope among the suffering Boston partisans.

The last decade of the old millennium had been a total disaster in Boston, and in many respects it had also been a disaster for the league as a whole. In 1999, labor troubles soured fans when the NBA's first-ever player lockout shortened the league schedule to 50 games in a curtailed season that didn't open until February and went without the traditional midseason All-Star Game. A huge dip in fan enthusiasm also followed the long-dreaded but inevitable retirement of icon Michael Jordan. (When Air Jordan surprisingly returned in Washington after a two-year exile he would be only a mere shadow of what he had once been.) The level and style of play seemingly sagged in Jordan's wake for most hardcore basketball purists. Even the revival of the storied Los Angeles Lakers with Shaquille O'Neal, Kobe Bryant, coach Phil Jackson and a three-peat run that matched Jordan's in Chicago a decade earlier couldn't quite seem to rekindle the now-lusterless NBA. And in Boston the teams that were now wearing the Celtics logo appeared to be little more than inept impostors of teams that had once terrorized the league for decades.

1999-2000 Celtics Capsule Review

Regular Season Results: 35-47 (.427); 5th in Atlantic Division, 17.0 games behind Miami; 6th worst record in Eastern Conference, ahead of New Jersey, Washington, Cleveland, Atlanta and Chicago.
Post-Season Results: Did not qualify for playoffs
Head Coach: Rick Pitino (90-124 record as Boston Head Coach)
Team Leaders: PPG: Antoine Walker (20.5); **Points:** Walker (1680); **Field Goals:** Walker (648); **Free Throws:** Paul Pierce (359); **Three-Pointers:** Pierce (96); **Rebounds:** Walker (652); **Assists:** Kenny Anderson (420); **Steals:** Pierce (152); **Blocks:** Tony Battie (70); **Minutes:** Walker (3003).
Celtics Among NBA Leaders: Paul Pierce (2nd in NBA Steals)

Player	G-GS	MIN	FG-FGA (Pct)	FT-FTA (Pct)	Pts	PPG	High
Walker, Antoine (F)	82-82	3003	648-1506 (.430)	311-445 (.699)	1680	20.5	39
Pierce, Paul (F-G)	73-72	2583	486-1099 (.442)	359-450 (.798)	1427	19.5	38
Anderson, Kenny (G)	82-82	2593	434-986 (.440)	196-253 (.775)	1149	14.0	33
Potapenko, Vitaly (C)	79-72	1797	307-615 (.499)	109-160 (.681)	723	9.2	22
Fortson, Danny (F)	55-5	856	140-265 (.528)	139-189 (.735)	419	7.6	23
Williams, Eric (F)	68-17	1378	165-386 (.427)	134-169 (.793)	489	7.2	22
Barros, Dana (G)	72-0	1139	196-435 (.451)	66-76 (.868)	517	7.2	19
Griffin, Adrian (G-F)	72-47	1927	175-413 (.424)	119-158 (.753)	485	6.7	23
Battie, Tony (F-C)	82-82	1505	219-459 (.477)	102-151 (.675)	541	6.6	18
Cheaney, Calbert (G-F)	67-19	1309	120-273 (.440)	9-21 (.429)	267	4.0	12
McCarty, Walter (F)	61-5	879	78-230 (.339)	39-54 (.722)	229	3.8	20
Thomas, Jamel (F)	3-0	19	5-10 (.500)	1-1 (1.000)	11	3.7	5
Overton, Doug (G)	48-0	432	61-154 (.396)	20-21 (.952)	152	3.2	11
Ellison, Pervis (C)	30-5	269	19-43 (.442)	15-21 (.714)	53	1.8	5
Turner, Wayne (G)	3-0	41	1-6 (.167)	2-6 (.333)	4	1.3	3

The only bright spots for the Celtics were the play of 1998 first-round draft pick Paul Pierce, who debuted with a 16.9 scoring average but lost Rookie of the Year honors to Toronto's Vince Carter, and third-year star Antoine Walker, who fell off slightly from his sophomore 22.4 average but carried the offensive burden. The two were practically the only entertaining show in town in the fourth season at the impressive new Fleet Center. But Pierce and Walker could hardly carry the burden alone, and the rebuilding program of club president and head coach Rick Pitino had already taken a sharp detour south only two years after its inception. At the end of the dismal 1999-2000 season only five league teams claimed worse records than Boston's 35-47 fifth-place Atlantic Division finish. The deathwatch was now out in full force on Pitino's already shaky tenure in Boston. A few notable personnel moves, like the acquisition of veteran guard Kenny Anderson (in a February 1998 seven-player swap with Toronto) and also that of small forward Danny Fortson (acquired from Denver in exchange for Ron Mercer on the eve of the 2000 season), had only minor impact on righting the sinking Celtics ship.

Boston had now suffered the worst three-year run (at least ten games under .500 each and every winter) in almost fifty full seasons. Pitino's days certainly were now numbered. If there was any optimism in the Celtics camp it was rarely seen among players, coaching staff or front office management—and certainly not among the downtrodden fans. Boston faithful openly wondered if Pierce and Walker would remain the hoped-for building blocks or instead would themselves abandon ship with their trade demands. Walker, who was billed as the franchise player and signed to a seven-year $72 million deal before the strike-shortened 1999 season, was being publicly shopped around to clubs willing to assume his contract only a single season later. There seemed a more than even chance that the ball club playing before disgruntled fans in the Fleet Center might yet show further deterioration before it ever displayed any signs of marked improvement.

In retrospect, the season that opened in November 2000 and drew to a close in April 2001 was an important year of transition, even if there was no substantial improvement in the league standings. The painful Rick Pitino era mercifully ended 34 games into the new season. Assistant Jim O'Brien inherited the team when it was already nose-diving at 12-22 and yet somehow managed to produce a break-even ball club (24-24) for the remainder of the winter. That in itself was remarkable progress, even if it might not seem so by past-era Celtics standards. O'Brien was now in charge of picking up the pieces as the NBA moved into the third season of a new century, and changes had to come fast while the careers of franchise stars Pierce and Walker were still peaking.

Together through it all, Paul Pierce and Antoine Walker have weathered some tough times in Boston. AP/Wide World Photos

New head coach Jim O'Brien stepped in to lead the
Celtics to a brighter future. AP/Wide World Photos

Pierce and Walker at the forward slots continued to provide the main cause for optimism around the Fleet Center. There were few frontcourt pairs their equal anywhere in the league. Pierce enjoyed another the banner season during 2001 (25.3 ppg and the league's third highest point total) as the two continued to flip-flop alternate seasons as the team's offensive leader. Pierce ranked eighth among the league's scoring leaders (in per-game average) and Walker (23.4 ppg) missed by a fraction of also cracking the top ten. Only the Lakers (with Shaquille O'Neal and Kobe Bryant) could offer a comparable double-barreled offensive pair. But rebuilding the backcourt and finding a reliable center to share the offensive burden while providing more intimidating defense were now the highest of priorities. Without those moves at the very least it was not at all difficult for the opposition to repeatedly neutralize Boston's high-powered frontline pair while at the same time exploiting the team's obvious defensive liabilities.

2000-2001 Celtics Capsule Review

Regular Season Results: 36-46 (.439); 5th in Atlantic Division, 20.0 games behind Philadelphia; 7th worst record in East, ahead of Detroit, Cleveland, New Jersey, Atlanta, Washington, Chicago.

Post-Season Results: Did not qualify for playoffs

Head Coach: Jim O'Brien (24-24), replacing Rick Pitino (102-146 record as Boston Head Coach)

Team Leaders: PPG: Paul Pierce (25.3); **Points:** Pierce (2071); **Field Goals:** Antoine Walker (711); **Free Throws:** Pierce (550); **Three-Pointers:** Walker (221); **Rebounds:** Walker (719); **Assists:** Walker (445); **Steals:** Pierce, Walker (138); **Blocks:** Mark Blount (76); **Minutes:** Walker (3396).

Celtics Among NBA Leaders: Paul Pierce (8th in NBA Scoring)

Boston Celtics 2000-2001 Roster and Individual Statistics

Player	Games	MIN	FG-FGA (Pct)	FT-FTA (Pct)	Pts	PPG	High
Pierce, Paul (F)	82	3120	687-1513 (.454)	550-738 (.745)	2071	25.3	44
Walker, Antoine (F)	81	3396	711-1720 (.413)	249-348 (.716)	1892	23.4	47
Stith, Bryant (F)	78	2504	245-611 (.401)	175-207 (.845)	756	9.7	29
Anderson, Kenny (G)	33	849	88-227 (.388)	59-71 (.831)	246	7.5	20
Potapenko, Vitaly (C)	82	1901	248-521 (.476)	115-158 (.728)	611	7.5	16
Williams, Eric (F)	81	1745	162-448 (.362)	165-231 (.714)	535	6.6	22
Battie, Tony (F-C)	40	845	108-201 (.537)	44-69 (.638)	260	6.5	19
Palacio, Milt (G)	58	1141	126-267 (.472)	78-92 (.848)	342	5.9	19
Overton, Doug (G)	7	144	15-44 (.341)	7-11 (.636)	38	5.4	10
Carr, Chris (F)	35	309	53-112 (.473)	46-60 (.767)	169	4.8	15
Brown, Randy (G)	54	1238	100-237 (.422)	23-40 (.575)	223	4.1	16
Blount, Mark (C)	64	1098	101-200 (.505)	46-66 (.697)	248	3.9	12
Brunson, Rick (G)	7	142	10-35 (.286)	4-9 (.444)	26	3.7	7
Herren, Chris (G)	25	408	29-96 (.302)	9-12 (.750)	83	3.3	13
McCarty, Walter (F)	60	478	45-126 (.357)	22-28 (.786)	131	2.2	27
Griffin, Adrian (G-F)	44	377	33-97 (.340)	18-24 (.750)	93	2.1	10
Moiso, Jerome (C-F)	24	135	12-30 (.400)	11-26 (.423)	35	1.5	5

In the end the 2001 campaign provided very little measurable improvement other than the second half .500 record posted after O'Brien's promotion. A step had apparently been taken in the right direction—hiring a coach who inspired player confidence. Trade talk surrounding Walker had subsided and the core nucleus of the team had been kept together for four seasons through thick and thin. The biggest lack in the Boston camp continued to be an adequate supporting cast to surround Pierce and Walker. Pierce had become a true superstar, and in the upcoming 2002 season he would emphasize that fact in spades by becoming the first Celtics player in franchise history to lead the entire NBA in points scored. It was a feat that had escaped Cousy, Havlicek, Cowens, Bird and all the other heavy artillery that had ever worn a Boston uniform. But Pierce needed more support than Walker alone, and the third season of the new century—the first under O'Brien from start to finish—would likely be altogether crucial to the revival of a storied Boston franchise.

Rodney Rogers's move to Boston added much-needed depth to the Celtics' frontcourt. AP/Wide World Photos

Boston superstar Paul Pierce hauls down one of his career-high 17 rebounds against the Detroit Pistons in the 2002 Eastern Conference semifinals. AP/Wide World Photos

Signs that the resurgence of the Celtics was close at hand came in the opening weeks of the 2001-2002 NBA season, the first in which O'Brien could mold his own preseason roster and shape his own season-long strategy. Playing only a game above .500 for the first month, the Celtics surged in December and moved to eight games above the break-even point by the first week of January. Boston was but one of several early-season surprises in an Atlantic Division that had now seemingly been turned upside down. Having roared to the top of the pack a year earlier on the strength of the volatile Allen Iverson and a rather patchwork supporting cast, the Philadelphia Sixers had fully collapsed before the new season was a third over. New Jersey and Boston were now the reloaded former also-rans bent on duplicating the Sixers' miracle of a year earlier. And it would remain that way—a two-horse race between Boston and New Jersey—for the remainder of the season.

Arguably the Nets under rookie mentor Byron Scott were an even bigger 2002 surprise than the Celtics of second-year coach Jim O'Brien. New Jersey had finished ten games behind the struggling Celtics in 2001, after all, and were now in the process of doubling their win total from the previous winter. Yet the Nets had retooled successfully with Jason Kidd in the backcourt and had benefited from one of the league's best defenses and the continued rapid maturation of Kenyon Martin, Keith Van Horn and Terry Kittles. But Boston's resurgence—also built on improved defensive play—was hardly any less remarkable. Walker and Pierce still carried the entire offensive load, one or the other earning team-high scoring honors in every one of the club's first forty games. Coming up big time after time, Walker beat the Lakers on a three-point buzzer shot in Los Angeles and Pierce did the same against the Heat in Miami. Despite all the fireworks from the one-two punch front line, it was unlikely that the run would have continued all season but for a fortuitous late-February trade with the Phoenix Suns for powerful forward Rodney Rogers and versatile guard Tony Delk. It was a costly deal since the price included giving up the coming summer's top draft pick, but in the end the gamble paid off handsomely. Delk assumed an immediate starting backcourt role while Rogers added some much-needed frontcourt bench strength; the pair finished the year as the club's third and fifth leading scorers.

Tony Delk didn't disappoint when he was added to the roster to bolster the Celtics' 2002 offensive fireworks. AP/Wide World Photos

In late April—with the third best record in the Eastern Conference—Boston returned to the NBA second-season playoffs for the first time in seven long years. And unlike the Chris Ford-coached clubs that had managed only one victory each in the last pair of postseason visits in 1993 and 1995, this Boston club seemed quite capable of making some authentic noise during the always-frantic postseason shootout. An opening series with sixth-seeded Philadelphia provided numerous thrills and went all the way to the wire before Paul Pierce exploded for 46 points at the Fleet Center to sink the vaunted Sixers defense. The conference semifinals versus Detroit opened on a largely sour note when Boston dropped its third straight road game of the playoffs by twelve in the Motor City, but the Celtics team quickly pulled itself together to prove beyond a doubt that it was indeed for real. Detroit scoring machine Jerry Stackhouse was shut down sufficiently night after night by a revived Boston defense for the number three-seeded Celtics to rub out the number two-seeded Pistons in four consecutive games.

By the time the conference finals with New Jersey rolled around in mid-May, the prospect had suddenly emerged of a most unlikely Boston-Los Angeles matchup for the 56th edition of the NBA Finals. That storied series was the most colorful rivalry in NBA history, and the league's top two dynasty franchises had previously met head to head nine different times with the championship up for grabs. Another Boston-LA finale—the first in fifteen years—would perhaps be just what a sagging league needed to close the gaping void in fan interest left by Jordan's absence and the current scarcity of genuine league superstars. But in the end, of course, it was not meant to be, as the Celtics' spunk was no true match for Jason Kidd and the rigid New Jersey defense. Yet before they were over the conference finals nonetheless did supply their own share of considerable thrills.

The three entertaining series of the 2002 playoffs would provide a handful of highlight moments to add to the substantial ledger of storied Boston Celtics playoff history. First came an impressive finish in the opening round against Philadelphia which saw a lopsided 120-87 Fleet Center blowout in the deciding game against the defending Eastern Conference champions. Next there was a display of total dominance against high-scoring Jerry Stackhouse and the Detroit Pistons. On the heels of a 12-point opening road loss, the Celts swept four straight, including a

2001-2002 Celtics Capsule Review

Regular Season Results: 49-33 (.598); 2nd in Atlantic Division, 3.0 games behind New Jersey Nets; 3rd best record in Eastern Conference, behind New Jersey Nets (52-30) and Detroit Pistons (52-30).

Post-Season Results: Eliminated by New Jersey Nets in Eastern Conference Finals (in six games)

Head Coach: Jim O'Brien (73-57 record as Boston Head Coach)

Team Leaders: PPG: Paul Pierce (26.1); **Points:** Pierce (2144); **Field Goals:** Pierce (707); **Free Throws:** Pierce (520); **Three-Pointers:** Antoine Walker (222); **Rebounds:** Walker (714); **Assists:** Walker (407); **Steals:** Pierce (154); **Blocks:** Pierce (86); **Minutes:** Walker (3406).

Celtics Among NBA Leaders: Paul Pierce (1st in points scored; 3rd in scoring average; All-NBA Third Team, 11th in NBA MVP Voting)

Boston Celtics 2001-2002 Roster and Individual Statistics

Player	G-GS	MIN	FG-FGA (Pct)	FT-FTA (Pct)	Pts	PPG	High
Pierce, Paul (F)	82-82	3302	707-1598 (.442)	520-643 (.809)	2144	26.1	48
Walker, Antoine (F)	81-81	3406	666-1689 (.394)	240-324 (.741)	1794	22.1	42
Rogers, Rodney (F)	27-1	626	107-222 (.482)	35-50 (.700)	288	10.7	25
Anderson, Kenny (G)	76-76	2430	312-716 (.436)	98-132 (.742)	731	9.6	19
Delk, Tony (G)	22-16	570	60-172 (.349)	22-30 (.733)	162	7.4	19
Strickland, Eric (G)	79-4	1643	190-488 (.389)	131-155 (.845)	606	7.7	23
Battie, Tony (F-C)	74-73	1819	211-390 (.541)	88-130 (.677)	510	6.9	20
Williams, Eric (G-F)	74-30	1747	144-385 (.374)	160-219 (.731)	472	6.4	19
Potapenko, Vitaly (C)	79-9	1343	137-301 (.455)	89-120 (.742)	363	4.6	14
McCarty, Walter (F)	56-0	718	80-180 (.444)	13-19 (.684)	212	3.8	18
Brown, Kedrick (F)	29-5	245	23-70 (.329)	12-20 (.600)	63	2.2	12
Blount, Mark (C)	44-0	415	32-76 (.421)	30-37 (.811)	94	2.1	11
Forte, Joseph (G)	8-0	39	1-12 (.083)	4-4 (1.000)	6	0.8	1

gutsy fifth-game victory preserved by sterling play from the bench when both Walker and Pierce were sidelined with foul trouble in the late going. And finally there was the greatest single-game fourth-quarter comeback in NBA playoff history in Game 3 of the conference finals with New Jersey. Together these and other dramatic moments (like the near-record 29-point first-half performance by Paul Pierce in the deciding game versus Philadelphia) turned the 2002 playoffs into a joyous month-long event that will long remain alive in the minds of the renewed Boston faithful.

A single highlight moment was the truly remarkable comeback against New Jersey in Game 3 of the conference finals. This game has to rank among the greatest Celtics moments from past championship eras with Cousy, Russell, Havlicek and Bird. Trailing by 21 at intermission and nearly run off the Fleet Center floor, O'Brien's stunned crew received an emotional display of leadership from Antoine Walker in the form of a halftime tongue lashing that challenged his teammates to play with more pride and refuse to be humiliated without putting up a noble fight. Still down by 21 after three quarters but now refusing to roll over and play dead, the seemingly outmanned Celtics suddenly unleashed the biggest fourth-quarter playoff comeback

in league annals. Outscoring the Nets 41-16 down the final stretch, Walker and company wrote one of the most memorable chapters of the already crammed franchise playoff history. In the chaos following the final horn ending a stunning 94-90 triumph, both

Antoine Walker drives against the New Jersey Nets' Kenyon Martin during the first half of Game 3 of the 2002 Eastern Conference finals. AP/Wide World Photos

Walker and Pierce leaped upon the center court press table to inspire postgame cheers from a near-delirious Fleet Center crowd.

Boston's remarkable postseason run of 2002 has now left only wild optimism in Beantown on the eve of the 2003 NBA season. That optimism was only stretched further by a major trade in midsummer that appears to have provided one of the biggest puzzle pieces in the rebuilding of the recently lackluster franchise. In a blockbuster deal on July 22, Boston landed top-rated center Vin Baker from the Seattle Sonics in exchange for aging veteran point guard Kenny Anderson, workhorse center Vitaly Potapenko, and little-used backcourt role player Joseph Forte. With Baker in the deal, Boston also claimed foÅ·-year veteran guard Shammond Williams, an original second-round draft pick of the Chicago Bulls. Baker was the center-piece of the deal, a star in Milwaukee for three seasons (where he led the NBA in minutes played in 1995) before joining Seattle in September 1997. A four-time NBA All-Star and member of the 2000 USA Olympic Team, Baker boasts high-powered career averages of 16.9 points and 8.2 rebounds; the University of Hartford alum twice posted season scoring averages above 20 in Milwaukee. Boston fans can now savor dreams of a front line of Baker, Pierce and Walker as the equal of any board-crashing trio in the league.

The arrival of 6-11 Vin Baker to anchor the front wall was the primary catalyst for all the optimism now surrounding Boston's return to the NBA wars on the heels of their first playoff run of the decade. In Baker the Celtics finally have the offensive powerhouse under the basket that has been missing since the retirement of Robert Parrish. But there are numerous other causes for broad smiles in the Boston camp. Primarily there is the measurable improvement in defensive play since Jim O'Brien's takeover on the bench. O'Brien's first step was to scrap the trapping college-style defenses installed by Pitino (and so unpopular with the players). Walker and Pierce showed signs last season of finally understanding that all-out effort on both ends of the floor is the final hallmark of the complete NBA star. If Baker may not be the intimidating defensive force Potapenko represented, the trade-off is that he is a better shot blocker than the post man they gave up. The risk seems a worthy one, though, since a player of Baker's potential might be just the ingredient needed to rekindle franchise fortunes.

There can be many pitfalls in an NBA season, and injuries to any of the big three up front could prove fatal to Boston's playoff hopes. But there can be little question that the nightmare years are now a thing of the past. Boston is finally back in the hunt for yet another championship banner to accompany sixteen already hanging from the rafters, and that more than anything else also signals a long-anticipated return to normalcy for the NBA wars of the foreseeable future.

Shammond Williams and Vin Baker show off their new Boston Celtics jerseys. AP/Wide World Photos